Fodor's

NAPA AND SONOMA

T0003017

Welcome to Napa and Sonoma

In California's premier wine region, the pleasures of eating and drinking are celebrated daily. It's easy to join in at famous wineries and rising newcomers off country roads, or at trendy in-town tasting rooms. Luxurious inns, hotels, restaurants, and spas abound, yet the natural setting is equally sublime, whether experienced from a canoe on the Russian River or the deck of a winery overlooking endless rows of vines. As you plan your upcoming travels to Napa and Sonoma, please confirm that places are still open and let us know when we need to make updates by writing to us at this address: editors@fodors.com.

TOP REASONS TO GO

★ **Fine Wine:** Rutherford Cabernets, Carneros Chardonnays, Russian River Pinots.

★ **Spectacular Food:** Marquee chefs, farmers' markets, and public markets.

★ **Cool Towns:** From chic Healdsburg to laid-back Calistoga, a place to suit every mood.

★ **Spas:** Mud baths, herbal wraps, couples' massages, and more in soothing settings.

★ **Winery Architecture:** Stone classics like Buena Vista, all-glass dazzlers like Hall.

★ **Outdoor Fun:** Biking past bright-green vineyards, hot-air ballooning over golden hills.

Contents

MAPS

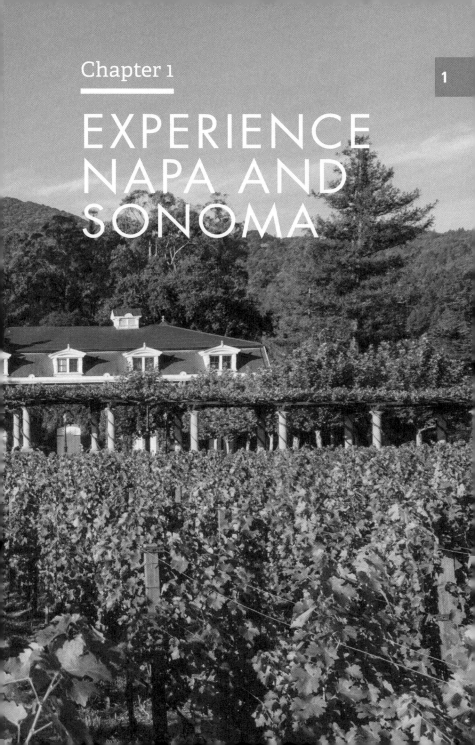

Chapter 1

EXPERIENCE NAPA AND SONOMA

15 ULTIMATE EXPERIENCES

Napa and Sonoma offer terrific experiences that should be on every traveler's list. Here are Fodor's top picks for a memorable trip.

1 Take to the Skies

It's worth waking before sunrise for a hot-air balloon ride over the vineyards. The experience is breathtaking, and oh-so-romantic for couples. Flights end before noon, so you can easily add lunch and wine tasting to the day's activities. *(Ch. 4, 6)*

2 Ogle the Art

Museum-quality artworks enhance a visit at several wineries, but you can also ogle street art and visit artists' studios and arts centers. *(Ch. 4, 5, 6)*

3 Ride the Rails

The romance of the rails and vineyard views make for a crowd-pleasing excursion on the Napa Valley Wine Train, often with winery stops. *(Ch. 4)*

4 Sip Sparkling Wine

A few wineries focus on sparkling wines. Wine making at Schramsberg and Korbel dates back to the 19th century; sip in style at Domaine Carneros, Gloria Ferrer, and Iron Horse. *(Ch. 4, 5, 6)*

5 Paddle a River

Several outfits offer guided or self-guided kayaking or canoe trips on the Napa and Russian Rivers. Pack a picnic, and you're ready to go! *(Ch. 4, 6)*

6 Splurge on a Meal

Celebrated chefs operate Wine Country restaurants, often using ingredients grown steps from the kitchen. Food this refined is worth at least one splurge. *(Ch. 4, 5, 6)*

7 Shop Till You Stop

Among the Wine Country's charms is that it's not overrun with cutesy boutiques or chains. Healdsburg earns top honors for its diverse shopping ops. *(Ch. 4, 5, 6)*

8 Play Winemaker

Learn to blend wine at entertaining sessions exploring the winemaker's art. At some wineries you'll bottle and label your creation to take home. *(Ch. 4, 6)*

9 Sample Spirits

At distillery tasting rooms you can sample spirits and learn about the production process and how it differs from wine and beer making. *(Ch. 4, 5, 6)*

10 Taste on a Hilltop

That Cab or Chard tastes all the better with hilltop valley vistas. In Napa, try Barnett or Pride; in Sonoma, Kunde, Jordan, or Trattore Farms. *(Ch. 4, 5, 6)*

11 Be a Pinot Pilgrim

To get a feel for the climate and terrain that foster world-class Pinot Noir, explore the Carneros District, Russian River Valley, and Sonoma Coast. *(Ch. 4, 5, 6)*

12 Hone Your Skills

Instructors and guest chefs beguile students and visitors during cooking demonstrations at the Culinary Institute of America's CIA at Copia campus. *(Ch. 4)*

13 Luxuriate at a Spa

For pure unadulterated luxuriating, Wine Country spas rank among the world's finest, with the emphasis on wellness as much as working out kinks. *(Ch. 4, 5, 6)*

14 Bike Past Vines

The Wine Country's many valleys make for leisurely guided or self-guided bike rides past gently rolling vineyards and sometimes through them. *(Ch. 4, 5, 6)*

15 Hit the Beach

Windswept, photogenic beaches and dramatically craggy cliffs are the norm along the Sonoma Coast. The drive north from Bodega Bay to Fort Ross is spectacular. *(Ch. 6)*

WHAT'S WHERE

1 Napa Valley. By far the best known of the California wine regions, Napa is home to some of the biggest names in wine, many of which still produce the same bottles of Cabernet Sauvignon that first put the valley on the map. Densely populated with winery after winery, especially along Highway 29 and the Silverado Trail, it's also home to luxury accommodations, some of the country's best restaurants, and spas with deluxe treatments, some incorporating grape seeds and other wine-making by-products.

2 Sonoma Valley and Petaluma. Centered on the historic town of Sonoma, the Sonoma Valley goes easier on the glitz but contains sophisticated wineries and excellent restaurants. Key moments in California and wine-industry history took place here. Part of the Carneros District viticultural area lies within the southern Sonoma Valley. Those who venture into the

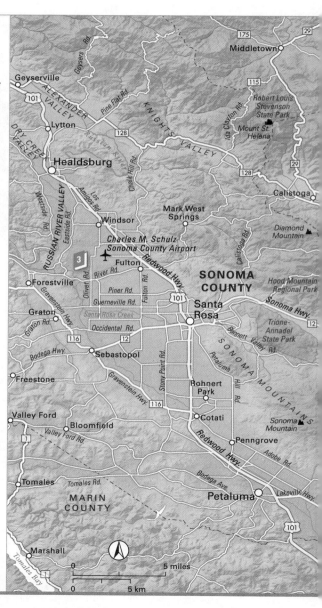

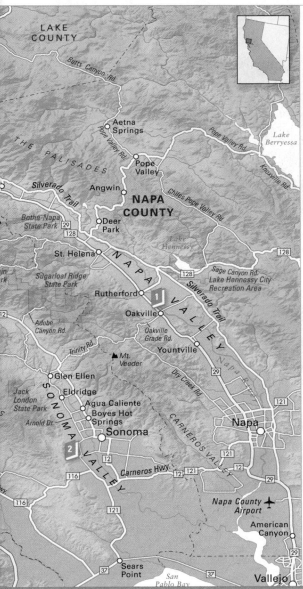

Carneros and west of the Sonoma Valley into the Petaluma Gap appellation will discover wineries specializing in Pinot Noir and Chardonnay. Both grapes thrive in the comparatively cooler climate. Farther north, Cabernet Sauvignon and other warm-weather varietals are grown.

3 Northern Sonoma, Russian River, and West County. Ritzy Healdsburg is a popular base for exploring three important grape-growing areas: the Russian River, Dry Creek, and Alexander valleys. Everything from Chardonnay and Pinot Noir to Cabernet Sauvignon, Zinfandel, and Petite Sirah grows here. Closer to the ocean lie the West Sonoma Coast wineries, beloved by connoisseurs for European-style wines from cool-climate grapes.

What to Eat and Drink in Napa and Sonoma

DAY BOAT SCALLOPS AT VALETTE
Sublime execution and heavenly ingredients—butter, fresh local fennel and leeks, Pernod, fennel pollen, scallops flown in from Maine, caviar, champagne beurre blanc (more butter), and a light, fluffy pastry—make chef Dustin Valette's signature day boat scallops *en croûte* a Healdsburg must-try.

STEAK AND A LIBRARY CAB
Since at least the 1960s, the iconic Wine Country food-wine pairing has been a juicy steak and Cabernet Sauvignon. Maximize your bliss with a Napa Valley Cab from the extensive wine libraries at Cole's (Napa), Press (above, St. Helena), and Stark's (Santa Rosa).

MAD FRITZ ALE
Master brewer Nile Zacherle and wife Whitney Fisher made a lot of wine for boutique wineries before opening their craft brewery specializing in "origin-specific beers," with each ingredient's source acknowledged on the back label. Tales from a Renaissance-era Aesop's Fables edition provide most of the beers' names and all the front-label illustrations.

DUNGENESS CRAB
Crab season along the Sonoma Coast runs from late fall or early winter through April or May. Establishments from seaside shacks to fine-dining spots serve the delectable crustaceans—steamed, as crab cakes and funnel cakes, and in chowder, salads, pasta, and myriad other preparations.

MUSHROOMY MUSHROOM SOUP AT KITCHEN DOOR

"It's so mushroomy, how does he do it?" ask many patrons at star chef Todd Humphries's Kitchen Door in downtown Napa. His soup's secrets of success? A heavy stock, his mushroom combo, and a splash of Marsala, says Humphries.

CHARLIE PALMER'S LOBSTER CORN DOG

Chef Charlie Palmer's trademark lobster corn dog is simple in conception—a lump of lobster surrounded by deep-fried cornbread, served on a stick with remoulade—yet somehow much more than the sum of its parts. Enjoy one at the Archer Hotel's Sky & Vine bar.

SORBET BRUNCH MIMOSA

Brunch isn't brunch at Calistoga's Lovina restaurant without a zesty mimosa with a scoop of seasonal-fruit sorbet. On a sunny day, the scene on the outdoor patios fronting Lovina's two-story bungalows feels like a backyard party.

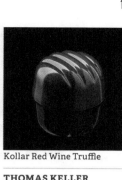

Kollar Red Wine Truffle

THOMAS KELLER CUISINE

Dining at Thomas Keller's The French Laundry costs hundreds, but you needn't break the bank to experience his cuisine. The chef's other Yountville restaurants include Ad Hoc (comfort food), Bouchon (French), Bouchon Bakery (fabulous pastries), and La Calenda (Oaxacan). He co-owns the Regiis Ova Champagne & Caviar Lounge.

RED WINE TRUFFLES AT KOLLAR CHOCOLATES

Chocolatier Chris Kollar installed an open kitchen in his downtown Yountville shop so patrons could see him and his crew at work, experimenting with new confections or whipping up another batch of red wine truffles, made with Napa Valley Zinfandel.

MODEL BAKERY ENGLISH MUFFINS

The Model Bakery's fluffy, doughy, orgasmically delicious signature baked good seduces on every level. Oprah swoons for these muffins, available at the bakery's Napa, Yountville, and St. Helena locations.

Best Bars in Napa and Sonoma

DUKE'S SPIRITED COCKTAILS

Happy hour is active in Healdsburg as winery employees unwind and visitors transition from wine-tasting to dining mode. Among the liveliest downtown spots is Duke's, whose "farm-to-bar" cocktails cleanse weary palates.

HEALDSBURG'S ROOFTOP BARS

Two rooftop bars in Healdsburg serve specialty cocktails and bar bites alfresco. Roof 106 at The Matheson restaurant attracts a chic crowd for predinner drinks. At the boutique Harmon Guest House's mellower The Rooftop (*above*), the draws include comfort-food bites and views of 991-foot Fitch Mountain.

BE BUBBLY AND SIGH!

Life's a perpetually effervescent party at Be Bubbly and Sigh! (*above*), sparkling-wine bars in downtown Napa and Sonoma. Cozy and festive, both pour local and international selections. Be Bubbly draws tourists and the hospitality crowd. Quotes from Dom Perignon, Coco Chanel, and Churchill extolling Champagne's virtues adorn the mirrors at Sigh!

ERNIE'S TIN BAR

Roadside Ernie's is as famous for its no-cell-phone policy—use your phone, and the next round's on you—as its 20 brews on tap and convivial vibe. The Petaluma watering hole, a long narrow bar with a few tables inside and an outdoor patio, shares a corrugated-tin building with a garage. Warning: the dude wearing the Stetson is as apt to be a millionaire as a ranch hand.

GOOSE & GANDER

A Craftsman bungalow off St. Helena's Main Street houses this popular eatery and its cool basement bar. The low ceiling and subdued lighting add speakeasy appeal that G&G comes by honestly: the bungalow's original owner allegedly used the cellar for Prohibition-era bootlegging.

GEYSERVILLE GUN CLUB

Historic, retro, and au courant, this bar occupies a ground-floor sliver of Geyserville's circa-1900 Odd Fellows Hall. Some cocktails change seasonally, with classic Bloody Marys and margaritas among the staples.

EL BARRIO

Guerneville's hole-in-the-wall with south-of-the-border flair specializes in craft cocktails based on tequila and mescal. If you can't decide what to order, La Casa, the house margarita, is a good bet.

Sky & Vine

LO & BEHOLD

Two bartenders with a knack for catchy cocktails teamed with a chef fascinated by international street cuisine to create this farm-to-bar hole-in-the-wall a block south of Healdsburg Plaza. The garden patio's a magnet on sunny days and warm evenings.

SKY & VINE

The Archer Hotel Napa's sixth-floor rooftop bar seduces with valley views, snappy libations, and snacks and bites from chef Charlie Palmer and crew. If zero proof's your thing, there are always a few delicious and so-good-for-you options. During "reverse happy hour" (a bit before closing except Friday and Saturday), Sky & Vine is almost a bargain.

WILFRED'S LOUNGE

Father-son vintners sold the family winery and opened this homage to mid-century Hawaii's Tiki-bar scene. What could have been retro and campy is tasteful and respectful, and the cocktails and cuisine are clean and contemporary. Enjoy Napa River views while downing a mai tai or something more exotic.

What to Buy in Napa and Sonoma

OLIVE OIL

By tradition dating to antiquity, grapes and olives have supplied two staples of the southern European diet: wine and olive oil. Visitors to several wineries with olive mills, including Petaluma's McEvoy Ranch, can taste and purchase extra-virgin oils produced entirely on-site.

POTTERY

For their farm-to-plate cuisine, some Wine Country restaurants extend their support of local purveyors to the second part of the equation, serving meals on elegant ceramic dinner-ware sometimes crafted within a few miles. Napa Valley artisans of note include Amanda Wright and Richard Carter, both with studios in St. Helena, and Nikki and Will Callnan of NBC Pottery in Angwin.

WINE GLASSES

High-end wineries take pride in serving wines in high-quality stemware. After a few tastings, you might catch on that the quality and shape of a glass really do enhance wines' aromatics and other attributes. Some winery gift shops sell the brand featured in the tasting room.

FASHION JEWELRY

"Everyday wearable chic" is the goal of many local jewelry artisans, some of whom put a bohemian spin on their output by incorporating leather or oxidized metals. Look for jewelry at winery gift shops and in downtown Sonoma, St. Helena, Healdsburg, Yountville, and Napa.

WINE

Yes, this one is obvious— buy wine in the Wine Country—but perhaps for reasons you haven't considered. Familiar brands have a few widely distrib-uted wines you can easily purchase back home. At the winery, though, the focus will be on higher-quality small-production offerings sold only in the tasting room. Wines in a custom box make an excellent gift for someone back home.

GIFT BOOKS

With their photogenic mountains, valleys, vineyards, and architecture, the Napa Valley and Sonoma County inspire large-format gift books devoted to wine, food, and other topics. Perennial favorites include titles about winery dogs and cats or containing aerial photography.

WINE-BARREL FURNITURE AND ACCESSORIES

What happens to oak barrels after they're used to make wine? Most are sold off, their staves, metal hoops, and lids transformed into Adirondack chairs, barstools, planters, wine racks, lazy Susans, chandeliers, swings, jewelry, and anything else enterprising artisans dream up.

TERROIR-DRIVEN BEAUTY PRODUCTS

"Terroir" is the French term for soil, climate, and related conditions that make a vineyard, and therefore its wines, unique. Several Napa and Sonoma companies apply this concept to sourcing ingredients for beauty and skin-care products found throughout the Wine Country.

ALL-NATURAL SOAPS

The catchy names of Napa Soap Company's all-natural soaps—Cabernet Soapignon, Clean O Noir—reflect their local ingredients: grape-seed oil (a wine-making by-product) and sometimes wine itself. Customers swoon over the fragrances. Find them at owner Sheila Rockwood's St. Helena shop at 655 Main Street and elsewhere in Napa and Sonoma.

WINE-BOTTLE CANDLES

Wine bottles are even more ubiquitous than barrels as a wine-making by-product in need of recycling and reuse. Many bottles are indeed recycled, with others finding a second life as water glasses, chandeliers, and vessels for candles. Feast it Forward, in Napa, carries wine-scented candles made from natural soy wax.

An Art Lover's Guide to Napa and Sonoma

HESS PERSSON ESTATES

Artworks by heavy hitters like Robert Rauschenberg fill the two-floor gallery of Hess Persson Estates. Swiss-born founder Donald Hess acquired the pieces over several decades. Some tastings at the Mt. Veeder winery include a gallery tour.

THE DONUM ESTATE

It's fitting that most of The Donum Estate's three dozen–plus large-scale outdoor sculptures grace the winery's lush vineyards, where the wine-growing team's farming skills yield Pinot Noirs and Chardonnays that are works of art themselves. The visual feast begins with Jaume Plensa's marble *Sanna, Giant Head*, which looms over a driveway curling toward a tasting pavilion with a multicolor conical canopy. Collection highlights include Chinese artist-activist Ai Weiwei's bronze *Circle of Animals/Zodiac Heads*, displayed in a grassy meadow. A Louise Bourgeois spider occupies its own indoor pavilion.

HALL ST. HELENA

Lawrence Argent's 35-foot polished-stainless-steel sculpture of a leaping rabbit marks the entrance to Hall St. Helena, which devotes a private tour (reservations required, tasting included) to the contemporary artworks collected by owners Kathryn and Craig Hall. You can view much of the collection before or after a standard tasting or on other tours. Hall is known for Cabernet Sauvignons, a few of which have earned 100-point scores from wine critics.

DI ROSA CENTER FOR CONTEMPORARY ART

The late Rene di Rosa founded this Carneros District art park that focuses on Northern California works from the mid-20th century to the present. Two galleries display some of the permanent collection and host temporary exhibitions, and the Sculpture Meadow and the area around di Rosa's former residence contain outdoor sculptures.

GEYSERVILLE SCULPTURE TRAIL

Enormous sculptures grab the eye north and south of downtown Geyserville. The figurative and abstract artworks change as they're sold or loans expire, but there's always plenty to view. From the south, take U.S. 101's Geyserville/Highway 128 East exit, turn right, then quickly left, onto Geyserville Avenue. From the north, exit at Canyon Road, turn left, then right, onto the avenue.

RAD NAPA

Full-scale murals adorn warehouses and other structures in Napa courtesy of artists funded by RAD Napa (Rail Arts District Napa). One of the flashiest examples, painted on the two-story CIA at Copia building, was inspired by the culinary gardens out front. Napa Valley Wine Train passengers and hikers and bikers along the Napa Valley Vine Trail have the best views. RAD Napa's website has a touring map.

di Rosa Center for Contemporary Art

HEALDSBURG GALLERIES

Downtown Healdsburg is awash with tasting rooms and fancy eateries, but the arts are also an enduring presence. Most spaces exhibit contemporary art. The 9,000-square-foot Paul Mahder Gallery, inside a vintage Quonset hut at 222 Healdsburg Avenue, has the largest selection: paintings, sculptures, and works in other media. Gallery Lulo (art, jewelry, design), at 303 Center Street, and Aerena Gallery Healdsburg (painting and sculpture), at 115 Plaza Street, are also worth checking out.

PATRICK AMIOT JUNK ART

All over Sonoma County, you'll see the sculptures Sebastopol resident Patrick Amiot fashions out of sheet metal and found objects, rendered all the more whimsical by the wild colors his wife, Brigitte Laurent, paints on them.

For the most significant concentration of sculptures, head two blocks west of Main Street to Florence Avenue, where many residents, including the two artists, proudly display the fanciful fabrications.

CA' TOGA GALLERIA D'ARTE

For sheer exuberance, it's hard to imagine anything topping Italian artist Carlo Marchiori's storefront Ca' Toga Galleria d'Arte in downtown Calistoga. This place is all about Marchiori's creativity, as expressed in everything from paintings and sculptures to ceramic housewares. Be sure to look up—the ceiling's a trip. The pièce de résistance is the artist's over-the-top Palladian-style villa. Heavy on the trompe l'oeil, it's open for visits on a limited basis.

FRANCIS FORD COPPOLA WINERY

The famous director sold his Geyserville winery, but its gallery of movie memorabilia remains. There isn't much art per se, but the collection contains props and other items related to his films, among them some of late-20th-century cinema's defining works. Two selfie stars are Don Corleone's desk from *The Godfather* and the namesake 1948 vehicle from *Tucker: The Man and His Dream.* Displayed on a car-showroom platform and one of only 51 produced, the auto is worth more than a million dollars. The gallery's supporting cast includes costumes from *Bram Stoker's Dracula,* models from daughter-director Sofia Coppola's films, five FFC Oscars, and hundreds of other items.

Top Napa Wineries

CHAPPELLET WINERY
The founders of this winery established in 1967 took a leap of faith purchasing land high above the valley floor, but the Pritchard Hill location yielded wines of distinction from the start. The views of Lake Hennessey and Mt. St. Helena continue to astound as well.

DOMAINE CARNEROS
The main building of this Napa winery was modeled after an 18th-century French château owned by the Champagne-making Taittinger family, one of whose members selected the site Domaine Carneros now occupies. On a sunny day, the experience of sipping a crisp sparkling wine on the outdoor terrace feels noble indeed.

INGLENOOK
History buffs will want to visit Inglenook, founded in the 19th century by a Finnish sea captain and rejuvenated over the past several decades by filmmaker Francis Ford Coppola. You can learn all about this fabled property during elegant tastings— or just sip a glass peacefully at a wine bar with a picturesque courtyard.

JOSEPH PHELPS VINEYARDS
There are few more glorious tasting spots in the Napa Valley than the terrace at this St. Helena winery. Phelps is known for its Cabernet Sauvignons and Insignia, a red Bordeaux blend. The wine-related seminars here are smart and entertaining.

LARKMEAD
Founded in 1895 but planted to grapes even before that, 150-acre Larkmead is one of the Napa Valley's storied estates. Hosts pour collector-quality Cabernets in a chic barn or outdoors in view of grapevines and the colorful garden.

SCHRAMSBERG
The 19th-century cellars at sparkling-wine producer Schramsberg hold millions of bottles. During a visit you'll learn how the bubblies at this Calistoga mainstay are made using the *méthode traditionelle* and how the bottles are "riddled" (turned every few days) by hand.

SMITH-MADRONE WINERY
Step back in time at this Spring Mountain winery where two brothers named Smith craft wines in a weathered, no-frills redwood barn. Founder Stu has been doing the farming, and Charlie has been making the wines for more than four decades at this place with splendid valley views.

THEOREM VINEYARDS
New to the business when they founded their winery in 2012, the owners of this Diamond Mountain property assembled sterling wine-making, culinary, and hospitality teams. Although you can taste the mostly Bordeaux-style wines by themselves, the food-and-wine pairings here rank among the valley's finest.

TREFETHEN FAMILY VINEYARDS
The main tasting space at Trefethen, a three-story wooden former winery building dating to 1886, was completely renovated following the 2014 Napa earthquake. More than a half-century old itself, Trefethen makes Riesling, Chardonnay, and Merlot in addition to Cabernet Sauvignon and a Malbec-oriented red blend.

VGS CHATEAU POTELLE
Small bites from an acclaimed Napa restaurant and Cabernet and other reds made from mountain fruit pair perfectly in Chateau Potelle's whimsically decorated St. Helena bungalow. In good weather, tastings take place under an open-air Moroccan tent. In either setting, owner Jean-Noel Fourmeaux's hospitality shines.

Top Sonoma Wineries

APERTURE CELLARS

In 2009, still in his 20s, celebrated winemaker Jesse Katz started Aperture, whose focus is single-vineyard Cabernets and Bordeaux-style red blends. The architecture of Katz's Russian River Valley tasting room riffs off photography, a nod to his dad and winery partner, Andy Katz, a world-famous photographer.

CHENOWETH WINES

Distinguished producers purchase grapes farmed by the Chenoweth family, whose ancestors settled northwest of Sebastopol in the mid-1800s. Some grapes are held back for the Chenoweth label's Pinot Noirs and rosé of Pinot. Family members, including winemaker Amy Chenoweth, conduct the down-home tastings.

THE DONUM ESTATE

Single-vineyard Pinot Noirs exhibiting "power yet elegance" made the reputation of this Carneros District winery also known for smooth, balanced Chardonnays. The three dozen–plus large-scale, museum-quality outdoor sculptures by the likes of Anselm Kiefer add a touch of culture to a visit.

HANZELL VINEYARDS

Most tastings at this Chardonnay and Pinot pioneer that opened in 1953 unfold at outdoor platforms positioned to take maximum advantage of the Sonoma Valley views. The gracious hosts provide details about the winery's legacy, organic farming practices, and studiously crafted wines.

IRON HORSE VINEYARDS

Proof that tasting sparkling wine doesn't have to be stuffy, this winery on the outskirts of Sebastopol pours its selections outdoors, with tremendous views of vine-covered hills that make the bubblies (and a few still wines) taste even better.

LIMERICK LANE

This winery's tasting room, in a restored stone farm building, is hardly Sonoma County's grandest, but the Zinfandel, Syrah, and Petite Sirah are arguably among the entire state's best. If you're curious about Zinfandel, don't miss Limerick Lane, whose oldest vines date back a century-plus.

RIDGE VINEYARDS

Oenophiles will be familiar with Ridge, which produces some of California's best Cabernet Sauvignon, Chardonnay, and Zinfandel. You can taste wines from grapes grown at Ridge's Sonoma County vineyards, and some from its neighbors, along with ones produced at its older Santa Cruz Mountains winery.

ROBERT YOUNG ESTATE WINERY

Guests at this longtime grower's hilltop tasting room enjoy views down the Alexander Valley while sipping Chardonnay and other whites and Bordeaux-style reds. The first Youngs settled in Geyserville in 1858; the entire history of local agriculture unfolded on this historic site.

SILVER OAK

"Only one wine can be your best," was cofounder Justin Meyer's rationale for Silver Oak's decision to focus solely on Cabernet. The winery pours its two yearly offerings (one from Napa, the other from Sonoma) in a glass-walled eco-friendly tasting room in the Alexander Valley.

THREE STICKS WINES

The Chardonnays and Pinot Noirs at Three Sticks come from Durell, Gap's Crown, and four other prized vineyards of owner Bill Price. They're served west of Sonoma Plaza at the lavishly restored Adobe, which dates to 1842. Seasonal tastings pair the Chardonnays with oysters and caviar.

What to Read and Watch

Books

COOKBOOKS

Bouchon Bakery **(2012), by Thomas Keller and Sebastien Rouxel.** The legendary Keller and his executive pastry chef share recipes that made Yountville's Bouchon Bakery an instant hit.

The Essential Thomas Keller: The French Laundry Cookbook & Ad Hoc at Home **(2010), by Thomas Keller.** Recipes inspired by Keller's upscale and down-home Yountville establishments show the chef's range.

Mustards Grill Napa Valley Cookbook **(2001), by Cindy Pawlcyn and Brigid Callinan.** Pawlcyn describes her iconic eatery as "a cross between a roadside rib joint and a French country restaurant." She shares recipes and expounds on her culinary philosophy.

Plats du Jour: The Girl & the Fig's Journey Through the Seasons in Wine Country **(2011), by Sondra Bernstein.** The chef who founded Sonoma County's two "fig" restaurants reveals her cooking secrets and adapts some of her signature dishes.

Wine Country Women of Sonoma **(2020), by Michelle Mandro.** In this sequel to a similar large-format photography book about the Napa Valley (2017), winemakers, chefs, executives, and women holding other key positions share insights and recipes.

FICTION

Eight Hundred Grapes **(2017), by Laura Dave.** At a personal crossroads, the protagonist returns to her family's Sebastopol vineyard as harvest season begins.

Murder Uncorked **(2005),** *Murder by the Glass: A Wine-Lover's Mystery* **(2006),** and *Silenced by Syrah* **(2007), by Michele Scott.** Vineyard manager Nikki Sands is the protagonist of this light and humorous mystery series that unfolds in the Napa Valley.

Nose: A Novel **(2013), by James Conaway.** A fictitious Northern California wine-making region—couldn't be Napa or Sonoma, could it?—is the setting for a mystery.

NONFICTION

Chinese in Napa Valley: The Forgotten Community That Built Wine Country **(2023), by John McCormick.** Among their many accomplishments, Chinese immigrants dug caves and planted vineyards while enduring severe prejudice and seeing their neighborhoods and much of their history erased.

Harvests of Joy: How the Good Life Became Great Business **(1999), by Robert Mondavi and Paul Chutkow.** Wine tycoon Robert Mondavi tells his story.

Hidden History of Napa Valley **(2019), by Alexandria Brown.** A local historian chronicles the activities and lives of Native Americans, Chinese and Mexican immigrants, African Americans, and other "marginalized people" in the valley.

The House of Mondavi: The Rise and Fall of an American Wine Dynasty **(2007), by Julia Flynn Siler.** The author ruffled many a Napa feather when she published this tell-all book.

Judgment of Paris: California vs. France and the Historic 1976 Paris Tasting That Revolutionized Wine **(2005), by George M. Taber.** The journalist who broke the story of the pivotal event analyzes its history and repercussions.

Lost Napa Valley **(2021), by Lauren Coodley.** With chapters detailing where Napans of yore farmed, worked, lived, played, and shopped, this book fondly recalls the days before the valley became an upscale destination.

Murder & Mayhem in the Napa Valley (2012), **by Todd L. Shulman.** A Napa police officer recounts a century and a half of crime in the land of fine wine.

Napa at Last Light: America's Eden in an Age of Calamity (2018), **by James Conaway.** The author of two previous bestsellers *(Napa,* 1990; *The Far Side of Eden,* 2002) about the Napa Valley reflects on more recent challenges.

The Napa Murder of Anita Fagiani Andrews (2021), **by Raymond A. Guadagni.** The trial judge of a downtown Napa bar owner's killer documents the nearly four-decade quest to achieve justice for her.

Napa Valley: The Land, the Wine, the People (2011), **by Charles O'Rear.** A former *National Geographic* photographer portrays the valley in this lush book.

Napa Valley Then & Now (2015), **by Kelli A. White.** A well-regarded sommelier's encyclopedic book details the valley's wines, wineries, and history.

A New Napa Cuisine (2014), **by Christopher Kostow.** The much-lauded chef of the Restaurant at Meadowood in St. Helena describes his evolution as a chef and his land-focused approach to cooking.

Sonoma Wine and the Story of Buena Vista (2013), **by Charles L. Sullivan.** California's first winery provides the hook for this survey of Sonoma County's wine-making history.

Tangled Vines: Greed, Murder, Obsession, and an Arsonist in the Vineyards of California (2015), **by Frances Dinkelspiel.** Rare vintages by the author's great-great-grandfather were among the 4½ million bottles destroyed in a deliberately set warehouse fire south of Napa.

When the Rivers Ran Red: An Amazing Story of Courage and Triumph in America's Wine Country (2009), **by Vivienne Sosnowski.** The author chronicles the devastating effect of Prohibition on Northern California winemakers.

Movies and TV

Bottle Shock (2008). Filmed primarily in the Napa and Sonoma Valleys, Randall Miller's fictionalized feature about the 1976 Paris tasting focuses on Calistoga's Chateau Montelena.

Call of the Valley: The Enduring Lure of Sonoma (2020). Julie Morrison's documentary surveys Sonoma's history with interviews and archival and new footage.

Falcon Crest (1981–90). This soap opera centered on a winery in the fictional "Tuscany Valley" (aka Napa) may not have aged as well as wines made during its era, but it's acquired a nostalgic patina. At its best, it's pulpy good fun.

Pretty Problems (2022). Sonoma County comes off as a bougie paradise, "the new Napa" (perhaps even worse) in this edgy, sassy IFC film about affluent millennials in the Wine Country.

Promised Land (2022). A sudsy multigenerational saga revolves around a Hispanic-owned Sonoma Valley winery.

Somm, Somm into the Bottle, Somm 3 (2012–18). The Napa Valley plays a role in these documentaries about, respectively, the master sommelier exam, the world of wine through 10 bottles, and three influential experts.

Wine Country (2019). Napa-Sonoma locations make cameo appearances in this comedy about a 50th-birthday celebration; Amy Poehler directed and co-stars (with Tina Fey).

Kids and Families

The Wine Country isn't a particularly child-oriented destination, so don't expect to find tons of activities organized with kids in mind. That said, you'll find plenty of playgrounds (there's one in Sonoma Plaza, for instance) and the occasional family-friendly attraction.

CHOOSING A PLACE TO STAY

If you're traveling with kids, always mention it when making reservations. Most of the smaller, more romantic inns and bed-and-breakfasts discourage or prohibit children, and those places that do allow them may prefer to put such families in a particular cottage or room so that any noise is less disruptive to other guests. Larger hotels are a mixed bag. Some actively discourage children, whereas others are more welcoming. The Carneros Resort and Spa tends to be the most child friendly of the large, luxurious hotels.

EATING OUT

Unless your kid is a budding Thomas Keller, it's best to call ahead to see if a restaurant can accommodate those under 12 with a special menu. You'll find inexpensive cafés in almost every town, and places like Gott's Roadside, a retro burger stand in St. Helena, are big hits with kids and their parents.

FAMILY-FRIENDLY ATTRACTIONS

One especially family-friendly attraction is the Charles M. Schulz Museum in Santa Rosa. Its intelligent exhibits generally appeal to adults; younger kids may or may not enjoy the level of detail. The sure bets for kids are the play area outside and the education room, where they can color, draw, and create their own cartoons. Another place for a family outing, also in Santa Rosa, is Safari West, an African wildlife preserve on 400 acres. The highlight is the two-hour tour of the property in open-air vehicles that sometimes come within a few feet of giraffes, zebras, and other animals. You can spend the night in tent cabins here. At Sonoma Zipline Adventures, north of Occidental, families zipline through the redwoods together. A mile south of Sonoma Plaza, Sonoma TrainTown Railroad dazzles the under-10 set with a 4-mile ride on a quarter-scale train, a petting zoo, and amusement rides.

AT THE WINERIES

Although some wineries prohibit children under 21 (more since the pandemic), kids are a common Wine Country sight. Hosts generally greet well-behaved kids with a smile and possibly a treat—grape juice or another beverage, sometimes coloring books or a similar distraction.

When booking a tour, ask if kids are allowed (for insurance and other reasons, wineries sometimes exclude children under a certain age), how long it lasts, and whether another option would be more suitable.

A few particularly kid-friendly wineries include Calistoga's Castello di Amorosa (what's not to like about a 107-room medieval castle, complete with a dungeon?) and Yountville's Oasis by Hoopes, whose rescue farm animals and acre-plus organic garden keep kids occupied. There are lawn games at Abbot's Passage in Glen Ellen, and Belden Barns in Santa Rosa sets up a scavenger hunt.

You'll find plenty of kids poolside at the Francis Ford Coppola Winery in Geyserville, and Honig Vineyard & Winery in Rutherford prides itself on making sure kids enjoy a visit as much as their parents do.

Chapter 2

TRAVEL SMART

Updated by
Daniel Mangin

★ **CAPITAL:**
Sacramento

👫 **POPULATION:**
39.1 million

$ **CURRENCY**
U.S. dollar

☎ **AREA CODE**
707

⚠ **EMERGENCIES:**
911

🚘 **DRIVING**
On the right

⚡ **ELECTRICITY:**
120–240 v/60 cycles;
plugs have two or three
rectangular prongs

🕐 **TIME:**
Three hours behind
New York

🌐 **WEB RESOURCES:**
www.visitnapavalley.com,
www.sonomacounty.com,
www.visitcalifornia.com,
travel.state.gov

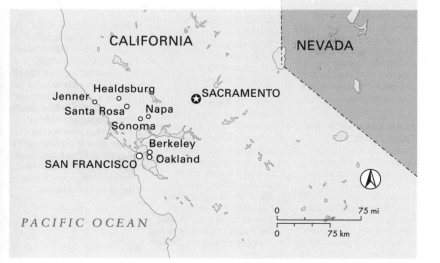

Know Before You Go

Given the region's popularity and the expense involved in a trip to Napa, Sonoma, or both, planning ahead is essential for any wine-country trip. Here are a few helpful things to know before you go.

THE WINE COUNTRY IS EXPENSIVE BUT NOT UNAFFORDABLE

"Has Wine Country Become Too Expensive for Its Own Good?" screamed a local newspaper's headline in late 2022. The ensuing piece spotlighted a trend toward higher-priced, appointment-only seated tastings—partly a response to social-distancing requirements relative to COVID-19. ("It's what our customers have told us they want," responds one winery owner.) It's possible to spend a small fortune on a Wine Country vacation, but there are ways to rein in costs, starting with the most important one: choosing affordable lodging (⇨ *see below for some tips*). Also, keeping a watch on meal costs. Tasting fees are indeed higher than before, but excellent lower-priced options remain.

PLAN AHEAD FOR THE FRENCH LAUNDRY

Chef Thomas Keller's highly praised Yountville restaurant remains a hot Wine Country ticket. At a few hundred dollars, not counting wine pairings, it's also among the most expensive dining experiences. And "ticket" here is literal. When you reserve a table, you're purchasing a seat, as at the theater; if you miss the show, there's no refund. Here's how it works: at specific times (usually the first of the month), the Tock online reservation service releases seats for the following month or two. Click the FAQs link on the restaurant's Tock page for the latest on how bookings are being released. Reservations for Single-Thread Farms Restaurant and Cyrus, Sonoma County's most luxurious fine-dining experiences, are released through Tock in a similar fashion.

AVOID STICKER SHOCK AT RESTAURANTS

Even if you're not dining at The French Laundry, eating out in Napa and Sonoma can induce sticker shock. There are several ways to avoid this. Have the day's fancy meal at brunch or lunch, when prices tend to be lower. Happy hour, when a restaurant might serve a signature appetizer or a smaller version of a famous plate at a lower price, is another option. Nearly every Wine Country town has a purveyor or two of gourmet food to go, making picnicking in a park or eating back at your lodging a viable strategy, too.

AVOID STICKER SHOCK AT HOTELS

Unlike many other U.S. destinations where rates are highest from Memorial Day to Labor Day, the Wine Country in typical (that is, nonfire) years is the busiest—and most expensive—between September and October, during harvest. Year-round you can save money by traveling midweek, when rates tend to be lower. The shoulder seasons of mid-to-late spring and early November, just after harvest, often bring beautiful weather and more reasonable prices. It's cheaper still in the off-season, from December to March, when, for instance, some hotels with spas offer packages that include massages, mud baths, or other treatments.

HOW TASTING ROOM HOURS WORK

Some wineries welcome walk-ins, but many require an appointment for all visits or ones involving tours or food pairings. It's still possible to visit some tasting rooms on short notice, but keep in mind that unlike at restaurants, you can't pop in three minutes before closing and expect to be served. If you arrive at a tasting room 15 or 20 minutes before closing time, you might receive a courtesy pour and an invitation to return another day for the full experience. If you arrive five minutes before closing, you likely won't be served at all.

FEES AND TIPPING

One of the easiest ways to save on tasting fees—two people sharing a tasting—fell out of favor because of COVID-19, but check at visitor centers and lodgings for complimentary or two-for-the-price-of-one passes. Some wineries will waive the charge if you join the wine club, purchase a few bottles, or spend a particular dollar amount. In industry parlance, fees at others are "exclusive of purchase." By long-standing tradition, tipping was neither required nor expected, but although you'll rarely see a jar to prod you, showing your server monetary appreciation has evolved into the norm these days. Five or $10 per person is sufficient if you've had a standard tasting not involving food. Instances that might require a larger tip include when your server has given you a few extra pours, otherwise provided outstanding service, or offered a discount on your purchases.

SONOMA COUNTY IS WORTH IT

The 1976 Judgment of Paris blind tasting of French and California reds and whites sealed the Napa Valley's fame when the all-French judging panel unwittingly awarded top honors in both categories to Napa wineries. Less-known fact: half the grapes in the winning white, a Chardonnay from Calistoga's Chateau Montelena, came from Sonoma County's Baciga-lupi Vineyard, among the early clues that the region west of the Napa Valley also produces world-class grapes. If you love Chardonnay and Pinot Noir, you're probably already planning to visit Sonoma County, but Cabernet Sauvignon, Zinfandel, and cool-climate Syrah are among the other stars. With coastal beaches, whale-watching, and parks full of redwoods, there are nonwine diversions, too.

DRIVING AND TRAFFIC

Traffic in Napa and Sonoma is generally straight-forward, the critical issue being negotiating rush-hour traffic. The Napa Valley is relatively compact, but there are only two main north–south roads. At rush hour and on weekends, when Bay Area locals descend, you're likely to get caught in traffic, so it's wise to plan your day's last winery stop away from busy Highway 29. In Sonoma County, it's best to avoid the U.S. 101 corridor during the morning and evening commutes.

ALTERNATIVES TO DRIVING

Police look for signs of driver intoxication, making it wise to have a designated driver or avail yourself of the many driver services and tour-company options. Uber and Lyft are also possible, except for trips far from urban areas, because you may have difficulty getting a ride back. If you'll be carless, consider staying in Yountville, downtown Napa, Sonoma, or Healdsburg, all of which have numerous tasting rooms within walking distance of each other. A short walk or bike ride will transport you to the countryside in each of these places.

SHIPPING WINE

Because individual states regulate alcoholic beverages, shipping wine back home can be easy or complicated, depending on where you live. Some states prohibit all direct shipments from wineries. Others allow limited quantities—a certain number of gallons or cases per year—if a winery has purchased a permit to do so. The penalties for noncompliance can be steep: it's a felony, for instance, to ship wines to Utah residents. Since selling wine is their business, tasting room hosts are well versed in the regulations. If you send wines back home, keep in mind that most states require someone 21 or older to sign for the delivery. Alaska Airlines allows passengers on domestic flights out of the Charles M. Schulz Sonoma County Airport (STS) to check up to one case of wine for free.

Getting Here and Around

Air

Nonstop flights from New York to San Francisco take about 6½ hours. Some flights require changing planes, making the total excursion between 8½ and 10 hours.

AIRPORTS
The Wine Country's primary gateway is San Francisco International Airport (SFO), 60 miles from the city of Napa and 57 miles from Sonoma. Oakland International Airport (OAK), almost directly across San Francisco Bay, is closer to Napa, 50 miles away. Most visitors choose SFO, though, because it has more daily flights. Another option is to fly into Sacramento International Airport (SMF), about 68 miles from Napa and 76 miles from Sonoma. Wine Country regulars often fly into Santa Rosa's Charles M. Schulz Sonoma County Airport (STS), which receives daily nonstop flights from several western cities. The airport is 15 miles from Healdsburg.

AIRPORT TRANSFERS
Sonoma County Airport Express (up to $45) shuttles passengers to Petaluma and Santa Rosa. There isn't an equivalent service for Napa.

The smallest Uber or Lyft vehicle from SFO costs from $110 to southern Sonoma or Napa and $135 to Healdsburg or Calistoga. A private service like Pleasant Limo charges up to $325, depending on how far north you're going.

Bicycle

Much of the Wine Country is flat. With all the vineyard scenery, if you're fit at all you can spend a great day touring the countryside by bike. Some lodgings provide bicycles free of charge, and you can rent them or book guided tours in Napa,

Yountville, St. Helena, and Calistoga; in Sonoma County, you'll find rental places in Sonoma, Healdsburg, Santa Rosa, and a few other towns.

Boat

Except for Napa Valley Gondola's romantic Napa River excursions, there's no real boat service here. You can rent a canoe for a glide along the Russian River and book guided and self-guided kayak tours on the Napa and Russian Rivers. The San Francisco Bay Ferry connects San Francisco and the city of Vallejo, where you can board a VINE bus to downtown Napa.

Bus

The knee-jerk local reaction to the notion of getting to tasting rooms—or the Wine Country—via public transit is that it's impossible or will take forever, but it's definitely possible. Napa, Petaluma, Santa Rosa, and Sonoma are the easiest to visit by bus. Napa and Sonoma both have fairly compact downtowns with numerous tasting rooms, restaurants, and lodgings. VINE buses connect Napa Valley towns; Sonoma County Transit serves its entire county. Golden Gate Transit Bus 101 heads north from San Francisco to Petaluma and Santa Rosa.

Car

A car is the most convenient way to navigate Napa and Sonoma. If you're flying into the area, it's almost always easiest to pick up a car at the airport. You'll also find rental companies in the larger Wine Country towns. A few rules to note: smartphone use for any purpose while driving is prohibited, including mapping applications unless the device is mounted to a car's windshield or dashboard and can be activated with a single swipe or finger tap. A right turn after stopping at a red light is legal unless posted otherwise.

PARKING
Parking is rarely a problem. Most wineries have ample free lots, as do most hotels (some charge). In some communities, street parking is limited to two or three hours during the day, but municipal lots are usually available for free or at a low rate.

ROAD CONDITIONS
Roads in the Wine Country are generally well maintained and, except on weekdays between 7 and 9:30 am and 4 and 6 pm and on some weekends, scenic and relatively uncrowded.

DRIVER AND CAR SERVICES
Several companies supply designated drivers to operate your rental or personal vehicle for winery visits. The fees are reasonable, and many patrons appreciate a knowledgeable local's stories and on-the-fly schedule adjustments. Most outfits will provide the car if necessary. Wine Tasting Driver serves Napa and Sonoma.

Another option is a private customized tour in a car, SUV, or van. Perata Luxury Tours allows clients to create their own itineraries or will tailor one to their interests. With Platypus Tours, you can join an existing tour with other guests or book a private one. Both companies have contacts with high-profile and off-the-beaten-path wineries in Napa and Sonoma. The full-service Wine Country Concierge, which specializes in itineraries involving luxury properties, can arrange transportation, too.

Ride-Sharing
Lyft and Uber are generally dependable, though securing a ride can be challenging after 10 pm or if you're seeking a winery pickup far from a town.

Taxi
Traditional taxis are nearly extinct in the Wine Country, and the few remaining companies provide so-so service. A better option is to use limousine or car services that charge by the hour or trip. Executive Car Service Napa Valley is a solid Napa outfit. In Sonoma County, try Sonoma Sterling Limousines.

Train
SMART (Sonoma-Marin Area Rail Transit) trains travel between San Rafael in Marin County north to Santa Rosa's Airport, with Sonoma County stops that include Petaluma and downtown Santa Rosa. If you're carless and traveling light, you can take Golden Gate Transit Bus 101 and then a SMART train from San Francisco into Sonoma County. Trains don't run late, though. Napa has no commuter train service, but the Napa Valley Wine Train's historic cars travel between Napa and St. Helena, offering meals, on-board wine tasting, and in many cases winery stops.

Essentials

🏃 Activities

Driving from winery to winery, you may find yourself captivated by the incredible landscape. To experience it up close, hop on a bike, paddle a canoe or a kayak, or hike a trail. Balloon rides depart early in the morning. Packages at bicycle outfitters may include bikes, winery tours, and a guide—or you can rent a bike and head off on your own. The Napa and Russian Rivers provide serene settings for canoe and kayaking trips past trees, meadows, vineyards, and small towns. Among the area state parks with hiking trails are Robert Louis Stevenson in the Napa Valley and Jack London and Armstrong Woods in Sonoma County.

🍴 Dining

Top Wine Country chefs tend to apply French and Italian techniques to dishes incorporating fresh, local products. Menus are often vegan- and vegetarian-friendly, with gluten-free options.

DISCOUNTS AND DEALS

Dining out for lunch or brunch can be a cost-effective strategy at pricey restaurants, as can sitting at the bar and ordering appetizers rather than entrées. Some places eliminate corkage fees one night a week or more.

MEALS AND MEALTIMES

Lunch is typically served from 11 or 11:30 to 2:30 or 3, with dinner service starting at 5 or 5:30 and lasting until 9 or 10. Restaurants that serve breakfast usually open by 7, sometimes earlier, with some serving breakfast through the lunch hour. Most weekend brunches start at 10 or 11 and go at least until 2.

PAYING

In 2020, most restaurants began taking only credit cards and not cash, though many have relaxed this policy. A few places don't accept credit cards. In most establishments, tipping is the norm, but some include the service in the menu price or add it to the bill.

⇨ *For guidelines on tipping see Tipping, below.*

PRICES

⇨ *Prices in the reviews are the average cost of a main course at dinner or, if dinner is not served, at lunch. Restaurant reviews have been shortened. For full information, visit Fodors.com.*

What It Costs in U.S. Dollars			
$	$$	$$$	$$$$
RESTAURANTS			
under $20	$20–$30	$31–$40	over $40

RESERVATIONS AND DRESS

Where reservations are indicated as essential, book a week or more ahead in summer and early fall. Except as noted in individual listings, dress is informal.

➕ Health/Safety

The Wine Country is a safe place. Still, the largest cities, Napa and Santa Rosa, have a few rougher sections (typically far from the tourist spots). Car break-ins are rare but do happen; don't leave valuables in sight. Wildfires often occur away from populated areas, but not always: if ordered to evacuate, heed immediately.

COVID-19

Most travel restrictions, including vaccination and masking requirements, have been lifted across the United

States except in health-care facilities and nursing homes. Some travelers may still wish to wear a mask in confined spaces, including on airplanes, on public transportation, and at large indoor gatherings, but that is increasingly a personal choice.

Lodging

Inns and hotels range from low-key to sumptuous, with the broadest selection of moderately priced rooms in Napa, Petaluma, and Santa Rosa. Reservations are a good idea, especially during the fall harvest season and on weekends. Minimum stays of two or three nights are common, though some lodgings are flexible about this in winter. Some places aren't suitable for kids, so ask before you book.

APARTMENT AND HOUSE RENTALS

Although Napa and other cities restrict Airbnb and similar rentals, you'll find listings online for accommodations throughout the Wine Country.

HOTELS

Newer hotels tend to have a more modern, streamlined aesthetic and spalike bathrooms, and many have excellent restaurants. Most hotels have Wi-Fi, sometimes free. Most large properties have pools and fitness rooms; those without sometimes have arrangements with nearby facilities.

INNS

Many inns occupy historic Victorian-era buildings. When rates include breakfast, the preparations often involve fresh, local produce. Most inns have Wi-Fi, but some may not have air-conditioning—be sure to ask if visiting in July or August, when temperatures can reach 90°F.

PRICES

⇨ *Prices in the reviews are the lowest cost of a standard double room in high season. Hotel reviews have been shortened. For full information, visit Fodors.com.*

What It Costs in U.S. Dollars			
$	$$	$$$	$$$$
HOTELS			
under $200	$200– $350	$351– $500	over $500

Nightlife

The Wine Country's two largest cities, Santa Rosa and Napa, offer the most in the way of nightlife, with Healdsburg and Petaluma two additional possibilities. Healdsburg has a sophisticated bar scene—and like Napa popular rooftop bars—though beer lovers might favor the Russian River Brewing Company's original Santa Rosa pub or its full-scale brewpub and beer garden in Windsor (between Santa Rosa and Healdsburg). The beer garden at Lagunitas Brewing Co. in Petaluma is among the other options for a fresh Sonoma County brew. In downtown Napa, try Napa Yard or head upvalley to Calistoga Inn Restaurant & Brewery. If you're into sparkling wine, Be Bubbly in Napa and Sigh! in downtown Sonoma pour an international selection of bubbles.

Packing

You needn't pack anything for a Wine Country excursion you wouldn't include for any other domestic U.S. trip. Dressy-casual attire is the norm at most wineries, restaurants, and accommodations, though except at resorts and fine-dining establishments no one will pay much

Essentials

attention to what you wear. Pack a sweater or light jacket even in summer—it gets chilly when the fog rolls in. It rarely rains from May through October; an umbrella can come in handy the rest of the year.

Performing Arts

Most A-list talents who perform in the Napa Valley do so as part of one of several festivals, most notably BottleRock Napa Valley (major and indie bands), Festival Napa Valley (opera, theater, dance, and classical music), and the Napa Valley Film Festival (more to promote a film than to perform, but sometimes both). Because of the city of Napa's size and proximity to San Francisco, a few downtown venues, among them Blue Note Napa, attract big-name musical acts. Over in Sonoma County, the Luther Burbank Center for the Arts in Santa Rosa and the Green Music Center in nearby Rohnert Park draw top musicians in all genres and present plays and musicals.

Shopping

Fine wine attracts fine everything else—dining, lodging, and spas—and shopping is no exception. Sonoma County's Healdsburg and Sonoma and the Napa Valley's Napa, St. Helena, and Yountville stand out for quality, selection, and their walkable downtowns.

Hands-down the Wine Country's best shopping town, Healdsburg supports establishments selling one-of-a-kind artworks, housewares, and clothing. Heading south 37 miles, shops and galleries ring Sonoma's historic plaza and fill adjacent arcades and side streets.

Taxes

Sales tax is 7¾%–8¼% in Napa County and 8½%–9½% in Sonoma County. The tax on hotel rooms adds 14%–15% to your bill in Sonoma County and 15% in Napa County.

Tipping

Tipping Guidelines for Napa and Sonoma	
Bartender	15%–20%, starting at $1 per drink at casual places
Bellhop	$3–$5 per bag, depending on the level of the hotel
Hotel concierge	$5 or more, if concierge performs a service for you
Hotel doorman, room service, or valet	$5
Hotel maid	$5–$10 a day (either daily or at the end of your stay, in cash)
Tasting-room server	$10 per couple basic tasting, $10–$20 per person hosted seated tasting, a little more at ultra-high-end tastings with food
Tour guide	10%–15% of the cost of the tour
Waiter	18%–22%, with 20% being the minimum at high-end restaurants; nothing additional if a service charge is added to the bill

Contacts

Air

AIRPORTS Charles M. Schulz Sonoma County Airport. (*STS*). ✉ *2200 Airport Blvd., Santa Rosa* ☎ *707/565–7240* ⊕ *www. sonomacountyairport. org.* **Oakland International Airport.** (*OAK*). ✉ *1 Airport Dr., Oakland* ☎ *510/563–3300* ⊕ *www. oaklandairport.com.* **Sacramento International Airport.** (*SMF*). ✉ *6900 Airport Blvd., Sacramento* ☎ *916/929–5411* ⊕ *www. sacramento.aero/smf.* **San Francisco International Airport.** (*SFO*). ✉ *McDonnell and Links Rds., San Francisco* ☎ *800/435–9736, 650/821–8211* ⊕ *www. flysfo.com.*

AIRLINES Alaska Airlines. ☎ *800/252–7522* ⊕ *www. alaskaair.com.* **Allegiant.** ☎ *702/505–8888* ⊕ *www. allegiantair.com.* **American Airlines.** ☎ *800/433–7300* ⊕ *www.aa.com.* **Sun Country Airlines.** ☎ *651/905–2737* ⊕ *www.suncountry. com.*

Boat

San Francisco Bay Ferry. ☎ *707/643–3779, 877/643–3779* ⊕ *sanfranciscobayferry.com.*

Bus

Golden Gate Transit. ☎ *415/455–2000* ⊕ *www. goldengate.org.* **Sonoma County Transit.** ☎ *707/576–7433, 800/345–7433* ⊕ *www.sctransit.com.* **VINE.** ✉ *Soscol Gateway Transit Center, 625 Burnell St., Napa* ☎ *707/251–2800, 800/696–6443* ⊕ *vinetransit.com.*

Car

511 SF Bay Traffic/Transit Alerts. ⊕ *511.org.*

RENTAL AGENCIES Exotic Car Collection by Enterprise. ☎ *415/542–6023, 866/458–9227* ⊕ *www. enterprise.com/exotic.*

CAR SERVICES AND SHUTTLES Executive Car Service Napa Valley. ☎ *707/479–4247* ⊕ *executivecarservice-napa.com.* **Perata Luxury Tours.** ☎ *707/227–8271* ⊕ *perataluxurycarservic-es.com.* **Platypus Wine Tours.** ☎ *707/253–2723* ⊕ *www.platypustours. com.* **Pleasant Limo.** ☎ *650/697–9999* ⊕ *www. pleasantlimo.com.* **Sonoma County Airport Express.** ☎ *707/837–8700* ⊕ *www. airportexpressinc.com.* **Sonoma Sterling Limousines.** ☎ *707/542–5444* ⊕ *sono-masterlinglimo.com.* **Wine Country Concierge.** ☎ *707/965–2400* ⊕ *www.*

winetrip.com. **Wine Tasting Driver.** ☎ *707/681–7050* ⊕ *wine-tasting-driver.com.*

Health/Safety

Ambulance, fire, police. ☎ *911 emergency.* **Queen of the Valley Medical Center.** ✉ *1000 Trancas St., At Villa La., Napa* ☎ *707/252–4411* ⊕ *www.thequeen.org.* **Santa Rosa Memorial Hospital.** ✉ *1165 Montgomery Dr., off 3rd St., Santa Rosa* ☎ *707/546–3210* ⊕ *www. stjoesonoma.org.*

🚆 Train

Bay Area Rapid Transit. (*BART*). ☎ *510/465–2278* ⊕ *www.bart.gov.* **SMART.** (*Sonoma-Marin Area Rapid Transit*). ☎ *707/794–3330* ⊕ *sonomamarintrain. org.*

◉ Visitor Information

CONTACTS Napa Valley Welcome Center. ✉ *1300 1st St., Suite 313, Napa* ✛ *At Franklin St.* ☎ *707/251–5895, 855/847–6272* ⊕ *www. visitnapavalley.com.* **Sonoma Valley Visitors Bureau.** ✉ *453 1st St. E, Sonoma* ☎ *707/996–1090, 866/996–1090* ⊕ *www. sonomavalley.com.*

Great Itineraries

First-Timer's Napa Tour

On this two-day Napa Valley survey you'll tour key wineries, taste fine wine, learn some history, and shop and dine. This itinerary is best done from Thursday through Sunday, when all the wineries (which all require an appointment) are open.

DAY 1: HISTORY, TASTING, SHOPPING, DINING

Start your first morning at downtown Napa's **Oxbow Public Market.** Pick up a brew at Ritual Coffee Roasters. If in need of something more substantial, drop by **Loveski** for bagels and bagel-egg sandwiches or the nearby **Model Bakery** for a doughy English muffin. Afterward, tour the culinary garden at the adjacent **CIA at Copia** campus and, if the building's open, pop inside and peruse the Wine Hall of Fame plaques on the ground floor. Inductees include Gustave Niebaum and John Daniel of the day's first stop, Inglenook, and Joseph Phelps, whose namesake winery is an afternoon alternate. The second-floor **Chuck Williams Culinary Arts Museum** contains kitchen implements dating back more than a century.

From the market, drive north on Highway 29 to Rutherford, where film director Francis Ford Coppola spent decades acquiring and restoring **Inglenook,** one of the 19th-century Napa Valley's grand estates. The winery's hosts provide a fascinating overview of area wine making, and the Cabernets, most notably the flagship Rubicon, are superb. If you can't get an appointment at Inglenook, try **Trefethen Family Vineyards.** The main tasting space of this winery founded in 1968 is a wooden winery built in 1886.

Departing Inglenook, continue north 3¾ miles on Highway 29 to St. Helena for lunch at **Farmstead at Long Meadow Ranch,** where many ingredients and some of the wines come from the ranch's properties in Rutherford and elsewhere.

Plan your after-lunch tasting based on your preferences in wine and atmosphere. The Super Tuscan wines at Calistoga's always lively **Castello di Amorosa,** off Highway 29 about 6½ miles north of Farmstead, are as over-the-top as the 107-room structure's medieval-style architecture. More serene in both setting and wines is **Joseph Phelps Vineyards,** off the Silverado Trail about 3 miles from Farmstead. In good weather, the St. Helena operation's flagship Terrace Tasting of its collector-worthy wines, including the Cabernet-heavy Insignia Bordeaux red blend, takes place alfresco overlooking grapevines and oaks. Reach Phelps from Farmstead by heading north briefly on Highway 29, east on Pope Street, south on the Silverado Trail, and east on Taplin Road.

Check into your St. Helena lodgings—the **Harvest Inn** and **Wydown Hotel,** both on Main Street, are good options. Poke around St. Helena's shops until dinner, perhaps at **Press, The Charter Oak,** or **Goose & Gander.**

DAY 2: TASTINGS, A TOUR, LUNCH, AND A TOAST

If your lodging doesn't serve breakfast, begin your day in downtown St. Helena with a pastry, quiche, or granola parfait at the original **Model Bakery** location or **The Station** nearby.

After breakfast, drive about 6 miles (south on Highway 29, east on Zinfandel Lane, south on the Silverado Trail, and west on Highway 128, also signed

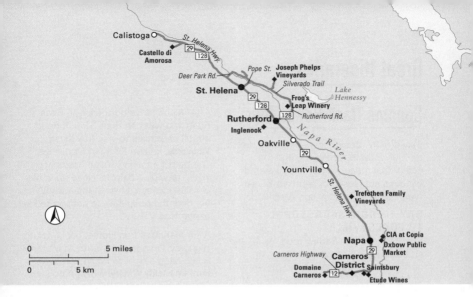

as Conn Creek Road) to **Frog's Leap.** The Rutherford winery's guided tour is educational and entertaining, but you can also taste Sauvignon Blanc, Cabernet Sauvignon, and other wines without the tour.

Spend the afternoon in the Carneros District, known for Chardonnay, Pinot Noir, and sparkling wine. From Frog's Leap, head south on Conn Creek Road and east on Skellenger Lane to the Silverado Trail, where you'll turn south. After about 8 miles, turn west on Oak Knoll Road, which in 2 miles runs into Highway 29. Drive south 7 miles, then turn west on Highway 121 (aka Carneros Highway) for 1¾ miles to reach your lunchtime stop, the **Boon Fly Café.** Part of the Carneros Resort and Spa, the casual café serves fried chicken, gourmet pizzas, and burgers.

From Boon Fly, backtrack ¼ mile east on Highway 121 to Cuttings Wharf Road, which leads south (turn right) to **Etude Wines,** known for Chardonnay, Pinot Noir, and Cabernet Sauvignon. If you're not hungry, visit Etude first and then stop by Boon Fly for a late lunch—the restaurant

serves food all day. Nearby Saintsbury, where reservations are always required, is another famed Pinot house that merits a visit if you have time.

From Etude (or Boon Fly), continue west on Highway 121 to **Domaine Carneros,** whose stately château was modeled after one in France by the winery's founders, the makers of Taittinger Champagne. The original winemaker here was fond of comparing the sophisticated sparkling wines to "Audrey Hepburn in a little black dress." If the weather's fine, sit on the vineyard-view outdoor terrace.

After your tasting, take the scenic route—Old Sonoma Road, north off Highway 121 less than ¼ mile east of Domaine Carneros—to downtown Napa. In town, turn north on Jefferson Street and east on 1st Street. Consider **Angèle** (French), **Kitchen Door** (modern American), or **ZuZu** (Spanish tapas) for dinner.

Great Itineraries

Sonoma Back Roads Tour

Stay strictly rural on this easygoing trek through forests, vineyards, and the occasional meadow. Some suggested wineries are closed one or two days a week, usually Tuesday and Wednesday.

DAY 1: FROM SEBASTOPOL TO FORESTVILLE

Start Day 1 at **The Barlow** food, wine, and art complex in Sebastopol; it's on the north side of Highway 12 two blocks east of Main Street. Have coffee and a pastry at **Taylor Lane Organic Coffee** and mosey around. Most of the shops won't be open yet, but you can catch a whiff of the complex's maker vibe and plot a return visit.

From The Barlow, pick up the Gravenstein Highway (also signed as Main Street and Highway 116 just west of The Barlow), heading north 3½ miles to Graton Road and **Dutton-Goldfield Winery.** The winery, a collaboration between a major grape grower, Steve Dutton of Dutton Ranch, and Dan Goldfield, a celebrated winemaker, built its reputation on Chardonnay and Pinot Noir grown in the Russian River Valley and other vineyards that benefit from coastal fog and wind. Dutton-Goldfield also makes a few other whites and reds.

If your tasting goes quickly, you can sample more cool-climate Chardonnays and Pinot Noirs at nearby **Red Car Wines** without even getting into your car—the two spaces share the same parking lot. When you're ready to move on, take Graton Road west half a mile to Graton. Browse the shops and gallery on the hamlet's one-block main drag and have lunch at the **Willow Wood Market Cafe.** The creamy polenta with roasted-vegetable ragout is a signature dish.

After lunch, drive northeast on Ross Road and west on Ross Station Road a total of 3 miles to visit **Iron Horse Vineyards,** known for sparkling wines. The barnlike tasting space has only three walls, providing patrons close-up views of rolling vineyard hills steps away. When needed, the hosts fire up heaters to keep things toasty.

After tasting at Iron Horse, backtrack to Highway 116 and turn north. At Martinelli Road, hang a right to reach Forestville's **Hartford Family Winery,** which produces Chardonnay, Pinot Noir, and old-vine Zinfandel.

Splurge on a night's rest at Forestville's **The Farmhouse Inn** and dine at its stellar restaurant. A less-expensive option: stay in Guerneville at **AutoCamp Russian River** or **Dawn Ranch Inn** and have dinner at **boon eat + drink** or the affiliated **Brot.**

DAY 2: HEALDSBURG AND GEYSERVILLE

Have a leisurely breakfast at your lodging or start Day 2 with a stop at **Pascaline Patisserie & Café,** a treat as much for its French-country ambience as for its exquisite pastries. (If you stayed in Guerneville, head downtown to Big Bottom Market.) You can dawdle on weekdays because the first stop, **MacRostie Estate House,** doesn't open until 11 (tastings start at 10 on weekends). From River Road, head north on Wohler Road (which begins across from The Farmhouse Inn) and then Westside Road, a 6½-mile drive. Owner Steve MacRostie has grown grapes for decades. His Healdsburg winery sources Chardonnay and Pinot Noir from his vineyards but also many other all-star sites.

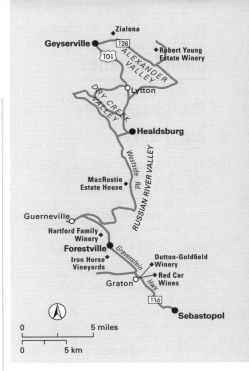

After tasting, continue on Westside to West Dry Creek Road, proceed north, and turn east at Lambert Bridge Road. The road dead-ends at your next stop, the **Dry Creek General Store,** which opened in 1881. Order inside and have lunch on the covered front porch.

Cabernet is the focus at Geyserville's **Robert Young Estate Winery.** From the general store, head south on Dry Creek Road for ¾ mile, turning left onto Lytton Springs Road, and left again (after 2¾ miles) on Lytton Station Road. Turn left again onto Alexander Valley Road 1½ miles later and left once more onto Highway 128 after 2 miles. When the highway curves sharply right after about ½ mile, continue straight onto Geysers Road and turn right onto Red Winery Road. The namesake founder has two Chardonnay clones named for him, but the robust Cabernet Sauvignons and other wines from red Bordeaux grapes are the reason to come here—oh yes, and the view down the entire Alexander Valley from the winery's knoll-top hospitality center. (Robert Young is closed on Tuesday; visit **Zialena** instead.)

Departing Robert Young, backtrack to U.S. 101 and head south to Healdsburg. Check out the shops on the streets bordering Healdsburg Plaza, then stop for a cocktail at **Duke's Spirited Cocktails** or the rooftop bar at **The Matheson.** Have dinner at The Matheson or walk to nearby **Barndiva** or **Valette.** Dine at Little Saint for plant-based cuisine.

Great Itineraries

The Ultimate Wine Trip, 4 Days

On this four-day extravaganza, you'll taste well-known and under-the-radar wines, bed down in plush hotels, and dine at restaurants operated by celebrity chefs. Reservations are required for all winery visits and recommended for dinner.

DAY 1: NORTHERN SONOMA

Begin your tour in the Alexander Valley at the French-style château of Healdsburg's **Jordan Vineyard & Winery.** Jordan produces one Russian River Valley Chardonnay and one Alexander Valley Cabernet Sauvignon each year. From spring to fall, book an outdoor tasting. To reach Jordan from downtown Healdsburg, drive north 3 miles on Healdsburg Avenue and northeast (turn right) about 1½ miles on Alexander Valley Road.

Have lunch in nearby Geyserville at **Diavola** or **Catelli's**. From Jordan, backtrack west ¼ mile on Alexander Valley Road, turning north (right) onto Lytton Station Road and following it about 1½ miles before turning west (right) on Lytton Springs Road. After 250 feet (before the highway), turn north (right) onto Geyserville Avenue.

Take the scenic route back to **Healdsburg Plaza,** south on Geyserville Avenue to Healdsburg Avenue. (You'll pass under U.S. 101 twice along the way.) Explore the shops near the plaza or stop for a Pinot Noir tasting at Cartograph Wines or Marine Layer Wines. **Hôtel Les Mars** and **Harmon Guest House** are two spots near the plaza to spend the night; stay at the **River Belle Inn** for a more traditional bed-and-breakfast experience or **Montage Healdsburg** for high design amid 250 acres of vineyards and oaks.

The Matheson restaurant's rooftop bar is a swank spot for a predinner cocktail before moving on to a meal downstairs or walking over to nearby **Bravas Bar de Tapas** or **Valette.** If you're in the mood to splurge, reserve (well in advance) a table at **SingleThread Farms Restaurant,** across from Valette. **Little Saint,** near SingleThread, serves plant-based cuisine.

DAY 2: HEALDSBURG AND GLEN ELLEN

Hike in the early morning or midafternoon, whichever suits you best, before or after visiting a few wineries or tasting rooms. If you're an early riser, begin the morning 2¾ miles north of Healdsburg Plaza strolling some of the **Healdsburg Ridge Open Space Preserve.** Wineries dot the Dry Creek Valley countryside, among them **Ridge Vineyards.** After tasting, have lunch in Healdsburg at **Troubadour Bread & Bistro, Little Saint,** or **Willi's Seafood & Raw Bar** before heading south on U.S. 101 and east on scenic Highway 12 to the Sonoma Valley town of Glen Ellen. If you've already hiked, drop by the tasting room of **Laurel Glen Vineyards** or **Talisman Wine,** both downtown. **Benziger Family Winery,** on London Ranch Road on the way to **Jack London State Historic Park,** is another good choice. If headed to the park, hike part of the Vineyard Trail, bordering land where the famous writer grew grapes, afterward stopping at the memorabilia-filled House of Happy Walls Museum. Have dinner at **Glen Ellen Star** and stay at the **Olea Hotel** or **Gaige House.**

DAY 3: NORTHERN NAPA VALLEY

Head east 11 miles from Glen Ellen on Trinity Road, which twists and turns over the Mayacamas Mountains, eventually becoming the Oakville Grade. Unless you're the driver, bask in the stupendous Napa Valley views as you descend into Oakville. At Highway 29, drive 7½ miles

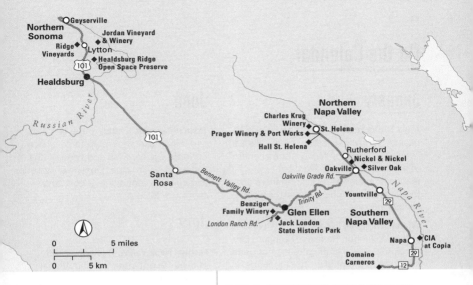

north through downtown **St. Helena** to **Charles Krug Winery,** established in 1861.

After tasting at Charles Krug, take lunch downtown at **Market, Crisp Kitchen & Juice,** or **The Station** and check out Main Street's shops before heading south on Highway 29 to **Hall St. Helena** (high-scoring Cabernets, impressive art collection) or its homey neighbor, **Prager Winery & Port Works.**

When done tasting, continue south on Highway 29 to Yountville for more shopping. Start in the north end of town at Restoration Hardware's **RH Yountville** and work your way south on Washington Street, stopping in the middle of town anywhere that catches your eye but most definitely at **Montecristi Panama Hats.**

Stay overnight at **Bardessono** or the **North Block Hotel,** both within walking distance of Yountville's famous restaurants. A meal at Thomas Keller's **The French Laundry** is many visitors' holy grail, but dining at **Bistro Jeanty** or Keller's **Bouchon Bistro** will also leave you feeling well served. Head to the **North Block Restaurant** for modern American or chef Michael Chiarello's **Coqueta Napa Valley** for tapas and larger Spanish plates. The specialty cocktails at both are exceptional.

DAY 4: SOUTHERN NAPA VALLEY

Take breakfast at your lodging or Southside Yountville at Stewart Cellars, then head north 3 miles on Highway 29 to **Oakville,** where sipping wine at **Nickel & Nickel** or **Silver Oak** will make clear why collectors covet Oakville Cabernet Sauvignons. Nickel & Nickel is on Highway 29; Silver Oak is east of it on Oakville Cross Road. After your tasting, have a picnic at **Oakville Grocery,** in business on Highway 29 since 1881, or lunch at **Brix Napa Valley** or **Mustards Grill.** You're liable to see winery folk at either Brix or Mustards.

Your meal completed, head south on Highway 29, exiting at 1st Street to visit downtown Napa's **CIA at Copia** food and wine complex (if it's open, don't miss the museum of culinary equipment upstairs). Backtrack on 1st Street to Highway 29 and head south to Highway 121. Turn west to reach the Carneros District, whose **Domaine Carneros** makes French-style sparkling wines. There's hardly a more elegant way to bid the Wine Country adieu than from the château's vineyard-view terrace.

On the Calendar

January

Napa Truffle Festival. Chef Ken Frank's passion for truffles is boundless. His La Toque restaurant in Napa is the scene of a fancy dinner, the highlight of this festival that also includes seminars and foraging expeditions. ⊕ *www.napatrufflefestival.com*

Winter Wineland. In mid-January, wineries in the Alexander, Russian River, and Dry Creek Valleys—including many not generally open to the public—host tastings and other events. ⊕ *www.wineroad.com*

March

Wine Road Barrel Tasting. In early March, northern Sonoma County wineries open their cellars for tastings of wines yet to be bottled. ⊕ *www.wineroad.com*

April

Passport to Dry Creek Valley. Participants at this two-day northern Sonoma County event sample the Zinfandels that made the valley's name, along with wines from the many other varietals that grow here. ⊕ *www.drycreekvalley.org/passport*

May

BottleRock Napa Valley. A three-day end-of-May food, wine, and music festival, BottleRock gets the summer rocking (and rolling) with artists like Metallica, Bruno Mars, Pink, Halsey, and Skip Marley. Tickets sell out in early January when the lineup is announced (VIP and other passes often before then). ⊕ *www.bottlerocknapavalley.com*

June

Taste of Sonoma. Chefs, grape growers, and winemakers team up to celebrate Sonoma County food and wine on the last Saturday in June. Dozens of wineries and culinary vendors take part. ⊕ *tasteofsonoma.com*

July

Festival Napa Valley. This acclaimed mid-July event attracts international opera, theater, dance, and classical-music performers to Castello di Amorosa and other venues. ⊕ *www.festivalnapavalley.org*

September and October

Sonoma County Harvest Fair. This three-week festival honors Sonoma agriculture with grape-stomping, wine, and olive-oil competitions, cooking demos, flower and livestock shows, carnival rides, and local entertainers. Grand tastings of award-winning wines and foods take place in early October. ⊕ *www.sonomacountyfair.com*

November

A Wine & Food Affair. For this November event, wineries prepare a favorite recipe and serve it with wine. Participants travel from winery to winery to sample the fare. ⊕ *www.wineroad.com*

Chapter 3

VISITING WINERIES AND TASTING ROOMS

Updated by
Daniel Mangin

Whether you're a serious wine collector making your annual pilgrimage to Napa and Sonoma or a newbie who doesn't know the difference between Merlot and Mourvèdre but is eager to learn, you can have a great time touring the Wine Country. Your gateway to the wine world is the tasting room, where staff members—occasionally even the winemaker—are happy to chat with curious guests.

Tasting rooms range from the grand to the humble, offering everything from a few sips of wine to in-depth tours of facilities and vineyards. First-time visitors frequently enjoy the history-oriented focus at Beaulieu, Beringer, Charles Krug, and Inglenook. The environments at some wineries reflect their founders' or current owners' other interests: horses at Nickel & Nickel and Tamber Bey, moviemaking at Francis Ford Coppola, contemporary art and architecture at The Donum Estate and Hall St. Helena, and medieval history at the Castello di Amorosa.

To prepare you for a winery visit, we've covered the fundamentals: how to taste wine, tasting rooms and what to expect, and the types of tours wineries typically offer. A list of common tasting terms will help you interpret what your mouth is experiencing as you sip. We've also described the major grape varietals and the specific techniques employed to craft white, red, sparkling, and rosé wines. Because great wines begin in the vineyard, we've included a section on soils, climates, and organic and biodynamic farming methods. A handy Wine Lover's Glossary of terms, from *acidity* to *zymology,* covers ones you may come across in the tasting room or on a tour.

Wine Tasting 101

At its core, wine tasting is simply about determining which wines you like best. "We're all experts at that," notes vintner Lloyd Davis of Sonoma's Corner 103 tasting room. "Think about it: no one knows your palate better than you do." That said, knowing a few basic terms and some of the strategies seasoned wine drinkers follow can enhance the experience. Follow your instincts: there's no right or wrong way to perceive or describe wine. If you watch the pros, you may notice that they inspect, swirl, and sniff before sipping a wine. Do the same. Take it slow, involving all your senses as you proceed through the steps outlined below.

USE YOUR EYES

Before you taste it, take a good look at the wine in your glass. Holding the glass by the stem, raise it to the light. Whether white, rosé, or red, your wine should be clear, without cloudiness or sediments. Some unfiltered wines may initially seem cloudy, but most clear as the sediments settle.

In natural light, place the glass in front of a white background such as a blank sheet of paper or a tablecloth. **Check the color.** Is it right for the wine? A California white should be golden: straw, medium, or deep, depending on the type. A rich, sweet dessert wine will have more intense color, but Chardonnay and Sauvignon Blanc will be paler. A rosé should be a clear pink, from pale to deep, without too much red. Reds may lean toward ruby or garnet coloring; some have a purple tinge. Pinot Noir can be pale yet still have character. In any color of wine, a brownish tinge is a flaw that indicates the wine is too old, has been incorrectly stored, or has gone bad.

BREATHE DEEP

After observing the wine, **sniff once or twice** and try to identify its aromas. Then softly move your glass in a circular motion to swirl the wine around. Aerating the wine this way releases more aromas. (It's called "volatilizing the esters," if you're trying to impress someone.) Stick your nose into the glass and take another long sniff. You might pick up the scent of apricots, peaches, ripe melon, and wildflowers in white wine; black pepper, cherry, violets, and cedar in a red. Rosés, made from red-wine grapes, smell something like a red, but in a scaled-back way, with hints of raspberry, strawberry, and sometimes rose petal. You might encounter surprising scents such as leather or graphite, which some people appreciate in certain (generally expensive) red wines.

For the most part, a wine's aroma should be clean and pleasing. If you find a wine's odor unpleasant, there's probably

something wrong. A vinegar smell indicates that the wine has started to spoil. A rotten wood or soggy cardboard smell usually means the cork has gone bad, ruining the wine. It's rare to find these faults in wines poured in the tasting rooms, however, because staffers usually taste from each bottle before pouring from it.

JUST A SIP

Once you've checked its appearance and aroma, **take a sip**—not a swig or a gulp—of the wine. As you sip a wine, **gently swish it around in your mouth**—this releases more aromas for your nose to explore. Do the aroma and the flavor complement each other, improve each other? While moving the wine around in your mouth, think about how it feels: Silky or crisp? Does it coat your tongue or is it thinner? Does it fill your mouth with flavor or is it weak? This combination of weight and intensity is referred to as *body*: a good wine may be light-, medium-, or full-bodied.

The more complex a wine, the more flavors you will detect while tasting. You might experience different things when you first take a sip (*up front*), when you swish (*in the middle* or *midpalate*), and just before you swallow (*at the end* or *back-palate*).

SPIT OR SWALLOW?

You may choose to spit out the wine (into the cup or receptacle provided) or swallow it. The pros typically spit because they want to preserve their palates (and sobriety) for the wines to come, but you'll find that swallowers far outnumber spitters in tasting rooms. Either way, **pay attention to what happens after the wine leaves your mouth**—this is the finish, and it can be spectacular. What sensations stay behind or appear? Does the flavor fade away quickly or linger pleasantly? A long finish is a sign of quality; wine with no perceptible finish is inferior.

Filmmaker Francis Ford Coppola owns Inglenook, one of the Napa Valley's great wine estates.

Tasting Rooms and Winery Tours

At most wineries you'll have to pay for the privilege of tasting. In the Napa Valley expect to pay $35–$125 for a tasting of current releases and $85–$150 or more for reserve, estate, or library wines. Sonoma County tastings generally cost $30–$75 for the former and $55–$125 for the latter. To experience wine making at its highest level, consider splurging for a special tasting at one winery at least.

For years it was the norm in tasting rooms not to tip, but with today's more personalized service, you might consider doing so. For a wine-only tasting overseen by a server assisting multiple tables, $10 per couple will suffice; for a hosted seated tasting, $10–$20 per person, perhaps more for extra attention or a high-end experience.

Many wineries are open to the public daily from around 10 or 11 am to 5 pm. A few countryside wineries and some in-town tasting rooms stay open until 6 or 7. However, most wineries stop serving new visitors from 15 to 30 minutes before the posted closing time, so don't expect to skate in at the last moment.

IN THE TASTING ROOM

In most tasting rooms, the server will provide a list of the wines being poured. The wines will be listed in a suggested tasting order, generally starting with the lightest-bodied whites and progressing to the most intense reds. Dessert wines will come at the end.

If you haven't reserved a set tasting experience—all Cabernets, for example—you may be able to choose several wines from the winery's available lineup. Whatever the case, if you prefer whites or reds, make this known. If possible, the server will adjust the offerings. Many wineries limit the number of pours to four or five, so don't waste a taste on something you know you don't prefer.

Each pour will be about an ounce. If your tasting doesn't involve a food pairing, crackers or breadsticks might be provided; nibble them to clear your palate between selections. If you don't like a wine or have tasted enough, don't feel obligated to finish it.

TAKING A TOUR

Even if you're not a devoted wine drinker, seeing how grapes become wine can be fascinating. Tours tend to be most exciting in September and October, when harvest and crush are under way. Depending on the winery's size, tours range from a few people to large groups and typically last from 30 minutes to an hour.

■ **TIP→ Wear comfortable shoes because you might be walking on wet floors or stepping over hoses or other equipment.**

Some winery tours are free, in which case you usually pay a separate fee to taste wine. If you've paid for the tour, your tasting is likely included in the price.

At large wineries, tours are typically offered on a regular basis. Less frequent are specialized experiences and seminars focusing on growing techniques, sensory evaluation, wine blending, food-and-wine pairing, and related topics.

VISITING SAFELY

Expect adherence to current CDC and California state guidelines regarding COVID-19. Winery websites usually describe what to expect during a tasting or tour. Call ahead if you have any specific concerns. To maintain proper sanitation and control patron flow, most wineries receive guests by appointment only. Some allow walk-ins space permitting, but many don't. Be aware, too, that many wineries that previously allowed picnicking, guests under age 21, or pets no longer do. Check ahead to avoid disappointment.

Wine Clubs

If several of a winery's offerings appeal to you and you live in a state that allows you to order wines directly from a producer, consider joining the wine club. You'll receive offers for members-only releases, invitations to winery events, and a discount on purchases.

Top Varietals

Several dozen grape varietals are grown in Napa and Sonoma, from favorites like Chardonnay and Cabernet Sauvignon to less familiar types like Albariño and Tempranillo. You may come across the following varietals as you visit wineries and tasting rooms.

WHITE

Albariño. Popular in Spain and a staple of Portuguese wine making, this cool-climate grape creates light, citrusy wines, often with overtones of mango or kiwi.

Chardonnay. A grape originally from relatively cool Burgundy, France, Chardonnay in Napa and Sonoma can be fruit-forward or restrained, buttery or highly acidic, depending on where it's grown, when during harvest it's picked, and the wine-making techniques applied.

Gewürztraminer. Cooler climes such as the Russian River Valley are great for growing this German-Alsatian grape, which is turned into a boldly perfumed, fruity wine.

Marsanne. A white-wine grape of France's northern Rhône Valley, Marsanne can produce a dry or sweet wine depending on how it is handled.

Pinot Gris. Known in Italy as Pinot Grigio, this varietal in Napa and Sonoma yields a more deeply colored, less acidic wine with medium to full body.

Riesling. Also called White Riesling, this cool-climate German grape has a sweet reputation in America. When made in a dry style, though, it can be crisply refreshing, with lush aromas.

Roussanne. This grape from the Rhône Valley makes a fragrant wine balancing fruitiness and acidity.

Sauvignon Blanc. Hailing from Bordeaux and the Loire Valley, this white grape does very well almost anywhere in Napa and Sonoma. Sauvignon Blancs display a range of personalities, from herbaceous to tropical-fruit.

Viognier. A grape from France's Rhône Valley, Viognier is usually made in a dry style. The best Viogniers often have an intense bouquet.

RED

Barbera. Prevalent in California thanks to 19th-century Italian immigrants, Barbera yields low-tannin, high-acid wines with ample fruit.

Cabernet Franc. Often used in blends to add complexity to Cabernet Sauvignon, this French grape can produce aromatic, soft, and subtle wines.

Cabernet Sauvignon. The king of California reds, this Bordeaux grape is at home in well-drained soils. It can require an extended aging period, so it's often softened with Cabernet Franc, Merlot, and other red varieties for earlier drinking.

Grenache. This Spanish grape, which makes some of the southern Rhône Valley's most distinguished wines, ripens best in hot, dry conditions. Medium-bodied, often light in color, Grenache is sometimes blended with a little Syrah to add tannin and texture.

Merlot. This blue-black Bordeaux varietal makes soft, full-bodied wines. Often fruity, it can be complex even when young.

Mourvèdre. A native of France's Rhône Valley, this grape makes wine that is deeply colored, very dense, and high in alcohol. When young it can seem harsh, but it mellows with aging.

Petite Sirah. A cross between the Rhône grapes Syrah and Peloursin, Petite Sirah, which loves a warm climate, produces a hearty wine.

Pinot Noir. The darling of grape growers in cooler parts of Napa and Sonoma, including the Carneros region and the Russian River Valley, Pinot Noir is also called the "heartbreak grape" because it's hard to cultivate. At its best it has a subtle but addictive earthy quality.

Sangiovese. Dominant in the Chianti region and much of central Italy, Sangiovese can be made into vibrant, light-to medium-bodied wines or complex reds, depending on how it's grown and vinified.

Syrah. Another big California red, this grape originated in the Rhône Valley. With good tannins, it can become a full-bodied, almost smoky beauty.

Tempranillo. The primary varietal in Spain's Rioja region, sturdy Tempranillo makes inky purple wines with a rich texture. Wines from this grape can be outstanding on their own but often excel paired with red-meat and game dishes.

Zinfandel. Celebrated as California's own (though it has distant old-world origins), Zinfandel is rich and spicy. Its tannins can make it complex and well suited for aging.

How Wine Is Made

THE CRUSH

Turning grapes into wine generally starts at the **crush pad,** where the grapes are brought in from the vineyards. Good winemakers keep tabs on the fruit throughout the year, but their presence is critical

From a balloon you'll see how compact the Napa Valley is.

at harvest, when ripeness determines the proper day for picking. Once that day arrives, the crush begins.

Wineries pick grapes by machine or hand, depending on the terrain and the type of grape. Harvesting often takes place at night with the help of powerful floodlights. Why at night? In addition to it being easier on the workers (daytime temperatures frequently reach 90°F [32°C] or more from August well into October), the fruit-acid content in the grape's pulp and juice peaks in the cool night air. The acids—an essential component during fermentation and aging and an important part of wine's flavor—plummet in the heat of the day.

Grapes arrive at the crush pad in large containers called gondolas. Unless the winemaker intends to ferment the entire clusters, which is generally done only for red wines, they are dropped onto a conveyor belt that deposits them into a **stemmer-crusher,** which separates the grapes from their stems. Then the sorting process begins. At most wineries this is done by hand at sorting tables, where workers remove remaining stems and leaves and reject any damaged berries.

Because anything not sorted out will wind up in the fermenting tank, some wineries double or even triple sort to achieve higher quality. Stems, for instance, can add unwanted tannins or, if not sufficiently ripe, "greenness" to a finished wine. On the other hand, winemakers sometimes desire those tannins and allow some stems through. A few high-end wineries use optical grape sorters that scan and assess the fruit. Berries deemed too small or otherwise defective are whisked away, along with any extraneous vegetal matter.

No matter the process used, the sorted grapes are then ready for transfer to a press or vat. After this step the production process goes one of four ways, depending on whether a white, red, rosé, or sparkling wine is being made.

WHITE WINES

The juice of white-wine grapes first goes to **settling tanks,** where the skins and solids sink to the bottom, separating from the free-run juice on top. The material in the settling tanks still contains a lot of liquid, so after the free-run juice is pumped off, the rest goes into a **press.** By one of several methods, additional liquid is squeezed from the solids. Like the free-run juice, the press juice is usually pumped into a stainless-steel **fermenter.**

During fermentation, yeast feeds on the sugar in the grape juice and converts it to alcohol and carbon dioxide. Wine yeast dies and fermentation naturally stops in two to four weeks, when the alcohol level reaches between 13% and 15% (or sometimes more).

To prevent oxidation that damages wine's color and flavor, winemakers almost always add sulfur dioxide, in the form of sulfites, before fermenting. A winemaker may also encourage **malolactic fermentation** (or simply *malo*) to soften a wine's acidity or deepen its flavor and complexity. This is done either by inoculating the wine with lactic bacteria soon after fermentation begins or right after it ends, or by transferring the new wine to wooden vats that harbor the bacteria.

For richer results, free-run juice from Chardonnay and other white grapes might be fermented in oak barrels. In many cases the barrels used to make white wines are older, "neutral" barrels previously used to make other wines. These **neutral barrels** can add fullness to a wine without adding wood flavors. In recent years wineries have begun using fermenting tanks made out of concrete. Initially these vessels, some shaped like eggs, others square or cone-shaped, were mainly employed to make white wines, but more wineries are also using them for rosés and reds. Bigger than an oak barrel but smaller than most stainless tanks, the vessels, like barrels, are porous enough to "breathe," but unlike wood don't impart flavors or tannins to wines. The notion of fermenting wines in concrete receptacles may sound newfangled, but their use dates back to the 19th century (and some say even further).

When the wine has finished fermenting, whether in a tank or a barrel, it is generally **racked**—moved into a clean tank or barrel to separate it from any remaining grape solids. Sometimes wines are left "on the lees"—atop the spent yeast, grape solids, and other matter in the fermenting tank—for an extended period before being racked to pick up extra complexity. Wine may be racked several times as the sediment continues to settle out.

After the first racking the wine may be **filtered** to remove solid particles that can cloud the wine and any stray yeast or bacteria that can spoil it. Some whites are filtered several times before bottling. Most commercial producers filter their wines, but many fine-wine makers don't, as they believe it leads to less complex wines that don't age as well.

White wine may also be **fined** by mixing in a fine clay called bentonite, albumen from egg whites, or other agents to absorb substances that can cloud the wine. As with filtering, the process is more common with ordinary table wines than fine wines.

New wine is stored in stainless-steel, wood (predominantly oak), concrete, and occasionally terra-cotta containers to rest and develop before bottling. This stage, called **maturation** or **aging,** may last anywhere from a few months to a year or more. Barrel rooms are kept dark to protect the wine from light and heat, which can be damaging. Some wineries keep their wines in air-conditioned rooms or warehouses; others use long, tunnel-like caves bored into hillsides, where the wine remains at a constant temperature.

Before bottling (sometimes earlier), winemakers typically blend two or more wine batches to balance flavor. **Blending** provides an extra chance to create a perfect single-varietal wine or combine several varietals that complement each other. On the other hand, a winemaker might forgo blending to highlight the attributes of grapes from a single vineyard.

If wine is aged for any length of time before bottling, it may be racked and perhaps filtered several times. Once bottled, the wine is stored for **bottle aging** in a cool, dark space. In a few months most white wines will be ready for release.

RED WINES

Red-wine production differs slightly from that of white wine. Red-wine grapes are crushed in the same way, but the juice is not separated from the grape skins and pulp before fermentation. This is what gives red wine its color and flavor. After crushing, the red-wine **must**—the thick slurry of juice, pulp, and skins—is fermented in vats. The juice is "left on the skins" from a few days to a few weeks. The length of time depends on the grape type and how much color and flavor the winemaker wants to extract.

Fermentation also extracts chemical compounds such as **tannins** from the skins and seeds, making red wines more robust than whites. Tannin levels are kept down in a red designed for drinking soon after bottling; they should have a greater presence in wine meant for aging. In a young red not ready for drinking, tannins feel dry or coarse in the mouth, but they soften over time. A wine with well-balanced tannins will maintain its fruitiness and backbone as its flavor develops. Without adequate tannins and acidity, a wine will not age well.

Creating the **oak barrels** that age the wine is a craft in its own right. At Demptos Napa Cooperage, a French-owned company that employs French barrel-making techniques, the process involves several elaborate production phases. Oak staves are formed into the shape

of a barrel using metal bands, and then the rough edges of the bound planks are smoothed. Finally, the barrels are toasted (exposed to fire) to give the oak its characteristic flavor, which will be imparted to the wine over time. Depending on the winemaker's preferences and goals, a barrel might have a "light," "medium," or "heavy" toast.

At the end of fermentation, the free-run wine is drained off. The grape skins and pulp are sent to a press, where the remaining liquid is extracted. As with white wines, the winemaker may blend a little of the press wine into the free-run wine to add complexity. Otherwise, the press juice goes into bulk wine—the lower-quality, less expensive stuff.

Next up is **oak-barrel aging,** which takes from a half year to a year or longer. Oak, like grapes, contains natural tannins, and the wine extracts these tannins from the barrels. The wood also has countless tiny pores through which water slowly evaporates, making the wine more concentrated. To ensure the aging wine does not oxidize, the barrels are regularly **topped off** with wine from the same vintage, reducing oxygen exposure.

New, or virgin, oak barrels impart the most tannins to a wine. With each successive use the tannins diminish, until the barrel is said to be "neutral." Depending on the varietal, winemakers might blend juice aged in virgin oak barrels with juice aged in neutral barrels. In the tasting room you may hear, for instance, that a Pinot Noir was aged in 30% new oak and 70% two-year-old oak, meaning that the bulk of the wine was aged in oak used for two previous agings.

SPARKLING WINES

Despite the mystique surrounding them, sparkling wines are nothing more or less than wines in which carbon dioxide is suspended, making them bubbly. Good sparkling wine will always be fairly expensive because a great deal of work goes into making it.

White sparkling wines can be made from either white or red grapes. In France, champagne is traditionally made from Chardonnay, Pinot Meunier, and Pinot Noir. That's mostly the case in Napa and Sonoma, though fewer sparklers have Pinot Meunier. Occasionally Albariño, Pinot Gris, and other grapes are used.

The freshly pressed juice and pulp, or must, is **fermented with special yeasts** that preserve the characteristic fruit flavor of the grape variety used. Before bottling, this finished "still" wine (without bubbles) is mixed with a *liqueur de tirage,* a blend of wine, sugar, and yeast. This mixture causes the wine to ferment again—in the bottle, where it stays for up to 12 weeks. **Carbon dioxide,** a by-product of fermentation, is produced and trapped in the bottle, where it dissolves into the wine (instead of escaping into the air, as happens during fermentation in a barrel, vat, or tank). This captive carbon dioxide transforms a still wine into a sparkler.

New bottles of sparkling wine are stored on their sides. The wine now ages *sur lie,* or "on the lees" (the dead yeast cells and other deposits trapped in the bottle). This aging process enriches the wine's texture and increases the complexity of its bouquet. The amount of time spent sur lie relates directly to its quality: the longer the aging, the more complex the wine.

The lees must be removed from the bottle before a sparkling wine can be enjoyed. This is achieved in a process whose first step is called **riddling.** In the past, each bottle, head tilted slightly downward, was placed in a riddling rack, an A-frame with many holes of bottle-neck size. Riddlers gave each bottle a slight shake and a downward turn—every day, if possible. This continued for six weeks, until each bottle rested upside down in the hole and the sediment

had collected in the neck. Today most sparkling wines are riddled in ingeniously designed machines called gyro palettes, which can handle 500 or more bottles at a time, though at a few wineries, such as Schramsberg, some of the work is still done by hand.

After riddling, the bottles are **disgorged.** The upside-down bottles are placed in a very cold solution, freezing the sediments in a block that attaches itself to the crown cap that seals the bottle. The cap and frozen plug are then removed. In most cases the bottle is topped off with a wine-and-sugar mixture called **dosage** and recorked with the traditional Champagne cork. The dosage ultimately determines the sparkler's sweetness.

Most sparkling wines are not vintage dated but are *assembled* (the term sparkling-wine makers use instead of *blended)* to create a **cuvée,** a mix of different wines and sometimes different vintages consistent with the house style. Nevertheless, sparkling wines may be vintage dated in particularly great years.

Sparkling wine may also be made by time- and cost-saving bulk methods. In the **Charmat process,** invented by Eugene Charmat early in the 20th century, secondary fermentation takes place in large tanks rather than individual bottles. Basically, each tank is treated as one huge bottle. This comes at a price: although the sparkling wine may be ready in as little as a month, it has neither the complexity nor the bubble quality of traditional sparklers.

ROSÉ WINES

Rosé or blush wines come from red-wine grapes, but the juicy pulp is left on the skins for a matter of hours—typically from 12 to 36—rather than days. When the winemaker decides that the juice has reached the desired color, it is drained off and filtered. Yeast is added, and the juice is left to ferment. Because the juice stays on the skins for a shorter time, fewer tannins

How to Read a Wine Label

A wine's label will tell you a lot about what's inside. To decode the details, look for the following information:

■ **Alcohol content:** In most cases, U.S. law requires wineries to list the alcohol content, which typically hovers around 13% or 14%, though big reds like Zinfandel can soar to 16% or more.

■ **Appellation:** At least 85% of the grapes must have come from the AVA (American Viticultural Area) listed on the bottle. A bottle that says "Mt. Veeder," for example, contains mostly grapes grown in the compact Mt. Veeder appellation, but if the label says "California," the grapes could be from anywhere in the state.

■ **Estate or Estate Grown:** Wines with this label must be made entirely of grapes grown on land owned or farmed by the winery.

■ **Reserve:** An inexact term meaning "special" (and therefore usually costing more), *reserve* can refer to how or where the grapes were grown, how the wine was made, or how long it was aged.

■ **Varietal:** If the label lists a single grape type, it means that at least 75% of the wine's grapes are of that varietal. If no grape is named, the wine is likely a blend of different types.

■ **Vineyard name:** If the label lists a vineyard, at least 95% of the grapes must have been harvested there.

■ **Vintage:** If a year appears on the label, at least 95% of the grapes were harvested that year (85% for wines not designated with an AVA). If no vintage is listed, the grapes may come from more than one year's harvest.

are leached from them, and the resulting wine is not as full flavored as a red.

The range of tastes and textures is remarkable. Rosé of Cabernet Sauvignon, for instance, can have a velvety and almost savory taste, while rosé of Pinot Noir or Syrah might have a crisp and mineral taste.

Grape Growing: The Basics

Most kinds of wine grapes are touchy. If the weather is too hot, they can produce too much sugar and not enough acid, resulting in overly alcoholic wines. Too cool and they won't ripen properly, and some will develop an unpleasant vegetal taste. And rain at the wrong time of year can wreak havoc on vineyards, causing

grapes to rot on the vine. These and many other conditions must be just right to coax the best out of persnickety wine grapes, and Napa and Sonoma have that magical combination of sun, rain, fog, slope, and soil that allows the fruit to thrive.

APPELLATIONS: LOCATION, LOCATION, LOCATION

Winemakers generally agree that despite the high-tech equipment at their disposal, wine is made in the vineyard. This emphasis on *terroir* (a French term that encompasses a region's soil, climate, and overall growing conditions) reflects a belief that what happens before grapes are crushed determines a wine's quality.

In the United States, the Alcohol and Tobacco Tax and Trade Bureau (TTB) designates **appellations of origin** based on political boundaries or unique soil, climate, or other characteristics.

Pinot Noir and Chardonnay are widely grown in the Russian River Valley.

California, for instance, is an appellation, as are Napa and Sonoma Counties. More significantly to wine lovers, the TTB can designate a unique grape-growing region as an American Viticultural Area (AVA), more commonly called an appellation. Whether the appellation of origin is based on politics or terroir, it refers to the source of a wine's grapes, not where it was made.

Many appellations are renowned for particular wines. The Napa Valley is known for Cabernet Sauvignon, for example, the Russian River Valley for Chardonnay and Pinot Noir, and the Dry Creek Valley for Zinfandel. As of early 2023, the Napa Valley contained 16 subappellations and Sonoma County 19. Wineries can indicate the appellation or AVA on a bottle's label only if at least 85% of the grapes were grown within it.

What makes things confusing is that appellations often overlap, allowing for increased levels of specificity. The Napa Valley AVA is, of course, part of the California appellation, but the Napa Valley AVA is itself divided into 16 smaller sub-appellations, the Oakville and Rutherford AVAs being among the most famous of these. Another well-known AVA, Los Carneros, overlaps Napa and Sonoma Counties, and there are even subappellations within subappellations. Sonoma County's Russian River Valley AVA, for example, contains the smaller Green Valley of the Russian River Valley AVA. The latter earned status as a separate viticultural area because of its soils and a climate cooler and foggier than much of the Russian River Valley.

GEOLOGY 101

"Site trumps everything," says Napa Valley winemaker Todd Graff, meaning that the specific land where vines grow is more significant than grape clones, farming techniques, and even wine making. In other words, geology matters. Grapevines are among the few plants that give their best fruit when grown in poor, rocky soil. On the other hand, they don't like wet feet: the ideal vineyard soil is easily permeable by water for good drainage.

Grape varieties thrive in different types of soil. For instance, Cabernet Sauvignon does best in well-drained, gravelly soil. If it's too wet or contains too much heavy clay or organic matter, the soil will give the wine an obnoxious vegetative quality. Merlot, however, can grow in soil with more clay and still be made into rich, delicious wine. Chardonnay likes well-drained vineyards but will also take heavy soil.

Napa Valley and Sonoma County soils are dizzyingly diverse, which helps account for the inordinate variety of grapes grown here. Some soils are composed of dense, heavy, sedimentary clays washed from the mountains; others are very rocky clays, loams, or silts of alluvial fans. These fertile, well-drained soils cover the valley floors in large swaths of the two regions. There are about 60 soil types in the Napa Valley and Sonoma County.

DOWN ON THE FARM

Much like a fruit or nut orchard, a vineyard can produce excellent grapes for decades—with varietals like Zinfandel even a century or more—if given the proper attention. The growing cycle starts in winter, when the vines are bare and dormant. While the plants rest, the grower enriches the soil and repairs the trellising system (if there is one) that holds up the vines. This is also when **pruning** takes place to regulate the vine's growth and crop size.

In spring the soil is aerated by plowing or other methods, and new vines go in. The grower trains established vines so they grow, with or without trellising, in the shape most beneficial for the grapes. **Bud break** occurs when the first bits of green emerge from the vines, and a pale green veil appears over the winter's gray-black vineyards. A late frost can be devastating at this time of year. Springtime brings the flowering of the vines, when clusters of tiny green blossoms appear, followed by **fruit set,** when grapes form from the blossoms.

As the vineyards turn luxuriant and leafy in summer, more pruning and leaf pulling keep foliage in check so the vine directs nutrients to the grapes and the proper amount of sunlight can reach the fruit. During what's known as **veraison** (pronounced "vuh-ray-SAHN"), grapes begin to change color from green to yellow (for most whites) or purple (for reds). Before or after veraison (sometimes both), the grower will **"drop fruit,"** cutting off some clusters so the remaining grapes intensify in flavor.

Fall is the busiest season in the vineyard. Growers and winemakers carefully monitor grape ripeness, sometimes with equipment that tests sugar and acid levels and sometimes simply by tasting them. As soon as the grapes are ripe, **harvest** begins. In Napa and Sonoma this generally starts in August and continues into November. Once grapes are ripe, picking must be done as quickly as possible, within just a day or two, to prevent them from passing their peak. Most grapes are harvested mechanically, but some are picked by hand. After harvest, the vines start to regenerate for the next year.

Many wineries purchase at least some of their fruit. Some negotiate contracts, often long-term, that allow the winery a say in farming decisions. This way, the winemaker can control the consistency and quality of the grapes, just as if they came from the winery's vineyard. Some wineries buy from several growers, and many growers sell to more than one winery.

ORGANIC AND BIODYNAMIC

If, as many grape growers insist, a wine is only as good as the vineyard it comes from, those who have adopted organic and biodynamic agricultural methods may be on to something. But when using terms like *organic* and *biodynamic,* what do vintners mean? It boils down to rejecting chemical fertilizers, pesticides, and fungicides. Biodynamic farmers also reject these artificial agents, and their vineyard maintenance often involves metaphysical principles as well.

Even rarer than wines produced from organically grown grapes are completely organic wines. For a wine to be certified as organic, the grapes must come from organic vineyards, and the processing must use a minimum of chemical additives and no added sulfites. (Remember that some wines made from certified organic grapes still contain naturally occurring sulfites.) Some winemakers argue that it is impossible to make outstanding wine without using additives like sulfur dioxide, an antioxidant that protects the wine's color, aroma, flavor, and longevity. Very few producers make completely organic wine.

Biodynamic farmers view the land as a living, self-sustaining organism requiring a healthy, unified ecosystem to thrive. To nurture the soil, for instance, vineyard workers spray specially formulated herbal "teas" (the ingredients include yarrow, dandelion, valerian, and stinging nettle flowers) onto compost spread in the fields. Grazing animals such as sheep maintain the ground cover between the vines (and the animals' manure provides natural fertilizer). Natural predators, among them insect-eating bats, control pests that might damage the crop. Biodynamic farmers believe that the movements of the sun and the moon influence plant development, so astronomical calendars play a role in the timing of many vineyard activities.

At its most elevated level, the biodynamic philosophy recognizes a farm as a metaphysical entity requiring its human inhabitants not merely to tend it but to form a spiritual bond with it. Other organic farmers share this notion in theory, even if their methods sometimes diverge. Among wineries whose practices have been certified organic are Hall St. Helena in the Napa Valley and Preston Family Winery in Northern Sonoma County. The Napa Valley's Raymond Vineyards

is certified organic and biodynamic, as is the Sonoma Valley's Hamel Family Wines.

SUSTAINABLE, REGENERATIVE

Two other terms you may hear in tasting rooms are "sustainable practices" and "regenerative farming." Sonoma County Winegrowers, a trade organization of grape producers, touts the fact that more than 99% of its members have been certified by third-party auditors for eco-friendly practices in the vineyard, winery, or both.

At its heart, sustainable viticulture strives to reduce the impact of farming on the land and maintain its usefulness for agriculture. Regenerative farming takes things a step further, exploring techniques that protect the soil and enhance a piece of land's viability. Many organic farmers, for instance, till their land to control weeds without using herbicides, but soil oxidation is a consequence of this approach. By not tilling, some farmers have been able to increase the amount of organic matter in the soil, allowing the land, said one farmer, to "store an extra 25,000 gallons of water per acre."

In Northern California, where drought years have outnumbered ones with average rainfall, the results from not tilling can be significant. Several local vintners have joined the International Wineries for Climate Action, which advises winegrowers about farming for maximum ecological effect.

Wine Lover's Glossary

Wine making and tasting require specialized vocabularies. Some words are merely show-off jargon, but many are specific and helpful.

Acidity. A wine's tartness, derived from grapes' fruit acids. These stabilize a wine (i.e., preserve its character), balance its sweetness, and bring out its flavors.

Tartaric acid is the primary acid in wine, but malic, lactic, and citric acids also occur.

Aging. The process by which some wines improve over time, becoming smoother and more complex. Wine is often aged in oak vats or barrels, slowly interacting with the air through the wood's pores. Sometimes wine is cellared for bottle aging.

Alcohol. Ethyl alcohol is a colorless, volatile, pungent spirit that gives wine its stimulating effect and some of its flavor. Alcohol also acts as a preservative, stabilizing the wine and allowing it to age.

American Viticultural Area (AVA). More commonly termed an *appellation*. A region with unique soil, climate, and other conditions can be designated an AVA by the Alcohol and Tobacco Tax and Trade Bureau. When a label lists an AVA—Napa Valley or Mt. Veeder, for example—at least 85% of the grapes used to make the wine must come from that AVA.

Ampelography. The science of identifying varietals by their leaves, grapevines, and, more recently, DNA.

Appellation. *See American Viticultural Area.*

Aroma. The scent of a wine derived from its grapes. It diminishes with fermentation and is replaced by a more complex bouquet as the wine ages. The term may also describe particular fruity odors in a wine, such as black cherry, green olive, ripe raspberry, or apple.

Balance. A quality of wine in which all desirable elements (fruit, acid, tannin) are in the proper proportion.

Barrel fermenting. The fermenting of wine in small oak or other barrels instead of large tanks or vats. This method keeps grape lots separate before wine blending. The cost of oak barrels makes this method expensive.

Biodynamic. An approach to agriculture that regards the land as a living thing; it incorporates organic farming techniques and the use of the astronomical calendar to cultivate a healthy balance in the vineyard ecosystem.

Blanc de blancs. Sparkling or still white wine made solely from white grapes.

Blanc de noirs. White wine made with red grapes by removing the skins during crush. Some sparkling whites, for example, are made with red Pinot Noir grapes.

Blending. Mixing multiple wines to create one of greater complexity or appeal, as when a heavy wine is blended with a lighter one to make a more approachable medium-bodied wine.

Body. The wine's heft or density as experienced by the palate. *See also Mouthfeel.*

Bordeaux blend. A red wine blended from varietals native to France's Bordeaux region. The primary ones are Cabernet Sauvignon, Cabernet Franc, Malbec, Merlot, and Petit Verdot.

Bouquet. The odors a mature wine gives off when opened. They should be pleasantly complex and hint at the wine's grape variety, origin, age, and quality.

Brix. A method of ascertaining whether grapes are ready for picking by measuring their sugars.

Brut. French term for the driest category of sparkling wine. *See also Demi-sec, Sec.*

Champagne. The northernmost wine district of France, where the world's only genuine champagne is made. The term is often used loosely in America to denote sparkling wines.

Cloudiness. The presence of particles that do not settle out of a wine, causing it to look and taste dusty or muddy.

Cluster. A single bunch of grapes.

Complexity. The qualities of good wine that provide a multilayered sensory experience. Balanced flavors, harmonious

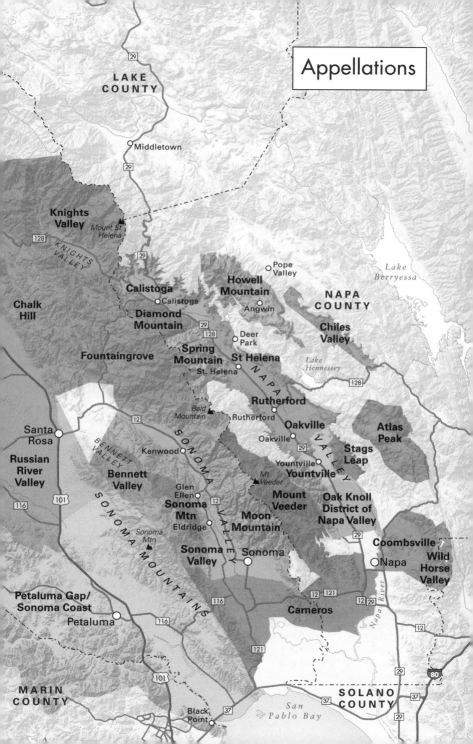

aromas or bouquet, and a long finish are components of complexity.

Cork taint. Describes wine flawed by the musty, wet-cardboard flavor imparted by cork mold, technically known as TCA, or 2,4,6-Trichloroanisole.

Crush. American term for the harvest season. Also refers to the year's crop of grapes crushed for wine.

Cuvée. Generally a sparkling wine, but sometimes a still wine, that is a blend of different wines and sometimes different vintages.

Decant. To pour a wine from its bottle into another container to expose it to air or eliminate sediment. Decanting for sediment pours out the clear wine and leaves the residue in the original bottle.

Demi-sec. French term that translates as "half-dry." It is applied to sweet wines that contain 3.5%–5% sugar.

Dessert wines. Sweet wines that are big in flavor and aroma. Some are relatively low in alcohol; others, such as port-style wines, are fortified with brandy or another spirit and may be 17%–21% alcohol.

Dry. Having very little sweetness or residual sugar. Most wines are dry, although some whites, such as Rieslings, are made to be "off-dry," meaning "on the sweet side."

Estate bottled. A wine entirely made by one winery at a single facility. In general the grapes come from the vineyards the winery owns or farms within the same appellation (which must be printed on the label).

Fermentation. The biochemical process by which grape juice becomes wine. Enzymes generated by yeast cells convert grape sugars into alcohol and carbon dioxide. Fermentation stops when the sugar is depleted and the yeast starves or when high alcohol levels kill the yeast.

Filtering, Filtration. A purification process in which wine is pumped through filters to rid it of suspended particles.

Fining. A method of clarifying wine by adding egg whites, bentonite (a type of clay), or other substances to a barrel. Most wine meant for everyday drinking is fined; however, better wines are fined less often.

Finish. The flavors that remain in the mouth after swallowing wine. Good wine has a long finish with complex flavors and aromas.

Flight. A few wines—usually from three to five—selected for tasting together.

Fortification. Adding brandy or another spirit to wine to stop fermentation and increase the alcohol level, as with port-style dessert wines.

Fruity. Having aromatic nuances of fresh fruit, such as fig, raspberry, or apple. Fruitiness, a sign of quality in young wines, is replaced by bouquet in aged wines.

Late harvest. Wine made from grapes harvested later in the season than the main lot and thus higher in sugar levels. Many dessert wines are late harvest.

Lees. The spent yeast, grape solids, and tartrates that drop to the bottom of the barrel or tank as wine ages. Wine, particularly white wine, gains complexity when left on the lees for a time.

Library wine. An older vintage than the winery's current releases.

Malolactic fermentation. A secondary fermentation, aka *ML* or *malo,* that changes harsh malic acid into softer lactic acid and carbon dioxide. Wine is sometimes inoculated with lactic bacteria or placed in wooden containers harboring the bacteria to enhance this process.

Meritage. A trademarked name for American Bordeaux-style white and red blends.

Méthode champenoise. The traditional, time-consuming method of making sparkling wines by fermenting them in individual bottles. By agreement with the European Union, sparkling wines made in California this way are labeled *méthode traditionelle.*

Mouthfeel. Literally, the way wine feels in the mouth.

Neutral oak. The wood of older barrels or vats that no longer pass much flavor or tannin to the wine stored within.

New oak. The wood of a fresh barrel or vat that has not previously been used to ferment or age wine. It can impart desirable flavors and enhance a wine's complexity, but if used to excess it can overpower a wine's true character.

Nonvintage. A blend of wines from different years. Nonvintage wines have no date on their labels.

Nose. The overall fragrance (aroma or bouquet) a wine gives off.

Oaky. A vanilla-woody flavor that develops when wine ages in oak barrels.

Organic viticulture. The technique of growing grapes without chemical fertilizers, pesticides, or fungicides.

Oxidation. Undesirable flavor and color changes to juice or wine caused by too much air contact, either during processing or because of a leaky barrel or cork.

Pétillant naturel. Usually shortened to "pét-nat," a recent term for the oldest way of making sparkling wine (aka *méthode ancien,* or "ancient method"), in which the wine is bottled while still fermenting, trapping carbon dioxide and generating carbonation.

pH. Technical term for a measure of acidity. It is a reverse measure: the lower the pH level, the higher the acidity, with the most desirable level between 3.2 and 3.5.

Phylloxera. A disease caused by the root louse *Phylloxera vastatrix,* which attacks and ultimately destroys vines' roots.

Regenerative farming. Recent agricultural movement aiming to progress beyond sustainability, prioritizing the sequestering of carbon, building soil health, and other strategies that improve or "regenerate" the land.

Residual sugar. The natural sugar left in a wine after fermentation, which converts sugar into alcohol. In general, the higher the sugar levels, the sweeter the wine.

Rhône blend. A wine made from grapes hailing from France's Rhône Valley, such as Grenache, Syrah, and Mourvèdre.

Rosé. Pink wine, usually made from red-wine grapes of any variety. The juice is left on the skins only long enough to give it a tinge of color.

Sec. French for "dry." The term is generally applied within the sparkling or sweet categories, indicating the wine has 1.7%–3.5% residual sugar. Sec is drier than demi-sec but not as dry as brut.

Sediment. Dissolved or suspended solids that drop out of most red wines as they age in the bottle, thus clarifying their appearance, flavors, and aromas. Sediment is not a defect in old wine or unfiltered new wine.

Sparkling wines. Wines in which carbon dioxide is dissolved, making them bubbly. Examples are French Champagne, Italian prosecco, and Spanish cava.

Sugar. Source of grapes' natural sweetness. When yeast feeds on sugar, it produces alcohol and carbon dioxide. The higher the grape's sugar content, the higher the wine's potential alcohol level or sweetness.

Sulfites. Compounds of sulfur dioxide almost always added before fermentation to prevent oxidation and kill bacteria and wild yeasts that can cause off-flavors.

Sustainable viticulture. Farming that aims to bring the vineyard into harmony with the environment. Organic and other techniques are used to minimize agricultural impact and promote biodiversity.

Table wine. Any wine with at least 7% but not more than 14% alcohol by volume. The term doesn't necessarily imply anything about the wine's quality or price—both superpremium and jug wines can be labeled as table wine.

Tannins. You can tell when they're there, but their origins are still a mystery. These natural grape compounds produce a sensation of drying or astringency in the mouth and throat. Tannins settle out as wine ages; they're a big player in many red wines.

Terroir. French for "soil." Typically used to describe the soil and climate conditions influencing the quality and characteristics of grapes and wine.

Varietal. A grape type. According to U.S. law, at least 75% of a wine must come from a particular grape to be labeled with a varietal name.

Veraison. The time during the ripening process when grapes change their color from green to red or yellow and sugar levels rise.

Vertical tasting. A tasting of several vintages of the same wine.

Vintage. A given year's grape harvest. A vintage date (e.g., 2023) on a label indicates the year the wine's grapes were harvested rather than the year the wine was bottled.

Yeast. A minute, single-celled fungus that germinates and multiplies rapidly as it feeds on sugar with the help of enzymes, creating alcohol and releasing carbon dioxide in the fermentation process.

Zymology. The science of fermentation.

NAPA VALLEY

Updated by
Daniel Mangin

◉ Sights	🍴 Restaurants	🛏 Hotels	🛍 Shopping	🍸 Nightlife
★★★★★	★★★★★	★★★★★	★★★★☆	★★★☆☆

WELCOME TO NAPA VALLEY

TOP REASONS TO GO

★ **Wine tasting:** Whether you're on a pilgrimage to famous Cabernet houses or searching for hidden-gem wineries and obscure varietals, the valley supplies plenty of both.

★ **Fine dining:** It might sound like hype, but a meal at one of the valley's top-tier restaurants can be a revelation—about the level of artistry intuitive chefs can achieve and how successfully quality wines pair with food.

★ **Art and architecture:** Several wineries are owned by art collectors whose holdings grace indoor and outdoor spaces, and the valley contains remarkable specimens of winery architecture.

★ **Spa treatments:** Work-hard, play-hard types and inveterate sybarites flock to spas for pampering.

★ **Balloon rides:** By the dawn's early light, hot-air balloons soar over the vineyards, a magical sight from the ground and even more thrilling from above.

1 Napa. The valley's largest town has plenty of wineries and tasting rooms, and downtown has evolved into a shopping and fine-dining haven.

2 Yountville. Find several must-visit restaurants, a well-groomed main street, and downtown tasting rooms; most of Yountville's wineries are to the east, with a few to the north and south.

3 Oakville. With a population of less than 100, this town is all about its mostly Cabernet vineyards.

4 Rutherford. "It takes Rutherford dust to grow great Cabernet," a legendary winemaker once said, and with several dozen wineries in this appellation, there are plenty of opportunities to ponder what this means.

5 St. Helena. Genteel St. Helena's Main Street evokes images of classic Americana; its wineries range from valley stalwarts Beringer and Charles Krug to boutique wineries in the hills.

6 Calistoga. This spa town still has its Old West–style false fronts, but it's now also home to luxurious lodgings and spas with 21st-century panache.

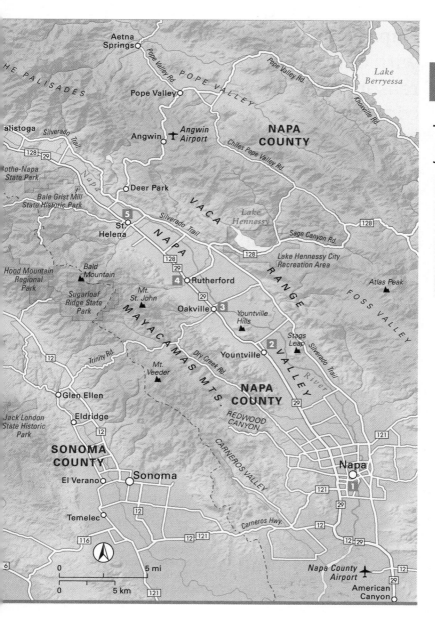

With more than 500 wineries and many of the industry's biggest brands, the Napa Valley is the Wine Country's star. Napa, the largest town, lures visitors with cultural attractions and (relatively) reasonably priced lodgings. A bit north, compact Yountville is packed with top-notch restaurants and hotels, and Oakville and Rutherford are extolled for their Cabernet Sauvignon–friendly soils. Beyond them, St. Helena teems with boutiques and wineries, and casual Calistoga, known for its spas, feels like an Old West frontier town, albeit one with luxury resorts.

The Napa Valley contains only about an eighth of the acreage planted in Bordeaux, but past volcanic and other seismic activity have bequeathed the valley diverse soils and microclimates that provide winemakers with the raw materials to craft wines of consistently high quality. More land is devoted to Cabernet Sauvignon and Chardonnay than any other varietals, but Cabernet Franc, Merlot, Pinot Noir, Petite Sirah, Sauvignon Blanc, Syrah, Zinfandel, and other wines are also made here. In terms of output, though, the valley's reputation far exceeds the mere 4% of California's total wine-grape harvest it represents.

So what makes the Napa Valley one of the state's top tourist destinations and a playground for San Francisco Bay Area residents? For one thing, variety: for every blockbuster winery whose name you'll recognize from the shelves of wine stores and the pages of *Wine Spectator*—Robert Mondavi, Beringer, and Caymus, to name a very few—you'll also find lower-profile operations that will warmly invite you into their modest tasting rooms. The local viticulture has in turn inspired a passion for food, and several marquee chefs have solidified the valley's position as one of the country's great restaurant destinations. You'll also get a glimpse of California's history, from wine cellars dating back to the late 1800s to the flurry of Steamboat Gothic architecture dressing up Calistoga. Binding all these temptations together is the sheer scenic beauty of the place. Much of Napa Valley's landscape unspools in orderly, densely planted rows of vines. Even the climate cooperates, as the warm summer days and refreshingly cool evenings so favorable for grape growing also make fine weather for traveling.

MAJOR REGIONS

The Napa Valley has 16 American Viticultural Areas (⇨ See Appellations, below) but practically speaking can be divided into its southern and northern parts. The southern Napa Valley encompasses the relatively cooler grape-growing areas and the towns of Napa and Yountville, along with slightly warmer Oakville. The northern Napa Valley begins around Rutherford and continues north to even hotter St. Helena and Calistoga.

Planning

When to Go

The Napa Valley is a year-round destination whose charms vary depending on the season. Watching a rainy winter day's misty fog rising off dark, gnarly grapevines, for example, can be just as captivating as witnessing a summer sunset backlighting flourishing vineyard rows. Because the Napa Valley is the most-visited Wine Country locale, summers draw hordes of tourists, making late spring and early fall, when it's less crowded and temperatures are often cooler, among the best times to come. Harvesttime— from August through October, depending on the grape type and the year's weather—is the best time to visit to see wine making in action. Weekends can be busy year-round. To avoid heavy traffic on summer weekends, it almost always works best to arrive by midmorning, especially if you need to be back in San Francisco by early evening.

Getting Here and Around

BUS

VINE buses, which pick up passengers from the BART (Bay Area Rapid Transit) El Cerrito Del Norte station and the Vallejo Ferry Terminal, run between Napa and Calistoga, with one stop or more in Yountville, Oakville, Rutherford, St. Helena, and Calistoga. Buses don't operate on all routes on Sunday (sometimes Saturday).

⇨ For more information about arriving by bus, see the Bus section in the Travel Smart chapter.

CONTACT VINE. ✉ Napa ☎ 707/251–2800, 800/696–6443 ⊕ www.vinetransit.com.

CAR

Traveling by car is the most convenient way to tour the Napa Valley. In normal traffic both of the main routes from San Francisco will get you here in about an hour. You can head north across the Golden Gate Bridge and U.S. 101, east on Highway 37 and then Highway 121, and north on Highway 29; or east across the San Francisco–Oakland Bay Bridge and north on Interstate 80, west on Highway 37, and north on Highway 29.

Highway 29 can become congested, especially on summer weekends. Traffic can be slow in St. Helena during morning and afternoon rush hours. You might find slightly less traffic on the Silverado Trail, which roughly parallels Highway 29 between Napa and Calistoga. Every few miles, cross streets connect the two highways like rungs on a ladder, making it easy to cross from one to the other.

■ TIP➔ **Although the Silverado Trail can get busy in the late afternoon, it's often a better option than Highway 29 if you're traveling between, say, St. Helena or Calistoga and the city of Napa.**

⇨ For information about car services and limos, see Getting Here and Around in the Travel Smart chapter.

Restaurants

Dining out is one of the deep pleasures of a Napa Valley visit. Cuisine here tends to focus on seasonal produce, some of it from gardens the restaurants maintain themselves, and many chefs endeavor to source their proteins locally, too. The French Laundry, La Toque, Bouchon Bistro, Bistro Jeanty, Press, Solbar, and the Restaurant at Auberge du Soleil often appear at the top of visitors' agendas, and rightfully so: in addition to stellar cuisine they all have sommeliers or waiters capable of helping you select wines that will enhance your enjoyment of your meal immeasurably, and the level of service matches the food and surroundings. Another dozen restaurants provide experiences nearly on a par with those at the above establishments.

⇨ *Restaurant prices are the average cost of a main course at dinner, or if dinner isn't served, at lunch. Restaurant reviews have been shortened. For full information, visit Fodors.com.*

Hotels

With the price of accommodations at high-end inns and hotels *starting* at $1,000 or more a night, when it comes to Napa Valley lodging the question is how much are you willing to pay? If you have the means, you can ensconce yourself between plush linens at exclusive hillside retreats with fancy architecture and even fancier amenities, and you're more or less guaranteed to have a fine time. As with Napa Valley restaurants, though, the decor and amenities the most stylish hotels and inns provide have upped the ante for all hoteliers and innkeepers, so even if you're on a budget you can live well. Many smaller inns, hotels, and even motels provide pleasant stays for a fairly reasonable price. The main problem with these establishments is that they can book up quickly, so if you're visiting between late May and October, it's wise to reserve your room as far ahead as possible.

⇨ *Hotel prices are the lowest cost of a standard double room in high season. Hotel reviews have been shortened. For full information, visit Fodors.com.*

What It Costs in U.S. Dollars			
$	$$	$$$	$$$$
RESTAURANTS			
under $17	$17–$26	$27–$36	over $36
HOTELS			
under $201	$201–$300	$301–$400	over $400

Planning Your Time

First things first: even in a month it's impossible to "do" the Napa Valley—there are simply too many wineries here. Many visitors find that tasting at three or at most four a day and spending quality time at each of them, with a leisurely lunch to rest the palate, is preferable to cramming in as many visits as possible. You can, of course, add variety with a spa treatment (these can take up to a half day), a balloon ride (expect to rise early and finish in the late morning), shopping, or a bicycle ride.

The town of Napa is the valley's most affordable base, and it's especially convenient if most of your touring will be in the southern half. If you'll be dining a lot in Yountville, staying there is a good idea because you can walk or take the Yountville Bee shuttle back to your lodging. Calistoga is the most affordable base in the northern Napa Valley, though it's not always convenient for touring southern Napa wineries.

Visitor Information

CONTACT Visit Napa Valley. ✉ *Napa* ☎ *707/226–5813* ⊕ *www.visitnapavalley. com.*

Appellations

Nearly all of Napa County, which stretches from the Mayacamas Mountains in the west to Lake Berryessa in the east, makes up the Napa Valley American Viticultural Area (AVA). This region is divided into smaller "nested" AVAs, or subappellations, each with unique characteristics.

Los Carneros AVA, often called the Carneros District or just Carneros, stretches west from the Napa River, across the southern Napa Valley, and into the southern Sonoma Valley. Pinot Noir and Chardonnay are the main grapes grown in this cool, windswept region just north of San Pablo Bay, but Merlot, Syrah, and, in the warmer portions, Cabernet Sauvignon also do well here. Pinot Noir and Chardonnay are also the stars of the **Wild Horse Valley AVA,** which lies east of Los Carneros and is the valley's coolest subappellation. Between Wild Horse Valley and Carneros, the **Coombsville AVA** also benefits from San Pablo Bay breezes. Cabernet Sauvignon grows on the western-facing slopes, with Merlot, Chardonnay, Syrah, and Pinot Noir more prevalent in the cooler lower elevations.

Four subappellations north of the Carneros District—Oak Knoll, Oakville, Rutherford, and St. Helena—stretch across the valley floor. Morning fog often covers the **Oak Knoll District of Napa Valley AVA,** which warms up during summer afternoons. A dozen and a half varietals do well here. The **Oakville AVA,** just north of Yountville, is studded with big-name wineries such as Robert Mondavi and Silver Oak and boutique labels that include the superexclusive Screaming Eagle. Oakville's gravelly, well-drained soil is especially good for Cabernet Sauvignon.

A sunny climate and well-drained soil also make **Rutherford AVA** one of the best locations for Cabernet Sauvignon in California, if not the world. North of Rutherford, the **St. Helena AVA** is one of Napa's toastiest, as the slopes surrounding the narrow valley reflect the sun's heat. Bordeaux varietals are the most popular grapes grown here—particularly Cabernet Sauvignon, but also Merlot. Just north, at the foot of Mt. St. Helena, is the **Calistoga AVA**; Cabernet Sauvignon does well here, as do Zinfandel, Petite Sirah, and Charbono (aka "Calistoga's cult grape").

The **Stags Leap District AVA,** a small section of the valley's eastern floor and hillsides, is marked by steep volcanic palisades. As with the neighboring **Yountville AVA,** Cabernet Sauvignon and Merlot are by far the favored grapes. In both subappellations, cool evening breezes encourage a long growing season and intense fruit flavors. Some describe the resulting wines as "rock soft" or an "iron fist in a velvet glove."

The **Mt. Veeder, Spring Mountain,** and **Diamond Mountain District AVAs,** stretching south to north amid the Mayacamas Mountains to the valley's west, and the **Atlas Peak, Chiles Valley,** and **Howell Mountain AVAs,** east across the valley within the Vaca Mountains, each demonstrate how stressing out grapevines can yield outstanding results. The big winner is Cabernet Sauvignon, which loves this type of terrain. Many of the vineyards on these slopes are so steep that they must be tilled and harvested by hand.

The valley's great variety of climates and soils explains why vintners here can make so many different wines, and so well, in a relatively compact region.

Top Tastings

Classic Cabs

Joseph Phelps Vineyards, St. Helena. Tastings of Phelps's Cabernet Sauvignon and flagship Insignia Bordeaux-style blend unfold like everything else here: with class, grace, and precision—an apt description of the wines themselves.

Shafer Vineyards, Napa. The Hillside Select Cabernet Sauvignon, most of its grapes grown within sight of the tasting room, concludes sessions at this hallowed Stags Leap District winery.

Silver Oak, Oakville. The sole wine Silver Oak produces is a Napa Valley Cabernet Sauvignon; hosts pour in a stone building constructed of materials from a 19th-century flour mill.

Setting

Fontanella Family Winery, Napa. Head partway up Mt. Veeder to sip Chardonnay, Cabernet, and other wines on the vineyard-view patio of this husband-and-wife team's boutique winery.

Quixote Winery, Napa. An eccentric structure by a world-famous European architect, and Cabernets and Petite Sirahs overseen by elite consultant Philippe Melka, make for a memorable outing at this Stags Leap District winery.

Schweiger Vineyards, St. Helena. The northern Napa Valley views from this winery atop Spring Mountain never fail to astonish; neither does the Schweiger family's hospitality.

Food Pairing

Theorem Vineyards, Calistoga. The winery's chef prepares intricate bites for pairing with Sauvignon Blanc, Merlot, Syrah, and Cabernet Sauvignon at this Diamond Mountain estate with vineyard and Mt. St. Helena views.

VGS Chateau Potelle, St. Helena. Sophisticated whimsy is on full display at this bungalowlike space where a top chef's small bites complement the mountain-grown wines.

Old-School Charm

Prager Winery & Port Works, St. Helena. Drift back in time at this homey, family-run operation specializing in fortified wines.

Tres Sabores, St. Helena. Tastings are low-key and fun at owner-winemaker Julie Johnson's down-home ranch, one of the Napa Valley's first with certified organic vineyards.

Napa

46 miles northeast of San Francisco.

After many years as a blue-collar burg detached from the Wine Country scene, the Napa Valley's largest town (population about 80,000) has evolved into its shining star. Masaharu Morimoto, Charlie Palmer, and other chefs of note operate restaurants here, and swank hotels and resorts can be found downtown and beyond. A walkway that follows the Napa River has made downtown more pedestrian-friendly, and the Oxbow Public Market, a complex of high-end food purveyors, is popular with locals and tourists.

The market is named for the nearby oxbow-shape bend in the Napa River, a bit north of where Napa was founded in 1848. The first wood-frame building was a saloon, and the downtown area

The Napa Valley's largest town has evolved into its shining star.

still projects an old-river-town vibe. Many Victorian houses have survived, some as bed-and-breakfast inns, and in the heart of downtown older buildings like the 1879 Italianate-style Napa Courthouse at 825 Brown Street have been preserved. The courthouse was among the numerous structures damaged during a magnitude 6.0 earthquake in 2014.

Napans are rightly proud of how the city responded to the quake and subsequent challenges—wildfires, fire-related power outages, and COVID-19—with support instantly materializing for first responders, health-care workers, stranded visitors, and fellow citizens in need. Downtown Napa emerged from the pandemic more robust than ever, and with several dozen sipping salons within a little more than a square mile of each other, it began billing itself as "the wine tasting room capital of the world."

■TIP→ **If based in Napa, in addition to exploring the wineries amid the surrounding countryside, plan on spending at least a half day strolling downtown.**

GETTING HERE AND AROUND

To get to downtown Napa from Highway 29, take the 1st Street exit and follow the signs. Most of downtown's sights and many of its restaurants are clustered in an easily walkable area around Main Street (you'll find street parking and garages nearby). Outside downtown, most wineries with Napa addresses are on or just off Highway 29 or the parallel Silverado Trail, except those in the Carneros District or Mt. Veeder AVA. Most of these are on or just off Highway 121. VINE buses serve downtown Napa and adjacent locales.

VISITOR INFORMATION

CONTACTS Do Napa. ⊠ *Napa* ☎ *707/257–0322* ⊕ *www.donapa.com.* **Napa Valley Welcome Center.** ⊠ *1300 1st St., Suite 313, Napa* ✠ *At Franklin St.* ☎ *707/251–5895, 855/847–6272* ⊕ *www.visitnapavalley.com.*

A mostly flat section of the Napa Valley Vine Trail connects Napa and Yountville.

⊙ Sights

SIGHTS IN DOWNTOWN NAPA

Acumen Wine Gallery

WINERY | Highly structured Cabernet Sauvignons from Atlas Peak grapes are the calling card of Acumen, which presents its wines in a combination tasting lounge and art gallery done up in glass, brass, copper, and reclaimed wood. Philip Titus, also the winemaker at the esteemed Chappellet Winery, has been making the affordable but well-crafted Mountainside tier and collector-quality Peak wines since 2020. Tastings at this downtown Napa salon require an appointment, though walk-ins are accommodated if possible, often the case if you're stopping by for a glass or bottle of sparkling or still wine. ✉ *1315 1st St., Napa* ✛ *Near Randolph St.* ☏ *707/492–8336* ⊕ *acumenwine.com* 🥂 *Tastings from $20 glass, $50 flight.*

Arch & Tower

WINERY | While its Oakville winery undergoes renovations, a project expected to last from Summer 2023 to Summer 2025, the Robert Mondavi Winery will pour its wines (along with a few other luxury brands) in downtown Napa's 1877 Borreo Building. Erected using stone quarried a few miles away in Soda Canyon, the two-story Italian Renaissance–style building has large windows and an outdoor terrace with views west to Main Street. A tireless promoter of the Napa Valley as California's preeminent wine-growing region, the late Robert Mondavi elevated Sauvignon Blanc by labeling his bottlings with the more exotic name Fumé Blanc and made Bordeaux-style reds of renown from To Kalon Vineyard in Oakville. Visits to taste these and other selections, many of them winery exclusives, require a reservation. At time of writing, there was no plan to keep the Borreo Building location open after the Oakville winery reopens in 2025. ✉ *930 3rd St., Napa* ✛ *At Soscol Ave.* ☏ *888/766–6328* ⊕ *robertmondaviwinery.com* 🥂 *Tastings from $65.*

Bazán Cellars

WINERY | In 1973, teenager Mario Bazán traveled north from Oaxaca, Mexico, intending to earn money to start a grocery business back home. Five decades later, he's still in the Napa Valley. After proving his mettle as a vineyard laborer and later foreman at Robert Mondavi, Opus One, and Stag's Leap Wine Cellars, Mario opened his own management company, these days overseeing a few hundred acres of vines. With his wife Gloria, a former pediatric dentist from Michoacán who makes glass jewelry, he founded Bazán Cellars in 2005. The gregarious Gloria manages the expat couple's modest downtown Napa tasting room, where Sauvignon Blanc, rosé, and Pinot Noir set up the stars, Cabernet Franc and Cabernet Sauvignon. Reservations are a good idea on weekends. ✉ *1000 Main St., Suite 150, Napa ✛ Near Main St.* 📞 *707/927–5564* ⊕ *www.bazan-cellars.com* 🎫 *Tastings from $14 glass, $55 flight.*

Brown Downtown Napa

WINERY | In 1980, the parents of the current owners of the Napa Valley's first Black-owned estate winery purchased 450 acres east of St. Helena in Chiles Valley, planting a vineyard in 1985. A decade later the second generation— siblings Doreen and David Brown, later joined by sister Coral—established the family's label. The estate Zinfandels and Cabernet Sauvignon, made by David, are perennial winners for their bold elegance, with another star the punchy, accessible Chaos Theory blend of Zinfandel, Cabernet Sauvignon, and a grape or two more. The Browns pour their wines in a high-ceilinged loftlike salon—exposed red brick and steel beams, tall arched windows, and teal walls—on the second floor of a 1905 downtown Napa structure that for its first six decades housed the *Napa Valley Register* newspaper. Reservations are required. ✉ *First Street Napa, 1005 Coombs St., 2nd fl., Napa ✛ At 1st St.* 📞 *707/963–2435* ⊕ *www.*

brownestate.com 🎫 *Tastings from $50* ⊘ *Closed Sun. and Mon.*

Chateau Buena Vista

WINERY | A palette of pink, lavender, teal, and gold, a blingy crystal chandelier, and a generous dose of leopard print and multicolor feathers buoy the atmosphere at the Napa outpost of the Wine Country's oldest winery, established in Sonoma in 1857. In this dapper setting, with Sinatra, Bublé, Fitzgerald, and other crooners and chanteuses on the playlist, you can sip sparkling wine by the glass or bottle, and Chardonnay, Pinot Noir, and Cabernet Sauvignon by the glass, bottle, or flight. Two experiences worth considering are a pairing of Cabernets with gourmet chocolates and another of sparkling wine with caviar. Walk-ins are usually welcome, though it's best to make a reservation for the tastings involving food. ✉ *1142 1st St., Napa ✛ Near Coombs St.* 📞 *707/703–5677* ⊕ *buenavistawinery.com/chateau-buena-vista-napa* 🎫 *Tastings from $20 glass, $40 flight.*

CIA at Copia

COLLEGE | Food fanatics and the merely curious achieve gastronomical bliss at the Culinary Institute of America's Oxbow District campus, its facade brightened by a wraparound mural inspired by the colorful garden that fronts the facility. You could easily spend a few hours checking out the wine and culinary options; visiting the well-curated shop, theme exhibitions, and Vintners Hall of Fame wall; or attending (book ahead) classes and demonstrations. Head upstairs to the Chuck Williams Culinary Arts Museum. Named for the Williams-Sonoma kitchenwares founder, it holds a fascinating collection of cooking, baking, and other food-related tools, tableware, gizmos, and gadgets, some dating back more than a century. ✉ *500 1st St., Napa ✛ Near McKinstry St.* 📞 *707/967–2500* ⊕ *www.ciaatcopia.com* 🎫 *Facility/museum free, class/demo fees vary.*

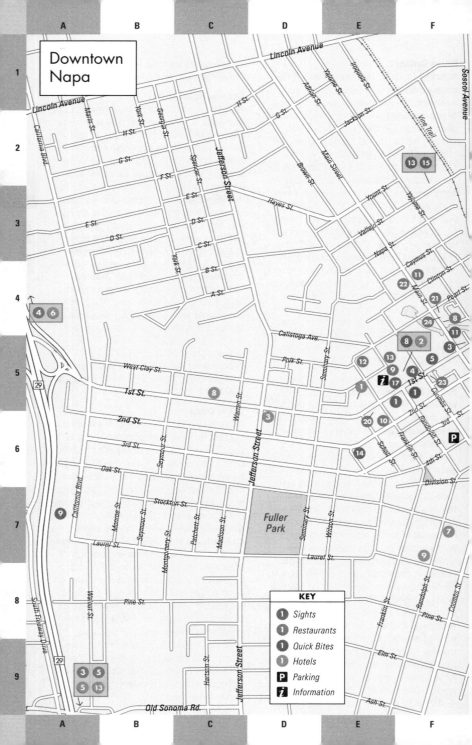

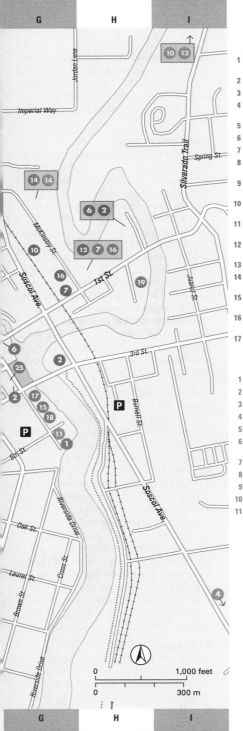

Sights ▼

1 Acumen Wine Gallery E5
2 Arch & Tower G5
3 Bazán Cellars F5
4 Brown Downtown Napa F5
5 Chateau Buena Vista.... F5
6 CIA at Copia H3
7 Mark Herold Wines..... G4
8 Mayacamas Downtown................ F5
9 Napa Valley Distillery A7
10 Napa Valley Wine Train............... G3
11 New Frontier Wine Co................... F4
12 Oxbow Public Market H4
13 RAD Napa F2
14 Robert Craig Winery Tasting Salon............ E6
15 St. Clair Brown Winery & Brewery....... F2
16 The Studio by Feast it Forward......... G4
17 Vineyard 29 Tasting Room............. E5

Restaurants ▼

1 Angèle G6
2 Avow Napa.............. G5
3 Bear A9
4 Bistro Don Giovanni ... A4
5 The Boon Fly Café A9
6 Bounty Hunter Wine Bar & Smokin' BBQ..... G5
7 C Casa.................... H4
8 Cole's Chop House....... F4
9 Compline................. E5
10 Grace's Table............ E6
11 Hal Yamashita Napa..... F4

12 Kenzo..................... E5
13 Kitchen Door E5
14 La Toque G3
15 Los Agaves Napa....... G6
16 Loveski Deli.............. H4
17 Morimoto Asia Napa... G5
18 Morimoto Napa G6
19 Napa Yard Oxbow Gardens......... H4
20 Oenotri E6
21 Osha Thai Napa.......... F4
22 The Q Restaurant and Bar...... F4
23 Scala Osteria & Bar F5
24 Torc....................... F4
25 ZuZu G5

Quick Bites ▼

1 Contimo Provisions...... F5
2 Lunch Box at Copia..... H3

Hotels ▼

1 Andaz Napa E5
2 Archer Hotel Napa F5
3 Blackbird Inn and Finch Guest House D6
4 Cambria Hotel Napa Valley................I8
5 Carneros Resort and Spa A9
6 Cottages of Napa Valley.............. A4
7 The George F7
8 The Inn On First C5
9 Inn on Randolph F7
10 Milliken Creek Inn I1
11 Napa River Inn G6
12 Silverado Resort and Spa I1
13 Stanly Ranch, Auberge Resorts Collection A9
14 Westin Verasa Napa ... G3

Mark Herold Wines

WINERY | Panama-born Mark Herold specializes in collector-quality Cabernet Sauvignons from the Atlas Peak, Coombsvillle, and Oakville AVAs. Herold also makes Uproar, a Cabernet blend from those three areas that astounds for its intense flavors and relatively accessible price. At the winemaker's Oxbow District storefront, where a wall sculpture of a hot-rod-green marlin surrounded by white lilies sets a peppy tone, you can sample four Cabernets at an Appellation Series tasting. The introductory Herold Highlights often begins with a Sauvignon Blanc and a Chardonnay (sometimes a dry rosé of Cabernet) before sips of Uproar and one of the appellation Cabs. All visits are by appointment, with last-minute ones often possible. ■TIP→ **A Taste of Place, an excursion to the winery's Coombsville vineyard, includes a tasting and a selection of cheeses.** ✉ 710 1st St., Napa ⊕ At McKinstry St. ☎ 707/256–3111 ⊕ www.markherold-wines.com ⊠ Tastings from $50.

★ **Mayacamas Downtown**

WINERY | Cabernets from Mayacamas Vineyards placed second and fifth respectively on *Wine Spectator* magazine's 2019 and 2020 "Top 100" lists of the world's best wines, two accolades among many for this winery founded atop Mt. Veeder in 1889. One of Napa's leading viticulturists, Annie Favia farms the organic vineyards, elevation 2,000-plus feet, without irrigation; her husband, Andy Erickson, is the consulting winemaker. The grapes for the Chardonnay come from 40-year-old vines. Aged in mostly neutral (previously used) French oak barrels to accentuate mountain minerality, the wine is a Napa Valley marvel. The Cabernet Sauvignon ages for three years, spending part of the time in oak barrels more than a century old. Erin Martin, a Napa Valley resident with a hip international reputation, designed the light-filled storefront tasting space. ■TIP→ **Experiencing these magnificent wines downtown—white wines-only** and red wines-only tastings possible—may entice you to visit the estate. ✉ First Street Napa, 1256 1st St., Napa ⊕ At Randolph St. ☎ 707/294–1433 ⊕ www.mayacamas.com ⊠ Tastings from $35 ⊗ Closed Mon. and Tues.

Napa Valley Distillery

DISTILLERY | Entertaining educators keep the proceedings light and lively at this distillery, which bills itself as Napa's first since Prohibition. NVD makes gin, rum, whiskey, and the flagship grape-based vodka, along with brandies and barrel-aged bottled cocktails that include Manhattans, mai tais, and negronis. Lesson number one at visits, always by appointment, is how to properly sip spirits (spoiler: don't swirl your glass as you would with wine). ■TIP→ **If you just want to sample the wares, the distillery operates a tasting bar at Oxbow Public Market.** ✉ 2485 Stockton St., Napa ⊕ Off California Blvd. ☎ 707/265–6272 ⊕ www.napadistillery.com ⊠ Tour and tasting $45 ⊗ Closed Mon.–Wed.

Napa Valley Wine Train

TRAIN/TRAIN STATION | Guests on this Napa Valley fixture travel the corridor established in 1864 to transport passengers as far north as Calistoga's spas. The rolling stock includes restored Pullman cars and a two-story Vista Dome coach with a curved glass roof. The train travels a leisurely, scenic route between Napa and St. Helena. Patrons on some tours enjoy a multicourse meal and tastings at one or more wineries. Some rides involve no winery stops, and themed trips are occasionally scheduled. ■TIP→ **It's best to make this trip during the day, when you can enjoy the vineyard views.** ✉ 1275 McKinstry St., Napa ⊕ Off 1st St. ☎ 707/253–2111, 800/427–4124 ⊕ www.winetrain.com ⊠ From $225.

New Frontier Wine Co.

WINERY | Heavyweights like Michel Rolland, Philippe Melka, and Maayan Koschitzky oversee the international collection of wines poured at New Frontier's downtown Napa tasting room. Many guests settling into the leather chairs and sofas in the exposed-brick storefront space opt for a California Flight of wines from largely Napa Valley and Sonoma County grapes, though adventurous sorts should consider a World Flight, which might showcase specimens from Argentina and Australia. You can also order wine by the glass or a two-glass "Side-by-Side" comparison, for example, of Chardonnays from the Russian River Valley and Patagonia. Ownership by Alejandro Bulgheroni, an Argentine-born entrepreneur whose worldwide holdings include an estate vineyard in St. Helena, is the through line on all these labels. ⊠ *1040 Main St., Suite 101, Napa ✛ Near 1st St.* ☎ *707/690–9923* ⊕ *www.new-frontierwines.com* 🍽 *Tastings from $15 glass, $65 flight.*

★ Oxbow Public Market

MARKET | The 40,000-square-foot market's two dozen stands provide an introduction to Northern California's diverse artisanal food products. Swoon over decadent charcuterie at the Fatted Calf (great sandwiches, too), slurp oysters at Hog Island, enjoy empanadas at El Porteño, or chow down on Moroccan street food at Moro. Sample wine (and cheese) at the Oxbow Cheese & Wine Merchant, ales at Fieldwork Brewing's taproom (at 1046 McKinstry, near Fatted Calf), and barrel-aged cocktails at the Napa Valley Distillery. The owner of Kara's Cupcakes operates the adjacent Bar Lucia for (mostly) sparkling wines and rosés. Milestone Provisions is a combination butchery, restaurant (California country cuisine including sublime fried-chicken sandwiches), and creamery known for velvety ice cream. Among the few nonfood vendors here is Napa Bookmine, which also operates a larger store elsewhere downtown. ⊠ *610 and 644 1st St., Napa ✛ At McKinstry St.* ☎ *No phone* ⊕ *www.oxbowpublicmarket.com.*

RAD Napa (*Rail Arts District Napa*)
PUBLIC ART | An ambitious beautification project also promoting democracy in art, outdoor wellness, and a few other ideals, RAD Napa commissions artists to paint murals on buildings, fences, and utility boxes along or near downtown Napa's railroad tracks. Sculptures and other installations are also involved. Many of the outdoor artworks can be viewed along the Napa Valley Vine Trail pedestrian and biking path or aboard the Napa Valley Wine Train. ■TIP➔ **Download a walking map on RAD Napa's website.** ⊠ *Napa* ☎ *707/501–5355* ⊕ *www.radnapa.org.*

★ Robert Craig Winery Tasting Salon

WINERY | Based way up Howell Mountain but with meticulously farmed hillside sources on both sides of the valley, Robert Craig has established a loyal following for its textured, full-flavored Cabernet Sauvignons. Hosts pour the wines inside a refurbished 1890s downtown Napa Folk Victorian and on its front porch and red-brick patio. Tastings, by appointment but usually possible on short notice, often begin with a Sonoma County Chardonnay or, while it lasts, La Fleur Craig Grenache Rosé from Howell Mountain. One trait all the wines share is how well they age. The Zinfandel from Howell Mountain's Black Sears Vineyard does its varietal proud. ⊠ *1553 2nd St. ✛ At Church St.* ☎ *707/252–2250* ⊕ *robertcraigwine.com* 🍽 *Tastings from $35.*

St. Clair Brown Winery & Brewery

WINERY | Tastings at this women-run "urban winery" and nanobrewery a few blocks north of downtown unfold in a colorful culinary garden. Winemaker Elaine St. Clair, well regarded for stints at Domaine Carneros and Black Stallion, produces elegant wines—crisp yet complex whites and smooth, French-style reds whose stars include Cabernet Sauvignon and Syrah. While pursuing her wine-making degree, St. Clair also studied brewing; a few of her light-, medium-, and full-bodied brews are always on tap.

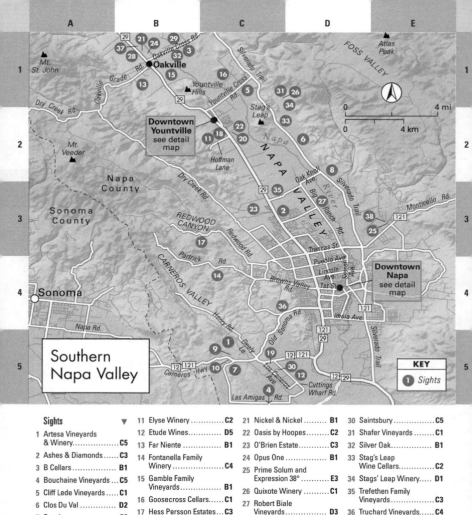

Southern Napa Valley

KEY

1 Sights

You can taste the wines or beers solo or enjoy them paired with appetizers that might include a selection of cheeses or addictive almonds roasted with rosemary, lemon zest, and lemon olive oil. ■TIP➜ **The tasting garden, anchored by an intimate, light-filled greenhouse, stays open until 8 pm on Friday and Saturday.** ✉ *816 Vallejo St., Napa* ✛ *Off Soscol Ave.* ☎ *707/255–5591* ⊕ *www.stclairbrown. com* 🍷 *Tastings from $25 beer, $55 wine* ⊘ *Closed Mon.–Wed.*

The Studio by Feast it Forward

WINERY | Fans of the online Feast it Forward lifestyle network flock to its brick-and-mortar location in downtown Napa to experience food, wine, and entertainment with a philanthropic component—at least 5% of the proceeds goes to charity. On any given day, tastings of impressive boutique selections by Feast it Forward member wineries might be happening downstairs, a sommelier-taught class upstairs, and a musician or other performer mesmerizing millennials in the covered, open-air performance space out back. The upbeat vibe, good intentions, high-quality food and kitchenware products, and well-curated events make this Oxbow District space worth investigating. ✉ *1031 McKinstry St., Napa* ✛ *Near 1st St.* ☎ *707/819–2403* ⊕ *www.feastitforward.com* 🍷 *Tastings from $13 glass, $35 flight* ⊘ *Closed Wed.*

Vineyard 29 Tasting Room

WINERY | Napa design star Richard von Saal's concept for this St. Helena winery's downtown tasting salon oozes cushy luxury with white walls, rich-green and charcoal-gray furniture, and brass trim everywhere. The glam setting suits Vineyard 29's two portfolio tiers: CRU for wines from grapes sourced from the Napa Valley to Oregon and Vineyard 29 for estate-grown wines. The latter label's focus is Cabernet Sauvignon, though the Aida Estate Zinfandel also shines. The introductory tasting of solely CRU wines reveals the wine-making sensibility, but

consider a sampling of current Vineyard 29 releases or, for a deeper dive, a Collectors or Library tasting. Walk-ins are welcome, but reservations are recommended on weekends. ■TIP➜ **You can also taste by the glass or bottle.** ✉ *1300 1st St., Suite 305* ✛ *At Randolph St.* ☎ *707/967–5405* ⊕ *vineyard29.com* 🍷 *Tastings from $40.*

SIGHTS BEYOND DOWNTOWN NAPA

Artesa Vineyards & Winery

WINERY | From a distance the modern, minimalist architecture of Artesa blends harmoniously with the surrounding Carneros landscape, but up close its pools, fountains, and large outdoor sculptures make their own impression. As might be expected in this region, Chardonnay and Pinot Noir from estate and sourced grapes predominate, but the winery also produces Albariño and sparkling wine, plus reds that include Cabernet Sauvignon, Merlot, and Tempranillo. By appointment you can sample them, sometimes paired with food, while enjoying views of estate and neighboring vineyards and, on a clear day, San Francisco. ✉ *1345 Henry Rd., Napa* ✛ *Off Old Sonoma Rd. and Dealy La.* ☎ *707/224–1668* ⊕ *www.artesawinery. com* 🍷 *Tastings from $60.*

Ashes & Diamonds

WINERY | Barbara Bestor's sleek white design for this appointment-only winery's glass-and-metal tasting space evokes mid-century modern architecture and with it the era and wines predating the Napa Valley's rise to prominence. Leading the wine-making team record producer Kashy Khaledi assembled are Steve Matthiasson, known for his restrained style and attention to viticultural detail, and Diana Snowden Seysses, who draws on experiences in Burgundy, Provence, and California. Bordeaux varietals are the focus, most notably Cabernet Sauvignon and Cabernet Franc but also the white blend of Sauvignon Blanc and Sémillon and even the rosé (of Cabernet Franc). With a label designer who was also responsible for a Jay-Z album cover and interiors that recall the *Mad Men* Palm Springs story arc, the pitch seems unabashedly intended to millennials, but the wines, low in alcohol and with high acidity (helpful with aging), enchant connoisseurs of all stripes. ⊠ *4130 Howard La., Napa ⊹ Off Hwy. 29* ☎ *707/666–4777* ⊕ *ashesdiamonds.com* ⊠ *Tastings from $60.*

Bouchaine Vineyards

WINERY | Tranquil Bouchaine lies just north of San Pablo Bay's tidal sloughs—to appreciate the off-the-beaten-path setting, step onto the terrace of the semicircular hilltop tasting room and scan the skies for hawks and golden eagles soaring above the vineyards. The alternately breezy and foggy weather in this part of the Carneros works well for Pinot Noir and Chardonnay. These account for most of the wines, but also look for Pinot Gris, Gewürztraminer, and Riesling whites, along with Cabernet Sauvignon, Merlot, Pinot Meunier, and Syrah. Some outdoor tastings take place on the terrace, others in the garden below it. ⊠ *1075 Buchli Station Rd., Napa ⊹ Off Duhig Rd., south of Hwy. 121* ☎ *707/252–9065* ⊕ *www. bouchaine.com* ⊠ *Tastings from $60.*

Clos du Val

WINERY | Searching in the early 1970s for the best non-European site to grow Cabernet Sauvignon, this French-owned outfit's founding winemaker selected land now called Hirondelle Vineyard. He chose well: Clos du Val (in French, "small vineyard of a small valley") built its reputation on its intense estate Cabernet, made with the Stags Leap District vineyard's fruit. Grapes for the much-praised Bordeaux-style red blend also come from Hirondelle, the French word for "swallow," a bird species prevalent here. Guests sample these wines plus Sauvignon Blanc, Cabernet Franc, and sometimes others in a glass-fronted

vineyard's-edge hospitality center (reservations required, same-day visits possible). In good weather, hosts retract the windows, unifying the tasting room, its flashy interiors by St. Helena–based designer Erin Martin, and the adjoining patio. ⊠ *5330 Silverado Trail, Napa ⊹ Near Capps Dr.* ☎ *707/261–5212* ⊕ *www. closduval.com* ⊠ *Tastings from $40 weekdays, $75 weekends.*

Cuvaison

WINERY | A hilly patchwork of vines fans out from this winery's contemporary glass-walled tasting room and spacious patio—on a sunny day, Cuvaison (pronounced "coo-vay-SAHN") is among the Napa Valley's most appealing spots to sip wine. Owned since 1979 by a Swiss family with the foresight to snap up 382 acres (about 150 now planted) of what's now prime Los Carneros real estate, the winery specializes in cool-climate Chardonnay, Sauvignon Blanc, and Pinot Noir. Longtime winemaker Steven Rogstad, well respected by his peers, describes the wines as "vineyard driven," but his mastery of technique elevates them further. The winery accommodates walkins when possible (try to call ahead), though it's best to have an appointment. ■**TIP**→ **Many guests pair a trip to Cuvaison with one to its across-the-street neighbor, sparkling-wine house Domaine Carneros.** ⊠ *1221 Duhig Rd. ⊹ At Hwy. 121* ☎ *707/942–2455* ⊕ *www.cuvaison.com* ⊠ *Tastings from $60.*

Darioush

WINERY | The visitor center at Darioush is unlike any other in the valley: 16 freestanding, sand-color columns loom in front of a travertine building whose exuberant architecture recalls the ancient Persian capital Persepolis. Exceptional hospitality and well-balanced wines from southern Napa Valley grapes are the winery's hallmarks. The signature Napa Valley Cabernet Sauvignon and other bottlings combine grapes grown high on Mt. Veeder with valley-floor fruit, the

At di Rosa, the art treasures can be found indoors and out.

former providing tannins and structure, the latter mellower, savory notes. Viognier, Chardonnay, Sauvignon Blanc, Merlot, Shiraz, and the Duel Cab-Shiraz blend are among other possible pours here. All visits are by appointment, best made at least a day or two ahead. ⊠ *4240 Silverado Trail, Napa* ✛ *Near Shady Oaks Dr.* ☎ *707/257–2345* ⊕ *www.darioush.com* 🖃 *Tastings from $90.*

di Rosa Center for Contemporary Art

ART MUSEUM | The late Rene di Rosa assembled an extensive collection of artworks created by Northern California artists from the 1960s to the present, displaying them on this 217-acre Carneros District property surrounded by Chardonnay and Pinot Noir vineyards. Two galleries at opposite ends of a 35-acre lake show works from the collection and host temporary exhibitions; the Sculpture Meadow behind the second gallery holds a few dozen large outdoor pieces. ⊠ *5200 Sonoma Hwy./Hwy. 121, Napa* ✛ *Near Duhig Rd.* ☎ *707/226–5991* ⊕ *www.dirosaart.org* 🖃 *$20* ⊗ *Closed Mon.–Thurs. (but check website).*

★ Domaine Carneros

WINERY | A visit to this majestic château is an opulent way to enjoy the Carneros District—especially in fine weather, when the vineyard views are spectacular. The château was modeled after an 18th-century French mansion owned by the Taittinger family. Carved into the hillside beneath the winery, the cellars produce sparkling wines reminiscent of those made by Taittinger, using only Los Carneros AVA grapes. Enjoy flights of sparkling wine or Pinot Noir with cheese and charcuterie plates, caviar, or smoked salmon. Tastings are by appointment only. ⊠ *1240 Duhig Rd., Napa* ✛ *At Hwy. 121* ☎ *707/257–0101, 800/716–2788* ⊕ *www.domainecarneros.com* 🖃 *Tastings from $40.*

Etude Wines

WINERY | You're apt to see or hear hawks, egrets, Canada geese, and other wildlife on the grounds of Etude, known for sophisticated Pinot Noirs. Although the

Both the art and the wine inspire at the Hess Persson Estates.

winery and its light-filled tasting room are in Napa County, the grapes for its flagship Carneros Estate Pinot Noir come from the Sonoma portion of Los Carneros, as do those for the rarer Heirloom Carneros Pinot Noir. Longtime winemaker Jon Priest also excels at single-vineyard Napa Valley Cabernets. In good weather, hosts pour Priest's reds, plus Chardonnay and Pinot Gris, on the patio outside the contemporary tasting room. Hosts of A Study of Pinot Noir, a private, seated experience, pour Pinot Noirs from different areas to illustrate how soil, climate, and growing conditions affect the finished wines. ⊠ 1250 Cuttings Wharf Rd., Napa ✛ 1 mile south of Hwy. 121 ☎ 707/257–5782 ⊕ www.etudewines. com ⌨ Tastings from $50.

★ Fontanella Family Winery

WINERY | Six miles from the downtown Napa whirl, husband-and-wife Jeff and Karen Fontanella's hillside spread seems a world apart. In addition to his formal studies, Jeff learned about wine making at three prestigious wineries before he

and Karen, a lawyer, established their own operation on 81 south-facing Mt. Veeder acres. The couple braved an economic recession, an earthquake, and wildfires in the first decade but emerged tougher, if no less gracious to guests lucky enough to find themselves tasting Viognier, Chardonnay, Zinfandel, and Cabernet Sauvignon on the patio here. Tastings often end with a Zinfandel-based port-style wine. ■ TIP → **Weather permitting, the reserve tasting includes the opportunity to stroll the estate, whose views south to San Francisco and east to Atlas Peak are terrific.** ⊠ 1721 Partrick Rd., Napa ✛ 1st St. to Browns Valley Rd. west of Hwy. 29 ☎ 707/252–1017 ⊕ www.fontanellawinery.com ⌨ Tastings from $65.

Hess Persson Estates

WINERY | About 9 miles northwest of Napa, up a winding road ascending Mt. Veeder, this appointment-only winery is a delightful discovery. The limestone structure, rustic from the outside but modern and airy within, contains Swiss founder Donald Hess's world-class art collection, including large-scale works by contemporary artists such as Andy Goldsworthy, Anselm Kiefer, and Robert Rauschenberg. Guided gallery tours are part of some tastings; other experiences might involve wine, cheese, chocolate, or small or large bites. An ATV vineyard tour is conducted some days, and there's a blending seminar. Mt. Veeder Cabernet Sauvignon is the star of the Hess Collection portfolio, with Chardonnay and Pinot Noir two other strong suits. The winery touts its accessible fruit-forward Lion's Head Collection tier as "next generation luxury wines." ✉ 4411 Redwood Rd., Napa ✛ West off Hwy. 29 at Trancas St./Redwood Rd. exit ☎ 707/255–1144 ⊕ www.hesspersssonestates.com ✉ Tastings from $85 ⊘ Closed Tues.–Thurs.

Hyde Estate Winery

WINERY | Dubbed "the wise man of Carneros" by *Wine Spectator* magazine, winegrower Larry Hyde began farming grapes in the southern Napa Valley in 1979. For years his fruit has gone into the high-scoring vineyard-designate Chardonnays of posh labels like Massican, DuMol, and Kistler, and Chardonnays and Pinot Noirs for Patz & Hall. With this exalted a pedigree—experts consider Hyde Vineyard not merely among California's finest vineyards but also the world—it was only a matter of time before wines bearing Hyde's name would debut. Pinot came first (2009), followed by Chardonnay (2012) and later Viognier, Sauvignon Blanc, Merlot, and Syrah. In 2017 Hyde and his son, Chris, opened a winery and appointment-only tasting room in the Carneros. When much of the valley is roasting during midsummer heat waves, San Pablo Bay breezes keep patrons on the vineyard's-edge terrace blessedly cool. ✉ 1044 Los Carneros Ave., Napa ✛ At Carneros Hwy. (121/12) ☎ 707/265–7626 ⊕ www.hydewines.com ✉ Tastings $75.

★ O'Brien Estate

WINERY | Barb and Bart O'Brien live on and operate this 40-acre Oak Knoll District estate, where in good weather guests sip wines at an outdoor tasting area adjoining the vineyard producing the fruit for them. It's a singular setting to enjoy Merlot, Cabernet Sauvignon, Bordeaux-style red blends, Sauvignon Blanc, and Chardonnay wines that indeed merit the mid-90s (sometimes higher) scores they garner from critics. Club members snap up most of the bottlings, with the rest sold at intimate tastings (reservations are required; book well ahead). All visits include vineyard and winery tours and an account of Barb and Bart's inspiring path to winery ownership. ◼TIP➜The superb wines and genial hosts make a stop here the highlight of many a Wine Country vacation. ✉ 1200 Orchard Ave., Napa ✛ Off Solano Ave. ☎ 707/252–8463 ⊕ www.obrienestate.com ✉ Tastings from $75.

Prime Solum and Expression 38°

WINERY | At a contemporary tasting barn with an outdoor patio and cabana seating, father-daughter wine-growing team William "Bill" Hill and Elana Hill showcase the Bordeaux-style reds of their Prime Solum label and the Chardonnays and Pinot Noirs of the Expression brand. Well-known in the Wine Country as a vineyard developer, Bill planted the nearby estate Brokenrock Vineyard, which supplies Cabernet Sauvignon to A-list wineries and Prime Solum, whose labels Elana, an accomplished painter, creates. Unlike many tastings where the wines are a few years old at most, sessions here focus on older vintages, not just of the Bordeaux reds but also the Pinots and even some of the Chardonnays. The Pinots come from as near as Sonoma County (at latitude 38°) and as far as Sta. Rita Hills (Expression 34°) and Oregon (Expression 44°). For guests who prefer lighter wines, the Endless Summer flight consists solely of whites and rosés. ✉ 1021 Atlas Peak Rd., Napa ✛ At

The Paris Wine Tasting of 1976

The event that changed the California wine industry forever took place half a world away in Paris. To celebrate America's 1976 Bicentennial, Steven Spurrier, a British wine merchant, sponsored a comparative blind tasting of California Cabernet Sauvignon and Chardonnay wines against Bordeaux Cabernet blends and French white Burgundies. The tasters were French and included journalists and producers.

Three California wines—Ridge's Montebello Cabernet Sauvignon and Chalone and David Bruce Chardonnays—were from the Santa Cruz Mountains. The rest—reds from Clos du Val, Freemark Abbey, Heitz, and Mayacamas; whites from Chateau Montelena, Freemark Abbey, Spring Mountain, and Veedercrest—were by Napa Valley producers.

And the Winners Were...

The 1973 Stag's Leap Wine Cellars Cabernet Sauvignon came in first among the reds, and the 1973 Chateau Montelena Chardonnay edged out the French and other California whites.

The so-called Judgment of Paris stunned the wine establishment, as it was the first serious challenge to French wines' supremacy.

Experts or Not?

In the prologue to his 2005 book *Judgment of Paris*, George M. Taber, the only reporter covering the event (for *Time* magazine), describes the panelists being "chattier" than wine judges usually are, an indication they weren't taking seriously a competition they were sure the French wines would win. Perhaps this inattention led one judge sipping a Napa Valley Chardonnay to exclaim, "Ah, back to France!" during the tasting or another to declare a French wine that ended up tallying poorly "definitely California." That some judges were so far off the mark begs the question of whether they were experts at all (or behaving as such that day), but no matter. When the shouting died down, the rush was on. Tourists and winemakers streamed into the Napa Valley, and interest grew so strong it also helped revitalize Sonoma County's wine industry.

Silverado Trail, 3½ miles from downtown Napa ☎ *707/492–3531* ⊕ *www.primesolum.com* 🍷 *Tastings from $60* ⊙ *Closed Tues. and Wed.*

★ Quixote Winery

WINERY | Extravagance infuses this boutique Stags Leap District operation, most notably in its architecture but also in the Petite Sirahs and Cabernets. Founder Carl Doumani spent years wooing the Austria-born architect Friedensreich Hundertwasser, whose sensibility has been compared to Antoni Gaudí's, to design the winery and production facility. Per Hundertwasser's insistence on replicating natural forms, the sod-roofed structure, clad in red brick and colorful ceramic tiles and topped with a gold onion dome, has no straight lines. Philippe Melka became the consulting winemaker in 2016, his rich, velvety style a complement to the ebullient setting. Winery visits are by appointment only. ■ TIP→ **The wine-and-food pairings here (book at least three days ahead) are exceptional.** ✉ *6126 Silverado Trail, Napa* ✛ *¾ mile south of Yountville Cross Rd.* ☎ *707/944–2659* ⊕ *quixotewinery.com* 🍷 *Tastings from $80.*

★ Robert Biale Vineyards

WINERY | Here's a surprise: a highly respected Napa Valley winery that doesn't sell a lick of Cabernet. Zinfandel from heritage vineyards, some with vines more than 100 years old, holds the spotlight, with luscious Petite Sirahs in supporting roles. Nearly every pour comes with a fascinating backstory, starting with the flagship Black Chicken Zinfandel. In the 1940s, the Biale family sold eggs, walnuts, and other farm staples, with bootleg Zinfandel a lucrative sideline. Because neighbors could eavesdrop on party-line phone conversations, "black chicken" became code for a jug of Zin. These days the wines are produced on the up-and-up, steps from the 10-acre property's tasting area. A stone's throw from Zinfandel vines, with far-off views of two mountain ranges, the open-air space has a back-porch feel. Visits are by appointment; call ahead for same-day. ⊠ *4038 Big Ranch Rd., Napa ✛ At Salvador Ave.* ☎ *707/257–7555* ⊕ *biale.com* ⊠ *Tastings from $50.*

Saintsbury

WINERY | In 1981, when Saintsbury released its first Pinot Noir, the Carneros District had yet to earn its reputation as a setting where the often finicky varietal could prosper. This pioneer helped disprove the conventional wisdom that only the French could produce great Pinot Noir; with their subtlety and balance Saintsbury's wines continue to please. In recent years the winery has expanded its reach to the Green Valley of the Russian River Valley, the Sonoma Coast, and Mendocino County's Anderson Valley with equally impressive results. Named for the English author and critic George Saintsbury (he wrote *Notes on a Cellar-Book*), this unpretentious operation also makes Chardonnay. Visits are by appointment only. ■ TIP→ **When the weather cooperates, tastings take place in a rose garden.** ⊠ *1500 Los Carneros Ave., Napa ✛ South off Hwy. 121 and east (left) on Withers Rd. for entrance* ☎ *707/252–0592* ⊕ *www.saintsbury.com* ⊠ *Tastings from $50.*

★ Shafer Vineyards

WINERY | Its Hillside Select Cabernet Sauvignon has long been one of the Napa Valley's most sought-after bottlings, and Shafer conducts small appointment-only tastings at a hospitality space with views of the rugged Stags Leap District incline where the prized wine's grapes grow. A Terrace View Tasting usually starts with the Red Shoulder Ranch Carneros Chardonnay, followed by TD-9 (a Cabernet Sauvignon–based Bordeaux blend), the One Point Five 100% Cabernet Sauvignon, and Relentless (a Syrah–Petite Sirah blend), concluding with the 100% Cabernet Hillside Select. The Private Collectors Experience includes an older Hillside Select vintage. Expertly farmed and masterfully balanced, Shafer's collector-quality wines deserve the high praise they receive. ⊠ *6154 Silverado Trail, Napa ✛ ¾ mile south of Yountville Cross Rd.* ☎ *707/944–2877* ⊕ *www.shafervineyards.com* ⊠ *Tastings from $125* ⊙ *Closed Sun.–Tues.*

Stag's Leap Wine Cellars

WINERY | A 1973 Stag's Leap Wine Cellars S.L.V. Cabernet Sauvignon put this winery and the Napa Valley on the enological map by placing first in the famous Judgment of Paris tasting of 1976. The grapes for that wine came from a vineyard visible from the stone-and-glass Fay Outlook & Visitor Center, which has broad views of a second fabled Cabernet vineyard (Fay) and the promontory that gives both the winery and the Stags Leap District AVA their names. The top-of-the-line Cabernets from these vineyards are poured at appointment-only tastings (call ahead for same-day visits), some of which include perceptive food pairings by the winery's executive chef. ■ TIP→ **When the weather's right, two patios with the same views as the tasting room fill up quickly.** ⊠ *5766 Silverado Trail, Napa ✛ At Wappo Hill Rd.* ☎ *707/261–6410* ⊕ *www.stagsleapwinecellars.com* ⊠ *Tastings from $75.*

Stags' Leap Winery

WINERY | A must for history buffs, this winery in a bowl-shape microvalley at the base of the Stags Leap Palisades dates to 1893. Three years earlier, its original owners erected the Manor House, noteworthy for its castlelike stone facade and redwood-paneled interior. The home, whose open-air porch seems out of a flapper-era movie set, hosts seated appointment-only tastings best booked a day or more ahead. Some tastings take place on the porch, others inside. Chardonnay and Cabernet Sauvignon are the calling cards, along with the Ne Cede Malis Petite Sirah, from vines planted in 1929. The winery also makes Sauvignon Blanc, Viognier, Malbec, and Merlot. ⊠ *6150 Silverado Trail, Napa* ✛ *¾ mile south of Yountville Cross Rd.* ☎ *707/257–5790* ⊕ *stagsleap.com* ⬛ *Tastings from $85* ⊘ *Closed Mon.*

★ Trefethen Family Vineyards

WINERY | Superior estate Chardonnay, dry Riesling, Cabernet Sauvignon, Merlot, Pinot Noir, and the Malbec-heavy Dragon's Tooth blend are the trademarks of this family-run winery founded in 1968. To find out how well Trefethen wines age, book a reserve tasting, which includes pours of limited-release wines and one or two older vintages. The terra-cotta-color historic winery on-site, built in 1886, was designed with a gravity-flow system, with the third story for crushing, the second for fermenting the resulting juice, and the first for aging. The wooden building suffered severe damage in the 2014 Napa earthquake, but after extensive renovations it reopened as the main tasting room. The early-1900s Arts and Crafts–style Villa, situated amid gardens, hosts reserve and elevated tastings. All visits require a reservation. ⊠ *1160 Oak Knoll Ave., Napa* ✛ *Off Hwy. 29* ☎ *707/255–7700* ⊕ *www.trefethen.com* ⬛ *Tastings from $50.*

The Battle of "Stags Leap"

The Stags Leap District AVA, named after a mythological stag, has no punctuation. In the 1970s (before the AVA came about), two wineries battled in court over ownership of "Stags Leap." After the Supreme Court of California ruled that Stags Leap is a geographical area, the case was settled over the position of apostrophes—before the "s" for Stag's Leap Wine Cellars and after it for Stags' Leap Winery. When the appellation was established in 1989, the AVA was allowed (after more litigation) to use "Stags Leap," without an apostrophe.

Truchard Vineyards

WINERY | Diversity is the name of the game at this family-owned winery on prime acreage amid the Carneros District's rolling hills. High-profile Napa Valley wineries purchase most of the grapes grown here, but some of the best are held back for estate-only wines—the Chardonnays and Pinot Noirs the region is known for, along with Roussanne, Zinfandel, Merlot, Syrah, Cabernet Sauvignon, and a few others. You must call ahead to taste, but a casual experience tailored to your interests awaits if you do. The included tour takes in the vineyards and the wine cave. ■ **TIP➜ Climb the small hill near the winery for a photo-op view of the pond and pen of Angora goats over the ridge.** ⊠ *3234 Old Sonoma Rd., Napa* ✛ *Off Hwy. 121* ☎ *707/253–7153* ⊕ *www.truchardvineyards.com* ⬛ *Tastings $55* ⊘ *Closed weekends.*

Whetstone Wine Cellars

WINERY | Pinot Noir, Syrah, and Viognier are the specialties of this boutique appointment-only winery with a tasting room inside a 19th-century French-style château. Hamden McIntyre, whose other Napa Valley wineries include the majestic Far Niente in Oakville and Inglenook in Rutherford, designed this less showy yet still princely 1885 structure. Its tree-shaded patio is a civilized spot to enjoy a flight in good weather. The influence of winemaker Jamey Whetstone's mentor Larry Turley, known for velvety Zinfandels, is most evident in the Pinots and the Syrah (there's also a Cabernet Sauvignon), but their élan is Whetstone's alone. ✉ *1075 Atlas Peak Rd., Napa* ✥ *Off Monticello Rd.* ☎ *707/254–0600* 🌐 *www.whetstonewinecellars.com* 🎫 *Tastings from $55.*

🍴 Restaurants

★ Angèle

$$$$ | FRENCH | A vaulted wood-beamed ceiling and paper-topped tables set the scene for romance at this softly lit French bistro inside an 1890s boathouse. Look for clever variations on classic dishes such as croque monsieur (grilled Parisian ham and Gruyère) and salade niçoise for lunch, with veal sweetbreads, cassoulet, beef bourguignon, and, in season, steamed mussels for dinner. **Known for:** classic bistro cuisine; romantic setting; outdoor seating under bright-yellow umbrellas. [$] *Average main: $38* ✉ *540 Main St., Napa* ✥ *At 5th St.* ☎ *707/252–8115* 🌐 *www.angelerestaurant.com.*

Avow Napa

$$$ | AMERICAN | The rooftop's the draw at this three-level brick-walled bar and restaurant opened by vintner Joseph Wagner, who grew up working at his family's Caymus Vineyards before starting Belle Glos Pinot Noir and other brands on his own. Small plates for pairing with updated classic cocktails might include caviar, oysters on the half shell, ceviche, and roasted bone marrow, but it's worth sticking around for dinner items like steelhead trout, pan-seared scallops, and cola-braised short rib. **Known for:** international wines and beers; carved-wood first-floor bar; affiliated Quilt & Co. tasting room next door for Wagner's small-lot wines. [$] *Average main: $32* ✉ *813 Main St., Napa* ✥ *At 3rd St.* ☎ *707/203–8900* 🌐 *avownapa.com* 🕒 *Closed Tues. and Wed. No lunch.*

Bear

$$$$ | MODERN AMERICAN | The culinary garden guests pass on their way to the Stanly Ranch resort's main restaurant supplies fruit, produce, and herbs for the artisanal cocktails and well-conceived dishes served inside the stone-and-glass structure. A salmon crudo appetizer exemplifies the approach: each of the pristinely fresh ingredients (yogurt, young dill, raw salmon, trout roe, green apple, Japanese spice) registers well enough separately but soars as an ensemble. **Known for:** grand yet comfortable interior; California-centric wine list with a global reach; patio dining with pool and villa views. [$] *Average main: $52* ✉ *Stanly Ranch, Auberge Resorts Collection, 200 Stanly Crossroad* ✥ *Stanly La., south off Hwy. 121/12* ☎ *707/699–6250* 🌐 *www.aubergeresorts.com/stanlyranch/dine.*

★ Bistro Don Giovanni

$$$ | ITALIAN | Giovanni Scala opened this boisterous roadhouse restaurant in the mid-1990s, and it's still a hangout of Napans who appreciate its Cal-Italian bistro cuisine, prepared with flair by Scott Warner, Scala's executive chef and partner. Warner augments the greatest-hits lineup—fritto misto (deep-fried calamari, onions, fennel, and rock shrimp), spinach ravioli with lemon-cream or tomato sauce, slow-braised lamb shank, and wood-fired pizzas—with daily specials based on seasonal ingredients. **Known for:** patio and garden dining; specialty cocktails and aperitifs; broad selection of Napa, Sonoma, and international wines. [$] *Average main: $36* ✉ *4110 Howard La., Napa* ✥ *5 miles north of downtown Napa off Hwy. 29* ☎ *707/224–3300* 🌐 *www.bistrodongiovanni.com.*

The Boon Fly Café

$$ | **MODERN AMERICAN** | This small spot that melds rural charm with industrial chic serves updated American classics such as fried chicken (free-range in this case), burgers (with Kobe beef), and beer-battered fish tacos (with lemon crème fraîche). The flatbreads, including a smoked salmon one made with *fromage blanc,* Parmesan, lemon crème fraîche, and capers, are worth a try. **Known for:** open all day; signature breakfast doughnuts; excellent cocktails and wines by the glass. [$] *Average main: $22* ✉ *Carneros Resort and Spa, 4048 Sonoma Hwy., Napa* ☎ *707/299–4870* 🌐 *www.boonflycafe.com.*

Bounty Hunter Wine Bar & Smokin' BBQ

$$ | **AMERICAN** | Every dish on the small menu at this wine store, wine bar, and restaurant is a standout, including the pulled-pork and smoked beef-brisket sandwiches served with three types of barbecue sauce, the meltingly tender St. Louis–style ribs, and the signature beer-can chicken (only Tecate will do). The space is whimsically rustic, with stuffed-game trophies mounted on the wall and leather saddles used as seats at a couple of tables. **Known for:** lively atmosphere; combo plates; sides and sauces. [$] *Average main: $22* ✉ *975 1st St., Napa* ✥ *Near Main St.* ☎ *707/226–3976* 🌐 *www.bountyhunterwinebar.com.*

C Casa

$$$ | **MODERN MEXICAN** | After running one of Oxbow Public Market's busiest stalls for more than a decade, owner Catherine Bergen jumped at the chance to occupy the complex's largest restaurant space, which her design team transformed into a hip-casual dining spot with a full bar specializing in artisanal tequilas and mescals. Bergen expanded her Baja-inspired menu with meat, fish, and tofu dishes prepared in a wood-fired grill and rotisserie. **Known for:** taqueria for to-go items from original space; breakfast tacos, huevos, and nachos; heated patio's Napa River views. [$] *Average main: $28* ✉ *Oxbow Public Market, 610 McKinstry St., Napa* ✥ *At 1st St.* ☎ *707/226–7700* 🌐 *www.myccasa.com.*

Cole's Chop House

$$$$ | **STEAKHOUSE** | When only a thick, flawlessly cooked New York or porterhouse (dry-aged by the eminent Allen Brothers of Chicago) will do, this steak house inside an 1886 stone building is just the ticket. New Zealand lamb chops are the nonbeef favorite, with oysters Rockefeller, beef carpaccio, and creamed spinach among the options for starters and sides. **Known for:** large outdoor patio; borderline-epic wine list; whiskey flights, cocktail classics done right. [$] *Average main: $54* ✉ *1122 Main St., Napa* ✥ *At Pearl St.* ☎ *707/224–6328* 🌐 *www.coleschophouse.com* ⏲ *No lunch.*

Compline

$$$ | **MODERN AMERICAN** | Sommelier Matt Stamp and restaurant wine vet Ryan Stetins opened this combination restaurant, wine bar, and wine shop. The place has evolved into a hot gathering spot for its youthful vibe and eclectic small and large plates that might include shrimp *lumpia* (a Filipino-style fried spring roll), half chicken, and the Compline burger, best enjoyed with duck-fat fries—and, per Stamp, Champagne. **Known for:** larger wine shop three doors away; pasta and vegetarian dishes; by-the-glass wines. [$] *Average main: $29* ✉ *1300 1st St., Suite 312* ☎ *707/492–8150* 🌐 *complinewine.com* ⏲ *Closed Tues.*

Grace's Table

$$$ | **ECLECTIC** | A dependable, varied menu makes this modest corner restaurant occupying a brick-and-glass storefront many Napans' go-to choice for a simple meal. Empanadas and iron-skillet corn bread with lavender honey and butter show up at all hours, with buttermilk pancakes and chilaquiles scrambled eggs among the brunch staples and cassoulet and roasted heirloom chicken popular for dinner. **Known for:** congenial staffers;

good beers on tap; eclectic menu focusing on France, Italy, and the Americas. $ *Average main: $30* ⊠ *1400 2nd St., Napa* ✚ *At Franklin St.* ☎ *707/226–6200* ⊕ *www.gracestable.net.*

Hal Yamashita Napa

$$$$ | JAPANESE | The owner of casual and fine-dining restaurants in Japan and elsewhere, Kobe-born chef Haruyuki Yamashita gained fame within his native land for techniques that modernized Japanese cuisine. At his sparsely decorated Napa location—black, gray, and brown tones, polished concrete floor, gleaming open kitchen—his team prepares prix-fixe multicourse meals, but you can also order sushi, tempura, and other items à la carte. **Known for:** superlative sushi; artisanal sake selection; happy hour (5–6 weekdays, 4–5 weekends). $ *Average main: $39* ⊠ *1300 Main St., Napa* ✚ *At Clinton St.* ☎ *707/699–1864* ⊕ *halnapa. com* ⊗ *Closed Tues. No lunch.*

★ Kenzo

$$$$ | JAPANESE | From the limestone floor to the cedar walls and cypress tabletops, most of the materials used to build this downtown Napa restaurant specializing in seasonally changing multicourse kaiseki meals were imported from Japan, as was the ceramic dinnerware. Delicate preparations of eel, abalone, bluefin tuna, and slow-roasted Wagyu tenderloin are typical of the offerings on the prix-fixe menu, which also includes impeccably fresh, artistically presented sashimi and sushi courses. **Known for:** spare aesthetic; delicate preparations; wine and sake selection. $ *Average main: $225* ⊠ *1339 Pearl St., Napa* ✚ *At Franklin St.* ☎ *707/294–2049* ⊕ *kenzonapa.com* ⊗ *Closed Mon. and Tues. No lunch.*

★ Kitchen Door

$$ | ECLECTIC | Todd Humphries has overseen swank haute-cuisine kitchens in Manhattan, San Francisco, and the Napa Valley, but he focuses on multicultural comfort plates at his high-ceilinged industrial-contemporary restaurant downtown.

The signature dishes include a silky cream of mushroom soup, flatbreads, pho, Thai fisherman's stew, duck banh mi sandwiches (go for the voluptuous duck jus add-on), and sweet, spicy, and succulent chicken wings among many other crowd-pleasers that keep this place hopping even in the off-season. **Known for:** specialty cocktails (bar a casual hangout); seasonally changing apps and entrées; outdoor patio. $ *Average main: $25* ⊠ *First Street Napa, 1300 1st St., Suite 272, Napa* ✚ *Near Clay St.* ☎ *707/226–1560* ⊕ *www.kitchendoornapa.com.*

★ La Toque

$$$$ | MODERN AMERICAN | Chef Ken Frank's La Toque is the complete package: his French-inspired cuisine, served in a formal dining space, is complemented by a wine lineup that consistently earns the restaurant a coveted *Wine Spectator* Grand Award. Ingredients appearing on the à la carte and prix-fixe tasting menus often include caviar, Alaskan halibut, Wagyu beef, and rich cheeses in dishes prepared and seasoned to pair with wines jointly chosen by the chefs and master sommelier. **Known for:** chef's tasting menu; astute wine pairings; vegetarian tasting menu. $ *Average main: $50* ⊠ *Westin Verasa Napa, 1314 McKinstry St., Napa* ✚ *Off Soscol Ave.* ☎ *707/257–5157* ⊕ *www.latoque.com* ⊗ *Closed Mon. and Tues. No lunch.*

Los Agaves Napa

$$ | MEXICAN | The vivid colors of the drinks, food, furnishings, and a mural by the Mexican urban artist Senkoe provide constant visual entertainment at this riverfront restaurant that evolved from a popular food truck. Oaxacan influences and spices like *chileajo* (vegetables, herbs, and chiles cooked and pureed) appear in the enchiladas, burritos, tacos, and other items, many inspired by southern Mexican street-food staples or recipes of the chef's extended family back home. **Known for:** daily-changing agua frescas; filling "wet" short-rib burrito

with half-red/half-green salsa; marvelous mole. $ *Average main: $26* ⊠ *660 Main St., Napa* ✛ *Near 5th St.* ☎ *707/266–1267* ⊕ *losagavesnapa.com.*

★ Loveski Deli

$$ | **JEWISH DELI** | Christopher Kostow gained fame as the award-winning chef of the Restaurant at Meadowood, the essence of Napa Valley haute fine dining, but the fare and mood are more down-to-earth at the order-at-the-counter deli he and his marketing-whiz wife, Martina Kostow, opened at the Oxbow Public Market. Bagels and bagel sandwiches anchor the breakfast menu, with pastrami and smoked-whitefish-salad sandwiches appearing for lunch and early dinner, along with matzoh ball soup, latkes, and other stalwarts. **Known for:** closing early; "always boiled," gluten-free bagels with trad (smoked salmon) and rad (miso vegetable) spreads; updated take on deli classics (kimchi with Reuben). $ *Average main: $17* ⊠ *610 1st St., Napa* ✛ *At McKinstry St.* ☎ *707/294–2525* ⊕ *www. loveskideli.com* ⊗ *No dinner.*

Morimoto Asia Napa

$$$ | **ASIAN FUSION** | Not to be confused with chef Masaharu Morimoto's flagship sushi palace a few doors south, his pan-Asian restaurant serves dim sum, spicy Szechuan *mapo* tofu, orange chicken, and a slew of other Chinese-inspired apps, soups, salads, and entrées in a light-filled space with Napa River views. This culinary concept, which worked well for the chef in Orlando and Waikiki, proved a Wine Country hit, too. **Known for:** lively atmosphere; river-view outdoor patio; full bar with numerous specialty cocktails. $ *Average main: $32* ⊠ *790 Main St., Napa* ✛ *At 3rd St.* ☎ *707/699–1737* ⊕ *morimotoasianapa.com.*

Morimoto Napa

$$$$ | **JAPANESE** | *Iron Chef* star Masaharu Morimoto is the big name behind this downtown Napa restaurant where everything is delightfully over the top, including the desserts. Organic materials

such as twisting grapevines above the bar and rough-hewn wooden tables seem simultaneously earthy and modern, creating a fitting setting for the gorgeously plated Japanese fare, from straightforward sashimi to more elaborate seafood, chicken, pork, and beef entrées. **Known for:** theatrical ambience; gorgeous plating; cocktail and sake menu. $ *Average main: $55* ⊠ *610 Main St., Napa* ✛ *At 5th St.* ☎ *707/252–1600* ⊕ *www.morimoto-apa.com.*

Napa Yard Oxbow Gardens

$$ | **AMERICAN** | **FAMILY** | Bookended by culinary gardens and constructed of corrugated-metal former shipping containers, redwoods felled by wildfires, and other ingeniously recycled materials, this 3½-acre open-air hangout has a block-party feel, especially at weekend brunch or when area musicians perform. The gardens inspire the seasonal comfort-food menu—summer tomatoes give way to fall beets in the salad, for instance—with staples like fish tacos, grilled chicken wings, tri-tip, and plant-based variations appearing year-round. **Known for:** local beers, wines, and spirits, including gin made on-site; family-friendly, dog-friendly space; weekend brunch, live music. $ *Average main: $19* ⊠ *585 1st St., Napa* ✛ *Across from Oxbow Public Market and CIA at Copia* ☎ *707/815–0398* ⊕ *www. napayard.com* ⊗ *Closed Mon. and Tues.*

Oenotri

$$ | **ITALIAN** | Often spotted at local farmers' markets and his restaurant's gardens, Oenotri's ebullient chef-owner and Napa native Tyler Rodde is ever on the lookout for fresh produce to incorporate into his rustic southern Italian cuisine. His restaurant, a brick-walled contemporary space with tall windows and wooden tables, is a lively spot to sample house-made *salumi* and pastas, thin-crust pizzas, and entrées that might include seared fresh fish or grilled rib eye. **Known for:** lively atmosphere; Margherita pizza with San Marzano tomatoes;

desserts with flair. $ *Average main: $26* ✉ *1425 1st St., Napa* ✛ *At Franklin St.* ☎ *707/252–1022* ⊕ *www.oenotri.com* ⊘ *Closed Mon. No lunch weekdays.*

★ Osha Thai Napa

$$$ | THAI | Northern Thailand–born chef-owner Lalita Souksamlane decorated her Wine Country restaurant with the same upscale flair—Thai wall ornaments, ornate wallpaper, cushy leatherette chairs, quartz tables adorned with roses—as her longtime San Francisco flagship. Beyond the aesthetic pleasure the decor provides, it also signals that in their delicacy and finesse her aromatic, flavorful entrées (some garnished with orchids) are on a par with similarly bedecked fine-dining establishments. **Known for:** wine offerings that complement the cuisine; pad Thai, ginger chicken, and other standbys but also a few rarities; weekday prix-fixe lunch a good deal. $ *Average main: $34* ✉ *1142 Main St., Napa* ✛ *At Pearl St.* ☎ *707/253–8880* ⊕ *oshathai.com/napa* ⊘ *Closed Mon. No lunch Sun.*

The Q Restaurant and Bar

$$ | AMERICAN | Tourists and loyalists from a previous location mingle at this lively spot whose perpetually in-motion chefs fry, barbecue, and smoke their way through a Southern-tinged menu that also includes pho, Italian chicken soup, and vinegar chicken. The baby back ribs, fried-chicken sandwich, cheddar-cheese burger, wedge salad, deviled eggs, and fried pickles score high with patrons, who somehow make room for the Q lime pie, brown-butter chocolate brownie, and other desserts. **Known for:** patio dining in back; craft cocktails and beers and short-but-sweet wine list; sides including four kinds of slaw, collard greens and ham hocks, and cast-iron-skillet corn bread. $ *Average main: $23* ✉ *1313 Main St., Napa* ✛ *Near Clinton St.* ☎ *707/224–6600* ⊕ *theqrandb.com* ⊘ *Closed Tues.*

★ Scala Osteria & Bar

$$$ | ITALIAN | The brightly lit dining room's mural map of the Naples coastline signals the chef's focus on *frutti di mare* (seafood) at this downtown homage to southern Italian cuisine the folks behind valley-fave Bistro Don Giovanni opened in 2023. Raw oysters, cooked whole fish, skillet-sautéed mussels, and halibut soup were among the early hits, along with pizzas hot out of a wood-fired oven. **Known for:** shareable plates and pasta dishes; Italian wine selection; late-night pizza, small bites, and desserts. $ *Average main: $30* ✉ *1141 1st St., Napa* ✛ *Near Coombs St.* ☎ *707/637–4380* ⊕ *scalaosteria.com.*

★ Torc

$$$$ | MODERN AMERICAN | *Torc* means "wild boar" in an early Celtic dialect, and owner-chef Sean O'Toole, who formerly helmed kitchens at top Manhattan, San Francisco, and Yountville establishments, occasionally incorporates the restaurant's namesake beast into his eclectic offerings. A recent menu featured tuna tartare, squash risotto, three hand-cut pasta dishes, a side of mushrooms foraged by a local pro, and Maine diver scallops in a lobster emulsion, all prepared by O'Toole and his team with style and precision. **Known for:** jolly only-at-the-bar happy hour (4–6 pm, nine seats total); specialty cocktails; Bengali sweet-potato pakora and deviled-egg appetizers. $ *Average main: $42* ✉ *1140 Main St., Napa* ✛ *At Pearl St.* ☎ *707/252–3292* ⊕ *www.torcnapa.com* ⊘ *Closed Sun. and Mon. No lunch.*

★ ZuZu

$$$ | SPANISH | The owner of this four-storefront empire touts it as a "mid-block party": ZuZu for paella, tapas, and other northern Spanish favorites; next door a gin bar (the spirit is big in Spain); third, a takeout window; and finally La Taberna for beer, wine, and *pintxos* (bar bites). The anchor, which opened in 2002, is still drawing crowds, who come for shareable plates that might include flounder ceviche, tender wood-fired octopus, *jamón ibérico,* and lamb chops with Moroccan barbecue glaze. **Known for:** range of gin flavors and tonics; paella of the day with bomba rice, chorizo, and shellfish; energetic crowds at gin bar and La Taberna. [$] *Average main: $35* ✉ *829 Main St., Napa* ✥ *Near 3rd St.* ☎ *707/224–8555* 🌐 *www.zuzunapa.com* 🕒 *Closed Mon. and Tues.*

Coffee and Quick Bites

Contimo Provisions

$ | AMERICAN | Two chefs who've starred at fine-dining restaurants shifted gears to open this humble shop, expanded with seating in 2023, where everything's made from scratch, either by them or their vendors. The ingredients are all of the highest quality, which explains the long lines at breakfast for the Ham & Jam (buttermilk biscuits with molasses-brined ham and seasonal jam) and at lunchtime for the Cuban, mortadella, and a few others. **Known for:** salads and other sides; cold and hot coffee drinks; ice-cream sandwich with homemade chocolate cookies. [$] *Average main: $14* ✉ *950 Randolph St.* ✥ *Near 1st St.* ☎ *707/782–6424* 🌐 *contimonapa.com* 🕒 *Closed Sun. and Mon. No dinner.*

Lunch Box at Copia

$ | AMERICAN | Relieve restaurant sticker shock (somewhat) and long waits by ordering bowls, salads, sandwiches, and desserts online for pickup at CIA at Copia's main-entrance takeout window. Some items' herbs, fruits, and vegetables are grown steps away at the culinary institute's garden. **Known for:** soft-serve ice cream; crab roll with crème fraîche dressing; open until 4 pm. [$] *Average main: $14* ✉ *500 1st St., Napa* ✥ *Near McKinstry St.* ☎ *707/967–2500* 🌐 *www.ciaatcopia.com/lunch-box* 🕒 *Closed weekends. No dinner.*

Hotels

Andaz Napa

$$$$ | HOTEL | Part of the Hyatt family, this boutique hotel with an urban-hip vibe has spacious guest rooms with white-marble bathrooms stocked with high-quality products. **Pros:** casual-chic feel; proximity to downtown restaurants, theaters, and tasting rooms; cheery, attentive service. **Cons:** unremarkable views from some rooms; expensive on weekends in high season; renovations planned for 2023 so ask for a room not affected by them. [$] *Rooms from: $458* ✉ *1450 1st St., Napa* ☎ *707/687–1234* 🌐 *andaznapa.com* 🛏 *141 rooms* 🍴 *No Meals.*

★ Archer Hotel Napa

$$$$ | HOTEL | Ideal for travelers seeking design pizzazz, a see-and-be-seen atmosphere, and first-class amenities, this five-story downtown Napa property fuses New York City chic and Las Vegas glamour. **Pros:** restaurants by chef Charlie Palmer; Sky & Vine rooftop bar; great views from upper-floor rooms (especially south and west). **Cons:** not particularly rustic; expensive in high season; occasional service and hospitality lapses. [$] *Rooms from: $459* ✉ *1230 1st St., Napa* ☎ *707/690–9800, 855/200–9052* 🌐 *archerhotel.com/napa* 🛏 *183 rooms* 🍴 *No Meals.*

Blackbird Inn and Finch Guest House

$$ | B&B/INN | Arts and Crafts style infuses the 1902 Blackbird Inn, from the lobby's fieldstone fireplace and lamps casting a warm glow over the impressive wooden staircase to the guest rooms' period-accurate, locally crafted oak beds and matching night tables. **Pros:** enthusiastic hosts; convenient to downtown; Victorian style in adjacent Finch house. **Cons:** per website "not an appropriate lodging for children"; some rooms are on the small side; street noise in rooms on Blackbird building's west side. [$] *Rooms from: $299* ✉ *1755 1st St., Napa*

☎ 707/226–2450 🌐 www.blackbirdinnnapa.com 🛏 12 rooms 🍴 Free Breakfast.

★ Cambria Hotel Napa Valley
$$ | **HOTEL** | Bright and spotless with a staff trained to please, this four-story Choice Hotels property provides value with a splash of boutique style in its public areas. **Pros:** fitness center and hot tub; excellent for the price; well-designed bathrooms (most with showers). **Cons:** no pool; on a busy road a mile from downtown (though no noise issues); short on Wine Country charm. *[$] Rooms from: $241 ✉ 320 Soscol Ave. ☎ 707/224–3400 🌐 cambrianapa.com 🛏 90 rooms 🍴 No Meals.*

★ Carneros Resort and Spa
$$$$ | **RESORT** | A winning combination of glamour, service, and pastoral seclusion makes this resort with freestanding board-and-batten cottages the perfect getaway for active lovebirds or families and groups seeking to unwind. **Pros:** cottages have lots of privacy; views from hilltop pool and hot tub; heaters on private patios. **Cons:** long drive to upvalley destinations; least expensive accommodations pick up highway noise; pricey pretty much year-round. *[$] Rooms from: $1099 ✉ 4048 Sonoma Hwy./Hwy. 121, Napa ☎ 707/299–4900, 888/400–9000 🌐 www.carnerosresort.com 🛏 100 rooms 🍴 No Meals.*

Cottages of Napa Valley
$$$$ | **B&B/INN** | Although most of the accommodations here date from the 1920s—when they rented for $5 *a month* (imagine that)—contemporary design touches and amenities, plush new furnishings, up-to-date bathrooms, and attentive service ensure a cozy, 21st-century experience. **Pros:** private porches and patios; basket of Bouchon pastries each morning; kitchen with utensils in each cottage. **Cons:** hum of highway traffic; extra-person charge for children under 12; weekend minimum-stay requirement. *[$] Rooms from: $499 ✉ 1012 Darms La., Napa ☎ 707/252–7810 🌐 www.napacottages.com 🛏 9 cottages 🍴 Free Breakfast.*

The George
$$ | **B&B/INN** | Tall palms tower over this restored three-story boutique inn, an elaborate 1891 Queen Anne–style structure once dubbed "the handsomest house in town." **Pros:** period character with contemporary style; in a quiet neighborhood but only a few blocks from downtown; high ceilings add to feeling of spaciousness. **Cons:** first-come first serve on-site parking (though ample street spaces in vicinity); no elevator (but one ground-floor ADA room); staff on-site for limited hours. *[$] Rooms from: $285 ✉ 492 Randolph St., Napa ☎ 707/596–5168 🌐 www.thegeorgenapa.com 🛏 9 rooms 🍴 Free Breakfast.*

★ The Inn on First
$$$$ | **B&B/INN** | Guests gush over the hospitality at this inn, where the painstakingly restored 1905 mansion facing 1st Street contains five rooms, with five additional accommodations, all suites, in a building behind a secluded patio and garden. **Pros:** full gourmet breakfast by hosts-with-the-most owners; gas fireplaces and whirlpool tubs in all rooms; away from downtown but not too far. **Cons:** no TVs; owners "respectfully request no children, no exceptions"; lacks pool, fitness center, and other amenities of larger properties. *[$] Rooms from: $430 ✉ 1938 1st St., Napa ☎ 707/253–1331 🌐 www.theinnonfirst.com 🛏 10 rooms 🍴 Free Breakfast.*

★ Inn on Randolph
$$$$ | **B&B/INN** | A few calm blocks from the downtown action on a nearly 1-acre lot with landscaped gardens, the Inn on Randolph—with a Gothic Revival–style main house and its five guest rooms plus five historic cottages out back—is a sophisticated haven celebrated for its gourmet gluten-free breakfasts and snacks. **Pros:** quiet residential neighborhood; spa tubs in cottages and two main-house rooms; romantic setting. **Cons:** a

bit of a walk from downtown; expensive in-season; weekend minimum-stay requirement. $ *Rooms from: $420* ✉ *411 Randolph St., Napa* ☎ *707/257–2886* 🌐 *www.innonrandolph.com* 🛏 *10 rooms* 🍴 *Free Breakfast.*

★ Milliken Creek Inn

$$$$ | **B&B/INN** | Perfect for a couple's weekend or midweek frolic, this secluded getaway with luxurious rooms is only a mile from the Oxbow Public Market and the Culinary Institute of America's CIA at Copia campus, and 1½ miles from downtown Napa's dining, shopping, and nightlife. **Pros:** countryside feeling but 1 mile from Oxbow Public Market area; larger Brookwood category rooms with stand-alone soaking tubs, fireplaces, and private decks with fire pits; breakfast delivered to your room or elsewhere on the grounds. **Cons:** expensive in-season; road noise audible in outdoor areas; no pool, fitness center, or bar. $ *Rooms from: $450* ✉ *1815 Silverado Trail, Napa* ☎ *707/255–1197* 🌐 *www.millikencreekinn.com* 🛏 *11 rooms* 🍴 *Free Breakfast.*

Napa River Inn

$$$ | **B&B/INN** | Part of a complex of restaurants and shops, this well-appointed if not showy waterfront inn is within walking distance of downtown hot spots. **Pros:** wide range of room sizes and prices; near downtown action; no parking or resort fees. **Cons:** river views could be more scenic; some rooms get noise from nearby restaurants; dated decor in some rooms. $ *Rooms from: $319* ✉ *500 Main St., Napa* ☎ *707/251–8500* 🌐 *www.napariverinn.com* 🛏 *66 rooms* 🍴 *Free Breakfast.*

Silverado Resort and Spa

$$$ | **RESORT** | If you like your resort to feel more country club than posh bastion, you'll likely find a stay at this 1,200-acre property satisfying. **Pros:** two championship golf courses, several pools, and more than a dozen tennis courts; The Grill for evening fine dining and Boost Café in the Market for grab-and-go breakfast and lunch; full-service spa. **Cons:** units rented out through Airbnb and VRBO can be problematic to book; not as luxurious as similar Napa Valley resorts (though hardly down at the heels); can be a madhouse during PGA events. $ *Rooms from: $391* ✉ *1600 Atlas Peak Rd., Napa* ☎ *844/421–6474* 🌐 *www.silveradoresort.com* 🛏 *340 rooms* 🍴 *No Meals.*

Stanly Ranch, Auberge Resorts Collection

$$$$ | **RESORT** | Grapevines surround this luxury property that opened in 2022 on 96 acres carved out of the titular, eight-times-larger Carneros ranch, whose grape-growing history dates to the 19th century. **Pros:** ultrahaute-rustic experience; wellness sanctuary with pool, spa, and high- and low-tech treatments; spacious villas and vineyard homes also available for overnight stays. **Cons:** location near San Pablo Bay can get breezy; extremely pricey; short drive to downtown restaurants and shops. $ *Rooms from: $1259* ✉ *200 Stanly Crossroad, Napa* ☎ *866/421–5122* 🌐 *aubergeresorts.com/stanlyranch* 🛏 *135 rooms* 🍴 *No Meals.*

Westin Verasa Napa

$$$ | **HOTEL** | Near the Napa Valley Wine Train depot and Oxbow Public Market, this spacious mostly suites resort is soothing and sophisticated, particularly in the guest quarters. **Pros:** woodsy Napa River setting but close to town; many rooms with well-equipped kitchenettes (some full kitchens); destination La Toque restaurant. **Cons:** amenities fee; slightly corporate feel; expensive in high season. $ *Rooms from: $388* ✉ *1314 McKinstry St., Napa* ☎ *707/257–1800* 🌐 *www.westinnapa.com* 🛏 *180 rooms* 🍴 *No Meals.*

🍸 Nightlife

ArBaretum

BARS | The husband and wife behind this energetic garden-theme bar (its name is a play on "arboretum") aim to provide patrons with more than a place to throw

Musical performances and other events take place at CIA at Copia's outdoor amphitheater.

a few back in a verdant indoor setting. It's a sit-down affair, with specialty cocktails, no two remotely alike, the focus. Some, like the San Remo, you may have heard of or tasted. The spicy concoction a bartender calls "carne asada in cocktail form" maybe not. ✉ 1149 1st St., Napa ⊹ At Coombs St. ☎ 707/265–6272 ⊕ napadistillery.com/visit-us.

★ Be Bubbly

WINE BARS | Fans of this storefront bar pouring dozens of Champagnes and sparkling wines from around the world call themselves Bubbleheads, fitting given the bubbly atmosphere owner-impresario Erin Riley, aka the Chief Bubblehead, has created. The knowledgeable servers will help you choose the right glass from the well-curated selection and keep you entertained with bingo, trivia contests, and other diversions. On some nights, Be Bubbly presents DJs and musicians. ✉ 1407 2nd St., Napa ⊹ At Franklin St. ☎ 707/637–4532 ⊙ Closed Tues.

Blue Note Napa

LIVE MUSIC | The famed New York jazz room's intimate West Coast club hosts national headliners such as Kenny Garrett, KT Tunstall, and Jody Watley. At Locals Night on many Wednesdays, homegrown talent performs. There's a full bar, and you can order a meal or small bites from the kitchen. The larger JaM Cellars Ballroom upstairs books similar artists. ✉ Napa Valley Opera House, 1030 Main St., Napa ⊹ At 1st St. ☎ 707/880–2300 ⊕ www.bluenotenapa.com.

Cadet Wine + Beer Bar

WINE BARS | Cadet plays things urban-style cool with a long bar, high-top tables, and a low-lit, loungelike feel. California wines and beers predominate, but the lineup circles the globe. Artisanal tequilas in cocktails or on their own will be the focus of Chispa, a new bar a few blocks away on 1st Street the same owners plan to open in 2023. ✉ 930 Franklin St., Napa ⊹ At end of pedestrian alley between 1st and 2nd Sts. ☎ 707/224–4400 ⊕ www.cadetbeerandwinebar.com.

Wilfred's Lounge

BARS | The effusive subtropical decor of this Tiki bar flirts with excess, but the artistry of the murals, carvings, and furnishings elicits respect. A noted mixologist's sensibly updated fruity drinks, adorned with orchids in lieu of umbrellas, are poured along with more straightforward cocktails and artisanal beers and wines. Hawaii-inflected dishes pair well with the libations, and a deck with Napa River views enhances the overall appeal. There's live music on some evenings. ⊠ *967 1st St.* ⊹ *Near Main St.* ☎ *707/690–9957* ⊕ *wilfredslounge.com* ⊗ *Closed Mon. and Tues.*

 Performing Arts

Uptown Theatre
MUSIC | At 860 seats, this art deco former movie house attracts performers like Ziggy Marley, Lyle Lovett, Roseanne Cash, Napa Valley resident Boz Scaggs, and others. ⊠ *1350 3rd St., Napa* ⊹ *At Franklin St.* ☎ *707/259–0123* ⊕ *www. uptowntheatrenapa.com.*

 Shopping

BOOKS

Copperfield's Books
BOOKS | Check the Napa page on this indie chain's website for local authors' readings and signings while you're in town. ⊠ *First Street Napa, 1300 1st St., Suite 398, Napa* ⊹ *At Franklin St.* ☎ *707/252–8002* ⊕ *www.copperfields-books.com/napa.*

Napa Bookmine
BOOKS | An indie shop scheduled to relocate during 2023 from its longtime site at 964 Pearl Street to the Register Square development, Napa Bookmine sells current magazines and new and used books and hosts author events. Specialties include children's and teen titles, travel books, and works by local writers. ⊠ *1625 2nd St., Napa* ⊹ *Near Wilson St.*

☎ *707/733–3199* ⊕ *www.napabookmine. com.*

SHOPPING CENTERS, MALLS

First Street Napa
MALL | The Archer Hotel Napa anchors this open-air downtown complex of mostly ground-level restaurants, tasting rooms, and national (Anthropologie, Lululemon) and homegrown (The Bennington Napa Valley, Habituate Lifestyle + Interiors, Napa Stäk) design, clothing, housewares, and culinary shops. Copperfield's Books and the Visit Napa Valley Welcome Center are also here, along with Milo and Friends for pet necessities and accessories. ⊠ *1300 1st St., Napa* ⊹ *Between Franklin and Coombs Sts.* ☎ *707/257–6900* ⊕ *www.firststreetnapa. com.*

 Activities

Enjoy Napa Valley
KAYAKING | Napa native Justin Perkins leads a history-oriented Napa River kayak tour that passes by downtown sights. On the leisurely paddle, Perkins points out the wildlife and regales participants with amusingly salacious tales of Napa's river-town past. ⊠ *Main St. Boat Dock, 670 Main St., Napa* ⊹ *Riverfront Promenade, south of 3rd St. Bridge* ☎ *707/227–7364* ⊕ *enjoy-napa-valley.com* ⊠ *$85* ⊗ *Closed Wed.*

Napa Valley Bike Shop
BIKING | This outfit that rents bikes is near the Napa Valley Vine Trail and another trail that follows the Napa River. Staffers will help with guided and self-guided trips booked through the affiliated Napa Valley Bike Tours in Yountville. ■**TIP→ The shop has an excellent map of Napa bike trails for all abilities.** ⊠ *950 Pearl St., Napa* ⊹ *At West St.* ☎ *707/251–8687* ⊕ *www. napavalleybiketours.com* ⊠ *Rentals from $55, tours from $149.*

Few experiences are as exhilarating yet serene as an early-morning balloon ride above the vineyards.

Napa Valley Gondola

ENTERTAINMENT CRUISE | Rides in authentic gondolas that seat up to six depart from downtown Napa's municipal dock. You'll never mistake the Napa River for the Grand Canal, but this is a diverting excursion that often includes a serenade. ⊠ *Main St. Boat Dock, 700 Main St., Napa* ⚓ *Riverfront Promenade, south of 3rd St. Bridge* ☎ *707/373–2100* ⊕ *napav-alleygondola.com* ⊠ *From $169 (up to 6 people).*

Yountville

9 miles north of downtown Napa; 9 miles south of St. Helena.

Yountville (population about 3,500) is something like Disneyland for food lovers, starting with The French Laundry, one of the best restaurants in the United States. Its chef, Thomas Keller, is also behind a few other Yountville enterprises—a French bistro, a bakery, American and Oaxacan restaurants, and a Champagne and caviar lounge among them. And that's only the tip of the iceberg: you could stay here several days and not exhaust all the options in this tiny town with an outsize culinary reputation.

Yountville is full of small inns and luxurious hotels catering to those who prefer to walk rather than drive to their lodgings after dinner. Although visitors use Yountville as a home base, touring Napa Valley wineries by day and returning to dine, you could easily while away a few hours downtown, wandering through the shops on or just off Washington Street or visiting the many tasting rooms. The Yountville Chamber of Commerce, on the southern end of town across from the Hotel Villagio, has maps with wine-tasting and history walks.

The town is named for George C. Yount, who in 1836 received the first of several large Napa Valley land grants from the Mexican government. Yount is credited with planting the valley's first vinifera grapevines in 1838. The vines are long gone, but wisps of Yountville's

19th-century past bleed through, most notably along Washington Street, where a restaurant at 6525 Washington occupies the redbrick former train depot, and shops and restaurants west of it inhabit the former Groezinger Winery, established in 1870.

GETTING HERE AND AROUND

If you're traveling north from Napa on Highway 29, take the Yountville/Veterans Home exit, make a right on California Drive and a left onto Washington Street. Traveling south on Highway 29, turn left onto Madison Street and right onto Washington Street. Nearly all of Yountville's businesses and restaurants are clustered along a 1-mile stretch of Washington Street. Yountville Cross Road connects downtown Yountville to the Silverado Trail, where you'll find several wineries. VINE buses serve Yountville. The free Yountville Bee electric bus circles the downtown area, hits a few spots beyond, and provides on-demand service via the Ride the Vine app.

VISITOR INFORMATION

CONTACT Yountville Chamber Of Commerce. ⊠ *6484 Washington St., Yountville ✛ At Oak Circle* ☎ *707/944–0904* ⊕ *yountville. com.*

Sights

SIGHTS IN DOWNTOWN YOUNTVILLE

Cornerstone Cellars

WINERY | Inside Yountville's whitewashed 19th-century passenger train depot, Cornerstone shares a space with an apparel shop and displays contemporary art curated by Aerena Galleries. The winery, started on something of a whim more than three decades ago (a Howell Mountain grower offered the founders some excess fruit late in the 1991 season), produces Cabernet Sauvignon from the valley's benchland and mountain sections. Because each Cabernet receives similar treatment from winemaker Kari Auringer,

the wines express what's unique about their subappellations, vineyard sources, and vintages. Cornerstone is a good place to find out what type of Napa Valley Cabernet you prefer—perhaps the smooth Benchlands blend, in recent years softened with Merlot and Cabernet Franc, or maybe the sturdier yet still lush Howell Mountain offering, usually 100% Cabernet or nearly so. ⊠ *6505 Washington St., Yountville* ☎ *707/945–0388* ⊕ *www.cornerstonecellars.com* 🥂 *Tastings from $40.*

Domaine Chandon

WINERY | On a knoll shaded by ancient oak trees, this sparkling-wine producer founded in 1973—the first in the Napa Valley by a French Champagne house—is owned by the luxury brand Louis Vuitton Moët Hennessy. Known for its lineup of brut, rosé, and demi-sec (half-dry, fairly sweet) bubblies, Domaine Chandon also makes Chardonnay, Pinot Meunier, Pinot Noir, and Cabernet Sauvignon still wines. In anticipation of its golden anniversary, the winery embarked on a comprehensive renovation of its indoor and outdoor tasting areas. After its scheduled completion in late 2023, Chandon will introduce some new tasting experiences, but The Epicurean, a multicourse pairing of larger bites with well-curated sparkling wines, is expected to continue. Offered most of the year, it's well worth the splurge. Other tastings involve food, but guests wishing to sip a few sparklers can choose four from the nearly two dozen the wine-making team crafts. ⊠ *1 California Dr., Yountville ✛ Off Hwy. 29* ☎ *888/242–6366* ⊕ *www.chandon.com* 🥂 *Tastings from $55.*

Handwritten Wines

WINERY | Handcrafted, 100% Cabernet Sauvignons from hillside and mountain vineyards 2 acres or smaller are this boutique winery's emphasis, with the wines from Mt. Veeder, Rutherford, and Calistoga often among the best. The lineup also includes Sauvignon Blanc

Domaine Chandon claims a prime piece of real estate.

and Chardonnay, along with a Pinot Noir from Santa Barbara County's Sta. Rita Hills AVA. Guests at appointment-only seated tastings sip either in a light-filled upscale-rustic space clad in reclaimed redwood wine-barrel staves or in the open-air courtyard the structure surrounds. ⊠ *6494 Washington St., Yountville ✛ Near Oak Circle* ☎ *707/944–8524* ⊕ *www.handwrittenwines.com* ✉ *Tastings from $75.*

Hestan Vineyards

WINERY | A contemporary structure of concrete, glass, hand-forged copper, and other materials, Hestan's downtown tasting room further impresses with its interior use of travertine and Venetian plaster. Gleaming cookware catches the eye before wine bottles do—the founder manufactures pots and pans for upscale outlets like Williams-Sonoma and in the 2020s introduced a line by chef Thomas Keller of The French Laundry. Sit down for a tasting, though, and attention quickly shifts to the polished, almost voluptuous wines that two acclaimed winemakers craft for four separate labels. The Meyer and Stephanie Cabernet Sauvignons and the Stephanie Petit Verdot, all from grapes grown amid the southern Vaca Range, are particularly successful, as is the Vincent Christopher Pinot Noir. ⊠ *6548 Washington St., Yountville ✛ At Humboldt St.* ☎ *707/945–1002* ⊕ *www. hestanvineyards.com* ✉ *Tastings from $40.*

JCB Tasting Salon

WINERY | Mirrors and gleaming surfaces abound in this eye-catching ode to indulgence named for its French owner, Jean-Charles Boisset (JCB). The JCB label first made its mark with sparkling wine, Chardonnay, and Pinot Noir, with Cabernet Sauvignon a more recent strong suit. In addition to providing a plush setting for sampling these wines, Boisset's downtown Yountville tasting space doubles as a showcase for home decor items from the likes of Lalique and Baccarat. ⊠ *6505 Washington St., Yountville ✛ At Mulberry St.* ☎ *707/934–8237* ⊕ *jcbcollection.com/ visit* ✉ *Tastings from $50.*

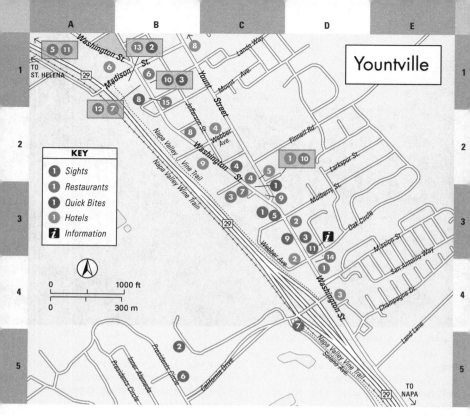

Yountville

KEY

- Sights
- Restaurants
- Quick Bites
- Hotels
- Information

| 0 | 1000 ft |
| 0 | 300 m |

Napa Valley Museum Yountville

ART MUSEUM | A permanent exhibition at this hillside museum near Domaine Chandon surveys the people and natural conditions that have shaped the valley's history. The well-curated temporary shows often surprise with their depth of cultural insight or the artistry involved. ✉ 55 Presidents Circle, Yountville ⊹ Off Hwy. 29 on California Veterans Home grounds ☎ 707/944–0500 ⊕ napavalleymuseum.org ☒ $15 ⊙ Closed Mon.–Wed.

Napa Valley Vine Trail

TRAIL | Dedicated locals conceived this multipurpose walking, biking, and jogging path they hope will run 47 miles from below Napa, north through the Napa Valley to Calistoga. A mostly flat 9-mile segment open for several years links Yountville and downtown Napa. Vineyard views predominate in the Yountville portion, giving way in Napa to the RAD Napa (Rail Arts District Napa) murals that grace warehouse walls and utility boxes. Markers let trail goers know where they are, interpretive signs convey some history, and shelters provide bike racks, pumps, and tools for minor repairs. An 8½-mile section expected to debut by fall 2023 will wind through vineyards and Bothe–Napa Valley State Park from St. Helena to Calistoga. Download the latest map on the trail's website. ■ TIP→ Napa Valley Bike Tours, with shops in Napa and Yountville, rents helmets and bikes, as do Trek Bicycle St. Helena and Calistoga Bikeshop. ⊹ Trailheads in Yountville at Hwy. 29 and Madison St., in Napa west of Soscol Ave. and Vallejo St. Expected trailheads in St. Helena on Pratt Ave. near Hwy. 29 and at Calistoga Depot off Lincoln Ave. ☎ 707/252–3547 ⊕ www.vinetrail.org.

RH Wine Vault

WINERY | Gargantuan crystal chandeliers, century-old olive trees, and strategically placed water features provide visual and aural continuity at Restoration Hardware's quadruple-threat food, wine, art, and design compound. An all-day café fronts two steel, glass, and concrete home-furnishings galleries, with a bluestone walkway connecting them to the wine salon. Centered on a two-story 1904 manor house constructed from Napa River stone, it's an excellent spot to learn about small-lot Napa and Sonoma wines, served by the glass, flight, or bottle. Collector-revered labels like Corison, Fisher, Lail, Matthiasson, Mayacamas, and Spottswoode are all represented, the wines in good weather poured in "outdoor living rooms" behind the stone structure. Oozing RH fabulousness as it does, the Wine Vault can feel like a scene on a busy day, but the wines are the real deal. All tastings are by appointment. ✉ 6725 Washington St., Yountville ⊹ At Pedroni St. ☎ 707/339–4654 ⊕ rh.com/yountville/winevault ☒ Tastings from $20 glass, $65 flight.

Silver Trident Winery

WINERY | At Silver Trident you can spring for the deluxe Potato Chip Extravaganza—wines paired with well-chosen gourmet chips—but the real splurge is on the decor: this tasteful downtown space doubles as a Ralph Lauren Home Collection showroom where everything's for sale. It's a fittingly ritzy setting for longtime winemaker Kari Auringer's subtly delicious Sauvignon Blanc, rosé, Pinot Noir (her strong suit), and Bordeaux-style reds (also quite good). In addition to the potato-chip experience, there's a tasting of current releases without food. All visits are by appointment, but with drop-ins accommodated when possible. ✉ 6495 Washington St., Yountville ⊹ Near Mulberry St. ☎ 707/945–0311 ⊕ silvertridentwinery.com ☒ Tastings from $50.

Stewart Cellars

WINERY | Three stone structures meant to mimic Scottish ruins coaxed into modernity form this complex with public and private tasting spaces and a bright outdoor patio. The attention to detail in the ensemble's design mirrors that of the wines, whose grapes come from coveted sources, most notably all six Beckstoffer Heritage Vineyards, among the Napa Valley's most historic sites for Cabernet Sauvignon. Although the Nomad Collection sextet of Cabs is the focus, winemaker Blair Guthrie also makes sparkling wine, Sauvignon Blanc, Chardonnay, rosé, Pinot Noir, and Zinfandel. Visits are by appointment, but except for Nomad tastings, walk-ins are usually accommodated. ⊠ *6752 Washington St., Yountville* ✛ *Near Pedroni St.* ☎ *707/963–9160* ⊕ *www.stewartcellars. com* ⌕ *Tastings from $40.*

Yountville Art Walk

PUBLIC ART | Nearly three dozen large-scale sculptures enliven Yountville's parks and sidewalks. Most are on or near Washington Street in downtown's southern and central sections. Download a map or pick one up at the visitor center (6484 Washington Street). Easier still, each work has a smartphone QR code linking to online information. ⊠ *Washington St., Yountville* ✛ *Between Champagne Dr. and Monroe St.* ⊕ *www. townofyountville.com/about.*

SIGHTS BEYOND DOWNTOWN YOUNTVILLE

★ Cliff Lede Vineyards

WINERY | Inspired by his passion for classic rock, owner and construction magnate Cliff Lede named the blocks in his Stags Leap District vineyard after hits by the Grateful Dead and other bands. Two other Lede obsessions are rock memorabilia and contemporary art like Jim Dine's outdoor sculpture *Twin 6' Hearts,* a magnet for the Instagram set. The vibe at this efficient, high-tech winery is anything but laid-back, however. Cutting-edge agricultural and enological science informs the vineyard management and wine making here. Lede produces Sauvignon Blanc, Cabernet Sauvignon, and Bordeaux-style red blends; tastings often include sparkling wine, Chardonnay, Pinot Gris, or Pinot Noir from sister winery FEL. All

the wines are well crafted, though the Cabs truly rock. ■ TIP➜ **Book a Backstage Tasting Lounge session to sip top-tier wines amid a rock music–related art exhibition.** ⊠ *1473 Yountville Cross Rd., Yountville* ✛ *Off Silverado Trail* ☎ *707/944–8642* ⊕ *clifflledevineyards.com* ⌕ *Tastings from $60.*

★ Elyse Winery

WINERY | One of his colleagues likens Elyse's winemaker, Russell Bevan, to "a water witch without the walking stick" for his ability to assess a vineyard's weather, soil, and vine positioning and intuit how particular viticultural techniques will affect wines' flavors. Bevan farms judiciously during the growing season, striving later in the cellar to preserve what nature and his efforts have yielded rather than rely on heavy manipulation. Elyse makes highly praised small-lot single-vineyard Zinfandels and Cabernet Sauvignons. Red blends containing as many as five varietals are another strong suit. A country lane edged by vines leads to this unassuming winery, whose unhurried tastings, often outdoors, have a backyard-casual feel. ■ TIP➜ **Costing much less than the average Napa Valley Cab, Elyse's Holbrook Mitchell Cabernet Sauvignon holds its own against peers priced appreciably higher.** ⊠ *2100 Hoffman La., Napa* ✛ *1¾ miles south of central Yountville, off Hwy. 29 or Solano Ave.* ☎ *707/944–2900* ⊕ *elysewinery.com* ⌕ *Tastings from $55.*

Goosecross Cellars

WINERY | Large retractable west-facing windows in this boutique winery's barn-like tasting space open up behind the bar to views of Cabernet Sauvignon vines—in fine weather, guests on the outdoor deck can practically touch them. Farther in the distance lie the Mayacamas Mountains. Goosecross makes Chardonnay and Pinot Noir from Carneros grapes, but the soul of this cordial operation is its 12-acre State Lane Vineyard, the 9.2 planted acres mostly Cabernet Sauvignon and Merlot with some Cabernet Franc, Malbec, and Petit Verdot. The State Lane Cabernet and Merlot are the stars, along with the Holly's Block 100% Cab and the Aeros Bordeaux-style blend of the vineyard's best grapes. The last two aren't always poured, but the intentionally big Branta red wine (the blend changes with each vintage), a crowd-pleaser, usually is. Visits to Goosecross are by appointment only. ✉ *1119 State La., Yountville* ✛ *Off Yountville Cross Rd.* ☎ *707/944–1986* ⊕ *www.goosecross.com* ☜ *Tastings from $60.*

Hill Family Estate Winery

WINERY | Doug Hill has farmed grapes for prominent Napa Valley wineries for years, but at the urging of his son, Ryan, the family began bottling its own Merlot, Cabernet Sauvignon, and other wines. Crafted by Alison Doran, a protégé of the late Napa winemaker André Tchelistcheff, these are refined reds you can sample, along with whites that include Albariño and Chardonnay, on a 7½-acre estate. Alfresco tastings take advantage of classic valley views—vineyards and the board-and-batten winery building up close, the Mayacamas Mountains farther west. Appointment-only visits are limited to a few guests per day, but the family also operates a tasting salon less than a mile away in downtown Yountville. ■TIP→ **Ask about seasonal tours (with tasting) of a "secret garden" that grows produce for The French Laundry and other top restaurants.** ✉ *6155 Solano Ave., Napa* ✛ *Near Hoffman La.* ☎ *707/944–9580* ⊕ *www.hillfamilyestate.com* ☜ *Tastings from $40 downtown, $75 at winery* ☾ *Closed Tues. and Wed.*

★ Mira Winery

WINERY | A close encounter of the wine kind—California winemaker and political communications expert (in this instance, Jim "Bear" Dyke) strike up a conversation in a Washington, D.C., bar—led to the formation of this winery devoted to single-vineyard wines from southern Napa Valley vineyards. At the time, the winemaker, Gustavo A. Gonzalez, headed up the red-wine program at Robert Mondavi Winery. Scaling down at Mira (from the Latin root word for "miracle"), he contributed his knowledge, connections, but most of all wise, restrained approach to creating Pinot Noir, Merlot, Syrah, Cabernet Sauvignon, and a few others. These unshowy but powerful wines, plus whites that include Chardonnay and a Sauvignon Gris fermented in a rare egg-shaped oak vessel, are served at a stone and glass hospitality house adjoining the winery. The structure's tall windows and outdoor seating areas take full advantage of Mira's setting between the Mayacamas Mountains and Wappo Hill. ✉ *6170 Washington St., Yountville* ✛ *1 mile south of downtown Yountville* ☎ *707/945–0881* ⊕ *miranapa.com* ☜ *Tastings from $50.*

Oasis by Hoopes

WINERY | Vineyards surround the walk-through organic garden and corral for rescue animals that anchor second-generation vintner Lindsay Hoopes's playfully pastoral wine venue. In conceiving this family- and dog-friendly outdoor-oriented spot—with ample patio and garden seating and a seasonal farmers' market—Hoopes aimed to expand the notion of what a Napa Valley wine tasting can entail. To that end, rather than pay a tasting fee, guests book a table, with the booking fee applied toward wine purchases (full bottles or "mini bottle flights") enjoyed on-site or to go. Lindsay's father started Hoopes Vineyard in the 1980s, selling his Oakville AVA Cabernet Sauvignon grapes to A-list producers before establishing his boutique label in 1999. The lineup now includes Sauvignon Blanc, Chardonnay, rosé, Merlot, and Syrah. Most are gems, particularly two Oakville Cabs and a Howell Mountain Merlot. ✉ *6204 Washington St., Yountville* ✛ *1 mile south of downtown* ☎ *707/944–1869* ⊕ *hoopesvineyard. com/oasis-by-hoopes* ☜ *Tastings from $100 (per person table reservation fee)* ☾ *Closed Mon.*

🍴 Restaurants

Ad Hoc

$$$$ | **AMERICAN** | At this low-key dining room with zinc-top tables, superstar chef Thomas Keller offers a changing daily fixed-price menu that might include smoked beef short ribs with creamy herb rice and charred broccolini or sesame chicken with radish kimchi and fried rice (check the website for that day's offerings). Ad Hoc also serves a small but decadent Sunday brunch, and Keller's Addendum annex, in a separate small building behind the restaurant, sells boxed lunches to go (including moist buttermilk fried chicken) from Thursday to Saturday except in winter. **Known for:** casual cuisine; don't-miss buttermilk-fried-chicken night; good prices for a Thomas Keller restaurant. [$] *Average main: $64* ✉ *6476 Washington St., Yountville* ✣ *At Oak Circle* ☎ *707/944–2487* 🌐 *www.thomaskeller.com/adhoc* 🕓 *Closed Tues. and Wed. No lunch weekdays and Sat.*

★ **Bistro Jeanty**

$$$ | **FRENCH** | Escargots, cassoulet, steak au poivre (pepper steak), and other French classics are prepared with precision inside this tan-brick country bistro whose flower-filled window boxes, extra-wide shutters, and red-and-white-striped awning hint at the Old World flair and joie de vivre that infuse the place. Regulars often start with the rich tomato soup in a flaky puff pastry before proceeding to sole meunière or coq au vin, completing the French sojourn with crème brûlée *au chocolat* or another authentic dessert. **Known for:** traditional preparations; oh-so-French atmosphere; patio seating. [$] *Average main: $34* ✉ *6510 Washington St., Yountville* ✣ *At Mulberry St.* ☎ *707/944–0103* 🌐 *www.bistrojeanty.com.*

Bottega

$$$ | **ITALIAN** | At his softly lit, exposed-redbrick downtown trattoria, which occupies sections of the 19th-century former Groezinger Winery, chef Michael Chiarello (Food Network, etc.) and his team transform local, seasonally changing ingredients into regional Italian cuisine. Staples like ricotta gnocchi with tomato sauce and smoked/braised short rib in espresso *agrodolce* (sweet-and-sour sauce) served with creamy ancient-grain polenta show the chef at his most rustic yet sophisticated. **Known for:** romantic setting; soulful craft cocktails; Italian and California wines. [$] *Average main: $33* ✉ *6525 Washington St., Yountville* ✣ *Near Mulberry St.* ☎ *707/945–1050* 🌐 *www.botteganapavalley.com.*

★ **Bouchon Bistro**

$$$ | **FRENCH** | The team that created The French Laundry is also behind this place, where everything—the zinc-topped bar, antique sconces, suave waitstaff, and traditional French onion soup—could have come straight from a Parisian bistro. Pan-seared flat iron steak with caramelized shallots and mussels steamed with white wine, saffron, and Dijon mustard—both served with crispy, addictive fries—are among the perfectly executed entrées. **Known for:** bistro classics; raw bar; Bouchon Bakery next door. [$] *Average main: $36* ✉ *6534 Washington St., Yountville* ✣ *Near Humboldt St.* ☎ *707/944–8037* 🌐 *thomaskeller.com/bouchonyountville.*

Brix Napa Valley

$$$ | **MODERN AMERICAN** | A roadside stop for specialty cocktails, casual lunches, and evening fine dining, Brix shares ownership with Kelleher Family Vineyards, whose Cabernet Sauvignon grapevines surround the restaurant on three sides. Pan-seared fish, juicy Brix burgers, house-made pasta, and risotto appear on both the lunch and dinner menus, with prime rib the crowd-pleaser on Sunday night. **Known for:** verdant outdoor dining areas; Napa/Sonoma-centric wine list with older-vintage surprises; Sunday brunch. [$] *Average main: $35* ✉ *7377 St.*

Helena Hwy., Napa ✥ 1½ miles north of Yountville ☎ 707/944–2749 🌐 www.brix.com 🕒 Closed Tues.

Ciccio

$$$ | ITALIAN | After a lengthy closure, an insider favorite for modern Italian was scheduled to reopen by summer 2023 with vintners Frank and Karen Altamura remaining as owners and Napa Valley culinary star and longtime Ciccio patron Christopher Kostow of The Restaurant at Meadowood and The Charter Oak stepping in as executive chef. The seasonal growing cycles of Meadowood's herb and produce garden dictate the menu, with fried-seafood appetizers, pasta dishes, and several wood-fired pizzas among the likely offerings. **Known for:** Negronis lineup; pizzas' flavorful cheeses; Napa and Italian wines. [$] *Average main: $33* ✉ *6770 Washington St., Yountville ✥ At Madison St. ☎ 707/945–1000 🌐 www.ciccionapavalley.com 🕒 No lunch (check website for days closed).*

★ Coqueta Napa Valley

$$$ | SPANISH | From pintxos and paellas to Iberian cheeses and fish *à la plancha* (flat-grilled), the chefs at this Wine Country offspring of Michael Chiarello's successful San Francisco restaurant Coqueta reimagine Spanish classics with a 21st-century farm-to-table sensibility. The frenetic pace in the flame-happy open kitchen, inside Yountville's redbrick former railroad depot, keeps the mood lively in the relatively small dining space, with the vibe on the patio out back even more so. **Known for:** sensual flavors; dynamic spicing; seasonal cocktails inspired by Spain and the Napa Valley. [$] *Average main: $33* ✉ *6525 Washington St., Yountville ✥ Near Yount St. ☎ 707/244–4350 🌐 www.coquetanv.com.*

★ The French Laundry

$$$$ | AMERICAN | Inside an ivy-laced old stone building and atop many a Napa Valley visitor's bucket list, chef Thomas Keller's destination restaurant lives up to the hype with intricate yet not overthought cuisine. Some courses on the two prix-fixe menus, one of which highlights vegetables, rely on luxe ingredients such as white quail; others take humble elements like carrots or fava beans and elevate them to art. **Known for:** signature starter "oysters and pearls"; "supplements" like white truffles, caviar, and Wagyu beef; superior wine list. [$] *Average main: $400* ✉ *6640 Washington St., Yountville ✥ At Creek St. ☎ 707/944–2380 🌐 www.frenchlaundry.com 🕒 No lunch Mon.–Thurs. 👔 Jacket required ☞ Reservations essential wks ahead.*

La Calenda

$$ | MEXICAN | A few steps south of his Bouchon Bistro, chef Thomas Keller opened this ivy-covered restaurant serving Oaxacan-inspired Mexican cuisine. The decor inside is airily upscale casual, though on sunny days most patrons head to the street-side patio to dine on dishes like tacos *al pastor* (with slow-grilled pork), chicken enchiladas with mole, and *pescado zarandeado verde* (grilled marinated fish with green salsa). **Known for:** house margarita; churros with dulce de leche for dessert; patio people-watching. [$] *Average main: $23* ✉ *6518 Washington St., Yountville ✥ At Yount St. ☎ 833/682–8226 🌐 www.lacalendamex.com 🕒 Closed Mon. and Tues. No lunch Wed. and Thurs.*

Lucy Restaurant & Bar

$$$ | MODERN AMERICAN | In a modern space radiating offhand elegance, the Bardessono's restaurant seduces with sophisticated flavors, many from fruits, vegetables, and herbs grown in the hotel's on-site culinary garden. Although the cuisine is ultimately modern American, the chef might incorporate Japanese, Mexican, or other techniques and ingredients depending on the dish. **Known for:** swank bar; posh patio; all-day menu good for odd-hours dining. [$] *Average main: $34* ✉ *Bardessono, 6526 Yount St., Yountville ✥ At Finell St.*

☎ *707/204–6030* ⊕ *www.lucyyountville. com.*

Mustards Grill

$$$ | **AMERICAN** | Cindy Pawlcyn's Mustards Grill fills day and night with fans of her hearty cuisine, equal parts updated renditions of traditional American dishes—what Pawlcyn dubs "deluxe truck stop classics"—and fanciful contemporary fare. Barbecued baby back pork ribs and a lemon-lime tart piled high with brown-sugar meringue fall squarely in the first category, and sweet corn tamales with tomatillo-avocado salsa and wild mushrooms represent the latter. **Known for:** roadhouse setting; convivial mood; hoppin' bar. ⓢ *Average main: $31* ⊠ *7399 St. Helena Hwy./Hwy. 29, Napa* ✛ *1 mile north of Yountville* ☎ *707/944–2424* ⊕ *www.mustardsgrill.com.*

North Block

$$$ | **MODERN AMERICAN** | Regionally farmed fish and other foraged and cultivated Northern California ingredients go into this restaurant's shareable seasonal plates, turned out in an open kitchen that faces a bar serving large-format cocktails as well as wines by up-and-coming producers and Wine Country mainstays. St. Helena–based designer Erin Martin supplied the mildly offbeat interiors, though most patrons dine on the Tuscan-theme courtyard patio in good weather. **Known for:** artisanal cocktails; oyster happy hour 4–6; atmospheric interior. ⓢ *Average main: $36* ⊠ *North Block Hotel, 6757 Washington St., Yountville* ✛ *Near Madison St.* ☎ *707/944–8080* ⊕ *www. northblockhotel.com/dining* ⊙ *Closed Sun. and Mon. No lunch.*

R+D Kitchen

$$ | **ECLECTIC** | As the name suggests, the chefs at this restaurant with an expansive patio often packed on weekends are willing to experiment, starting with sushi plates that include spicy *hiramasa* (yellowtail kingfish) rolls with rainbow-trout caviar. Rotisserie chicken, wild-mushroom meat loaf,

the buttermilk fried-chicken sandwich topped with Swiss, and a slow-roasted pork sandwich served with coleslaw are perennial favorites. **Known for:** good value; cheerful staff; Dip Duo (guacamole and pimento cheese with chips) on patio bar menu. ⓢ *Average main: $25* ⊠ *6795 Washington St., Yountville* ✛ *At Madison St.* ☎ *707/945–0920* ⊕ *rd-kitchen.com/ locations/yountville.*

★ Regiis Ova Caviar & Champagne Lounge

$$$ | **WINE BAR** | Even restaurateurs as famous as Thomas Keller test out concepts via pop-ups, though in retrospect his pairing of mostly French sparkling wines with caviar from a company (Regiis Ova) the chef co-owns was always destined for permanent glory. Intended as a palate-cleansing pit stop between Cab tasting and dinner, the place, furnished in insouciant, faintly decadent style by Bay Area celeb designer Ken Fulk, tempts patrons to stay put, order more bubbly and roe, and call it a meal. **Known for:** live jazz most days; sommelier-selected French Champagnes; chilled oysters, tartares, and crudités. ⓢ *Average main: $35* ⊠ *6480 Washington St., Yountville* ✛ *At Oak Circle* ☎ *707/947–7181* ⊕ *regiisovalounge.com* ⊙ *Closed Mon. and Wed. No lunch (but check).*

RH Yountville Restaurant

$$$ | **MODERN AMERICAN** | Crystal chandeliers and fountains worthy of a French château supply the pizzazz at Restoration Hardware's street-side café, and the all-day menu's starters (charcuterie, shrimp cocktail, crispy artichoke), salads, and mains (from a burger modeled on one from Chicago's Au Cheval restaurant to delicate Atlantic sole in brown butter) easily live up to it. The prosciutto is flown in from Parma and the burrata from Puglia, the greens are ever-so-fresh, and the plating impresses. **Known for:** street-side patio; shaved rib-eye sandwich; Bellini with prosecco and peach purée. ⓢ *Average main: $34* ⊠ *6725 Washington St., Yountville* ✛ *At Pedroni St.*

☏ 707/339–4654 ⊕ rh.com/yountville/restaurant.

☕ Coffee and Quick Bites

Bouchon Bakery

$ | BAKERY | There's almost always a line outside the bakery next door to Thomas Keller's Bouchon Bistro. The textbook golden-brown croissants star, and the brownies, macarons, *kouign-amanns,* artisanal breads, and savory sandwiches are equally alluring. **Known for:** pain au chocolat; lemon and other tarts; coffee and espresso drinks. Ⓢ *Average main: $9* ✉ *6528 Washington St., Yountville ✛ At Yount St.* ☏ *707/944–2253* ⊕ *thomaskel-ler.com/bouchonbakeryyountville.*

Kelly's Filling Station and Wine Shop

$ | AMERICAN | The fuel is more than petrol at this gas station–convenience store whose redbrick exterior recalls the heyday of Route 66 travel. The shop inside sells superb hot dogs, fresh scones from nearby R+D Kitchen, gourmet chocolates, and (in summer) ice cream—gas up, grab some picnic items, and be ever-so-merrily on your way. **Known for:** top-rated wines; picnic items; coffee, espresso, and cool drinks to go. Ⓢ *Average main: $8* ✉ *6795 Wash-ington St., Yountville ✛ At Madison St.* ☏ *707/944–8165.*

Madeleine's Macarons at Stewart Cellars

$ | BAKERY | With Edith Piaf as his background track, a waiter whose job at Yountville's Bistro Jeanty had become a pandemic casualty spent several months toiling to perfect the macaron, his wife's favorite cookie. Success selling his multiflavored confections at farmers' markets and placement at a few upscale grocers (Jeanty was the first restaurant customer) spurred the couple, Dennis and Aubrey McInnich, to expand into retail with this shop and café selling their brightly colored treats. **Known for:** savory macarons as well as sweet; six-packs (of macarons) to go; certified organic coffee

from San Francisco–based Linea roastery. Ⓢ *Average main: $5* ✉ *6752 Washing-ton St., Yountville ✛ Near Pedroni St.* ☏ *707/289–7499* ⊕ *www.madeleines-macarons.com* ⊙ *Closed Tues. and Wed. No dinner.*

Hotels

★ Bardessono

$$$$ | RESORT | Tranquillity and luxury with a low carbon footprint are among the goals of this ultragreen wood, steel, and glass resortlike property in downtown Yountville, but there's nothing spartan about the accommodations, arranged around four landscaped courtyards. **Pros:** large rooftop lap pool; in-room spa treatments; three luxury villas for extra privacy. **Cons:** expensive year-round; limit-ed view from some rooms; a bit of street traffic on hotel's west side. Ⓢ *Rooms from: $1100* ✉ *6526 Yount St., Yountville* ☏ *707/204–6000* ⊕ *www.bardessono.com* ⇥ *65 rooms* ꛩ *No Meals.*

Hotel Villagio

$$$$ | RESORT | At this slick yet inviting downtown haven, the streamlined furnishings, subdued color schemes, and high ceilings create a sense of spacious-ness in the rooms and suites, each of which has a wood-burning fireplace and a balcony or patio. **Pros:** central location; steps from restaurants and tasting rooms; 13,000-square-foot spa. **Cons:** staff could be more solicitous; highway noise audible from some rooms on property's west side; expensive on week-ends in high season. Ⓢ *Rooms from: $800* ✉ *6481 Washington St., Yountville* ☏ *707/927–2130, 877/351–1133* ⊕ *www.villagio.com* ⇥ *113 rooms* ꛩ *Free Breakfast.*

Hotel Yountville

$$$$ | HOTEL | The landscaped woodsy set-ting, resortlike pool area, and exclusive yet casual ambience of the Hotel Yount-ville attract travelers wanting to get away from it all yet still be close—but not too close—to fine dining and tasting rooms. **Pros:** chic rooms; close to Yountville fine dining; high ceilings in upper-floor rooms. **Cons:** occasional service lapses unusual at this price point; expensive in high season; minimum-stay requirement some weekends. ⓢ *Rooms from: $750* ✉ *6462 Washington St., Yountville* ☎ *707/967–7900, 855/232–0452* ⊕ *www.hotelyountville.com* ⇆ *80 rooms* ⦿ *No Meals.*

★ Lavender Inn

$$$ | B&B/INN | Travelers looking for personalized service from innkeepers who take the trouble to learn guests' names and preferences will enjoy this intimate inn just off Yountville's main drag. **Pros:** on-site free bikes; use of pool at nearby sister property; personalized service. **Cons:** hard to book in high season; lacks amenities of larger properties; not sceney enough for some guests. ⓢ *Rooms from: $400* ✉ *2020 Webber St., Yountville* ☎ *707/944–1388* ⊕ *www.lavendernapa.com* ⇆ *9 rooms* ⦿ *Free Breakfast.*

Maison Fleurie

$$ | B&B/INN | A stay at this comfortable, reasonably priced inn, said to be the oldest hotel in the Napa Valley, places you within walking distance of Yountville's fine restaurants. **Pros:** smallest rooms a bargain; outdoor hot tub and pool; free bikes. **Cons:** lacks amenities of a full-service hotel; some rooms pick up noise from nearby Bouchon Bakery; hard to book in high season. ⓢ *Rooms from: $260* ✉ *6529 Yount St., Yountville* ☎ *707/944–2056* ⊕ *www.maisonfleurienapa.com* ⇆ *13 rooms* ⦿ *Free Breakfast.*

Napa Valley Lodge

$$$$ | HOTEL | Clean rooms in a convenient motel-style setting draw travelers willing to pay more than at comparable lodgings in the city of Napa to be within walking distance of Yountville's tasting rooms, restaurants, and shops. **Pros:** well-maintained rooms; vineyard-view rooms on north and west sides; large pool area. **Cons:** no elevator; nice enough but lacks panache; pricey on weekends in high

season. ⓢ *Rooms from: $450* ✉ *2230 Madison St., Yountville* ☎ *707/944–2468, 888/944–3545* ⊕ *www.napavalleylodge.com* ⇆ *55 rooms* ⦿ *Free Breakfast.*

★ North Block Hotel

$$$$ | HOTEL | A two-story boutique property near downtown Yountville's northern edge, the North Block attracts sophisticated travelers who appreciate the clever but unpretentious style and offhand luxury. **Pros:** extremely comfortable beds; personalized service; spacious bathrooms. **Cons:** outdoor areas get some traffic noise; weekend minimum-stay requirement; rates soar on high-season weekends. ⓢ *Rooms from: $662* ✉ *6757 Washington St., Yountville* ☎ *707/944–8080* ⊕ *northblockhotel.com* ⇆ *20 rooms* ⦿ *No Meals.*

★ Poetry Inn

$$$$ | B&B/INN | All the rooms at this splurge-worthy hillside retreat have broad lower Napa Valley vistas from their westward-facing balconies; indoors the comfortably chic decor and amenities that include a private spa and a fully stocked wine cellar add to the pleasure of a stay at this exclusive hideaway. **Pros:** valley views; discreet service; gourmet breakfasts by on-staff chef. **Cons:** expensive pretty much year-round; party types might find atmosphere too low-key; shops and restaurants 3 miles away. ⓢ *Rooms from: $2250* ✉ *6380 Silverado Trail, Yountville* ☎ *707/944–0646* ⊕ *poetryinn.com* ⇆ *5 rooms* ⦿ *Free Breakfast.*

Vintage House

$$$$ | RESORT | Part of the 22-acre Estate Yountville complex—other sections include sister lodging Hotel Villagio, the 13,000-square-foot Spa at The Estate, and shops and restaurants—this downtown hotel consists of two-story brick buildings along verdant landscaped paths shaded by mature trees. **Pros:** aesthetically pleasing accommodations; private patios and balconies; secluded feeling yet near shops, tasting rooms, and restaurants. **Cons:** highway noise audible in some exterior rooms; very expensive

on summer and fall weekends; weekend minimum-stay requirement. $ *Rooms from: $800* ✉ *6541 Washington St., Yountville* ☎ *707/927–2130, 877/351–1153* ⊕ *www.vintagehouse.com* ⤴ *80 rooms* ❄️ *Free Breakfast.*

Shopping

CLOTHING
Montecristi Panama Hats

HATS & GLOVES | Rows of Panama hats from classic to contemporary line this colorful storefront boutique's walls. The owners, who import their headgear from a revered designer in their native Ecuador, also commission scarves and other accessories. Actor Johnny Depp is among the shop's customers, which claims to have the "largest inventory of genuine Panama hats" in the United States. ✉ *6496 Washington St., Yountville* ⊹ *Near Oak Circle* ☎ *707/944–2870* ⊕ *www.panamahatsco.com.*

FOOD AND WINE
Kollar Chocolates

CHOCOLATE | The aromas alone will lure you into this shop selling artisanal European-style chocolates created on-site. The truffles, many incorporating local ingredients, include lavender with dark chocolate and fennel pollen with milk chocolate. ✉ *The Estate Yountville, 6525 Washington St., 1st fl., Yountville* ☎ *707/738–6750* ⊕ *www.kollarchocolates.com* ◑ *Closed Tues.–Thurs.*

Activities

Balloons Above the Valley

BALLOONING | This company's personable and professional pilots make outings a delight. Hosts pick up guests at their lodgings and return them when the flight is over. ✉ *Napa* ☎ *707/253–2222, 800/464–6824* ⊕ *www.balloonrides.com* ⛴ *From $300.*

B Spa Therapy Center

SPAS | Many of this spa's patrons are Bardessono hotel guests who take their treatments in their rooms' large, customized bathrooms—all of them equipped with concealed massage tables—but the main facility is open to nonguests as well. An in-room treatment favored by couples starts with massages in front of the fireplace and ends with a bath and sparkling wine. The two-hour Yountville Signature Experience, which can be enjoyed in-room or at the spa, begins with a shea-butter-enriched sugar scrub, followed by a Chardonnay grape-seed-oil massage and a hydrating hair-and-scalp treatment. The spa engages massage therapists skilled in Swedish, Thai, and other techniques. In addition to massages, the services include facials and other skin-care treatments. ✉ *Bardessono, 6526 Yount St., Yountville* ⊹ *At Mulberry St.* ☎ *707/204–6050* ⊕ *www.bardessono.com/spa* ⛴ *Treatments from $195.*

Napa Valley Aloft

BALLOONING | Passengers soar over the Napa Valley in balloons that launch from downtown Yountville. Flights are from 40 minutes to an hour-plus, depending on the wind speed, with the entire experience taking from three to four hours. ✉ *The Estate Yountville, 6525 Washington St., Yountville* ⊹ *Near Mulberry St.* ☎ *707/944–4400, 855/944–4408* ⊕ *www.nvaloft.com* ⛴ *From $295.*

Napa Valley Bike Tours

BIKING | With dozens of wineries within 5 miles, this shop makes a fine starting point for guided and self-guided vineyard and wine-tasting excursions. Rental bikes are also available. ✉ *6500 Washington St., Yountville* ⊹ *At Mulberry St.* ☎ *707/251–8687* ⊕ *www.napavalleybiketours.com* ⛴ *From $169.*

The Spa at The Estate

SPAS | The joint 13,000-square-foot facility of Vintage House and the Hotel Villagio is a five-minute walk from the former's lobby, even less from the latter's. Private

Far Niente ages its Cabernets and Chardonnays in 40,000 square feet of caves.

spa suites are popular with couples, who enjoy the separate relaxation areas, indoor and outdoor fireplaces, steam showers, saunas, and extra-large tubs. Therapists customize the signature Estate Massage based on clients' needs. Other massages and treatments involve hot stones, grape-seed extract, mud, magnesium, CDB, or aromatherapy. Several types of facials are offered as well. The ground-floor retail area, open to the public, is well stocked with beauty products. ✉ *The Estate Yountville, 6481 Washington St., Yountville ✛ At Oak Circle* ☎ *707/948–5050* ⊕ *www.theestateyountville.com/spa* ✐ *Treatments from $225.*

Oakville

2 miles northwest of Yountville.

Barely a blip on the landscape as you drive north on Highway 29, Oakville is marked mainly by its grocery store, but the town's small size belies the big splash it makes in the wine-making world. Slightly warmer than Yountville and Carneros to the south, but a few degrees cooler than Rutherford and St. Helena to the north, the Oakville area benefits from gravelly, well-drained soil. This allows roots to go deep—sometimes more than 100 feet—so that the vines produce intensely flavored fruit. Cabernet Sauvignon from the most famous vineyard here, To Kalon, at the base of the Mayacamas range, goes into many top-rated wines from winemakers throughout the valley. Big-name wineries within this appellation include Silver Oak, Far Niente, and Opus One.

GETTING HERE AND AROUND

If you're driving along Highway 29, you'll know you've reached Oakville when you see the Oakville Grocery on the east side of the road. Here the Oakville Cross Road provides access to the Silverado Trail (head east). Oakville wineries are scattered along Highway 29, Oakville Cross Road, and the Silverado Trail in roughly equal measure.

You can reach Oakville from the town of Glen Ellen in Sonoma County by heading east on Trinity Road from Highway 12. The twisting route, along the mountain range that divides Napa and Sonoma Counties, eventually becomes the Oakville Grade. The views of both valleys on this drive are breathtaking, though the continual curves make it unsuitable for those who suffer from motion sickness. VINE buses serve Oakville.

◉ Sights

B Cellars

WINERY | The chefs take center stage in the open-hearth kitchen of this boutique winery's hospitality house, and with good reason: creating food-friendly wines is B Cellars' raison d'être. Visits to the Oakville facility—all steel beams, corrugated metal, and plate glass yet remarkably cozy—often begin with a tour of the winery's culinary garden and vineyard, with a pause for sips of wine still aging in barrel. A seated tasting of finished wines paired with small bites follows the tour. Another session surveys the Napa Valley and Sonoma County appellations that supply B Cellars fruit. Kirk Venge, whose fruit-forward style suits the winery's food-oriented approach, crafts red and white blends and single-vineyard Cabernets from estate fruit and grapes from Beckstoffer and other noteworthy vineyards. All visits are strictly by appointment. ⊠ 703 Oakville Cross Rd., Oakville ⊹ West of Silverado Trail ☎ 707/709–8787 ⊕ www.bcellars.com ⊠ Tastings from $125 ⏱ Closed Tues. and Wed.

Far Niente

WINERY | Hamden McIntyre, a prominent winery architect of his era also responsible for Inglenook and what's now the Culinary Institute of America at Greystone, designed the centerpiece 1885 stone winery here. Abandoned in the wake of Prohibition and only revived beginning in 1979, Far Niente now ranks as one of the Napa Valley's most beautiful properties. Guests participating in the Estate Tasting learn some of this history while sipping the flagship wines, a Chardonnay and a Cabernet Sauvignon blend, along with Russian River Valley Pinot Noir from the affiliated EnRoute label and Dolce, a late-harvest white dessert wine. The Extended Estate Tasting takes in the winery and its aging caves, while the Cave Collection library tasting pairs older vintages with seasonal bites. ■ **TIP→ Fall, when nearly 200 ginkgo trees lining the driveway glow yellow, is a fine time to visit.** ⊠ 1350 Acacia Dr., Oakville ⊹ Off Oakville Grade Rd. ☎ 707/944–2861 ⊕ www.farniente.com ⊠ Tastings from $100.

★ Gamble Family Vineyards

WINERY | Unlike most of his neighbors, third-generation farmer Tom Gamble doesn't trumpet his boutique winery's tasting room with a sign along St. Helena Highway. When confirming guests' (required) appointments, hosts describe the mailbox to look for. The low-key branding is among the clues that a visit here is less about flash and more about substance. Gamble, whose family settled in Oakville more than a century ago, sells grapes to A-list wineries, reserving a portion for single-vineyard Cabernet Sauvignons, a Bordeaux-style blend or two, and a knockout Sauvignon Blanc. The collector-quality reds, meticulously crafted, remarkably restrained, and reminiscent of Napa's Judgment of Paris heyday, are poured in a 2013 structure whose design pays tribute to 19th-century Napa Valley farmhouses. When he's around, the amiable Gamble often drops by tastings to say hi. ⊠ 7554 St. Helena Hwy./Hwy. 29, Oakville ⊹ ⅓ mile north of Yount Mill Rd. ☎ 707/944–2999 ⊕ www. gamblefamilyvineyards.com ⊠ Tastings from $150 ⏱ Closed Sun.

★ Nickel & Nickel

WINERY | A corral out front, antique barns, and a farm-style windmill add horse-country flair to this winery

Oakville's Nickel & Nickel pairs horse-country flair with single-vineyard Cabernets.

renowned for its smooth, almost sensual, single-vineyard Cabernet Sauvignons. Some of the best derive from the home-base Oakville AVA, including the John C. Sullenger Vineyard, which surrounds the property's 1884 Queen Anne residence. Cabernets from other Napa Valley appellations supply the contrast. For the splurge Terroir Tasting, hosts introduce eight Cabernets, paired with artisanal cheeses and charcuterie, describing how each vineyard's distinctive soils and microclimates influence the finished product. Two other tastings explore similar issues less comprehensively.

■ **TIP→ Cabernet lovers won't want to miss this sister winery to elegant Far Niente.** ⊠ *8164 St. Helena Hwy./Hwy. 129, Oakville ✛ North of Oakville Cross Rd.* ☎ *707/967–9600* ⊕ *www.nickelandnickel. com* ✉ *Tastings from $90.*

Opus One

WINERY | The Napa Valley's Robert Mondavi and France's Baron Philippe de Rothschild joined forces in the late 1970s to produce Opus One, a Bordeaux blend often credited as Napa's first ultrapremium wine. The Cabernet Sauvignon–dominant wine is made and presented at a low-slung limestone structure, much of it concealed by a crescent-shape berm of native grasses and plants. In its poise and varied, textured surfaces, the 1991 neoclassical building mirrors the polished complexity of the wine, whose grapes come from To Kalon across the street and three other estate vineyards. The Courtyard Experience provides a suitable introduction to winery and wine, but consider booking the Opus One Experience. Involving small gourmet bites and including a visit to the tour de force semicircular subterranean barrel room, it takes place in a contemporary salon. Unveiled in 2021, the sumptuous space has views through its north-facing glass wall up the valley to Mt. St. Helena. ⊠ *7900 St. Helena Hwy./Hwy. 29, Oakville ✛ At Oakville Cross Rd.* ☎ *707/944–9442* ⊕ *www.opusonewinery.com* ✉ *Tastings from $100.*

Robert Mondavi Winery

WINERY | Arguably the most influential participant in the Napa Valley's rise to international prominence, the late Robert Mondavi established his namesake winery in the 1960s. In an era when tasting rooms were downscale affairs, Mondavi commissioned architect Cliff May to create a grand Mission-style space to receive visitors. The winery planned to close in late spring 2023 for two years of extensive renovations of the production and hospitality facilities and expects to receive guests here again in summer 2025. ■TIP→ **From summer 2023 to summer 2025, all Robert Mondavi Winery tastings will take place in downtown Napa at Arch & Tower in the Borreo Building, 930 3rd Street.** ⊠ *7801 St. Helena Hwy./Hwy. 29, Oakville* ☎ *888/766–6328* ⊕ *www.robertmondaviwinery.com.*

Saddleback Cellars

WINERY | A short drive down a country lane leads to this winery whose founder, Nils Venge, made history as the first U.S. winemaker to earn a 100-point score from the wine critic Robert Parker. The wine that earned Venge this distinction was a Cabernet Sauvignon for nearby Groth. These days, he makes two Cabs for his own label, along with Pinot Blanc, Sangiovese, Zinfandel, Malbec, and several others guests sample by appointment at vineyard's-edge picnic tables. Saddleback's presentation is decidedly retro compared to its tonier Oakville neighbors, but the stories, wines, and mountain views east and west cast a memorable spell. ⊠ *7802 Money Rd., Oakville* ⊕ *Off Oakville Cross Rd.* ☎ *707/944–1305* ⊕ *www.saddlebackcellars.com* ⚑ *Tastings $40.*

★ Silver Oak

WINERY | The first review of this winery's Napa Valley Cabernet Sauvignon declared the debut 1972 vintage not all that good and overpriced at $6 a bottle. Oops. The now-celebrated Bordeaux-style blend, still the only Napa Valley Cab bearing the winery's label each year, evolved into a cult favorite, and founders Ray Duncan and Justin Meyer received worldwide recognition for their signature use of exclusively American oak to age the wines. Tastings take place in a hospitality center constructed out of reclaimed stone and other materials from a 19th-century Kansas flour mill. The standard session includes sips of the current Napa Valley vintage, its counterpart from Silver Oak's Alexander Valley operation in Sonoma County, and a library wine. Hosts of vertical tastings pour six Cabernet vintages. All visits require an appointment. ⊠ *915 Oakville Cross Rd., Oakville* ⊕ *Off Hwy. 29* ☎ *707/942–7022* ⊕ *www.silveroak.com* ⚑ *Tastings from $60.*

★ Turnbull Cellars

WINERY | It'd be easy to confuse this winery for its more famous neighbor to the north, Cakebread Cellars—William Turnbull designed the original buildings at each. Founded by the architect in 1979 and owned since 1993 by Patrick O'Dell, Turnbull produces richly textured Cabernets from Oakville and Calistoga vineyards. Winemaker Peter Heitz plays light with French oak or, in some cases, handmade Italian amphorae. Guests sip his estate wines indoors among curated shows of works from O'Dell's art and photography collection or outside on landscaped patios surrounded by vineyards. The hospitality exceeds millennials' expectations, and social media–friendly backdrops make for enticing shots, but there's an older-Napa gentility to this appointment-only winery that even many locals haven't gotten around to visiting. Beat them to the punch. This place is worth it. ⊠ *8210 St. Helena Hwy., Oakville* ⊕ *¼ mile south of Glos La.* ☎ *707/963–5839* ⊕ *www.turnbullwines.com* ⚑ *Tastings from $65.*

Coffee and Quick Bites

Oakville Grocery

$ | SANDWICHES | Built in 1881 as a general store, Oakville Grocery carries high-end groceries and prepared foods. On summer weekends, customers stocking up on picnic provisions—meats, cheeses, breads, pizzas, and gourmet sandwiches—pack the place, but during the week it serves as a mellow pit stop to sip an espresso out front, picnic out back, or taste wines at Oakville Wine Merchant next door. **Known for:** breakfast quiches, scones, muffins; BLTA and chicken Gruyère sandwiches; Oakville Wine Merchant next door for wine tasting, history museum. [$] *Average main: $15* ✉ *7856 St. Helena Hwy./Hwy. 29, Oakville* ✣ *At Oakville Cross Rd.* ☎ *707/944–8802* 🌐 *www.oakvillegrocery.com.*

Rutherford

2 miles northwest of Oakville.

The spot where Highway 29 meets Rutherford Road in the tiny community of Rutherford may well be the most significant wine-related intersection in the United States. With its singular microclimate and soil, Rutherford is an important viticultural center, with more big-name wineries than you can shake a corkscrew at, including Beaulieu, Inglenook, Mumm Napa, and St. Supéry.

Cabernet Sauvignon is king here. The soil is ideal for those vines, and since this part of the valley gets plenty of sun, the grapes develop intense flavors. The famous claim of longtime Beaulieu Vineyards winemaker André Tchelistcheff that "it takes Rutherford dust to grow great Cabernet" is quoted by just about every area winery that produces the stuff. That "dust," courtesy of the region's primarily gravel, sand, and loam soils, imparts faint chocolaty notes you may detect in the reds.

GETTING HERE AND AROUND

Wineries line Highway 29 and parallel Silverado Trail north and south of Rutherford Road/Conn Creek Road, which connects the two roads. VINE buses serve Rutherford.

VISITOR INFORMATION

CONTACT Rutherford Dust Society. ✉ *Rutherford* ☎ *707/585–8686* 🌐 *www.rutherforddust.org.*

Sights

Beaulieu Vineyard

WINERY | The influential André Tchelistcheff (1901–94), who helped define the California style of wine making, worked his magic here for many years. BV, founded in 1900 by Georges de Latour and his wife, Fernande, makes several widely distributed wines, but others are produced in small lots and are available only at the winery. The most famous of these is the Georges de Latour Private Reserve Cabernet Sauvignon, first crafted in the late 1930s. Still going strong under senior winemaker Trevor Durling, the wine earned a 100-point rave from a top critic in 2022. All visits to Beaulieu are by appointment. **■ TIP→ Book a Hewitt Vineyard Cabernet Tasting to sample wines from a heralded Rutherford vineyard.** ✉ *1960 St. Helena Hwy./Hwy. 29, Rutherford* ✣ *At Hwy. 128* ☎ *707/257–5749* 🌐 *www.bvwines.com* 🎫 *Tastings from $55.*

Cakebread Cellars

WINERY | The late Jack and Dolores Cakebread were among the wave of early-1970s vintners whose efforts raised the Napa Valley's wine-making profile and initiated what became known as the Wine Country lifestyle. Tasting experiences at the winery's redwood-lined hospitality center adapt that lifestyle to contemporary sensibilities while still honoring Cakebread's history. Chardonnay and Cabernet Sauvignon helped establish the company, which makes so many other

Prohibition and Depression

The National Prohibition Act, which passed in 1919 under the popular name of the Volstead Act, had far-reaching effects on California wineries. Prohibition forced many to shut down altogether, but some, particularly Napa operations such as Beaulieu Vineyard, Beringer, and (on the St. Helena site now occupied by the Culinary Institute of America) the Christian Brothers, stayed in business by making sacramental wines. Others took advantage of the exception permitting home wine making and sold grapes and in some cases do-it-yourself kits with "warnings" about the steps that would result in grape juice turning into wine. A few wineries kept their inventories in bond, storing their wine in warehouses certified by the Department of Internal Revenue and guaranteed secure by bonding agencies. Magically, wine flowed out the back doors of the bonded warehouses into barrels and jugs brought by customers, and just as magically it seemed to replenish itself. Now and then a revenuer would crack down, but enforcement was lax at best.

Struggle and Survival

Prohibition, which ended in 1933, did less damage in the Napa Valley, where grapes thrive but fruit trees grow poorly on the rocky and gravelly slopes, benchlands, and alluvial fans, than it did in Sonoma County, where plum, walnut, and other orchards had replaced many vineyards. Fewer Napa growers had been able to convert to other crops, and more had been able to survive with sacramental wine, so more vineyards could be brought back to fine-wine production after repeal. Several major wineries survived Prohibition, including Inglenook and Charles Krug (acquired in the 1940s by the Cesare Mondavi family), which made very good wines during this period. Nevertheless, the wine industry struggled well into the 1960s to regain its customer base.

4

Napa Valley RUTHERFORD

wines—Sauvignon Blanc, rosé, Merlot, Pinot Noir, Syrah, and sundry red blends among them—that you can opt for an all-reds or all-whites tasting. All visits are by appointment. ■TIP➜ **The Cakebread Classic survey of current releases provides a good introduction; for a deeper dive, book one of the wine-and-food pairings or the library tasting of older vintages.** ✉ *8300 St. Helena Hwy./Hwy. 29, Rutherford* ☎ *800/588–0298* ⊕ *www.cakebread.com* 🍷 *Tastings from $50.*

Caymus Vineyards

WINERY | This winery's Special Selection Cabernet Sauvignon twice won *Wine Spectator* wine of the year. In good weather, you can sample the latest vintage and a few other wines outdoors in a landscaped area in front of the tasting room. Chuck Wagner started making wine on this property in 1972 and still oversees Caymus production. His children craft wines for other brands within the Wagner Family of Wine portfolio, including oaked and unoaked Mer Soleil Chardonnays, a Pinot Noir, Conundrum white and red blends, Red Schooner Malbec, and Emmolo Sauvignon Blanc and Merlot. All Caymus visits require an appointment. ✉ *8700 Conn Creek Rd., Rutherford* ✛ *Off Rutherford Rd.* ☎ *707/967–3010* ⊕ *www.caymus.com* 🍷 *Tastings from $50.*

Elizabeth Spencer at Rutherford Cross Estate

WINERY | Although its first vintage (1998) debuted long after those of neighbors Inglenook and Beaulieu, this winery lays

Round Pond Estate makes sophisticated wines and extra-virgin olive oils.

claim to a slice of Rutherford history: guests gain entry to the verdant appointment-only courtyard tasting area via the town's 1872 redbrick former post office. Varietal and geographical diversity is a primary goal, with Cabernet Sauvignon, Grenache, Merlot, Pinot Noir, and Syrah among the reds produced from Napa, Sonoma, and Mendocino County grapes. Whites include Chardonnay, Viognier, and Sauvignon Blanc. After purchasing Elizabeth Spencer in 2021, new owner Boisset Collection brought aboard consultant Heidi Barrett to oversee the wines but retained longtime winemaker Sarah Vandendriessche. ■TIP➜ **The Kathleen Thompson Hill Kitchen Memories Collection, housed in a building off the parking lot, contains cooking utensils of nostalgic and historical value.** ✉ *1165 Rutherford Rd., Rutherford ✛ At Hwy. 29* ☎ *707/963–6067* ⊕ *www.elizabethspencerwinery. com* 🎫 *Tastings from $50* ☯ *Closed Tues. and Wed. in winter.*

★ **Frog's Leap**

WINERY | If you're a novice, the tour at eco-friendly Frog's Leap is a fun way to begin your education. Conducted by hosts with a sense of humor, the tour stops by a barn built in 1884, an acre of organic gardens, and a frog pond topped with lily pads. The winery produced its first vintage, small batches of Sauvignon Blanc and Zinfandel, in 1981, adding Chardonnay and Cabernet Sauvignon the next year. Merlot, Petite Sirah, and the Heritage Blend of classic Napa Valley varietals including Charbono and Valdiguié are among the other reds these days. All visits require a reservation, but walk-ins are accommodated when possible. ■TIP➜ **The tour is recommended, but you can forgo it and taste on a garden-view porch.** ✉ *8815 Conn Creek Rd., Rutherford* ☎ *707/963–4704* ⊕ *www.frogsleap. com* 🎫 *Tastings from $45.*

Honig Vineyard & Winery

WINERY | **FAMILY** | Sustainable farming is the big story at this family-run winery. When offered, the absorbing Eco-Tour and Tasting focuses on the Honig family's environmentally friendly farming and production methods, which include using biodiesel to fuel the tractors, monitoring water use in the vineyard and winery, and generating power with solar panels. Bluebirds, hawks, and owls patrol for insects, rodents, and other pests; trained golden retrievers spot vine-damaging mealybugs early, eliminating the need for heavy pesticides. Known for Sauvignon Blanc and Cabernet Sauvignon, the Honigs also make rosé of Cabernet and late-harvest Sauvignon Blanc. All tastings are by appointment; call ahead for last-minute availability. ⊠ *850 Rutherford Rd., Rutherford ✛ Near Conn Creek Rd.* ☎ *800/929-2217* ⊕ *www.honigwine.com* ✉ *Tastings from $40.*

★ **Inglenook**

WINERY | *Wine Enthusiast* magazine bestowed a lifetime-achievement award on vintner-filmmaker Francis Ford Coppola, whose wine-world contributions include resurrecting the historic Inglenook estate. Over the decades, he reunited the original property acquired by Inglenook founder Gustave Niebaum, remodeled Niebaum's ivy-covered 1880s château, and purchased the rights to the Inglenook name. Just in time for the 2022 harvest, the winery unveiled a 22,000-square-foot wine cave and production facility. The eco-friendly cave and Inglenook's place in Napa Valley history are among the topics discussed at tastings, some involving food pairings. Most sessions see a pour of the signature Rubicon, a Cabernet Sauvignon–based blend with a classic Rutherford profile. All visits require an appointment; call the winery or check at the visitor center for same-day availability. ■ **TIP→ In lieu of a tasting, you can book a table at The Bistro, a wine bar with a picturesque courtyard, to sip wine by the glass or bottle.** ⊠ *1991 St.*

Helena Hwy./Hwy. 29, Rutherford ✛ At Hwy.128 ☎ *707/968-1179* ⊕ *www.inglenook.com* ✉ *Tastings from $75* ⊗ *Closed Tues. and Wed., except for bistro.*

Mumm Napa

WINERY | When Champagne Mumm of France set about establishing a California sparkling-wine outpost, its winemaker chose the Napa Valley, where today the winery sources grapes from more than 50 local producers. Made in the *méthode traditionnelle* style from Chardonnay, Pinot Noir, Pinot Meunier, and occasionally Pinot Gris, the wines are all fermented in the bottle. Most guests enjoy them alfresco, by the glass or flight, on a patio above the surrounding vineyards or one at eye level. Book an Oak Terrace Tasting to sample top-of-the-line cuvées under the sprawling branches of a blue oak nearly two centuries old. Tasting is by appointment only, but walk-ins are accommodated when possible. ⊠ *8445 Silverado Trail, Rutherford ✛ 1 mile south of Rutherford Cross Rd.* ☎ *707/967-7700* ⊕ *www.mummnapa.com* ✉ *Tastings from $40.*

Piña Napa Valley

WINERY | The Piña family, whose Napa Valley heritage dates from the 1850s, is known locally as much for its first-rate vineyard-management company as its modest winery that specializes in single-vineyard, 100% Cabernet Sauvignon. Winemaker Anna Monticelli crafts these robust Cabs from mostly hillside fruit, all estate grown. Though she doesn't blend in other varietals, commonly done to soften Cabernet, the winery doesn't release its wines until age has mellowed them. If he's not busy elsewhere, Larry Piña, the genial managing partner and among his family's seventh generation involved in the wine business, often drops by during tastings. All require an appointment, with same-day guests accommodated when possible (but call ahead). ⊠ *8060 Silverado Trail, Rutherford ✛ 0.2 miles north of Skellenger La.* ☎ *707/738-9328*

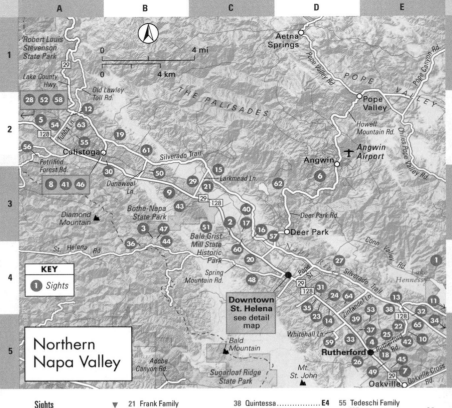

Northern Napa Valley

KEY

① Sights

⊕ *pinanapavalley.com* ▱ *Tastings $50* ☾ *Closed Tues. and Wed.*

Round Pond Estate

WINERY | Sophisticated wines come from Round Pond, but the valley-floor estate also produces premium olive oils, most from olives grown and crushed on the property. Guests participating in the olive oil tasting, held across the street from the winery, pass through the high-tech olive mill and sample the aromatic oils, both alone and with house-made red-wine vinegars. Hosts at the winery tasting room pour Round Pond's well-rounded red and other wines. The flagship Estate Cabernet Sauvignon has the structure and heft of the classic 1970s Rutherford Cabs but acknowledges 21st-century palates with smoother, if still sturdy, tannins. Tastings are by appointment only (48 hours in advance preferred for those involving food). ■TIP→ **The full Il Pranzo lunch incorporates products made and produce grown on-site.** ✉ *875 Rutherford Rd., Rutherford* ⊹ *Near Conn Creek Rd.* ☏ *707/302–2575* ⊕ *www.roundpond.com* ▱ *Tastings from $65* ☾ *Closed Mon. and Tues.*

★ Sequoia Grove

WINERY | Sequoias shade the outdoor areas and century-old barn of this winery acclaimed for its single-vineyard Cabernet Sauvignons. The winemaker supplements fruit grown on this property and another in Rutherford with grapes from other valley-floor and mountain vineyards. A current-release tasting might include a single-vineyard Cab—Sequoia Grove also makes Chardonnay, Cabernet Franc, Syrah, and a few more—but for a sense of how variations in terrain and microclimate influence Cabernet, choose the Single Vineyard experience. All visits require an appointment. ■TIP→ **For the insightful A Taste for Cabernet, the executive chef prepares a range of small bites, including fish and vegetarian, that demonstrate Cabernet Sauvignon's versatility.** ✉ *8338 St. Helena Hwy./Hwy. 29, Rutherford* ⊹ *Near* *Bella Oaks La.* ☏ *707/339–5757* ⊕ *www. sequoiagrove.com* ▱ *Tastings from $45.*

St. Supéry Estate Vineyards & Winery

WINERY | The French fashion company Chanel purchased St. Supéry in 2015, adding further glamour to this winery whose Rutherford vineyards surround its immaculate hospitality center and production facility. St. Supéry makes two widely distributed wines, a Sauvignon Blanc and a Cabernet Sauvignon, but most tastings revolve around limited-production efforts from the Rutherford property and the 1,500-acre Dollarhide Ranch on Howell Mountain. Hosts tailor sessions to guests' preferences, pouring, for instance, all whites or all reds. One of the latter tastings explores valley-floor and mountain Cabernet Sauvignon, another that varietal and four other Bordeaux grapes, Cabernet Franc, Malbec, Merlot, and Petit Verdot. Among the specialized experiences at this enthusiastic proponent of wine education is Aromatherapy with a Corkscrew, which involves blind sniffing and tasting to learn how to identify citrus, tropical, and other aromas in wines. ✉ *8440 St. Helena Hwy./Hwy. 29, Rutherford* ⊹ *Near Manley La.* ☏ *707/963–4507* ⊕ *www.stsupery.com* ▱ *Tastings from $45.*

Sullivan Rutherford Estate

WINERY | In 1972, James O'Neil Sullivan, a Hollywood graphic designer, moved his family to Rutherford to make Cabernet Sauvignon. Most of the wines (Merlot was another focus) came from grapes planted on his 26-acre estate, to which Mexico City–born Juan Pablo Torres Padilla, managing partner of a group that purchased the winery in 2018, added parcels in the Atlas Peak and St. Helena AVAs. Grapevines, a small lake bordered by a landscaped garden, and the 1978 Arts and Crafts–style home architect John Marsh Davis cantilevered over the vineyard supply a pastoral backdrop for leisurely appointment-only tastings best booked at least a day ahead. The winery expects to break ground in mid-to-late 2023 on a new combination production facility and hospitality center to be completed by 2025. ✉ *1090 Galleron Rd., Rutherford* ✣ *Off Hwy. 29* ☎ *707/963–9646* 🌐 *sullivanwine.com* 🎟 *Tastings from $150.*

ZD Wines

WINERY | Founded in 1969 and still run by the same family, this winery specializing in Chardonnay, Pinot Noir, and Cabernet Sauvignon is respected for its organic practices, local philanthropy, and Abacus blend. Made "solera-style," Abacus contains wine from every ZD Reserve Cabernet Sauvignon vintage since 1992. The Chardonnay and Pinot Noir come from a Carneros property, the Cabernet from the winery's Rutherford estate, where the wines are made and presented to the public. Appointment-only tastings (same-day often possible, but call ahead) take place in a second-floor space with broad valley views west to the Mayacamas Mountains. Book a current-release flight for an introduction to ZD and its wine-making philosophy. Barrel tastings, small bites, and small-batch reserve wines are all part of the Abacus Experience, which concludes with a current and older Abacus blend. ✉ *8383 Silverado Trail, Rutherford* ☎ *800/487–7757* 🌐 *www.zdwines.com* 🎟 *Tastings from $50.*

🍴 Restaurants

La Luna Market & Taqueria

$ | MEXICAN | The burritos, tacos, and quesadillas at this unassuming pit stop will fill you up before wine tasting or help absorb what you've imbibed. The super burrito laden with cheese, beans, sour cream, guacamole, and your choice of meat—winery workers swear by the crispy carnitas—provides a day's fuel in itself; for breakfast (before 11) there's a burrito with eggs, your choice of meat, and potatoes, beans, and salsa. **Known for:** vegetarian variations with chiles rellenos; homemade-tortilla nachos; outdoor seating. [$] *Average main: $11* ✉ *1153 Rutherford Rd., Rutherford* ✣ *Off Hwy. 29* ☎ *707/963–3211* 🌐 *www.lalunamarket.com* 🕒 *No dinner.*

★ Restaurant at Auberge du Soleil

$$$$ | AMERICAN | Possibly the most romantic roost for brunch, lunch, or dinner in all the Wine Country is a terrace seat at the Auberge du Soleil resort's illustrious restaurant, and the Mediterranean-inflected cuisine more than matches the dramatic vineyard views. The prix-fixe dinner menu (three or four courses), relying mainly on local produce, might include caviar or diver scallop starters, delicately prepared fish or vegetable middle-course options, and mains like prime beef pavé with béarnaise, spiced lamb loin, or Japanese Wagyu A5. **Known for:** six-course chef's tasting menu; comprehensive wine list; special-occasion feel. [$] *Average main: $150* ✉ *Auberge du Soleil, 180 Rutherford Hill Rd., Rutherford* ✣ *Off Silverado Trail* ☎ *707/963–1211* 🌐 *www.aubergedusoleil.com* 🕒 *Closed Mon. and Tues.*

Rutherford Grill

$$$ | AMERICAN | Dark-wood walls, subdued lighting, and red-leather banquettes make for a perpetually clubby mood at this Rutherford hangout where the patio, popular for its bar, fireplace, and rocking chairs, opens for full meal service or drinks and appetizers when the weather's right. Many entrées—steaks, burgers, fish, rotisserie chicken, and barbecued pork ribs—emerge from an oak-fired grill operated by master technicians. **Known for:** iron-skillet corn bread direct from the oven; signature French dip sandwich; reasonably priced wine list. [$] *Average main: $29* ✉ *1180 Rutherford Rd., Rutherford* ✣ *At Hwy. 29* ☎ *707/963–1792* 🌐 *www.rutherfordgrill.com.*

🛏 Hotels

★ Auberge du Soleil

$$$$ | RESORT | Taking a cue from the olive tree-studded landscape, this hotel with a renowned restaurant and spa cultivates a luxurious look that blends French and California style. **Pros:** stunning valley views; spectacular pool and spa areas; Deluxe-category suites fit for a superstar. **Cons:** stratospheric prices; least expensive rooms get some noise from the bar and restaurant; weekend minimum-stay requirement. [$] *Rooms from: $1575* ✉ *180 Rutherford Hill Rd., Rutherford* ☎ *707/963–1211, 800/348–5406* 🌐 *www.aubergedusoleil.com* 🛏 *52 rooms* 🍴 *Free Breakfast.*

★ Rancho Caymus Inn

$$$$ | HOTEL | A romantic hacienda-away-from-home that off-season may well be the Napa Valley's best value in its price range, this upscale-contemporary boutique hotel near Inglenook and the Rutherford Grill contains rooms whose decor and artworks evoke the area's Mexican heritage. **Pros:** courtyard pool area; smallest rooms are 400 square feet, with several 600 or more; well-trained staff. **Cons:** all rooms have only showers (albeit nice ones); king beds in all rooms (no sofa beds, though a few rollaways available); no spa or fitness center. [$] *Rooms from: $475* ✉ *1140 Rutherford Rd., Rutherford* ☎ *707/963–1777* 🌐 *www.ranchocaymusinn.com* 🛏 *26 rooms* 🍴 *Free Breakfast.*

St. Helena

2 miles northwest of Rutherford.

Downtown St. Helena is the very picture of good living in the Wine Country: sycamore trees arch over Main Street (Highway 29), where visitors flit between boutiques, cafés, and storefront tasting rooms housed in sun-faded redbrick buildings. The genteel district pulls in rafts of tourists during the day, though like most Wine Country towns St. Helena more or less rolls up the sidewalks after dark.

The Napa Valley floor narrows between the Mayacamas and Vaca Mountains around St. Helena. The slopes reflect heat onto the vineyards below, and since there's less fog and wind, things get pretty toasty. St. Helena is one of the valley's hottest AVAs, with midsummer temperatures often reaching the mid-90s. Bordeaux varietals predominate—mainly Cabernet Sauvignon but also Merlot, Cabernet Franc, and Sauvignon Blanc. High-profile wineries bearing a St. Helena address abound, with Beringer, Charles Krug, and Ehlers Estate among the ones whose stories begin in the 19th century. The successes of relatively more recent arrivals such as Stony Hill, Rombauer, Duckhorn, Hall, Phelps, and a few dozen others have only added to the town's enological cachet.

GETTING HERE AND AROUND

Highway 29 in downtown St. Helena is called Main Street, with many shops and restaurants between Pope and Adams Streets. Wineries are found north and south of downtown along Highway 29 and the Silverado Trail, but some less touristy spots are east of the trail on Howell Mountain and northwest of downtown on Spring Mountain. VINE buses stop along Main Street.

VISITOR INFORMATION

CONTACT St. Helena Chamber of Commerce. ✉ *1136 Main St., St. Helena* ✣ *Near Pope St.* ☎ *707/963–4456* 🌐 *www.sthelena.com.*

Sights

SIGHTS IN DOWNTOWN ST. HELENA

Beringer Vineyards

WINERY | Brothers Frederick and Jacob Beringer opened the winery that still bears their name in 1876. One of California's earliest bonded wineries, it's the oldest one in the Napa Valley never to have missed a vintage—no mean feat, given Prohibition. Some tastings take place inside or on the veranda of Frederick's grand Rhine House Mansion, completed in 1886 and surrounded by mature landscaped gardens worth a stroll themselves. Beringer is known for several widely distributed wines, but many poured here are winery exclusives. The Legacy Tasting & Tour surveys Beringer's history; the tasting takes place where the brothers crafted their first vintage. The winery prefers that all guests make a reservation, but same-day visits are often possible when no food is involved. ✉ *2000 Main St./Hwy. 29, St. Helena* ✛ *Near Pratt Ave.* ☎ *707/257–5771* ⊕ *www.beringer.com* 🍷 *Tastings from $20 glass, $45 flight.*

Charles Krug Winery

WINERY | A historically sensitive renovation of its 1874 Redwood Cellar Building transformed the former production facility of the Napa Valley's oldest winery into an epic hospitality center. Charles Krug, a Prussian immigrant, established the winery in 1861 and ran it until his death in 1892. Italian immigrants Cesare Mondavi and his wife, Rosa, purchased Charles Krug in 1943, operating it with their sons Peter Sr. and Robert (who later opened his own winery). Still run by Peter Sr.'s family, Charles Krug specializes in small-lot Yountville and Howell Mountain Cabernet Sauvignons plus Sauvignon Blanc, Chardonnay, Merlot, and Pinot Noir. All visits are by appointment. ✉ *2800 Main St./Hwy. 29, St. Helena* ✛ *Across from Culinary Institute of America* ☎ *707/967–2229* ⊕ *www.charleskrug. com* 🍷 *Tastings from $50.*

Clif Family Tasting Room

WINERY | Cyclists swarm to the tasting room of Gary Erickson and Kit Crawford, best known for the Clif energy bar, a staple of many a pedaling adventure. Cycling trips through Italian wine country inspired the couple to establish a Howell Mountain winery and organic farm whose bounty they share at some of this merry hangout's tastings. The estate Cabernets served at the Cima—King of Mountain Experience show winemaker

Laura Barrett at her most nuanced, but she crafts whites, a rosé of Grenache, and reds for all palates. If hungry, you can pair the wines with soups, salads, and *bruschette* (open-faced grilled-bread sandwiches) from the Bruschetteria food truck parked outside from Wednesday through Sunday. ✉ *709 Main St./Hwy. 29, St. Helena* ✛ *At Vidovich La.* ☎ *707/968– 0625* ⊕ *www.cliffamily.com* 🍷 *Tastings from $50.*

Crocker & Starr

WINERY | Cabernet Sauvignons expressing "power and elegance" and "a deep sense of place" are the main event at this winery jointly owned by businessman Charlie Crocker and founding winemaker Pam Starr. The wine-making team also crafts Sauvignon Blanc, Cabernet Franc, and Malbec, along with the Bridesmaid series Sauvignon Blanc and a Cabernet Franc–dominant red blend. Crocker & Starr was established in 1997, but James Dowdell, a St. Helena wine pioneer, planted grapes and built a winery and a brandy facility on this land in the late 1800s. Hosts of the Current Release Vineyard Experience recount the Dowdell family's story during a brief foray into the vineyards and peek at the winery, followed by a seated tasting in an arbor. There's also an exploration of estate reds. All visits require an appointment, same-day sometimes possible. ✉ *700 Dowdell La., St. Helena* ✛ *¼ mile east of Hwy. 29* ☎ *707/967–9111* ⊕ *www. crockerstarr.com* 🍷 *Tastings from $75.*

★ Lang & Reed Napa Valley

WINERY | Playful labels by artist Jeanne Greco, whose past clients include Aerosmith, Mattel (for Barbie), and the post office, are the first indication that something offbeat is afoot at Lang & Reed. The second: the wines themselves. In the land of Chardonnay, Sauvignon Blanc, and Cabernet Sauvignon, husband-wife owners John and Tracey Skupny focus on Cabernet Franc and Chenin Blanc. In making the Cab Francs, John strives to create wines that are "delicious and fruity but not simple." He succeeds. Son Reed Skupny's worldwide quest for wine knowledge found him in the Loire Valley, eventually becoming obsessed with crafting noteworthy Chenin Blanc. His Chenins, clean on the palate with pleasing acidity, achieve his objective. Lang & Reed pours its wines in a restored Victorian, sometimes on its front porch. A block from Main Street, the casual setting evokes the slower-paced Napa of yore. ⌧ *1244 Spring St., St. Helena ⊹ At Oak Ave.* ☎ *707/963–7547* ⊕ *langandreed.com* ⌱ *Tastings from $75* ☾ *Closed Mon.*

★ Spottswoode

WINERY | A historic winery with a forward-looking agricultural focus, Spottswoode makes a flagship Cabernet Sauvignon critics and collectors champion for its structure, grace, and purity of fruit. Tastings also include another Cabernet and a delectably suave Sauvignon Blanc. The estate vineyard, certified organic and biodynamic, sits at the base of the Mayacamas Mountains on a site where wine grapes have been cultivated since the 1880s. Three structures remain from that era, but Spottswoode's current cachet dates to 1972, when the Novak family purchased adjoining parcels totaling 46 acres. After selling grapes to other wineries for a decade, the family created its revered label. ■TIP→ **Appointment-only Spottswoode sees a few dozen visitors a week (book well ahead in summer).** ⌧ *1902 Madrona Ave., St. Helena ⊹ West ½ mile off Main St.* ☎ *707/963–0134* ⊕ *www. spottswoode.com* ⌱ *Tastings from $150* ☾ *Closed weekends.*

★ VGS Chateau Potelle

WINERY | Sophisticated whimsy is on full display at the Chateau Potelle tasting room. Jean-Noel Fourmeaux, its bon vivant owner, fashioned this jewel of a space out of a nondescript 1950s bungalow south of downtown St. Helena. The residence, decorated with contemporary art (some wine-themed), and the Moroccan-tented outdoor patio are the scene of leisurely paced, sit-down, appointment-only tastings, some accompanied by gourmet bites from Napa's La Toque restaurant. Fourmeaux prefers fruit grown at higher elevations because he believes the extended ripening time grapes require in a cooler environment produces more complex and flavorful wines. His Cabernet Sauvignon, Syrah, and other reds support this thesis. The Chardonnay stars among the whites. ■TIP→ **Be sure to ask what "VGS" stands for.** ⌧ *1200 Dowdell La., St. Helena ⊹ At Hwy. 29* ☎ *707/255–9440* ⊕ *www.vgs-chateaupotelle.com* ⌱ *Tastings from $75.*

SIGHTS BEYOND DOWNTOWN ST. HELENA

★ Aonair Wines

WINERY | A long, sometimes narrow road meanders east from the Silverado Trail through Conn Valley to this 17-acre Howell Mountain estate. Grant Long Jr., its resourceful proprietor, made his first batch of wine while still a teen. After proving his mettle at a few Napa wineries, he started his own label. While guests sip wines on the cliffside tasting room's lofty deck, taking in views of vineyard rows sloping sharply into the valley, uniformly cheery staffers fill in the details of Long's compelling wine journey. Cabernet Sauvignon and the Mountains Proprietary Blend, both Napa Valley, and a Sierra Foothills Grenache-heavy blend stand out among a mostly reds lineup. The appointment-only winery advises making a reservation at least a month ahead. ■TIP→ **Tastings and the wines are reasonably priced—how Long manages this in America's costliest growing region is part of the Aonair (pronounced "ay-oh-nair") mystique.** ⌧ *647 Greenfield Rd., St. Helena ⊹ 5 miles east of Silverado Trail, Howell Mountain Rd. to Conn Valley Rd. to Greenfield* ☎ *707/738–8352* ⊕ *www. aonairwine.com* ⌱ *Contact winery for tasting fee* ☾ *Closed Sun. and Mon.*

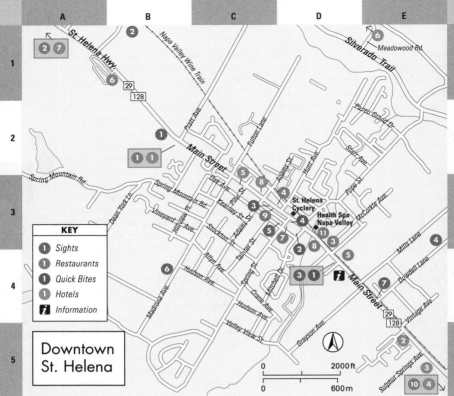

Downtown St. Helena

KEY

- 1 Sights
- 1 Restaurants
- 1 Quick Bites
- 1 Hotels
- 𝒊 Information

Sights	▼
1 Beringer Vineyards	**B2**
2 Charles Krug Winery	**B1**
3 Clif Family Tasting Room	**D4**
4 Crocker & Starr	**E3**
5 Lang & Reed Napa Valley	**D3**
6 Spottswoode	**B4**
7 VGS Chateau Potelle	**E4**

Restaurants	▼
1 Acacia House	**B2**
2 Brasswood Bar + Bakery + Kitchen	**A1**
3 The Charter Oak	**D3**
4 Cook St. Helena	**C3**
5 Farmstead at Long Meadow Ranch	**D4**
6 Gatehouse Restaurant	**B1**
7 Goose & Gander	**D3**
8 Gott's Roadside	**D3**
9 Market	**C3**
10 Press	**E5**
11 Tra Vigne Pizzeria and Restaurant	**D3**

Quick Bites	▼
1 Clif Family Bruschetteria Food Truck	**D4**
2 Crisp Kitchen & Juice	**D3**
3 Model Bakery	**C3**
4 The Station	**D3**

Hotels	▼
1 Alila Napa Valley	**B2**
2 El Bonita Motel	**E5**
3 Harvest Inn	**E5**
4 Ink House Napa Valley	**E5**
5 Inn St. Helena	**C3**
6 Meadowood Napa Valley	**E1**
7 Wine Country Inn	**A1**
8 Wydown Hotel	**C3**

★ AXR Napa Valley

WINERY | Three entrepreneur-investor types established AXR with a winemaker-partner, Jean Hoefliger, who describes a vineyard as "the soul of a wine" and his job in the cellar "to create an emotion." Hoefliger, who in 2021 completed a 15-year run with the Napa Valley's Alpha Omega Winery, crafts multilayer Chardonnays from sourced grapes (including an often highly rated entrant from Sonoma County's Ritchie Vineyard) and dense yet supple 100% Cabernet Sauvignons. The Cabs come from notable sites like Sleeping Lady in Yountville, Denali in St. Helena, and the estate V Madrone Vineyard. Hosts at one-on-one tastings convey the passion, science, and experience underlying Hoefliger's wines and the history of the redwood-studded AXR property. Some sessions unfold in a renovated barn, others in an 1876 house once part of a pre-Prohibition restaurant and inn that thrived here. ⊠ *3199 St. Helena Hwy. N (Hwy. 29), St. Helena ⊹ At Bea La., ½ mile south of Bale Grist Mill* ☎ *707/302–8181* ⊕ *www.axrnapavalley.com* ▨ *Tastings from $90.*

Barnett Vineyards

WINERY | Spring Mountain Road winds past oaks and madrones and, in springtime, sprays of wildflowers to this winery's lofty east-facing hillside setting. Most tastings are held outside to take advantage of views across the northern Napa Valley rivaling those from a balloon. Barnett's winemaker, David Tate, makes restrained balanced wines: Cabernet Sauvignon, Cabernet Franc, and Merlot from the steeply terraced mountain estate and Chardonnay and Pinot Noir sourced from prestigious vineyards. Quietly dazzling, the wines will draw your attention from those vistas. Tastings are by appointment. ⊠ *4070 Spring Mountain Rd., St. Helena ⊹ At Napa–Sonoma county line* ☎ *707/963–7075* ⊕ *www.barnettvineyards.com* ▨ *Tastings $100.*

CADE Estate Winery

WINERY | On a clear day, the views from this Howell Mountain winery's hospitality center and gravel patio—complete with infinity waterfall and Robinia shade trees—stretch south down the valley to Carneros. The exceptional tableau befits the collector-worthy Cabernets created by a team deservedly proud of its eco-friendly farming and production practices. Winemaker Danielle Cyrot's attention to detail begins in the vineyard and continues in the cellar, where she uses five dozen barrel types from two dozen coopers to bring out the best in the frisky (as in highly tannic) mountain fruit. All visits are by appointment, best made at least a day or two ahead. ⊠ *360 Howell Mountain Rd. S, Angwin ⊹ From Silverado Trail, head northeast on Deer Park Rd.* ☎ *707/690–1213* ⊕ *www.cadewinery.com* ▨ *Tastings from $100.*

★ Chappellet Winery

WINERY | When Donn and Molly Chappellet established their renowned Pritchard Hill winery in 1967, most Cabernet Sauvignon was grown on the Napa Valley floor, but the couple and other early adopters proved that mountain fruit could produce complex ageworthy wines. The Chappellets chose their rocky, tree-studded, now 640-acre property for its grape-growing potential, but the striking views north to Lake Hennessey and Mt. St. Helena undoubtedly played a role, too. The winemaker and vineyard manager have worked here for more than three decades, and with the family's second generation in charge, a sense of purpose and continuity prevails. Relaxed tastings of wines that might also include Chenin Blanc, Chardonnay, Pinot Noir, and Cabernet Franc often take place in the cavernous original winery amid rows of stacked oak barrels. ■**TIP**→ **A tasting of current releases follows the once-a-month group hike of Pritchard Hill, highly recommended for those in shape.** ⊠ *1581 Sage Canyon Rd., St. Helena ⊹ 4½ miles east of Silverado Trail* ☎ *707/286–4219*

⊕ www.chappellet.com 🖥 Tastings from $125.

Conn Creek Winery

WINERY | The grapes for this winery's Cabernet Sauvignons come from most of the Napa Valley's 16 subappellations. To provide insight into the factors winemakers consider when crafting a Bordeaux-style red, Conn Creek developed the Barrel Blending Experience. An affable educator supplies the lowdown on basics like the characteristics of five Bordeaux varietals and how variations in soils and microclimates of valley-floor and mountain vineyards affect tannin structure. Armed with this information, participants set about blending, bottling, corking, and labeling a wine to take home. Even among friends, the competition to produce a successful blend is sometimes intense. Trivia: Koerner Rombauer, who later founded the famous Chardonnay house bearing his name, got his Napa Valley wine-making start as a Conn Creek partner. ∎ TIP→ **The blending seminar is great fun.** ⊠ 8711 Silverado Trail, St. Helena ✛ At Hwy. 128 ☎ 800/793–7960 ⊕ www.conncreek.com 🖥 Tastings from $50 ⊘ Closed Tues. and Wed. mid-fall–mid-summer.

★ Corison Winery

WINERY | Respected for three 100% Cabernet Sauvignons, Corison Winery harks back to simpler days, with tastings alfresco in view of the half century–old Kronos Vineyard or amid oak barrels inside an unadorned, barnlike facility. The straightforward approach suits the style of Cathy Corison. One of post-1960s Napa Valley's first women owner-winemakers, she eschews blending because she believes her sunny St. Helena AVA vineyards (and other selected sites) can ripen Cabernet better than anywhere else in the world. Critics tend to agree with her approach, often waxing ecstatic about these classic wines. The highly recommended Library Tasting, which starts with a brief winery and vineyard tour, includes recent releases and older vintages that

together illustrate Corison's consistency as a winemaker and how gracefully her wines mature. All visits are by appointment. ⊠ 987 St. Helena Hwy., St. Helena ✛ At Stice La. ☎ 707/963–0826 ⊕ www. corison.com 🖥 Tastings from $95.

Duckhorn Vineyards

WINERY | Merlot's moment in the sun may have passed, but you wouldn't know it at Duckhorn, whose Three Palms Merlot was crowned wine of the year by *Wine Spectator* as recently as 2017. Duckhorn also makes Cabernet Sauvignon, Cabernet Franc, Chardonnay, Sauvignon Blanc, and a few other wines you can sip in the high-ceilinged tasting room or on a fetching wraparound porch overlooking carefully tended vines. "Elevated" experiences, some not offered daily, include a tasting of estate and single-vineyard wines and private hosted tastings guests can customize to suit their preferences. All visits are by appointment. ⊠ 1000 Lodi La., St. Helena ✛ At Silverado Trail N ☎ 707/963–7108 ⊕ www.duckhorn.com 🖥 Tastings from $60.

Ehlers Estate

WINERY | New and old blend seamlessly at this winery whose 1886 tasting room's contemporary decor benefits from the gravitas and sense of history the original stone walls and exposed redwood beams impart. Winemaker Laura Díaz Muñoz crafts complex Cabernet Sauvignon, Merlot, and other Bordeaux-style wines from 40 acres of organically farmed estate grapes. Seated appointment-only tastings focus on the growing practices and the winery's intriguing history, including its 19th-century glory days, Prohibition hijinks under new owners, and the property's late-20th-century revival by a dynamic French couple. ⊠ 3222 Ehlers La., St. Helena ✛ At Hwy. 29 ☎ 707/963–5972 ⊕ www.ehlersestate. com 🖥 Tastings from $125 ⊘ Closed Tues. and Wed.

Faust Haus

WINERY | An architect's spirited redesign of an 1876 Victorian—brooding exterior and heavy ground-floor hues contrasting with bright, open, and airy upstairs spaces—mimics the dark-and-light themes of Germany's Faust legend. Up a terraced hill from Highway 29, Faust Haus serves as a showcase for estate Coombsville AVA wines like The Pact (as in Faust's pact with the devil), a balanced, fruit-forward 100% Cabernet Sauvignon. Tastings, some including wine-friendly food, unfold inside the house or on exterior terraces, one of which looks east across the valley to Howell Mountain. All visits are by appointment, best made at least a day ahead. ⊠ *2867 St. Helena Hwy., St. Helena ⊹ Near Deer Park Rd.* ☎ *707/200–2560* ⊕ *faustwines.com* ☜ *Tastings from $75* ⊗ *Closed Tues. and Wed.*

Hall St. Helena

WINERY | The Cabernet Sauvignons produced here are works of art born of the latest in organic-farming science and wine-making technology. A glass-walled tasting room allows guests to see some of the high-tech equipment winemaker Megan Gunderson employs to craft wines that also include Merlot, Cabernet Franc, and Sauvignon Blanc. Looking westward from the second-floor tasting area, rows of neatly spaced Cabernet vines capture the eye, and beyond them the tree-studded Mayacamas Mountains. Hard to miss as you arrive along Highway 29, Lawrence Argent's 35-foot-tall *Bunny Foo Foo,* a stainless-steel sculpture of a rabbit leaping out of the vineyard, is one of many museum-quality artworks on display at appointment-only Hall (call for same-day). The Art of Cabernet tasting provides a solid introduction to this prominent producer's output. Another worthwhile tour takes in the grounds and the artworks. ∎ **TIP→ Sister winery Hall Rutherford hosts an exclusive wine-and-food pairing atop a Rutherford hillside.** ⊠ *401 St. Helena Hwy./Hwy. 29,* *St. Helena ⊹ Near White La.* ☎ *707/967– 2626* ⊕ *www.hallwines.com* ☜ *Tastings from $60.*

★ Heitz Cellar

WINERY | Since this winery founded in 1961 changed hands in 2018, its valley-floor tasting room has morphed from a humble site to sip collector-worthy single-vineyard Cabernets into a white-tablecloth salon with prices to match. The premier experience—an estate cellar tour 5 miles away, an excursion to two vineyards, and a tasting—tops out at $1,000 a person. A more straightforward session, culminating with the legendary Martha's Vineyard Oakville Cab, unfolds inside the Salon at Heitz Cellar or on the stone structure's terrace, which juts east into a Cabernet vineyard. Crafted from certified organic grapes, the wines are magnificent, and the reasonably priced optional food pairing reveals additional complexity. Nostalgic critics have decried Heitz's grander iteration as a marker of "the real Napa Valley" slipping away. Perhaps, but the wines' restrained style recalls the great Cabs (including Heitz's) of the 1960s–70s, and the present-day hospitality couldn't be more welcoming. ⊠ *436 St. Helena Hwy., St. Helena ⊹ Near White La.* ☎ *707/963–2047* ⊕ *www. heitzcellar.com* ☜ *Tastings from $125.*

★ Joseph Phelps Vineyards

WINERY | In 2022, LVMH's Moet Hennessy division purchased the winery the late Joseph Phelps founded a half-century before, a changing of the guard that reinforced Napa's stature as an international luxury-lifestyle player. Phelps produces excellent whites, along with Pinot Noir from its Sonoma Coast vineyards, but the blockbusters are the Bordeaux reds, particularly the Cabernet Sauvignons and Insignia, a luscious-yet-subtle Cab-dominant blend. Insignia, which often receives high-90s scores from respected wine publications, is always among the current releases poured at the one-hour seated Terrace Tasting overlooking grapevines and oaks. Other experiences, including one involving food pairings, unfold inside the main redwood structure, a classic of 1970s Northern California architecture. Participants in the Insignia Retrospective Tasting, offered a few times a month, sample several vintages of the flagship wine. ⊠ *200 Taplin Rd., St. Helena ✛ Off Silverado Trail* ☎ *707/963–2745, 800/707–5789* ⊕ *www.josephphelps.com* ☳ *Tastings from $115.*

Louis M. Martini Winery

WINERY | A 100-point score for its Lot No. 1 Cabernet Sauvignon and a snappy renovation of the original 1933 winery added 21st-century luster to this operation whose namesake was a founding Napa Valley Vintners member. Established well before the valley's preoccupation with Cabernet Sauvignon took hold, Martini, owned for more than two decades by E&J Gallo, also makes Sauvignon Blanc, Bordeaux-style red blends, Cabernet Franc, Merlot, Malbec, Muscat, Petite Sirah, Zinfandel, and dessert wines. A basic tasting includes a few of these. The more comprehensive Heritage Tasting of small-lot wines is highly recommended, with or without the optional food pairing. Fun fact: 10 of the St. Helena AVA acres the winery occupies cost Louis M. a whopping $3,000 (total) in 1933. ⊠ *254 St. Helena Hwy. S, St. Helena ✛ At Chaix La.* ☎ *707/968–3362* ⊕ *www.louismartini.com* ☳ *Tastings from $55.*

Pestoni Family Estate Winery

WINERY | A 19th-century wine-bottling contraption, a Prohibition-era safe with tales to tell, and photos and documents spanning five generations enhance a visit to this winery run by the descendants of Albino Pestoni, their Swiss-Italian forebear. Pourers share the Pestoni story while dispensing wines made from grapes grown in choice vineyards the family has acquired over the decades. The Howell Mountain Merlots and Cabernet Sauvignons at Legacy tastings always stand out. Heritage tastings of current releases often include Sauvignon Blanc, Sangiovese, and Cabernet grown on the Pestonis' Rutherford Bench property. The 1892 Field Blend from Lake County heirloom grapes—Zinfandel, Cabernet, and Petite Sirah—commemorates the year Albino entered the wine business. ■ **TIP➔ After a tasting, guests are welcome to picnic in the winery's tree-shaded pavilion.** ⊠ *1673 St. Helena Hwy. S/ Hwy. 29, St. Helena ✛ Near Galleron Rd.* ☎ *707/963–0544* ⊕ *www.pestonifamily.com* ☳ *Tastings from $50.*

Prager Winery & Port Works

WINERY | "If door is locked, ring bell," reads a sign outside the weathered-redwood tasting shack at this family-run winery known for red, white, and tawny ports. The sign, the bell, and the thousands of dollar bills tacked to the walls and ceilings inside are your first indications that you're drifting back in time with the old-school Pragers, who have been making regular and fortified wines in St. Helena since 1979. Five members of the second generation run this homespun operation founded by Jim and Imogene Prager. In addition to ports, the winery makes Petite Sirah and Sweet Claire, a late-harvest Riesling dessert wine. Some tastings take place in a garden outside the tasting room or on the crush pad. Visits are by appointment; call for same-day. ⊠ *1281 Lewelling La., St. Helena ✛ Off Hwy. 29* ☎ *707/963–7678* ⊕ *www.pragerport.com* ☳ *Tastings $40 (includes glass).*

★ Pride Mountain Vineyards

WINERY | This winery 2,200 feet up Spring Mountain straddles Napa and Sonoma counties, confusing enough for visitors but even more complicated for the wine-making staff: government regulations require separate wineries and paperwork for each side of the property. It's one of several Pride Mountain quirks, but the winery's "big red wines," including a Cabernet Sauvignon that earned 100-point scores from a prominent wine critic two years in a row, are serious

Tastings in Raymond's atmospheric Barrel Cellar include wines that are still aging.

business. On a visit, by appointment only, you can learn about the farming and cellar strategies behind Pride's acclaimed Cabs. The winery also produces Syrah, a Cab-like Merlot, Claret, Cabernet Franc, and noteworthy Chardonnay and Viognier whites. ■ TIP→ **The views here are knock-your-socks-off gorgeous.** ✉ *4026 Spring Mountain Rd., St. Helena ⊹ Off St. Helena Rd. (extension of Spring Mountain Rd. in Sonoma County)* ☎ *707/963–4949* ⊕ *www.pridewines.com* ✉ *Tastings from $30* ⊙ *Closed Tues.*

The Prisoner Wine Company

WINERY | The iconoclastic brand opened an industrial-chic space with interiors by the wildly original Napa-based designer Richard Von Saal to showcase its flagship The Prisoner red blend. "Getting the varietals to play together" is winemaker Chrissy Wittmann's mission with that wine (Cabernet Sauvignon, Petite Sirah, Syrah, and Charbono in a recent vintage). The goal's the same with siblings like the Blindfold Blanc de Noir—mostly white Pinot Noir (no skin contact, so no

purple color), with some Viognier, and Gewürztraminer. The Line-up Tasting of current releases unfolds in a lounge that's more hip hotel bar than traditional tasting room. Other experiences involve boldly flavored plates that pair well with Wittman's fruit-forward wines. Reservations are required for all visits. ✉ *1178 Galleron Rd., St. Helena ⊹ At Hwy. 29* ☎ *707/967–3823, 877/283–5934* ⊕ *www.theprisonerwinecompany.com* ✉ *Tastings from $85.*

★ Quintessa

WINERY | The enduring beauty of this 280-acre estate reveals itself most vividly atop an oak-laced vineyard's-edge ridge with views across much of the Rutherford appellation. Fortunately for guests, many tastings take place here, some at open-air seating areas, others in steel, glass, and stone pavilions that open or close to the elements as needed. This land was a cattle ranch until Agustin and Valeria Huneeus purchased the property in 1989, convinced it could produce collector-worthy wines. Time has proven them correct, as the single Bordeaux-style red blend made each vintage, aged in caves dug deep into the hillside, annually garners mid- to high-90s scores from top critics. Tastings, by appointment only, start with the Illumination Sauvignon Blanc and include at least one library (older) Cabernet for comparison. ⊠ 1601 Silverado Trail S, St. Helena ✛ ¼ mile north of Hwy. 128 ☎ 707/286–2730 ⊕ www.quintessa.com ✉ Tastings from $125 ⊘ Closed Tues. and Wed.

Raymond Vineyards

WINERY | All the world's a stage to Jean-Charles Boisset, Raymond's charismatic owner—even his vineyards, where his five-act Theater of Nature includes a series of gardens and displays that explain biodynamic agriculture. The theatrics continue indoors in the disco-dazzling Crystal Cellar tasting room (chandeliers and other accoutrements by Baccarat), along with several additional spaces, some sedate and others equally expressive. Despite goosing up the glamour—gal pals out for a fun afternoon love this place—Boisset and winemaker Stephanie Putnam have continued the winery's tradition of producing lush, flavorful wines. The Cabernet Sauvignons and Merlots often surprise. All visits are by appointment. ■ TIP➔ **The Winemaker for a Day blending seminars here are entertaining.** ⊠ 1584 St. Helena Hwy./Hwy. 29, St. Helena ✛ ¼ mile north of Galleron Rd. ☎ 707/963–3141 ⊕ www.raymondvineyards.com ✉ Tastings from $40 ⊘ Closed Tues. and Wed. in winter.

Rombauer Vineyards

WINERY | Irma S. Rombauer, the great-aunt of winery founder Koerner Rombauer (who passed away in 2018), defined generations of American home cuisine with her best-selling book *The Joy of Cooking,* but he laid claim to a similar triumph. "Iconic" is an adjective often associated with Rombauer Chardonnays, particularly the flagship Carneros bottling. Although often described simply as "buttery," at their best the wines express equal parts ripeness, acidity, and creaminess, with vanilla accents courtesy of skillful oak aging. Most guests book a full tasting—Rombauer also makes Sauvignon Blanc, Zinfandel, Cabernet Sauvignon, Merlot, and dessert wines—but it's also possible to sip by the glass, on the vineyard-view porch or while strolling the landscaped grounds. In either case you'll need a reservation (call for same-day visits). ⊠ 3522 Silverado Trail N, St. Helena ✛ ¾ mile north of Glass Mountain Rd. ☎ 866/280–2582 ⊕ rombauer.com ✉ Tastings from $14 glass, $25 flight.

★ Schweiger Vineyards

WINERY | Trying to sell his wife, Sally, on his late-1970s notion of planting a vineyard on their woodsy Spring Mountain property, contractor Fred Schweiger assured her, "It'll just be a hobby." Over time that hobby evolved into the lifestyle the family now shares with guests to its indoor and outdoor tasting spaces, whose gasp-worthy elevation-2,000-feet views include some of the original vines and extend across the Napa Valley to Howell Mountain. One of Fred's mentors advised him to plant the "king and queen of grapes," Chardonnay and Cabernet Sauvignon. For a decade the family sold all the fruit, but in 1994 son Andy began making Schweiger wines, eventually adding Sauvignon Blanc, more Bordeaux reds, Pinot Noir, and two port-style dessert offerings. ■ TIP➔ **For an exhilarating and educational spin through the vines, some on steeply terraced slopes, book (May–August) the All-Terrain Vineyard Experience.** ⊠ 4015 Spring Mountain Rd., St. Helena ✛ 500 feet from Sonoma County line ☎ 707/963–4882 ⊕ www.schweigervineyards.com ✉ Tastings from $65.

★ Smith-Madrone Vineyards & Winery

WINERY | For a glimpse of the Napa Valley before things got precious, head up Spring Mountain to the vineyard Stu Smith purchased in 1970 and still farms.

His low-tech winery is a family affair: brother Charlie has made Smith-Madrone's critically acclaimed wines for more than four decades, and son Sam is Charlie's assistant. Blissfully informal outdoor tours and tastings of Chardonnay, Cabernet Sauvignon, and Riesling take place by appointment three days a week, starting at the weather-worn no-frills redwood barn where Charlie makes the wines. He mostly lets the grapes do the talking, but profound wisdom underlies his restraint: these food-friendly wines are marvels of acidity, minerality, but most of all flavor. The view across the valley to Howell Mountain is often fantastic. ⊠ *4022 Spring Mountain Rd., St. Helena* ✛ *Near Napa/Sonoma county line* ☎ *707/963–2283* ⊕ *www.smithmadrone. com* ⬚ *Tastings from $65* ☾ *Closed Sun., Mon., Wed., and Fri.*

★ Spring Mountain Vineyard

WINERY | Until the 2020 Glass Fire swept through this historic property, the tales hosts shared revolved around the estate's illustrious past, but these days the topics also include heroism and resilience. Although several 19th-century buildings perished, the longtime vineyard manager helped save the 1885 Miravalle mansion (famous for a star turn in TV's *Falcon Crest*) even as his own home on-site burned to the ground. He fought as well to preserve the vineyard, most of which survived, as did caves holding many previous vintages. Spring Mountain produces Chardonnay, Sauvignon Blanc, and Pinot Noir, but the calling cards are the Estate Cabernet Sauvignon and signature Elivette Bordeaux-style blend, both bold and robust, reflecting their mountain origin. Despite its brush with disaster, the winery remains worth a visit (appointment required) for its wines, views, and staff's courtly hospitality. ⊠ *2805 Spring Mountain Rd., St. Helena* ✛ *Off Madrona Ave.* ☎ *707/967–4188* ⊕ *www.springmountainvineyard.com* ⬚ *Tastings from $50.*

Stony Hill Vineyard

WINERY | A winery whose Old World–style Chardonnay sommeliers love, Stony Hill was founded by the late Fred and Eleanor McCrea. During World War II, the couple purchased a 160-acre goat farm on Spring Mountain's eastern slope, first planting grapevines, some still bearing fruit, in 1948. Private tastings (reservations required) emphasize whites—Stony Hill also produces dry Gewürztraminer and Riesling, and in some years Semillon du Soleil, a dessert wine from grapes dried in the sun after harvesting to increase their sugars. A leaner-than-average Cabernet Sauvignon is the heaviest offering. ⊠ *3331 St. Helena Hwy. N, St. Helena* ✛ *Near Bale Grist Mill* ☎ *707/963–2636* ⊕ *stonyhillvineyard.com* ⬚ *Tastings from $125.*

★ Titus Vineyards

WINERY | Painterly westward-facing views of vineyards, the Napa River treeline, and Spring Mountain provide the backdrop for indoor and outdoor tastings at this low-key valley-floor winery. The concrete-and-glass production facility and hospitality center, completed in 2015, skews new, but the setting feels timeless. Grapes have been growing on this ranch for more than a century, and the agricultural history dates to the mid-1800s. After arriving in 1968, the first Titus family generation sold grapes to Beaulieu and other Napa Valley stalwarts. Next-generation brothers Eric and Phillip Titus (the latter famed Chappellet's longtime winemaker) oversaw significant replantings in the past quarter-century, ensuring a steady flow of mostly Bordeaux grapes for the family's label. Cabernet Sauvignon comprises more than half the production, with Viognier, Pinot Noir, Cabernet Franc, Merlot, and Zinfandel among the other bottlings. ⊠ *2971 Silverado Trail N, St. Helena* ✛ *¼ mile north of Deer Park Rd.* ☎ *707/963–3235* ⊕ *www.titusvineyards. com* ⬚ *Tastings from $60.*

★ Tres Sabores Winery

WINERY | A long, narrow lane with two sharp bends leads to workaday Tres Sabores, where the sight of sheep, golden retrievers, guinea hens, pomegranate and other trees and plants, a slew of birds and bees, and a heaping compost pile reinforces a simple point: despite the Napa Valley's penchant for glamour this is, first and foremost, farm country. Owner-winemaker Julie Johnson specializes in single-vineyard wines that include Cabernet Sauvignon and Zinfandel from estate-grown certified-organic Rutherford bench vines. She also excels with Petite Sirah from dry-farmed Calistoga fruit, Sauvignon Blanc, and the zippy ¿Por Qué No? (Why not?) red blend. *Tres sabores* is Spanish for "three flavors," which to Johnson represents the land, her vines, and, as she puts it, "the spirit of the company around the table." Tastings by appointment only are informal and usually held outside. ⊠ *1620 S. Whitehall La., St. Helena ✣ West of Hwy. 29* ☎ *707/967–8027* ⊕ *www.tressabores. com* 🍷 *Tastings from $55.*

Trinchero Napa Valley

WINERY | Sipping this winery's Malbec or Bordeaux red blends, it seems inconceivable that last century's White Zinfandel craze made these willfully tannic wines possible. Over the years, the Trinchero family, owners of Sutter Home, which invented White Zin and stills sells millions of bottles annually, assembled a quality portfolio of estate vineyards whose grapes go into wines that truly live up to the term "terroir-driven." The wowsers include the Single Vineyard Collection reds—several Cabs, Petit Verdot, Malbec, Merlot, and Petite Sirah—most from the Napa Valley's Atlas Peak, Calistoga, Mt. Veeder, and St. Helena subappellations. All are served in an elegant, exuberant tasting room designed by St. Helena's internationally acclaimed Erin Martin or in several outdoor spaces. All tastings require a reservation. ⊠ *3070 St. Helena Hwy. N, St. Helena ✣ Near Ehlers La.*

☎ *707/963–1160* ⊕ *www.trincheronapavalley.com* 🍷 *Tastings from $85 (sometimes lower Mon. and Thurs.)* ⊙ *Closed Tues. and Wed.*

★ Viader Vineyards & Winery

WINERY | On a 92-acre Howell Mountain property with valley views west to the Mayacamas range, this boutique winery was established in 1986. Founder Delia Viader bucked conventional wisdom by planting her vines vertically down a 32% slope instead of terracing them horizontally. Her three principal red blends, these days assembled by her son Alan, are similarly atypical in that they're not, per Delia, "trying to hijack your palate with high tannins or alcohol." Smooth and supple yet intense and aromatic, the wines are the product of tender yet exacting farming and wine-making processes. A curving knoll of oaks, madrones, and manzanitas separating the two vineyard sections holds the winery and nearby tasting room. The latter's vistas and terrace are as alluring as the much-sought-after wines. Visits to Viader require an appointment, preferably made at least a day or two ahead. ⊠ *1120 Deer Park Rd., Deer Park ✣ 3 miles northeast off Silverado Trail* ☎ *707/963–3816* ⊕ *viader. com* ⊙ *Tastings from $100.*

★ Wheeler Farms

WINERY | The Araujo family, renowned for elevating Calistoga's Eisele Vineyard to world-class status, celebrates an earlier Napa Valley clan at this 11-acre valley-floor property. Part of a larger late-19th-century parcel assembled by two generations of the Wheeler family, the current site contains a flower and culinary garden, a small fruit orchard, and 7-plus acres of mostly Cabernet Sauvignon, all farmed organically and biodynamically. One of two contemporary stained-cedar buildings holds a state-of-the-art winery and cellar, where the Wheeler and similarly collector-worthy brands' wines are made, the other a handsome hospitality center. The latter space, with views north through floor-to-ceiling windows to Mt. St. Helena, comes off more upscale Wine Country living room than tasting venue. In its unshowy elegance, the presentation here mirrors the wines, served with small bites prepared in an open kitchen. ✉ *588 Zinfandel La., St. Helena ✣ ½ mile east of Hwy. 29* ☎ *707/200–8500* 🌐 *www.wheelerfarmswine.com* 🎟 *Tastings from $145.*

🍴 Restaurants

Acacia House

$$$$ | MODERN AMERICAN | Inside the bright-white 1907 Georgian-style structure anchoring the otherwise contemporary Alila Napa Valley resort, Acacia House serves ambitious cuisine—sea urchin *cacio e pepe* (cheese and pepper pasta), perhaps, or jamón ibérico schnitzel—that generally lives up to the elegant setting. At lunch, the chefs, who source ingredients from top purveyors (the quality duly reflected in the prices), also turn out comfort fare like avocado toast with trout and a burger with slow-cooked tomato and caramelized onion. **Known for:** special-occasion feel; lounge menu 3–5; wraparound patio on a sunny day. [$] *Average main: $45* ✉ *1915 Main St., St. Helena ✣ At Pratt Ave.* ☎ *707/963–9004* 🌐 *www.acaciahouserestaurant.com.*

Brasswood Bar + Bakery + Kitchen

$$$ | ITALIAN | After Napa Valley fixture Tra Vigne lost its lease, many staffers regrouped a few miles north at the restaurant (the titular Kitchen) of the Brasswood complex, which also includes a bakery, shops, and a wine-tasting room. Along with dishes developed for the new location, the chefs incorporate Tra Vigne favorites such as mozzarella-stuffed arancini (rice balls) into the Mediterranean-leaning menu. **Known for:** mostly Napa-Sonoma wine list; bakery a good lunch stop for pizzas, salads, and sandwiches; patio seating. [$] *Average main: $33* ✉ *3111 St. Helena Hwy. N, St. Helena ✣ Near Ehlers La.* ☎ *707/302–5101* 🌐 *brasswood.com/brasswoodbarkitchen.*

The Charter Oak

$$$ | MODERN AMERICAN | Christopher Kostow's reputation rests on his swoon-worthy haute cuisine for the Meadowood resort, but he and his Charter Oak team adopt a more straightforward approach—fewer ingredients chosen for maximum effect—at this high-ceilinged, brown-brick downtown restaurant. With exceedingly fresh produce from Meadowood's nearby farm, this strategy might translate into dishes like red kuri squash with pickled peppers, almonds, and goat cheese; or pork collar with fermented pepper jam (or just go for the cheeseburger and thick hand-cut fries). **Known for:** monthly changing wings appetizer; patio dining in brick courtyard; weekday happy hour 2:30–5. [$] *Average main: $32* ✉ *1050 Charter Oak Ave., St. Helena ✣ At Hwy. 29* ☎ *707/302–6996* 🌐 *www.thecharteroak.com.*

★ Cook St. Helena

$$$ | ITALIAN | A curved marble bar spotlit by contemporary art-glass pendants adds a touch of style to this downtown restaurant whose northern Italian cuisine pleases with understated sophistication. Mussels with house-made sausage in a spicy tomato broth, chopped salad with pancetta and pecorino, and the daily changing risotto are among the dishes regulars revere. **Known for:** top-quality ingredients; reasonably priced local and international wines; intimate dining. [$] *Average main: $30* ✉ *1310 Main St., St. Helena ✣ Near Hunt Ave.* ☎ *707/963–7088* 🌐 *www.cooksthelena.com* 🕒 *Closed weekends.*

★ Farmstead at Long Meadow Ranch

$$$ | AMERICAN | In a high-ceilinged former barn with plenty of outside seating, Farmstead revolves around an open kitchen whose chefs prepare meals with grass-fed beef and lamb, fruits and vegetables, and eggs, olive oil, wine,

Long Meadow Ranch's St. Helena compound includes a general store, a café, and Farmstead restaurant.

honey, and other ingredients from nearby Long Meadow Ranch. Entrées might include wood-grilled trout with fennel and bacon-mustard vinaigrette; caramelized beets with goat cheese and chimichurri; or a wood-grilled heritage pork chop with jalapeño grits. **Known for:** heritage St. Louis–style ribs; Sunday brunch; on-site general store, café, and Long Meadow Wines tasting space. $ *Average main: $33* ✉ *738 Main St., St. Helena* ✛ *At Charter Oak Ave.* ☎ *707/963–4555* ⊕ *www.longmeadowranch.com/eat-drink/ restaurant.*

★ Gatehouse Restaurant

$$$$ | MODERN AMERICAN | Gung-ho Culinary Institute of America students in their final semester run this excellent if unheralded restaurant in a historic stone structure. A solid value, the three- or four-course prix-fixe meals—oft-changing, nicely plated dishes—emphasize local ingredients, some so local they're grown on-site or nearby. **Known for:** passionate service; many repeat customers; optional wine pairings. $ *Average main:*

$55 ✉ *2555 Main St., St. Helena* ✛ *Near Deer Park Rd.* ☎ *707/967–2300* ⊕ *www. ciagatehouserestaurant.com* ⊘ *Closed Sun. and Mon. and during semester breaks (check website or call for updates). No lunch.*

Goose & Gander

$$$$ | AMERICAN | A Craftsman bungalow whose 1920s owner reportedly used the cellar for bootlegging during Prohibition houses this restaurant where the pairing of food and drink is as likely to involve a craft cocktail as a sommelier-selected wine. Main courses such as wood-grilled chicken or salmon, wet-aged black Angus rib eye, and the grass-fed G&G burger with Gruyère follow starters that might include corn croquettes, sticky pig ears, and harissa sausage with fry bread and baba ghanoush. **Known for:** intimate main dining room with fireplace; alfresco patio dining; basement bar among Napa's best watering holes. $ *Average main: $41* ✉ *1245 Spring St., St. Helena* ✛ *At Oak St.* ☎ *707/967–8779* ⊕ *www.goosegander.com* ⊘ *No lunch.*

Gott's Roadside

$ | **AMERICAN** | A 1950s-style outdoor hamburger stand goes upscale at this spot whose customers brave long lines to order breakfast sandwiches, juicy burgers, root-beer floats, and garlic fries. Choices not available a half century ago include ahi-tuna and Impossible burgers and kale and Vietnamese chicken salads. **Known for:** tasty 21st-century diner cuisine; shaded picnic tables (arrive early or late for lunch to get one); second branch at Napa's Oxbow Public Market. [$] *Average main: $16* ✉ *933 Main St./Hwy. 29, St. Helena* ✣ *Near Charter Oak Ave.* ☎ *707/963–3486* 🌐 *www.gotts.com.*

Market

$$$ | **AMERICAN** | Ernesto Martinez, this easy-going eatery's Mexico City–born chef and co-owner, often puts a Latin spin on farm-to-table American classics. Although he plays things straight with the Caesar salad, champagne-battered fish-and-chips, and baby back ribs, the organic fried chicken comes with cheddar-jalapeño corn bread, and the fried calamari owes its piquancy to the accompanying peppers, nopales cactus, chipotle aioli, and avocado-tomatillo dip. **Known for:** dependable cuisine; full bar; wine-and-small-bites happy hour weekdays 3–6. [$] *Average main: $33* ✉ *1347 Main St., St. Helena* ✣ *Near Hunt Ave.* ☎ *707/963–3799* 🌐 *marketsthelena.com* 🕒 *Closed Sun. and Mon.*

★ Press

$$$$ | **AMERICAN** | For years this cavernous casual-chic restaurant with a contempo-barn interior and wraparound patio steps from neighboring vineyards was northern Napans' preferred stop for a top-shelf cocktail, dry-aged steak, and high-90s-scoring local Cabernet. You can still order a tomahawk or New York strip, but chef Philip Tessier, formerly of Yountville's The French Laundry and Bouchon Bistro and New York City's Le Bernardin, has introduced more refined cuisine, much of whose produce is grown nearby. **Known for:** impressive craft cocktails for pairing with dozen-plus apps; Wine Spectator Grand Award for wide-ranging list; prix-fixe tasting menu highly recommended. [$] *Average main: $56* ✉ *587 St. Helena Hwy./Hwy. 29, St. Helena* ✣ *At White La.* ☎ *707/967–0550* 🌐 *www.pressnapavalley.com* 🕒 *No lunch.*

Tra Vigne Pizzeria and Restaurant

$$ | **PIZZA** | Crisp, thin-crust Neapolitan-style pizzas—among them the unusual Positano, with sautéed shrimp, crescenza cheese, and fried lemons—are the specialties of this family-friendly offshoot of the famous, now departed, Tra Vigne restaurant. Hand-pulled mozzarella and a few other Tra Vigne dishes are on the menu, along with the salads, pizzas, and pastas. **Known for:** well-priced oysters at happy hour (4–6); relaxed atmosphere; create-your-own-pizza option. [$] *Average main: $19* ✉ *1016 Main St., St. Helena* ✣ *At Charter Oak Ave.* ☎ *707/967–9999* 🌐 *www.pizzeriatravigne.com.*

☕ Coffee and Quick Bites

Clif Family Bruschetteria Food Truck

$ | **ITALIAN** | Although it ventures out for special events, this walk-up food truck serving Italian-inflected fast food has a steady gig outside the Clif Family Tasting Room. From 11:30 to 4 (until 6 on Wednesday), order salads, panini, or a falafel, mushroom, pork, or vegetarian bruschetta to go or to enjoy in the tasting room or on its back patio. **Known for:** soups and salads; many organic ingredients; Wednesday's international street food menu. [$] *Average main: $15* ✉ *1284 Vidovich Ave., St. Helena* ✣ *At Hwy. 29* ☎ *707/968–0625 for tasting room* 🌐 *www.cliffamilyfoodtruck.com* 🕒 *Closed Mon. and Tues. No dinner.*

Crisp Kitchen & Juice

$$ | **AMERICAN** | "Elevate Your Everyday" glows a neon side at Crisp, whose spanking-clean interior mirrors the pristine food—avocado toast, beet-cured salmon

tartine, breakfast and lunch bowls, and inventive juices, soups, broths, and smoothies—this health-oriented café serves. The location next to Sunshine Market (easy parking out front) may lack glamour, but the place exudes wellness, and the menu acknowledges the requirements of vegans, vegetarians, and carnivores alike. **Known for:** grab-and-go bowls and salads; build-your-own granola bowls, breakfast sandwiches, and morning porridge; wellness and superfood lattes (regular coffee drinks, too). [$] *Average main: $17* ✉ *1111 Main St., Suite B, St. Helena* ✣ *At Mitchell Dr.* ☎ *707/657–4444* 🌐 *www.crispkitchenandjuice.com* 🕑 *Closed Sun. No dinner.*

Model Bakery

$ | BAKERY | Thanks to multiple plugs by Oprah, each day's fresh batch of English muffins here sells out quickly, but the scones, croissants, breads, and other baked goods also inspire. Breakfast brings pastries and sandwiches with scrambled eggs, cheddar, and bacon between a buttermilk biscuit; the lunch menu expands to include soups, salads, pizzas, and more sandwiches—turkey-pesto focaccia, ciabatta chicken-Asiago panini, and vegan veggies among them. **Known for:** signature English muffins; people-watching at outdoor tables; Yountville and downtown Napa satellite locations. [$] *Average main: $12* ✉ *1357 Main St., St. Helena* ✣ *Near Adams Ave.* ☎ *707/963–8192* 🌐 *www.themodelbakery.com* 🕑 *No dinner.*

The Station

$ | AMERICAN | Joel Gott of nearby Gott's Roadside purchased a downtown gas station and kept the pumps humming, spiffing up the interior retro style and adding shaded outdoor seating. Start the day with quiche, a chipotle-bacon and egg biscuit, or avocado-and-egg or cinnamon-sugar toast, or drop by for lunch wraps, grain bowls, salads, focaccia, and sandwiches. **Known for:** morning pastries; grab-and-go items; locally sourced ingredients. [$] *Average main: $13* ✉ *1153 Main St., St. Helena* ✣ *At Spring St.* ☎ *707/963–3356* 🌐 *www.stationsh.com* 🕑 *No dinner.*

🛏 Hotels

★ Alila Napa Valley

$$$$ | HOTEL | An upscale-casual ultracontemporary adults-only resort formerly known as Las Alcobas Napa Valley but now in the Hyatt Alila brand's fold, this hillside gem sits adjacent to Beringer Vineyards six blocks north of Main Street shopping and dining. **Pros:** vineyard views from most rooms; Acacia House restaurant; pool, spa, and fitness center. **Cons:** expensive much of the year; per website hotel is "adults only" (18-plus); sizable resort fee. [$] *Rooms from: $767* ✉ *1915 Main St., St. Helena* ☎ *707/963–7000* 🌐 *www.alilanapavalley.com* 🛏 *68 rooms* 🍴 *No Meals.*

El Bonita Motel

$$$ | MOTEL | A classic 1950s-style neon sign marks the driveway to this roadside motel that during the off-season offers solid value to budget-minded travelers. **Pros:** cheerful rooms; family friendly; microwaves and minirefrigerators. **Cons:** noise issues in roadside and ground-floor rooms; expensive in high season; lacks amenities of fancier properties. [$] *Rooms from: $339* ✉ *195 Main St./Hwy. 29, St. Helena* ☎ *707/963–3216* 🌐 *www.elbonita.com* 🛏 *52 rooms* 🍴 *Free Breakfast.*

Harvest Inn

$$$ | HOTEL | Although this inn sits just off Highway 29, its patrons remain mostly above the fray, strolling 8 acres of gardens, enjoying views of the vineyards adjoining the property, and drifting to sleep in beds adorned with fancy linens and down pillows. **Pros:** garden setting; spacious rooms; near choice wineries, restaurants, and shops. **Cons:** fair amount of wedding action; rooms could be nicer for the high-season price; occasional service lapses. [$] *Rooms from: $399* ✉ *1 Main St., St. Helena* ☎ *707/963–9463*

⊕ www.harvestinn.com ➷ 81 rooms ⭘ No Meals.

Ink House Napa Valley

$$$$ | **B&B/INN** | Two of the lavish ultracontemporary rooms of this 1885 Italianate pay homage to its most famous residents, Theron H. Ink, the 19th-century vintner, businessman, and local politician who commissioned the home, and Elvis Presley, who holed up here a few months while filming a movie. **Pros:** valley-floor views from cupola; custom-made furniture and chandeliers; wraparound porch. **Cons:** near the highway, though double-paned windows filter out most road noise; ground-floor ADA room but no elevator to upper floors; two-day minimum-stay requirement. $ Rooms from: $750 ✉ 1575 St. Helena Hwy. ☎ 707/331–4382 ⊕ www.inkhousenapavalley.com ➷ 4 rooms ⭘ Free Breakfast.

Inn St. Helena

$$$ | **B&B/INN** | A large room at this spiffed-up downtown St. Helena inn is named for author Ambrose Bierce (*The Devil's Dictionary*), who lived in the main Victorian structure in the early 1900s, but sensitive hospitality and modern amenities are what make a stay worth writing home about. **Pros:** aim-to-please staff and owner; outdoor porch and swing; convenient to shops, tasting rooms, and restaurants. **Cons:** no pool, gym, room service, or other typical amenities; two-night minimum on weekends (three or four with Monday holiday); per website "children 16 and older are welcome" except in one room. $ Rooms from: $318 ✉ 1515 Main St., St. Helena ☎ 707/963–3003 ⊕ www.innsthelena.com ➷ 8 rooms ⭘ Free Breakfast.

Meadowood Napa Valley

$$$$ | **RESORT** | This elite 250-acre resort's celebrated restaurant and more than half its accommodations were destroyed in the 2020 Glass Fire, but the spa, pools, tennis courts, fitness center, and a fair number of cottages in one part survived, with continuing reconstruction in other areas not expected to affect the guest experience. **Pros:** scrupulously maintained rooms; all-organic spa; gracious service. **Cons:** still recovering from fire; far from downtown St. Helena; weekend minimum-stay requirement. $ Rooms from: $1025 ✉ 900 Meadowood La. ☎ 707/531–4788 ⊕ meadowood.com ➷ 36 rooms ⭘ No Meals.

Wine Country Inn

$$$$ | **B&B/INN** | Vineyards flank the three buildings, containing 24 rooms and five cottages, of this pastoral retreat where blue oaks, maytens, and olive trees provide shade and gardens feature lantana (small butterflies love it) and lavender. **Pros:** no resort fee; good-size swimming pool; vineyard views from most rooms. **Cons:** some rooms let in noise from neighbors; expensive in high season; weekend minimum-stay requirement. $ Rooms from: $429 ✉ 1152 Lodi La., St. Helena ✛ East of Hwy. 29 ☎ 707/963–7077, 888/465–4608 ⊕ www.winecountryinn.com ➷ 29 rooms ⭘ Free Breakfast.

★ Wydown Hotel

$$$ | **HOTEL** | This smart boutique hotel near downtown shopping and dining delivers comfort with a heavy dose of style: the storefront lobby's high ceiling and earth tones, punctuated by rich-hued splashes of color, hint at the relaxed grandeur owner-hotelier Mark Hoffmeister and his design team achieved in the rooms upstairs. **Pros:** well run; eclectic decor; downtown location. **Cons:** lacks the amenities of larger properties; large corner rooms pick up some street noise; two-night minimum on weekends. $ Rooms from: $374 ✉ 1424 Main St., St. Helena ☎ 707/963–5100 ⊕ www.wydownhotel.com ➷ 12 rooms ⭘ No Meals.

Nightlife

The Saint
WINE BARS | This high-ceilinged downtown wine bar occupies a stone-walled late-19th-century former bank. Lit by chandeliers and decked out in contemporary style with plush sofas and chairs and Lucite stools at the bar, it's a classy, loungelike space to expand your enological horizons. ⊠ *1351 Main St., St. Helena* ⊹ *Near Adams St.* ☎ *707/302–5130* ⊕ *www.thesaintnapavalley.com* ⊘ *Closed Mon.*

 Performing Arts

Cameo Cinema
FILM | The art nouveau Cameo Cinema, built in 1913 and now beautifully restored, screens first-run and art-house movies. Equipped with Barco laser projection and Dolby Atmos sound systems, the 140-seat venue occasionally hosts live performances. ⊠ *1340 Main St., St. Helena* ⊹ *Near Hunt Ave.* ☎ *707/963–9779* ⊕ *www.cameocinema.com.*

 Shopping

BOOKS
Main Street Bookmine
BOOKS | St. Helena's treasured Main Street Books was headed for closure when the folks behind Napa Bookmine in downtown Napa rescued the indie. The tiny shop's specialties include Napa and Sonoma titles. ⊠ *1315 Main St., St. Helena* ⊹ *Near Hunt Ave.* ☎ *707/963–1338* ⊕ *napabookmine.com.*

CLOTHING
★ Pearl Wonderful Clothing
MIXED CLOTHING | Sweet Pearl carries the latest in women's fashions in a space that makes dramatic use of the section of the historic stone building the shop occupies. Celebs find bags, shoes, jewelry, and outfits here—and you might, too. ⊠ *1219C Main St., St. Helena* ☎ *707/963–3236* ⊕ *pearlwonderfulclothing.com.*

FOOD AND WINE
Gary's Wine & Marketplace
FOOD | Gary Fisch owns four New Jersey stores selling gourmet groceries and international wines but has such a soft spot for the Napa Valley that when the Dean & DeLuca chain abandoned this location, he swooped in and set up shop. The wine selection is as good as ever, and the prepared foods and deli items will ensure you'll picnic in style. ⊠ *607 St. Helena Hwy./Hwy. 29, St. Helena* ⊹ *At White La.* ☎ *707/531–7660* ⊕ *garyswine.com.*

Napa Valley Olive Oil Manufacturing Company
FOOD | "There's a crazy little shack beyond the tracks," the song goes, but in this case the 1870s barn east of the railroad tracks sells tickle-your-taste-buds olive oils and vinegars, along with cheeses, meats, breads, and other delectables to take on the road or enjoy at picnic tables outside. This is no-frills old Napa with a shout-out to old Italy. ⊠ *835 Charter Oak Ave., St. Helena* ⊹ *Off Main St.* ☎ *707/963–4173* ⊕ *www.nvoliveoilmfg.com* ⊘ *Closed Mon. and Tues.*

Woodhouse Chocolate
CHOCOLATE | Elaborate confections made on the premises are displayed like miniature works of art at this shop that resembles an 18th-century Parisian salon. ⊠ *1367 Main St., St. Helena* ⊹ *At Adams St.* ☎ *707/963–8413, 800/966–3468* ⊕ *www.woodhousechocolate.com.*

HOUSEHOLD ITEMS
★ Carter and Co.
CERAMICS | Ceramicist Richard Carter fires up his minimalist line of dinnerware at his 85-acre Pope Valley ranch, where he also creates sculptures and other works on display at his downtown store. Thoughtfully curated kitchenware, home-design items, and hand-crafted clothing by other artisans are also for sale. ⊠ *1231 Main St., near Hunt Ave., St. Helena* ☎ *707/963–5878* ⊕ *carterandco.com* ⊘ *Closed Sun. and Mon.*

NBC Pottery Gallery & Studio

CERAMICS | The French Laundry, Four Seasons Napa Valley, several wineries, and Martha Stewart herself rank among the fans of ceramicist spouses Nikki Ballere and William Callnan III. The two create artworks and dinnerware ceramics—and exhibit the works of other local artisans—in their studio east of St. Helena in Angwin. It's worth the 6-mile trip halfway up Howell Mountain to see what Ballere and Callnan, who also conduct lively classes, are up to. ✉ *410 Circle Dr., Angwin ✛ South off College Ave.* ☎ *707/965–1007* ⊕ *nbcpottery.com* ✆ *Closed Mon. and Sat. except by appointment.*

Activities

Health Spa Napa Valley

SPAS | The focus at this local favorite is on health, wellness, and fitness, so there are personal trainers offering advice and an outdoor lap pool in addition to the extensive regimen of massages and body treatments. The Harvest Mud Wrap, for which clients get slathered with grape-seed mud and Kaolin clay, is a more indulgent, less messy alternative to a traditional mud bath. Afterward, you can take advantage of the sauna, hot tub, and eucalyptus steam rooms. ✉ *1030 Main St., St. Helena ✛ At Pope St.* ☎ *707/967–8800* ⊕ *healthspanapavalley.com* ➳ *Treatments from $115.*

Calistoga

3 miles northwest of St. Helena.

The false-fronted shops, 19th-century buildings, and unpretentious tasting rooms lining the main drag of Lincoln Avenue give Calistoga a slightly rough-and-tumble feel that's unique in the Napa Valley. With Mt. St. Helena rising to the north and visible from downtown, Calistoga looks a bit like a cattle town tucked into a remote mountain valley.

In 1859 Sam Brannan—Mormon missionary, entrepreneur, and vineyard developer—learned about a place in the upper Napa Valley, called Agua Caliente by settlers, that was peppered with hot springs and even had its own "Old Faithful" geyser. He snapped up 2,000 acres of prime property and laid out a resort. Planning a place that would rival New York's famous Saratoga Hot Springs, he built an elegant hotel, bathhouses, cottages, stables, an observatory, and a distillery (the last a questionable choice for a Mormon missionary). Brannan's gamble didn't pay off as he'd hoped, but Californians kept coming to "take the waters," supporting small hotels and bathhouses built wherever a hot spring bubbled to the surface. In the 21st century, Calistoga began returning to its roots, with luxury properties like Solage (2007) springing up and Indian Springs and old standbys sprucing up. The trend continued in 2021 with the opening of the Four Seasons Napa Valley and a total makeover of Dr. Wilkinson's. (In 1952, the latter advertised "The Works"—mud and steam baths and a blanket wrap followed by a massage—for a whopping $3.50, a sum that even adjusted for inflation wouldn't come close to covering the current charges.) At the Brannan Cottage Inn (⇨ *see Hotels, below*), you can spend a night in part of the only Sam Brannan cottage still on its original site.

GETTING HERE AND AROUND

To get here from St. Helena or anywhere else farther south, take Highway 29 north and then turn right on Lincoln Avenue. Alternatively, you can head north on Silverado Trail and turn left on Lincoln. VINE buses serve Calistoga.

VISITOR INFORMATION

CONTACT Visit Calistoga. ✉ *1133 Washington St., Calistoga ✛ Near Lincoln Ave.* ☎ *707/942–6333* ⊕ *www.visitcalistoga.com.*

The astounding Castello di Amorosa has 107 rooms.

Sights

Bennett Lane Winery

WINERY | Winemaker Rob Hunter of Bennett Lane strives "to create the greatest Cabernet Sauvignon in the world." At this appointment-only winery's tastefully casual salon in the far northern Napa Valley, you can find out how close he and his team come. Although known for valley-floor Cabernet, Bennett Lane also produces Merlot and the Maximus Red Feasting Wine, a Cab-heavy red blend nicely priced considering the quality. On the lighter side are Chardonnay and the Maximus White Feasting Wine blend of Sauvignon Blanc, Chardonnay, and Muscat. The basic flight surveys current-release whites and reds. There's also a Cab-focused offering. Many tastings take place in a garden whose pergola frames vineyard and Calistoga Palisades views. ⊠ *3340 Hwy. 128, Calistoga* ✛ *3 miles north of downtown* ☎ *707/942–6684* ⊕ *www.bennettlane.com* 🖻 *Tastings from $35.*

Castello di Amorosa

WINERY | An astounding medieval structure complete with drawbridge and moat, chapel, stables, and secret passageways, the Castello commands Diamond Mountain's lower eastern slope. Some of the 107 rooms contain artist Fabio Sanzogni's replicas of 13th-century frescoes (cheekily signed with his website address), and the dungeon has an iron maiden from Nuremberg, Germany. You must pay for a tour to see most of Dario Sattui's extensive eight-level property, though with general admission you'll have access to part of the complex. Bottlings of note include Sangiovese and other Italian-style wines and Il Barone, a deliberately big Cab. All visits are by appointment. ⊠ *4045 N. St. Helena Hwy./ Hwy. 29, Calistoga* ✛ *Near Maple La.* ☎ *707/967–6272* ⊕ *www.castellodiamorosa.com* 🖻 *Tastings from $55.*

Ca' Toga Galleria d'Arte

ART GALLERY | The boundless wit, whimsy, and creativity of the Venetian-born Carlo Marchiori, this gallery's owner-artist, finds expression in paintings, watercolors, ceramics, sculptures, and other artworks. Marchiori often draws on mythology and folktales for his inspiration. A stop at this magical gallery might inspire you to tour Villa Ca' Toga, the artist's Palladian home, a tromp-l'oeil tour de force open for tours from May through October on Saturday morning only, by appointment. ✉ *1206 Cedar St., Calistoga* ✛ *Near Lincoln Ave.* ☎ *707/942–3900* ⊕ *www.catoga.com* ⊘ *Closed Mon.–Wed.*

Chateau Montelena

WINERY | Set amid a bucolic northern Calistoga landscape, this stately winery whose stone winery building was erected in 1888 helped establish the Napa Valley's reputation for high-quality wine making. At the pivotal Paris tasting of 1976, the Chateau Montelena 1973 Chardonnay took first place, beating out four white Burgundies from France and five other California Chardonnays, an event immortalized (with some liberties taken) in the 2008 movie *Bottle Shock*. A 21st-century Napa Valley Chardonnay is always part of A Taste of Montelena—the winery also makes Sauvignon Blanc, Riesling, a fine estate Zinfandel, and Cabernet Sauvignon—or you can opt for the Montelena Estate Collection tasting of Cabernets from several vintages. All visits require a reservation. ✉ *1429 Tubbs La., Calistoga* ✛ *Off Hwy. 29* ☎ *707/942–5105* ⊕ *www.montelena. com* 🥂 *Tastings from $60.*

★ Davis Estates

WINERY | Owners Mike and Sandy Davis transformed a ramshackle property into a plush winery whose predominantly Bordeaux-style wines live up to the magnificent setting. In fashioning the couple's haute-rustic appointment-only hospitality center, the celebrated Wine Country architect Howard Backen incorporated cedar, walnut, and other woods. In fine weather, many guests sit on the open-air terrace's huge swinging sofas, enjoying broad valley views while tasting Sauvignon Blanc and Chardonnay whites, with Pinot Noir, Merlot, Cabernet Franc, Petit Verdot, and Cabs and Cab-heavy blends among the reds. The wines can be paired with small bites by Mark Caldwell, the executive chef. Tastings are by appointment only. ✉ *4060 Silverado Trail N, Calistoga* ✛ *At Larkmead La.* ☎ *707/942–0700* ⊕ *www.davisestates. com* 🥂 *Tastings from $100.*

Elusa Winery

WINERY | The perks of staying at the Four Seasons Napa Valley include the resort's on-site winery and 4.7 acres of vines, but tastings at the classy-rustic hospitality center are also open to nonguests. One goal of consulting winemaker Thomas Rivers Brown is to bring more attention to the virtues of the Calistoga AVA, particularly the appellation's volcanic soils. The supple wines created from them prove his mission worthwhile. Tastings, always by appointment, qualify as a luxury experience, but the hospitality is warm, thoughtful, and unforced. ✉ *400 Silverado Trail N, Calistoga* ✛ *Near Rosedale Rd.* ☎ *707/403–6644* ⊕ *www. elusawinery.com* 🥂 *Tastings from $150.*

Frank Family Vineyards

WINERY | Former Disney film and television executive Rich Frank founded his namesake winery in 1992, but the wine-making history here dates to the 19th century—portions of an original 1884 structure, reclad in stone in 1906, remain standing today. From 1952 until 1990, Hanns Kornell made sparkling wines on this site. Frank Family, since 2022 part of the Treasury Wine Estates portfolio, also makes sparklers, but the high-profile wines are the Carneros Chardonnay and several Cabernet Sauvignons, particularly the Rutherford Reserve and the Winston Hill red blend. Tastings, some held in the glass-walled, vineyard's-edge The Miller House hospitality barn, which debuted in 2023, are sit-down affairs, with reservations required. ✉ *1091 Larkmead La., Calistoga* ✛ *Off Hwy. 29* ☎ *707/942–0859* ⊕ *www. frankfamilyvineyards.com* 🥂 *Tastings from $60.*

Knights Bridge Winery

WINERY | Two businessmen brothers founded this winery that produces collector-quality Chardonnay, Sauvignon Blanc, and Cabernet Sauvignon on a secluded Knights Valley AVA estate. All the wine production on this site, whose elevation varies from 200 to 1,200 feet, takes place underground in an ingeniously designed cave. Most visits begin with a UTV side-by-side property tour, passing by dry-farmed, head-trained Chardonnay vines more than three decades old and several Cabernet and other Bordeaux-grape blocks. **TIP→ Though in Sonoma County, the winery bears a Calistoga address; if using GPS, make sure to enter the correct coordinates.** ✉ *17138 Spencer La., Calistoga* ✥ *Off Hwy. 128* ☎ *707/341–3391* 🌐 *www.knightsbridgewinery.com* 🎫 *Tastings from $150.*

★ **Larkmead**

WINERY | Founded in 1895 but planted with grapes even before that by San Francisco's free-spirited Lillie Hitchcock Coit, Larkmead was named by her for the meadowlarks that once flitted through the northern Napa Valley. Intuitive artistry informs everything that unfolds on the 150-acre estate, from the vineyards and colorful gardens to the barn-chic interior design, five-star hospitality, and artworks by Kate Solari Baker, whose parents purchased Larkmead in 1948. A former winemaker describes the diverse soils here as "a 'snapshot' of the entire Napa Valley" and the reason why the winery's three top-of-the-line Cabernets taste so different despite their grapes growing in some cases mere yards from each other. Most tastings include a brief tour that passes by a 3-acre vineyard planted to research alternative varietals and viticultural techniques to cope with climate change. ✉ *1100 Larkmead La., Calistoga* ✥ *Off Hwy. 29* ☎ *707/942–0167* 🌐 *www.larkmead.com* 🎫 *Tastings from $90.*

Lola Wines

WINERY | A winery with personality galore, Lola earns plaudits from critics for owner-winemaker Seth Cripe's accessible, unconventional wines. The Chardonnay, Chenin Blanc, Malvasia Bianca, Riesling, and other whites favor acidity and "unripeness" over bombastic flavors. The rosé of Pinot Noir and reds including Pinot Noir, Zinfandel, and Cabernet Sauvignon also share this succulent trait. All the wines are from single vineyards and 100% their varietal. Cripe, who also runs a lucrative side business selling bottarga (fish roe) to fine-dining restaurants nationwide, presents his wines with wife and business partner Rafaela Costa at a redbrick 1892 former home a few blocks from the center of town. Some of her artworks adorn the walls inside. In good weather, most tastings take place on the tree-shaded patio out back. ✉ *916 Foothill Blvd., Calistoga* ✥ *At Pine St. south of Lincoln Ave.* ☎ *707/342–0623* 🌐 *www.lolawines.com* 🎫 *Tastings from $35* ⏲ *Closed Tues. and Wed.*

Romeo Vineyards & Cellars

WINERY | Redwoods and cedars tower over the downtown Calistoga garden patio of this under-the-radar producer of Bordeaux-varietal wines. Alison Doran, whose first wine-making gig was working as a harvest intern in the 1970s for André Tchelistcheff, the premier California winemaker of his era, extracts rich flavors from grapes grown a few miles away in Romeo's half-century-old southern Calistoga vineyard. The Napa Valley Cabernet is a bona fide bargain for the quality; the Malbec and Petit Verdot are also strong suits, as are the Sauvignon Blanc and Petit Verdot rosé. ✉ *1224 Lincoln Ave., Calistoga* ✥ *At Cedar St.* ☎ *707/942–8239* 🌐 *www.romeovineyards.com* 🎫 *Tastings from $35.*

★ **Schramsberg**

WINERY | On a Diamond Mountain site the German-born Jacob Schram planted to grapes in the early 1860s, Schramsberg

Chinese in the Caves and Vineyards

A scene in a Calistoga alley mural (⊠ *1429 Lincoln Ave.*) depicting the city's Chinatown, as well as a 1st Street Bridge plaque commemorating a larger riverbank settlement in downtown Napa, are among the scant present-day recognition of the contributions Chinese immigrants made to the 19th-century Napa Valley. Beringer, Schramsberg, Storybook Mountain, and a few other wineries credit Chinese workers with digging historic caves. They also built wineries, cleared land, grew and harvested grapes, made wine, and erected stone fences that still grace the Wine Country landscape. Some of the primarily male immigrants toiled in mines and quarries or ran laundries, restaurants, and other businesses.

Sizable Chinatowns
The earliest newcomers had initially traveled from Asia to participate in California's gold rush, which began in 1849. A decade-plus later, workers were recruited to lay track for the Transcontinental Railroad's California–Utah leg. Following the railroad's completion, many sought employment in the valley, laying the groundwork for what grew into sizable Chinatowns in Napa, St. Helena, and Calistoga (Rutherford contained a much smaller one).

Driven Out
Despite their contributions, long-simmering anti-Asian sentiment heated up in the 1880s, leading to many Chinese settlers being driven out of agriculture and the valley itself. Within a few years, newly arrived immigrants from Italy and other regions of southern Europe had filled the void.

4

Napa Valley CALISTOGA

pours its esteemed *méthode traditionnelle* sparkling wines. Author Robert Louis Stevenson was among Schram's early visitors. After the vintner's death in 1905, the winery closed and fell into disrepair, but in 1965 Jack and Jamie Davies purchased the 200-acre Schramsberg property and began restoring its buildings and caves. Chinese laborers dug some of the latter in the 1870s. In the 1990s, the family set about replanting the vineyard to Cabernet Sauvignon and other Bordeaux varietals for the Davies Vineyards label's still red wines. Tastings at Schramsberg can include pours of only sparkling wines, only still wines, or a combination of the two. All visits are by appointment. ⊠ *1400 Schramsberg Rd., Calistoga* ✛ *Off Hwy. 29* ☎ *707/942–2469, 800/877–3623* ⊕ *www.schramsberg.com* ⧉ *Tastings with cave tour from $80.*

Sharpsteen Museum of Calistoga History
HISTORY MUSEUM | Walt Disney animator Ben Sharpsteen, who retired to Calistoga, founded this old-school but compelling museum whose centerpiece is an intricate diorama depicting the Calistoga Hot Springs Resort during its 19th-century heyday. A restored cottage from the resort, moved to this site, sits next door to the museum but is entered through it. Other exhibits survey life in Calistoga through the decades and author Robert Louis Stevenson's time here in 1880. ⊠ *1311 Washington St., Calistoga* ✛ *At 1st St.* ☎ *707/942–5911* ⊕ *www.sharpsteenmuseum.org* ⧉ *$3.*

Sterling Vineyards
WINERY | **FAMILY** | An aerial tram whisks guests up a 300-foot hill to a white-washed Greek Mediterranean–style winery with sweeping Napa Valley views. Appointment-only Sterling, which

suffered severe damage during the 2020 wildfires, is expected to reopen in fall 2023 with a new tram and completely remodeled indoor and outdoor hospitality spaces. A self-guided tour allows guests to delve into the wine-making process. Or not. On a sunny day, the vistas south down the valley can be mighty distracting. Sterling, which released its first vintage in 1969, makes waves for its Cabernet Sauvignons like the top-of-the-line Iridium and another from Diamond Mountain; Chardonnay, a crowd-pleasing Malvasia Blanca, and sparkling wine are among the lighter bottlings. ■TIP➜ **For a more fulfilling visit, choose a tasting of upper-tier wines.** ⊠ *1111 Dunaweal La., Calistoga ✛ Off Hwy. 29* ☎ *707/942–3300, 800/726–6136* ⊕ *www.sterling-vineyards.com* ⌼ *Tastings from $45.*

★ Storybook Mountain Vineyards

WINERY | Tucked into a rock face in the Mayacamas range, this family-run winery established in 1976 occupies a picture-perfect site with rows of vines rising steeply in dramatic tiers. Zinfandel is king—there's even a dry Zin Gris rosé—but Viognier, Cabernet Sauvignon, and a Bordeaux blend are also in the mix. Visits, all by appointment, usually begin with a short walk up the hillside and a visit to the atmospheric aging caves, parts of which have the same rough-hewn look as they did when Chinese laborers dug them by hand in the late 1880s. Jerry Seps, who started Storybook with his wife, Sigrid, continues to make the wines, these days with their daughter, Colleen, whose husband, Rick Williams, handles marketing and sometimes leads tours. ⊠ *3835 Hwy. 128, Calistoga ✛ 4 miles northwest of town* ☎ *707/942–5310* ⊕ *www.storybookwines.com* ⌼ *Tastings $55* ⊙ *Closed Sun.*

Tamber Bey Vineyards

WINERY | Endurance riders Barry and Jennifer Waitte share their passion for horses and wine at their glam-rustic winery north of Calistoga. Their 22-acre Sundance Ranch remains a working equestrian facility, but the site has been revamped to include a state-of-the-art winery with separate fermenting tanks for grapes from Tamber Bey's vineyards in Yountville, Oakville, and elsewhere. The winemakers produce Chardonnay, Sauvignon Blanc, Grenache rosé, and Pinot Noir, but the showstoppers are several subtly powerful reds, including the flagship Oakville Estate Cabernet Sauvignon and a Yountville Merlot. The top-selling wine, Rabicano, is a Cabernet Sauvignon-heavy Bordeaux-style blend. Visits here require an appointment. ⊠ *1251 Tubbs La., Calistoga ✛ At Myrtledale Rd.* ☎ *707/942–2100* ⊕ *www. tamberbey.com* ⌼ *Tastings from $80.*

Tedeschi Family Winery

WINERY | Time-travel back to the days when the Napa Valley "lifestyle" revolved around a family rolling up its collective sleeves to grow grapes, make wines, and present them in a modest setting—these days on a patio between the crush pad and small estate vineyard. The first Tedeschi arrived in the valley in 1919 from Pisa, Italy, and the grandparents of the current winemaker, Mario, and general manager, his amiable brother Emilio, purchased the Calistoga property, then an orchard, in the 1950s. Mario makes the Estate Cabernet from an acre of grapes grown on-site, with fruit for Viognier, rosé of Valdigué, Malbec, Petite Sirah, and other wines from Napa Valley and Sonoma County sources. ■TIP➜ **An appointment to taste is required, but it's possible to make one same-day (just call ahead).** ⊠ *2779 Grant St., Napa ✛ At Greenwood Ave.* ☎ *707/501–0668* ⊕ *www.tedeschifamilywinery.com* ⌼ *Tastings from $35.*

★ Theorem Vineyards

WINERY | The sought-after consultant Thomas Rivers Brown oversees the collector-quality Cabernets of this winery on Diamond Mountain's northern slope. The Voir Dire Cabernet Sauvignon (one owner practices law), the luxury brand's layered and silky flagship, comes from the property's oldest vines. Younger plantings produce fruit for the friskier Hawk's Prey Cab and mellifluous Merlot, with Chardonnay, Sauvignon Blanc, and Syrah coming from a high-elevation estate in Sonoma County's Moon Mountain District. Catered bites that illustrate the wines' food-friendliness (and then some) accompany the wines at tastings, many held in a red replica barn with Mt. St. Helena views. Brown and team ply their craft inside a contemporary high-tech facility nearby. Two restored structures, one a schoolhouse, date to the 19th century. ■ TIP➔ **It's best to book visits a few days ahead.** ⊠ *255 Petrified Forest Rd., Calistoga ✛ 1¼ miles west of Hwy. 128* ☎ *707/942–4254* ⊕ *www.theoremvineyards.com* ⊡ *Tastings from $200.*

★ Tom Eddy Winery

WINERY | If you miss the driveway to Tom and Kerry Eddy's hillside slice of paradise, you'll soon find yourself in Sonoma County—their tree-studded 22-acre property, home to deer, wild turkeys, and winery dog Nala, is that far north. Tom, the winemaker, and Kerry, a sommelier and talented sculptor who hosts most of the tastings, pour their wines by appointment only. Except for the estate Kerry's Vineyard Cabernet Sauvignon, they're made from grapes sourced from as near as Calistoga and, in the case of the Sauvignon Blanc, as far away as New Zealand. A 1974 UC Davis graduate, Tom made his reputation crafting mountain Cabernets with structure and elegance. They're the winery's stars, but he also produces Chardonnay, Grenache Blanc, rosé of Pinot Noir, Pinot Noir, and Malbec. A visit here is enchanting. ⊠ *3870 Hwy. 128, Calistoga ✛ 4¼ miles north of downtown* ☎ *707/942–4267* ⊕ *tomeddywinery.com* ⊡ *Tastings from $125* ⊙ *Closed Sun.*

★ Venge Vineyards

WINERY | As the son of Nils Venge, the first winemaker to earn a 100-point score from the critic Robert Parker for a Napa Valley wine, Kirk Venge had a hard act to follow. Now a consultant to exclusive wineries himself, Kirk is an acknowledged master of fruit-forward but balanced Cabernet-heavy Bordeaux-style blends. At his casual ranch-house tasting room, flights that might start with Sauvignon Blanc, Chardonnay, Merlot, or Zinfandel set the stage for the Cabernet Sauvignon. With its views of the estate Bone Ash Vineyard and, west across the valley, Diamond Mountain, the ranch house's porch would make for a magical perch even if Venge's wines weren't treasures themselves. Tastings are by appointment only, with same-day visits unlikely. ⊠ *4708 Silverado Trail, Calistoga ✛ 1½ miles south of downtown, near Dunaweal La.* ☎ *707/942–9100* ⊕ *www. vengevineyards.com* ⊡ *Tastings from $65* ☞ *Reservations recommended 2–3 wks in advance for weekend visits.*

★ Vincent Arroyo Winery

WINERY | Fans of this down-home winery's flagship Petite Sirah snap it up so quickly that visitors to the plywood-paneled tasting room have to buy "futures" of wines still aging in barrels. The same holds true for the other small-lot wines. Vincent Arroyo, namesake original owner and winemaker, quit his mechanical engineering career in the 1970s to become a farmer, replacing a prune orchard with Petite Sirah and Cabernet Sauvignon, and these days Zinfandel, the winery's top sellers. Later came more acreage and other varietals, including Merlot, Tempranillo, Sangiovese, and Chardonnay—all dry-farmed. These days Vince's daughter, Adrian, and her husband, Matthew Moye (the current winemaker), own and run the winery. The presentation here, experienced by appointment only, is charmingly old-school, with Arroyo, Adrian, and Moye often on hand. ⊠ *2361 Greenwood Ave., Calistoga ✛ Off Hwy. 29* ☎ *707/942–6995* ⊕ *www.vincentarroyo.com* ⊡ *Tastings from $40.*

🍴 Restaurants

Cafe Sarafornia

$ | AMERICAN | Longtime upvalley restaurateurs run this down-home diner whose efficient chefs churn out comfort food with a touch more flair than the zingy Cal-hippie decor might lead you to expect. Huevos rancheros and other egg dishes top the breakfast (until 2:30 closing) menu along with pancakes, waffles, French toast, and vegetarian and corned-beef hash; burgers (beef, fish, or black bean), tuna melts, sandwiches, wraps, and several salads headline at lunch, with sides that include crispy-golden onion rings. **Known for:** huge portions; create-your-own omelets and egg scrambles; cakes and deep-dish pies. $ *Average main: $14* ✉ *1413 Lincoln Ave., Calistoga* ✛ *At Washington St.* ☎ *707/942–0555* ⊕ *cafesarafornia.com* ☾ *No dinner.*

Calistoga Inn Restaurant & Brewery

$$$ | AMERICAN | When the weather's nice, the inn's outdoor patio and beer garden edging the Napa River are swell places to hang out and sip some microbrews. Among the beer-friendly dishes, the garlic-crusted calamari appetizer and the country paella entrée stand out, along with several pizzas, the burger topped with Tillamook cheddar, and (for lunch) the Reuben with ale-braised corned beef. **Known for:** comfort food; kid-friendly patio; ales and beers. $ *Average main: $33* ✉ *1250 Lincoln Ave., Calistoga* ✛ *At Cedar St.* ☎ *707/942–4101* ⊕ *www.calistogainn.com.*

Evangeline

$$$ | AMERICAN | The gas-lamp-style lighting fixtures, charcoal-black hues, and bistro cuisine at Evangeline evoke old New Orleans with a California twist. The chefs put a jaunty spin on dishes that might include shrimp étouffée, duck confit, or steak *frites*; the elaborate weekend brunch, with *pamplemousse* (grapefruit) mimosas an acerbic intro to everything from raw oysters, avocado toast, and smoked salmon to shrimp and grits and prosciutto Benedict, is an upvalley favorite. **Known for:** outdoor courtyard; palate-cleansing Sazeracs; gumbo ya-ya and addictive fried pickles. $ *Average main: $29* ✉ *1226 Washington St., Calistoga* ✛ *Near Lincoln Ave.* ☎ *707/341–3131* ⊕ *www.evangelinenapa.com* ☾ *No lunch weekdays.*

Fleetwood Calistoga

$$$ | AMERICAN | Built-in wood-fired ovens anchor the open kitchen at this fun-casual spot with tile floors and bare light bulbs strung over the tables. Pizzas and pasta dishes made from farm-fresh ingredients dominate the menu, but straight-forward fish, chicken, and steak entrées appear as well. **Known for:** full bar's happy hour; wood-fired pizzas; Fleetwood burger with Gruyère. $ *Average main: $27* ✉ *Calistoga Motor Lodge, 1880 Lincoln Ave., Calistoga* ✛ *Near Silverado Trail* ☎ *707/709–4410* ⊕ *www.fleetwoodcalistoga.com* ☾ *No lunch weekdays.*

House of Better

$$ | SOUTHWESTERN | The chef at this casual, family-friendly, mostly open-air spa restaurant promotes wellness via Southwest-inspired "booster food" like a quinoa-and-kale salad and bowls containing sautéed kale, red quinoa, green chilies, and avocado. To reel in the wary, House of Better hedges its bet with cheesy flatbreads and nicely spiced fish tacos, going full carnivore with a green-chili cheeseburger and pepper steak add-ons to nachos, enchiladas, and tacos. **Known for:** green-chili apple pie; hearty soups and stews; casual atmosphere. $ *Average main: $18* ✉ *Dr. Wilkinson's Backyard Resort & Mineral Springs, 1507 Lincoln Ave., Calistoga* ✛ *At Fair Way* ☎ *707/942–6257* ⊕ *www.houseofbetter.com.*

★ Lovina

$$$$ | MODERN AMERICAN | A vintage-style neon sign outside this bungalow restaurant announces "Great Food," and the chefs deliver with well-plated dishes

served in two buildings, one a Craftsman gem, or on street-side patios that are especially festive during weekend brunch. The offerings at women-owned and-run Lovina change often, but a recent menu's roasted Cornish hen, lobster and prawn risotto, and seared wild halibut with gnocchi and wild mushrooms are typical of the imaginative cuisine. **Known for:** no-tipping policy; varied brunch menu; Wine Wednesdays no corkage fee and discounts on wine list. [$] *Average main: $45* ✉ *1107 Cedar St., Calistoga* ✣ *At Lincoln Ave.* ☎ *707/942–6500* 🌐 *www.lovinacalistoga.com* 🕐 *No lunch Mon.–Wed. and Fri.*

Sam's Social Club

$$$ | **AMERICAN** | Tourists, locals, and spa guests—some of the latter in bathrobes after treatments—assemble inside this casual resort restaurant or on its extensive patio for breakfast, lunch, bar snacks, or dinner. Lunch options include thin-crust pizzas, sandwiches, a cheddar burger, and entrées such as chicken paillard, with the burger reappearing for dinner along with fish, steak, the house-made pasta of the day, and similar fare. **Known for:** weekend slow-roasted prime rib; cocktail-friendly starters; hearty salads. [$] *Average main: $36* ✉ *Indian Springs Resort and Spa, 1712 Lincoln Ave., Calistoga* ✣ *At Wappo Ave.* ☎ *707/942–4969* 🌐 *www.samssocialclub.com.*

★ Solbar

$$$$ | **AMERICAN** | The restaurant at Solage attracts the resort's clientele, upvalley locals, and guests of nearby lodgings for sophisticated farm-to-table cuisine served in the high-ceilinged dining area or alfresco on a sprawling patio warmed by shapely heaters and a mesmerizing fire pit. Dishes on the lighter side might include house-made pasta or sake-marinated fish, with duck breast, crispy pork, or a tomahawk steak among the heartier options. **Known for:** artisanal cocktails; festive patio; lunchtime salads and sandwiches. [$] *Average main: $48* ✉ *Solage, 755 Silverado Trail, Calistoga* ✣ *At Rosedale Rd.* ☎ *707/226–0860* 🌐 *aubergeresorts.com/solage/dine.*

Sushi Mambo

$$ | **JAPANESE** | Preparations are traditional and unconventional at this sushi and country-Japanese restaurant whose owner vows diners will not leave hungry. The menu's diversity might daunt you into sticking to the familiar, but don't overlook offbeat items like the Fungus Among Us (tempura mushrooms stuffed with spicy tuna), Batman Roll (eel and cream cheese), and Hottie (deep-fried panko shrimp with spicy tuna). **Known for:** street-side patio; offbeat items; vegetarian options. [$] *Average main: $23* ✉ *1631 Lincoln Ave., Calistoga* ✣ *At Wappo Ave.* ☎ *707/942–4699* 🌐 *sushimambo.com* 🕐 *Closed Sun.*

Truss

$$$ | **MODERN AMERICAN** | Shades of brown and beige predominate in the Four Seasons resort's classy-casual indoor-outdoor "living room," which serves upmarket casual fare, and the adjacent Auro for an elaborate multicourse tasting menu. The kitchen for both restaurants, visible behind glass walls, turns out seasonally oriented cuisine overseen by Mexico City–born, Napa-raised Rogelio Garcia, previously of The French Laundry and Bravo's *Top Chef* cable show. **Known for:** Calistoga Palisades views; bar bites and specialty cocktails; artistry of Auro flavors and presentation. [$] *Average main: $32* ✉ *Four Seasons Napa Valley, 400 Silverado Trail N, Calistoga* ✣ *At Rosedale Rd.* ☎ *707/709–2100* 🌐 *www.trussrestaurantandbar.com* 🕐 *No lunch at Auro.*

Coffee and Quick Bites

Buster's Southern BarBeQue & Bakery

$$ | **BARBECUE** | A roadside stand at the west end of Calistoga's downtown, Buster's serves Louisiana-style barbecue basics, sweet-potato pies, and corn bread muffins. Local-fave sandwiches

Embrace Calistoga's many repeat visitors appreciate the attentive service and full breakfasts.

at lunch (best time to come) include the tri-tip, spicy hot links, and pulled pork, with tri-tip and pork or beef ribs the hits at dinner (which comes early at 6 or 7 in winter, 7 or 8 in summer). **Known for:** mild and searing hot sauces; slaw, baked beans, and other sides; Sunday jazz and blues concerts spring–fall. $ *Average main: $17* ✉ *1207 Foothill Blvd./Hwy. 29, Calistoga* ✛ *At Lincoln Ave.* ☎ *707/942–5605* ⊕ *www.busterssouthernbbq.com.*

★ Calistoga Depot

$$ | **AMERICAN** | Calistoga's flashy 19th-century entrepreneur Sam Brannan built the depot in 1868 to receive spa patrons, but it was looking careworn until his 21st-century equivalent, Wine Country vintner-showman Jean-Charles Boisset, restored the wood-frame building and opened a combination gourmet grocery, café, wine shop, distillery, and wine and beer garden. As at Boisset's historic Oakville Grocery, salads, artisanal sandwiches, and wood-fired pizzas headline. **Known for:** wine and craft-beer selection; all-day breakfast; patio seating.

$ *Average main: $17* ✉ *1458 Lincoln Ave., Calistoga* ✛ *At Fair Way* ☎ *707/963–6925* ⊕ *calistogadepot.com* ◷ *No dinner.*

Hotels

★ Brannan Cottage Inn

$$$ | **B&B/INN** | Stained oak floors, wainscoting, and retro bathroom fixtures recall Victorian times at this small inn whose centerpiece is an 1860s cottage from Calistoga's original spa era. **Pros:** short walk from downtown; helpful staff; Sam's General Store for coffee and light meals. **Cons:** noise from neighbors can be heard in some rooms; showers but no bathtubs in some rooms; lacks pool and other amenities of larger properties. $ *Rooms from: $329* ✉ *109 Wappo Ave., Calistoga* ✛ *At Lincoln Ave.* ☎ *707/942–4200* ⊕ *www.brannancottageinn.com* ⇗ *6 rooms* ⏐⊙⏐ *Free Breakfast.*

Bungalows at Calistoga

$$$ | **HOUSE** | These spacious (584–889-square-foot) contemporary bungalows provide guests with an

upscale, up-to-date home away from home, with fireplaces, outdoor patios and dining areas, wireless and streaming-service connectivity, fully equipped kitchens, and washers and dryers. **Pros:** contemporary style; five-minute walk to downtown Calistoga; rates include up to four guests. **Cons:** lacks room service and other hotel amenities; no pool or fitness center; two-night minimum. Ⓢ *Rooms from: $375* ✉ *207 Wappo Ave., Calistoga* ☏ *707/341–6544* ⊕ *thebungalowsatcalistoga.com* ⤳ *3 bungalows* ⟡ *No Meals.*

Calistoga Motor Lodge and Spa
$$$ | **MOTEL** | **FAMILY** | About half the lodge's rooms, decorated in mid-century modern style, date to its 1947 origins as a roadside motel, with the newer remaining ones (the most recent scheduled for completion by late summer 2023) edging this quasi resort into budget-boutique territory. **Pros:** 10-minute walk to downtown shops and restaurants; geothermal mineral pools; above-average restaurant and spa. **Cons:** some streetside rooms pick up traffic noise (ask for a room in back); best rooms pricey in high season; some rooms could use a refresh. Ⓢ *Rooms from: $305* ✉ *1880 Lincoln Ave., Calistoga* ☏ *707/942–0991* ⊕ *www.calistogamotorlodgeandspa.com* ⤳ *98 rooms* ⟡ *No Meals.*

Dr. Wilkinson's Backyard Resort & Mineral Springs
$$$ | **HOTEL** | In 2022, new owners completed the transformation of this Calistoga mainstay into a playfully retro mid-century-style resort with all the mod cons. **Pros:** easy walk to shops, restaurants, and tasting rooms; twin bunks in family rooms; heated mineral pools. **Cons:** some rooms pick up street noise; no room service; kitschy aesthetic may not work for some guests. Ⓢ *Rooms from: $343* ✉ *1507 Lincoln Ave., Calistoga* ☏ *707/942–4102* ⊕ *www.drwilkinson.com* ⤳ *50 rooms* ⟡ *No Meals.*

★ Embrace Calistoga
$$$ | **B&B/INN** | Extravagant hospitality defines the Napa Valley's luxury properties, but Embrace Calistoga takes the prize in the "small lodging" category. **Pros:** attentive service; brunch-style breakfasts; restaurants, tasting rooms, and shopping within walking distance. **Cons:** light hum of street traffic; no pool or spa; two-night minimum some weekends. Ⓢ *Rooms from: $369* ✉ *1139 Lincoln Ave., Calistoga* ☏ *707/942–9797* ⊕ *embracecalistoga.com* ⤳ *5 rooms* ⟡ *Free Breakfast.*

Four Seasons Resort and Residences Napa Valley
$$$$ | **RESORT** | Opened in 2021, this suave luxury resort entices high rollers with farmhouse-eclectic interiors and amenities that include a spa, a destination restaurant, two pools, 7-plus acres of vines, and a working winery. **Pros:** estate villa and one-bedroom suites offer maximum luxury and privacy; casual dining at indoor-outdoor Truss and five-course tasting menu at Auro; on-site vineyard and winery. **Cons:** expensive year-round; casual-chic yet may feel too formal for some guests; minimum weekend stay requirement. Ⓢ *Rooms from: $1491* ✉ *400 Silverado Trail N, Calistoga* ☏ *707/709–2100, 800/819–5053 for reservations* ⊕ *www.fourseasons.com/napavalley* ⤳ *83 rooms* ⟡ *No Meals.*

★ Francis House
$$$$ | **B&B/INN** | Built in 1886 of locally quarried tufa, abandoned for half a century but gloriously restored, the Second Empire–style Francis House is now a five-room luxury inn. **Pros:** ultrachic style evokes the past but feels utterly contemporary; winner of prestigious historic-preservation award; pool and lawn area in back. **Cons:** pricey for Calistoga (but less costly than the plushest resorts); more for romantic getaways than family adventures; weekend minimum-stay requirement. Ⓢ *Rooms from: $654* ✉ *1403 Myrtle St., Calistoga*

☎ 707/341–3536 🌐 thefrancishouse.com 🛏 5 rooms 🍴 Free Breakfast.

Indian Springs Calistoga

$$$ | RESORT | Palm-studded Indian Springs—operating as a spa since 1862—ably splits the difference between laid-back and chic in accommodations that include lodge rooms, suites, cottages, stand-alone bungalows, and two houses. **Pros:** sprawling grounds with outdoor seating areas; on-site Sam's Social Club restaurant; enormous mineral pool. **Cons:** lodge rooms are small; many rooms have showers but no tubs; two-night minimum on weekends (three with Monday holiday). *[$] Rooms from: $309 ✉ 1712 Lincoln Ave., Calistoga ☎ 707/709–8139 🌐 www.indianspringscalistoga.com 🛏 113 rooms 🍴 No Meals.*

Meadowlark Country House & Resort

$$$$ | B&B/INN | Two charming European gents run this informal yet sophisticated inn on 20 wooded acres 1½ miles north of downtown. **Pros:** social atmosphere during tasty full breakfasts; many repeat customers; per website welcomes "hetero, gay, bi, or any other lifestyle." **Cons:** clothing-optional pool policy isn't for everyone; adults-only (18-plus) policy; maximum occupancy in most rooms is two. *[$] Rooms from: $410 ✉ 601 Petrified Forest Rd., Calistoga ☎ 707/942–5651 🌐 www.meadowlarkinn.com 🛏 10 rooms 🍴 Free Breakfast.*

★ Solage

$$$$ | RESORT | The aesthetic at this 22-acre property where health and wellness are priorities is Napa Valley barn meets San Francisco loft: guest rooms have high ceilings, sleek contemporary furniture, all-natural fabrics in soothingly muted colors, and an outdoor patio. **Pros:** great service; complimentary bikes; separate pools for kids and adults. **Cons:** scene might not suit everyone; longish walk from some lodgings to spa and fitness center; expensive in season. *[$] Rooms from: $749 ✉ 755 Silverado Trail, Calistoga ☎ 866/942–7442, 707/226–0800 🌐 www.solagecalistoga.com 🛏 89 rooms 🍴 No Meals.*

Activities

Indian Springs Spa

SPAS | Even before Sam Brannan constructed a spa on this site in the 1860s, the Wappo Indians built sweat lodges over its thermal geysers. Treatments include a Calistoga-classic, pure volcanic-ash mud bath followed by a mineral bath and an infrared sauna, after which clients are wrapped in a flannel blanket for a 15-minute cool-down session or until called for a massage if they've booked one. Body scrubs—one with sea salt, the other with sugar—and facials are also popular. Before or following a treatment, guests unwind at the serene Buddha Pool, fed by one of the property's four geysers. *✉ 1712 Lincoln Ave., Calistoga ✥ At Wappo Ave. ☎ 707/709–8139 🌐 indianspringscalistoga.com/spa-overview 🎫 Treatments from $115.*

★ Spa Solage

SPAS | This 20,000-square-foot eco-conscious spa reinvented the traditional Calistoga mud-and-mineral-water regimen with the hour-long "Mudslide." The three-part treatment includes a mud body mask applied in a heated lounge, a soak in a thermal bath, and a power nap in a sound-vibration chair. The mud here, less gloppy than at other resorts, is a mix of clay, volcanic ash, and essential oils. Massage and other traditional services are available, along with hydration therapy, infrared saunas for exfoliation and relaxation, and wellness sessions. *✉ 755 Silverado Trail, Calistoga ✥ At Rosedale Rd. ☎ 855/790–6023 🌐 aubergeresorts.com/solage/wellness/spa 🎫 Treatments from $200.*

SONOMA VALLEY AND PETALUMA

Updated by
Daniel Mangin

◉ Sights	🍴 Restaurants	🛏 Hotels	🛍 Shopping	🍸 Nightlife
★★★★★	★★★★☆	★★★★☆	★★★☆☆	★★★☆☆

WELCOME TO SONOMA VALLEY AND PETALUMA

TOP REASONS TO GO

★ **California and wine history:** Sonoma's mission and nearby sites shine a light on California's history; at Buena Vista you can explore the wine industry's roots.

★ **Literary trails:** Work off the wine and fine cuisine—and just enjoy the scenery—while hiking the trails of Jack London State Park, which contains the ruins of London's Wolf House.

★ **Peaceful Glen Ellen:** As writers from Jack London to M. F. K. Fisher discovered, peaceful Glen Ellen is a good place to decompress and tap into one's creativity. (Though Hunter S. Thompson found it too sedate.)

★ **Seated Pinot Noir tastings:** Blue Farm, Sojourn, the Donum Estate, and other wineries host seated tastings of high-quality Pinots from Los Carneros and beyond.

★ **Wineries with a view:** The views from the outdoor tasting spaces at McEvoy Ranch, Ram's Gate, and Kunde encourage lingering over a glass of your favorite varietal.

1 Sonoma. The Wine Country's oldest town has it all: fine dining, historical sites, and wineries from down-home to high style. Much of the activity takes place around Sonoma Plaza, where in 1846 some American settlers declared independence from Mexico and established the California Republic. The republic lasted only a month, but during the next decade, Count Agoston Haraszthy laid the foundation for modern California wine making.

2 Glen Ellen. Sonoma Creek snakes through Glen Ellen's tiny "downtown." The lodgings here are small, and the town, home to Jack London State Park, has retained its rural character.

3 Kenwood. St. Francis and a few other name wineries straddle Highway 12 in Kenwood, whose vague center lies about 5 miles north of Glen Ellen.

4 Petaluma. This southern Sonoma County town's agricultural roots stretch back to the mid-1830s; the approval of the Petaluma Gap AVA recognized the area's potential for grape growing, especially Pinot Noir and Chardonnay.

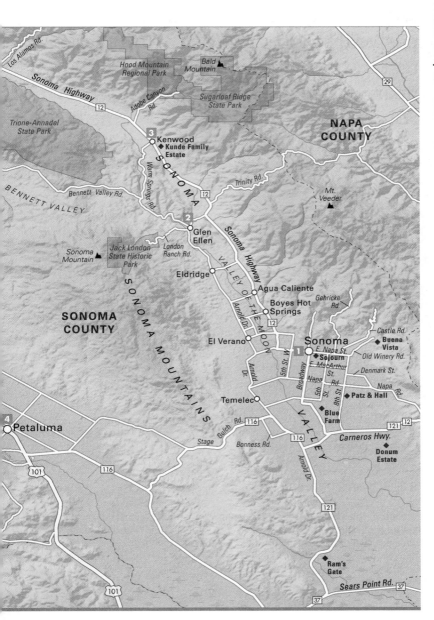

Los Alamos Rd.

Sonoma Highway

12

Trione-Annadel
State Park

Hood Mountain
Regional Park

Bald
Mountain

Sugarloaf Ridge
State Park

29

**NAPA
COUNTY**

Adobe Canyon Rd.

3 Kenwood
◆ **Kunde Family
Estate**

S O N O M A

12

Trinity Rd.

Mt.
Veeder

BENNETT VALLEY

Bennett Valley Rd.

Warm Springs Rd.

2 Glen
Ellen

Sonoma
Mountain

Jack London
State Historic
Park

London
Ranch Rd.

Sonoma Highway

VALLEY OF THE MOON

Eldridge

Agua Caliente

Gehricke Rd.

Boyes Hot
Springs

12

**SONOMA
COUNTY**

S O N O M A   M O U N T A I N S

Arnold Dr.

El Verano

5th St. W.

Sonoma
E. Napa St.
◆ **Sojourn**
E. MacArthur St.

1

Castle Rd.
◆ **Buena
Vista**
Old Winery Rd.

Denmark St.

Broadway

5th St. E.

8th St.

Napa Rd.

◆ **Patz & Hall**

Temelec

Arnold Dr.

VALLEY

**Blue
Farm**

121 **12**

Stage Gulch Rd.

116

Bonness Rd.

116

Carneros Hwy.

◆ **Donum
Estate**

4 Petaluma

101

116

Arnold Dr.

121

◆ **Ram's
Gate**

101

37

Sears Point Rd. **37**

The birthplace of modern California wine making, the Sonoma Valley seduces with its unpretentious attitude and pastoral landscape. Tasting rooms, restaurants, and historical sites abound near Sonoma Plaza. Beyond downtown Sonoma, wineries and attractions fan out along gently winding roads.

Sonoma County's half of the Carneros District lies within Sonoma Valley, whose other towns of note include Glen Ellen and Kenwood. To Sonoma Valley's west, bustling Petaluma has come into its own as a Wine Country destination. A walkable downtown, burgeoning dining scene, and relatively inexpensive lodgings add to its allure.

Sonoma Valley tasting rooms are often less crowded than those in Napa or northern Sonoma County, especially midweek, and the vibe here, though sophisticated, is less sceney. That's not to suggest that the Sonoma Valley is undiscovered territory. On the contrary, along Highway 12, the main corridor through the Sonoma Valley, you'll spot classy inns, restaurants, and spas in addition to wineries. In high season Glen Ellen and Kenwood are filled with well-heeled wine buffs, and the best restaurants can be crowded.

The historic Sonoma Valley towns offer glimpses of the past. Sonoma, with its tree-filled central plaza, is rich with 19th-century buildings. Two names pop up on many plaques affixed to them: General Mariano Guadalupe Vallejo, who in the 1830s and 1840s was Mexico's highest-ranking military officer in these parts, and Count Agoston Haraszthy, who opened Buena Vista Winery in 1857. Glen Ellen, meanwhile, has a special connection with the author Jack London. Kenwood claims a more recent distinction: in 1999 a winery here was the first in Sonoma County to earn a wine of the year award from *Wine Spectator* magazine, one of several signs that Sonoma Valley wine making had come of age.

Bounded by the Mayacamas Mountains on the east and Sonoma Mountain on the west, this scenic valley extends north from San Pablo Bay nearly 20 miles to the eastern outskirts of Santa Rosa. The varied terrain, soils, and climate—cooler in the south because of the bay influence and hotter toward the north—allow grape growers to raise cool-weather varietals such as Chardonnay and Pinot Noir as well as Cabernet Sauvignon and other heat-seeking grapes.

In 1836 General Vallejo established the Rancho de Petaluma as an agricultural concern. The oldest surviving structure, the Petaluma Adobe, is now a state park. The surrounding land is still primarily used for farming, some of it grapes.

MAJOR REGIONS

The Sonoma Valley lies north of San Pablo Bay, an extension of the larger San Francisco Bay. The largest town, Sonoma, about 41 miles north of San Francisco's Golden Gate Bridge, is bisected by Highway 12, which continues north to Glen Ellen and Kenwood. About 41,000 people live in the Sonoma Valley: 11,000 in Sonoma proper, with another 29,000 or so within the town's orbit or in other unincorporated areas; Glen Ellen and Kenwood have about 1,000 residents each. West of the Sonoma Valley in southern Sonoma County—a straight shot north from the Golden Gate Bridge—U.S. 101 bisects Petaluma. With about 60,000 residents, Petaluma is the county's second-largest city after Santa Rosa.

Planning

Getting Here and Around

BUS

Sonoma Transit buses provide service within Sonoma and Petaluma and to Glen Ellen and Kenwood.

⇨ See the Bus section in the Travel Smart chapter for more information about arriving by bus. For local service, see the Bus sections for this chapter's individual towns.

CAR

Traveling by car is the easiest way to tour the Sonoma Valley. Highway 12, also called the Sonoma Highway, is the main thoroughfare through the valley, running north–south through Sonoma, Glen Ellen, and Kenwood into Santa Rosa. Arnold Drive heads north from Highway 121 in southern Sonoma to Glen Ellen. On the north side of town, it reconnects with (and dead-ends at) Highway 12. A turn left (north) leads to Kenwood. You can

access Petaluma, which lies southwest of Sonoma, off U.S. 101.

From San Francisco: To get to the Sonoma Valley from San Francisco, travel north on U.S. 101 to the Highway 37 turnoff (Exit 460A), driving east for about 7 miles to Highway 121, the main route through the Carneros District. Highway 12 leads north from Highway 121 into the town of Sonoma. For Petaluma, continue on U.S. 101 to Kastania Road (Exit 472A), turn right and then quickly left, and follow signs on Petaluma Boulevard South to downtown.

From the Napa Valley: To reach the Sonoma Valley from Napa, turn west off Highway 29 onto Highway 121/12 and drive north on Highway 12 when it splits off from Highway 121. For Petaluma, turn west off Highway 12 onto Watmaugh Road 2 miles before Sonoma Plaza and follow Highway 116 west; for Sonoma, continue north on Highway 12, by this time signed as Broadway. A more adventurous route (not for the carsick) leads west over the Mayacamas range on highly scenic—but slow and winding—Oakville Grade Road, which turns into Trinity Road before it reaches Highway 12 in Glen Ellen. If coming to the Sonoma Valley from Calistoga, head west from Highway 128 on Petrified Forest Road and Calistoga Road to Highway 12 in Santa Rosa. From there, head south into the valley.

Avoiding confusion: In the Carneros District, Highway 121 is signposted as Carneros Highway, Sonoma Highway (the parts coinciding with Highway 12), and Arnold Drive. It's all the same road.

Restaurants

When *Esquire* magazine named Animo one of the nation's top new restaurants of 2022, it joined Cafe La Haye, the Girl and the Fig, and LaSalette as a place to experience complex cuisine emphasizing locally produced meat, fish, cheese, vegetables, and fruit. Glen Ellen Star is its town's must-do, but you can't go wrong at any of the fine-dining restaurants here. In Kenwood, Salt & Stone serves bistro favorites; New Orleans inspires Tips Roadside's menu. Petaluma's restaurant scene is centered on downtown. Central Market for Cal-Med is a longtime star, with Table Culture Provisions (modern American) a more recent critical darling.

⇨ *Restaurant prices are the average cost of a main course at dinner, or if dinner isn't served, at lunch. Restaurant reviews have been shortened. For full information, visit Fodors.com.*

Hotels

Sonoma has the valley's most varied accommodations, with motels and small inns, vacation condos, and boutique hotels. Small inns are the norm in Glen Ellen and Kenwood. Spa lovers have several high-end choices at either end of the valley, among them the large and splashy Fairmont Sonoma Mission Inn & Spa in Sonoma and the Mediterranean-style Kenwood Inn and Spa in Kenwood. Chain motels predominate in Petaluma, though the Hampton Inn is inside a former silk mill.

For weekend stays it's wise to book ahead from late May through October. Most small lodgings require a two-night minimum stay on weekends at this time, three if Monday is a holiday.

⇨ *Hotel prices are the lowest cost of a standard double room in high season. Hotel reviews have been shortened. For full information, visit Fodors.com.*

What It Costs in U.S. Dollars			
$	$$	$$$	$$$$
RESTAURANTS			
under $17	$17–$26	$27–$36	over $36
HOTELS			
under $201	$201–$300	$301–$400	over $400

Planning Your Time

You can hit Sonoma Valley's highlights in a day or two—a half or a full day exploring western Carneros District wineries and some in Sonoma proper, and the same amount of time to check out Glen Ellen and Kenwood. Traffic usually isn't an issue, except on Highway 12 north of Sonoma Plaza and the intersection of Highways 116 and 121 during the morning and afternoon commutes. It takes at least half a day to get to know Petaluma.

Many valley wineries receive visitors by appointment only. On weekdays at some, you may be able to reserve a space on short notice, but for weekend visits, especially during the summer and early fall, booking ahead is essential even when food pairings (which wineries need time to plan for) are not involved.

Visitor Information

CONTACTS Sonoma Valley Visitors Bureau. ✉ *Sonoma Plaza, 453 1st St. E, Sonoma* ☏ *707/996–1090* ⊕ *www.sonomavalley. com.*

When to Go

The best time to visit the Sonoma Valley is between late spring and early fall, when the weather is warm and wineries bustle with activity. September and October, when grape harvesting and crushing are in full swing, are the busiest

Top Tastings

Setting

Blue Farm Wines, Sonoma. A few miles south of Sonoma Plaza, Chardonnay and Pinot Noir winegrower Anne Moller-Racke's idyllic 13-acre estate, complete with rose garden and aging pepper tree, recalls old Sonoma.

Hanzell Vineyards, Sonoma. From a hillside perch a few miles north of Sonoma Plaza, guests here enjoy vast Sonoma Valley views while sipping the Chardonnays and Pinot Noirs of this pioneering winery.

The Donum Estate, Sonoma. Known for Pinot Noirs displaying both power and elegance, Donum pours its wines in a hilltop tasting room whose views include museum-quality outdoor sculptures.

McEvoy Ranch, Petaluma. The bucolic ranch's Taste of the Season—a wine flight (Chardonnay, Pinot Noir, Syrah, others) served with artisanal cheeses, charcuterie, and seasonal edibles—unfolds on a pond's-edge flagstone patio.

History

Bedrock Wine Co., Sonoma. Zinfandel and other varietals grown in heritage vineyards are Bedrock's passion. A famous Civil War general once owned Bedrock's estate vineyard; the wines are poured a few miles away at his former in-town dwelling.

Kunde Family Winery, Kenwood. At tastings that might take place in the caves or on a valley-floor patio or hillside with panoramic views, you'll learn all about the family that established this now 1,850-acre ranch in 1904.

Buena Vista Winery, Sonoma. The restoration of a 19th-century wine-making structure revived interest in Sonoma's oldest winery, founded in 1857.

Food Pairing

St. Francis Winery, Kenwood. The executive chef's five petite plates pair well with this famous winery's Zins, Cabs, and other wines.

Three Sticks Wines, Sonoma. Well-conceived pairings—offered year-round in a restored 1842 adobe—show the versatility of Chardonnay and Pinot Noir. Seasonal Chardonnay-only pairings include one with caviar and another with oysters.

Just Plain Fun

Winery Sixteen 600 Tasting House, Sonoma. A hippie sensibility infuses the bungalow showcasing serious wines from grapes farmed by legendary vineyardist Phil Coturri. Guests choose which rock or jazz vinyl they'd like to accompany well-balanced whites and mostly reds.

months. At this time—and on all summer weekends—lodging prices tend to be at their highest. Tasting rooms throughout the Sonoma Valley are generally not too crowded during the week, even in high season, except perhaps on holiday Mondays.

Appellations

Although Sonoma *County* is a vast growing region that encompasses several different appellations, the much smaller Sonoma *Valley*, at the southern end of Sonoma County, is comparatively compact. It consists mainly of the **Sonoma Valley AVA,** which stretches northwest from San Pablo Bay toward Santa Rosa. The weather and soils here are unusually diverse. Pinot Noir and Chardonnay vineyards are most likely to be found in the AVA's southernmost parts, the sections cooled by fog from San Pablo Bay. (This part of the Sonoma Valley AVA overlaps with the Sonoma County portions of **Los Carneros AVA.**) Zinfandel, Cabernet Sauvignon, and Sauvignon Blanc are more plentiful farther north, near Glen Ellen and Kenwood, both of which in summer tend to be a few degrees warmer than the southern Sonoma Valley.

The **Sonoma Mountain AVA** rises west of Glen Ellen on the Sonoma Valley AVA's western border. Benefiting from a sunny location and rocky soil, the vineyards here produce deep-rooted vines and intensely flavored grapes that are made into complex red wines, often Cabernet Sauvignon. Opposite Sonoma Mountain southeast across the Sonoma Valley lies the **Moon Mountain District Sonoma County AVA.** On the Mayacamas range's western slopes, this sliver due west of the Napa Valley's Mt. Veeder subappellation contains some of California's oldest Zinfandel and Cabernet Sauvignon vines. Steep terrain and rocky soils result in smaller berries relative to valley-floor vines, and the higher skin-to-juice ratio yields intense flavor.

Portions of the **Sonoma Coast AVA** overlap Los Carneros and the Sonoma Valley. The tiny **Bennett Valley AVA,** also part of the Sonoma Valley AVA, falls within the city of Santa Rosa (⇨ *See Chapter 6*). West of the Sonoma Valley AVA is the **Petaluma Gap AVA,** whose name references a break in the Coast Range that permits cooling Pacific Ocean fog and wind to flow through. Except for a wee bit that edges into Marin County, this subappellation lies within the Sonoma Coast AVA.

Sonoma

14 miles west of Napa; 45 miles northeast of San Francisco.

One of the few towns in the valley with multiple attractions unrelated to food and wine, Sonoma has plenty to keep you busy for a couple of hours before you head out to the wineries. And you needn't leave town to taste wine: about three dozen tasting rooms do business on or near Sonoma Plaza.

The valley's cultural center, Sonoma, founded in 1835 when California was still part of Mexico, is built around tree-filled Sonoma Plaza. If you arrive from the south, on Broadway (Highway 12), you'll be retracing the last stretch of what long ago was California's most important road—El Camino Real, or "the royal road," the only overland route through the state. During California's Spanish and Mexican periods, it ran past all of the state's 21 missions, beginning at San Diego de Alcalá (1769) and ending at Mission San Francisco Solano (1823). This last mission still sits in the center of Sonoma.

GETTING HERE AND AROUND

Highway 12 from the south (San Francisco) or north (Santa Rosa) is the main route into Sonoma. North from Highway 121 to Sonoma Plaza the road is also called Broadway. There are two- and three-hour unmetered parking spaces around the plaza, and free all-day parking can be found a block or two off the plaza. Once you've parked, a pleasant stroll takes you past many of the town's restaurants, shops, and tasting rooms. High-profile and boutique wineries can be found a mile or so east; arrow-shape signs on East Spain Street and East Napa Street will direct you.

Sonoma Transit buses connect Sonoma with other Sonoma County towns.

Wine-Making Pioneer

Born in Hungary, Count Agoston Haraszthy—though of his native land's aristocracy, his noble title was self-awarded—arrived in Sonoma in 1857 and set out to make fine wine commercially. He planted European vinifera varietals rather than mission grapes (varietals brought to the Americas by Spanish missionaries) and founded Buena Vista Winery the year he arrived. Bucking custom, Haraszthy grew grapes on dry hillsides instead of in the wetter lowlands, his accomplishment demonstrating that Sonoma's climate was sufficiently moist to sustain vines without irrigation.

Adaptable Zinfandel
Despite producing inferior wines, the prolific mission grapes were preferred by California growers over better varieties of French, German, and Italian vinifera grapes through the 1860s and into the 1870s. But Haraszthy's success had begun to make an impression. A new red-wine grape, Zinfandel, was becoming popular because it made excellent Claret (as good red wine was then called) and adapted to the area's climate.

Balance Lost
By this time, however, Haraszthy had disappeared, literally, from the scene. After a business setback during the 1860s, the count lost control of Buena Vista and ventured to Nicaragua to restore his fortune in the sugar and rum industries. While crossing a stream infested with alligators, the count lost his balance and plunged into the water below. The body of modern California wine making's first promoter and pioneer was never recovered.

◉ Sights

SIGHTS IN DOWNTOWN SONOMA

Bedrock Wine Co.

WINERY | Zinfandel and other varietals grown in heritage vineyards throughout California are the focus of Bedrock, a young winery whose backstory involves several historical figures. Tastings take place in a home east of Sonoma Plaza owned in the 1850s by General Joseph Hooker. General William Tecumseh Sherman was his partner in the vineyard a few miles away (a spat over it affected their Civil War interactions); the next owner, newspaper magnate William Randolph Hearst's father, George, replanted it in the late 1880s. Some Hearst vines still produce grapes, whose current owner-winemaker, Morgan Twain-Peterson, learned about Zinfandel from his dad, Ravenswood founder Joel Peterson.

Twain-Peterson's bottlings, many of them field blends containing multiple varietals grown and fermented together, are as richly textured as his winery's prehistory. ⊠ *General Joseph Hooker House, 414 1st St. E, Sonoma* ⚓ *Near E. Spain St.* ☎ *707/343–1478* ⊕ *www.bedrockwineco. com* 🍷 *Tastings from $45* ⊙ *Closed Wed.*

Corner 103

WINERY | After leading an effort to revive a local winery, Lloyd Davis, an African American financier and oenophile, turned his attention to making the experience of learning about wine and food-wine pairings less daunting. To that end he opened a light-filled space, diagonally across from Sonoma Plaza, for tastings of Sonoma County wines guests can pair with cheeses or small bites. The lineup includes a brut rosé sparkler, Chardonnay and Marsanne-Roussanne whites, a rosé of Pinot Noir, and several reds. Corner

103's welcoming atmosphere, which in recent years has earned it a ranking at or near the top of *USA Today*'s Best Tasting Room list, makes it an excellent choice for wine novices seeking to expand their knowledge. Visits are by appointment, though hosts usually accommodate drop-ins seeking wine-only tastings. ⊠ *103 W. Napa St., Sonoma* ⌖ *At 1st St. W* ☎ *707/931–6141* ⊕ *www.corner103.com* ▣ *Tastings from $30.*

Pangloss Cellars Tasting Lounge

WINERY | The high-ceilinged tasting room of this winery named for the optimistic doctor from Voltaire's satire Candide occupies a restored 1902 stone building across from Sonoma Plaza. Originally a general store, it's a striking setting to enjoy wines by Erich Bradley, also the winemaker at nearby Sojourn Cellars. The Pangloss roster includes white and red blends, a brut rosé sparkling wine, Chardonnay, Grenache, Mourvèdre, Pinot Noir, Syrah, Zinfandel, and Cabernet Sauvignon. You can sip wines by the flight or glass or enjoy them with cheese and charcuterie or a caviar plate. The winery prefers guests make a reservation, but walk-ins for wine-only tastings are usually possible on weekdays. ■TIP➔ **Bradley also makes the collector-worthy wines of the affiliated Texture winery; they're poured in a dedicated room in the back of the Pangloss building.** ⊠ *35 E. Napa St., Sonoma* ⌖ *At 1st St. E* ☎ *707/933–8565* ⊕ *www.panglosscellars.com* ▣ *Tastings from $35.*

Prohibition Spirits Tasting Room & Bar Shop

DISTILLERY | Zesty limoncello was the first claim to fame of this distillery whose nearly three dozen artisanal offerings also include other "cellos" (try the fig if it's being poured), gins, brandies, liqueurs, and bottled cocktails. You can sample six at the tasting room, down an alley due east of Sonoma Plaza. In addition to the alcoholic beverages, the shop sells bar paraphernalia, cocktail-related books, a few snacks, and coffee aged in bourbon barrels. ⊠ *Mercato Courtyard, 452 1st St. E, Sonoma* ⌖ *East of Sonoma Plaza* ☎ *707/933–7507* ⊕ *www.prohibition-spirits.com* ⊘ *Tastings from $25.*

Sojourn Cellars

WINERY | Stellar fruit sources and a winemaker with a light touch have earned Sojourn Cellars high ratings from critics for its Chardonnays, Pinot Noirs, and Cabernet Sauvignons. Founded in 2001, the winery started out producing Cabernet and still makes several from the Napa Valley and Sonoma County, but the more than a dozen well-balanced Sonoma Coast, Petaluma Gap, and Russian River Valley Pinot Noirs capture most of the attention. Comparative tastings (by appointment) at a bungalow just east of Sonoma Plaza explore the subtle variations in the Pinots caused by climate, terrain, and clone type depending on the grape sources. ■TIP➔ **By 2024, Sojourn hopes to be making wine and receiving guests at the former Ravenswood Winery site a few miles away but plans to retain the bungalow space for in-town sessions.** ⊠ *141 E. Napa St., Sonoma* ⌖ *½ block east of Sonoma Plaza* ☎ *707/938–7212* ⊕ *www.sojourncellars.com* ▣ *Tastings from $45.*

Sonoma Mission

CHURCH | The northernmost of the 21 missions established by Franciscan friars in California, Sonoma Mission was founded in 1823 as Mission San Francisco Solano. These days it serves as the centerpiece of Sonoma State Historic Park, which includes several other sites in Sonoma and nearby Petaluma. Some early mission structures fell into ruin, but all or part of several remaining buildings date to the era of Mexican rule over California. The Sonoma Barracks, a half block west of the mission at 20 East Spain Street, housed troops under the command of General Mariano Guadalupe Vallejo, who controlled vast tracts of land in the region. General Vallejo's Home, a Victorian-era structure, is a few blocks west.

Downtown Sonoma

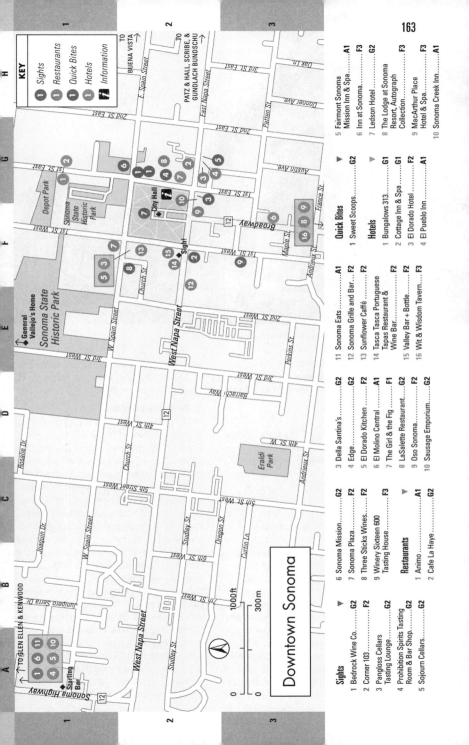

KEY

- 1 Sights
- 1 Restaurants
- 1 Quick Bites
- 1 Hotels
- 🛈 Information

Sights ▶

1 Bedrock Wine Co. **G2**
2 Corner 103 .... **F2**
3 Pangloss Cellars Tasting Lounge **G2**
4 Prohibition Spirits Tasting Room & Bar Shop **G2**
5 Sojourn Cellars **G2**
6 Sonoma Mission **G2**
7 Sonoma Plaza **F2**
8 Three Sticks Wines **F2**
9 Winery Sixteen 600 Tasting House **F3**

Restaurants ▶

1 Animo **A1**
2 Cafe La Haye **G2**
3 Della Santina's **G2**
4 Edge **G2**
5 El Dorado Kitchen **F2**
6 El Molino Central **A1**
7 The Girl & the Fig **F1**
8 LaSalette Restaurant **G2**
9 Oso Sonoma **F2**
10 Sausage Emporium **G2**
11 Sonoma Eats **A1**
12 Sonoma Grille and Bar ... **F2**
13 Sunflower Caffé **F2**
14 Tasca Tasca Portuguese Tapas Restaurant & Wine Bar **F2**
15 Valley Bar + Bottle **F2**
16 Wit & Wisdom Tavern **F3**

Quick Bites ▶

1 Sweet Scoops **G2**

Hotels ▶

1 Bungalows 313 .... **G1**
2 Cottage Inn & Spa **G1**
3 El Dorado Hotel **F2**
4 El Pueblo Inn **A1**
5 Fairmont Sonoma Mission Inn & Spa **A1**
6 Inn at Sonoma **F3**
7 Ledson Hotel **G2**
8 The Lodge at Sonoma Resort, Autograph Collection **F3**
9 MacArthur Place Hotel & Spa **F3**
10 Sonoma Creek Inn **A1**

Sonoma Mission was the last of California's 21 missions.

✉ *114 E. Spain St., Sonoma* ⌖ *At 1st St.
E* ☎ *707/938–9560* ⊕ *www.parks.ca.gov*
🎟 *$3, includes same-day admission to
other historic sites.*

Sonoma Plaza

PLAZA/SQUARE | Dating to the mission era,
Sonoma Plaza is surrounded by 19th-cen-
tury adobes, atmospheric hotels, and
the swooping marquee of the Depres-
sion-era Sebastiani Theatre. A statue
on the plaza's northeastern side marks
the spot where California proclaimed its
independence from Mexico on June 14,
1846. Despite its historical roots, the plaza is not a museum piece. On summer
days it's a hive of activity, with children
blowing off steam in the playground,
couples enjoying picnics from gourmet
shops, and groups listening to live music
at the small amphitheater. The stone **city
hall** is also here. If you're wondering why
the 1906 structure looks the same from
all angles, here's why: its four sides were
purposely made identical so that none of
the plaza's merchants would feel that city
hall had turned its back to them. ✉ *North*

end of Broadway/Hwy. 12, Sonoma
⌖ *Bordered by E. Napa St., 1st St. E, E.
Spain St., and 1st St. W.*

★ Three Sticks Wines

WINERY | The grapes for the Chardonnays
and Pinot Noirs of Three Sticks come
from six estate vineyards, including Durell and Gap's Crown, of winery founder
Bill Price. Winemaker Ryan Prichard also
crafts Rhône-style wines that bear the
Casteñeda label in honor of the restored
1842 Vallejo-Casteñeda Adobe, where
the entire lineup is poured. San Francisco–based designer Ken Fulk transformed
the structure, Sonoma's longest-occupied
residence, into a showcase both lavish
and refined. Seated private tastings
might unfold at a long elm table inside
the adobe or a cast-stone one under a
willow-covered arbor. The winery's food
pairings, which rank among Sonoma County's best, demonstrate the
wines' versatility. Two Chardonnay-only
sessions, one involving caviar, the other
oysters, are offered seasonally; a superb
one offered year-round also includes Pinot

Noir. ✉ *143 W. Spain St., Sonoma* ✥ *At 1st St. W* ☎ *707/996–3328* ⊕ *www.threestickswines.com* 🍷 *Tastings from $75.*

★ Winery Sixteen 600 Tasting House

WINERY | Don't be surprised if someone in tie-dye greets you at the downtown salon of this winery whose labels psychedelic art whiz Stanley Mouse—known for his rock posters and Grateful Dead album covers—designs. The hippie ethos that begat the 1960s back-to-the-land movement and the original Earth Day survives and thrives in the wines, whose grapes come from vineyards cofounder Phil Coturri manages. Dubbed by *Wine Spectator* magazine the "Wizard of Green," Coturri is an expert at organic and biodynamic viticulture. Grenache is a particular jam, but in several decades of farming he's proven adept at coaxing the best out of whatever varietals he's tending. Tastings might include rosé, Viognier, Grenache, Zinfandel, Syrah, Cabernet Franc, or other wines. If you're interested, the hosts are happy to explain Coturri's winegrowing philosophy—but only after you've selected some vinyl (classic jazz or rock) to accompany your pours. ✉ *589 1st St. W, Sonoma* ✥ *Near McDonnell St.* ☎ *707/721–1805* ⊕ *www. winerysixteen600.com* 🍷 *Tastings from $42.*

SIGHTS BEYOND DOWNTOWN SONOMA

Anaba Wines

WINERY | Reprising the greatest hits of Burgundy (Chardonnay, Pinot Noir) and the Rhône (Grenache, Syrah, Viognier), Anaba hosts guests in a whitewashed board-and-batten hospitality center whose breezeway frames windswept Coast Range views to the west. When John Sweazey founded Anaba in 2006, he named it for the Carneros District's up-sweeping anabatic winds, a few years later installing a turbine to harness them for electricity. When planning the hospitality center and adjacent production facility, both completed in 2019, Sweazey and son John Michael continued the alternative-energy commitment by ordering solar panels that, supplemented by the turbine, supply the winery's power. Lower on the radar than many of its Carneros peers, appointment-only Anaba receives high marks from critics for its wines, particularly the Roberts Road Pinot Noir, Bismark Syrah, and late-harvest Viognier. For their quality, they're reasonably priced. ✉ *62 Bonneau Rd., Sonoma* ✥ *At Hwys. 116 and 121* ☎ *707/996–4188* ⊕ *www.anabawines. com* 🍷 *Tastings from $45.*

Bartholomew Estate Vineyards and Winery

WINERY | Grape growing at this winery surrounded by 375-acre Bartholomew Park dates back to an 1840s vineyard a Native American planted during California's Mexican era. These days, the park's nonprofit foundation makes wines from its own organically farmed estate vines. The Garden Block Zinfandel, Viviano's Block Syrah, and Estate Cabernet Sauvignon score well in local wine competitions; lighter wines include Sauvignon Blanc, a Marsanne-Roussanne blend, and rosé of Zinfandel. Tastings often take place on an oak knoll overlooking the vines, with Sonoma Valley and the mountains as the bucolic backdrop. You can also purchase a bottle and picnic in a separate grove. ■TIP→ **It's not necessary to taste wine to enjoy the park's 3-plus miles of hiking trails; park in the lot and follow signs to the trailheads.** ✉ *1000 Vineyard La., Sonoma* ✥ *Take Castle Rd. east 1 mile off 7th St.* ☎ *707/509–0540* ⊕ *bartholomewestate.com* 🍷 *Tastings from $35.*

★ Blue Farm Wines

WINERY | Anne Moller-Racke, founder of the Pinot Noir powerhouse The Donum Estate and its president for nearly two decades, established this smaller label also devoted to serious Chardonnay and Pinot Noir. Moller-Racke, who describes herself as a winegrower in the French *vigneron* tradition that places agriculture at the pinnacle of wine making, practices "precision farming" to produce the best possible fruit. Hosts of private tastings at her 13-acre estate explain her philosophy and the five Sonoma County appellations where she cultivates grapes. Anchored by a circa-1880 Victorian and adjacent pump house, the former horse farm is now planted to 7 acres of grapes. Near the residence, a formidable century-old pepper tree and a rose garden with dozens of varieties catch the eye, the Mayacamas Mountains supplying the idyllic setting's backdrop. The appointment-only winery requests prospective guests inquire about visits at least 48 hours in advance. ⊠ *San Luis Rd., off Hwy. 12, Sonoma* ☎ *707/721–6773* ⊕ *bluefarmwines.com* ⊠ *Tastings $65* ⊗ *Closed weekends.*

Buena Vista Winery

WINERY | A local actor in top hat and 19th-century garb sometimes greets guests as Count Agoston Haraszthy at this homage to the birthplace of modern California wine making. Haraszthy's rehabilitated former press house (used for pressing grapes into wine), completed in 1864, is the architectural focal point, with photos, banners, plaques, and artifacts providing historical context. Chardonnay, Pinot Noir, Cabernet Sauvignon, and several Bordeaux-style red blends are the strong suits among the several dozen wines produced. During appointment-only visits (weekday walk-ins generally possible), you can taste some of them solo or preorder a cheese plate or box lunch from the affiliated Oakville Grocery. ⊠ *18000 Old Winery Rd., Sonoma* ✛ *Off E. Napa St.* ☎ *800/926–1266* ⊕ *www.buenavistawinery.com* ⊠ *Tastings from $30.*

★ The Donum Estate

WINERY | The team at this prominent Chardonnay and Pinot Noir producer prizes viticulture—selecting vineyards with superior soils and microclimates, planting compatible clones, and farming organically with rigor—over wine-making wizardry. Tasting areas that include a contemporary white board-and-batten structure and a pavilion with a conical multicolor glass canopy afford guests hilltop views of Los Carneros, San Pablo Bay, and beyond. The wines, from several Sonoma County appellations and one in Mendocino County, continue to exhibit the "power yet elegance" that sealed the winery's fame in the 2000s. Tastings are by appointment only (last-minute unlikely). The more than three dozen large-scale museum-quality contemporary sculptures placed amid the vines, including works by Ai Weiwei, Lynda Benglis, Louise Bourgeois, Keith Haring, and Anselm Kiefer, add a touch of high culture to a visit here. ⊠ *24500 Ramal Rd., Sonoma* ✛ *Off Hwy. 121/12* ☎ *707/732–2200* ⊕ *www.thedonumestate.com* ⊠ *Tastings from $125.*

Gloria Ferrer Caves and Vineyards

WINERY | On a clear day this Spanish hacienda–style winery's Vista Terrace lives up to its name as guests at seated tastings sip delicate sparkling wines while taking in east-facing views of Los Carneros AVA and beyond it San Pablo Bay. The Chardonnay and Pinot Noir grapes from the vineyards in the foreground are the product of old-world wine-making knowledge—generations of the founding Ferrer family made cava in Spain—but also contemporary soil management techniques and clonal research. Hosts well-acquainted with the winery's sustainability practices and history as the Carneros District's first sparkling-wine house serve the wines, either solo or accompanied by food that varies from cheese and charcuterie to caviar or a full lunch. Except on Wednesday, visits are by appointment. ■TIP➜ **On Wednesday only, the winery is open for by-the-glass pours and bottle service (no flights), reservations not required.** ⊠ *23555 Carneros Hwy./Hwy. 121, Sonoma* ☎ *707/933–1986* ⊕ *www.gloriaferrer.com* ⊠ *Tastings from $65* ⊗ *Closed Tues.*

No flights (only bottle and by-the-glass service) Wed.

Gundlach Bundschu

WINERY | "Gun lock bun shoe" gets you close to pronouncing this winery's name correctly, though everyone here shortens it to Gun Bun. The Bundschu family, which has owned most of this property since 1858, still uses parts of an 1870 stone winery for production. Reds from estate grapes include Cabernet Franc, Cabernet Sauvignon, Merlot, and the Bordeaux-style Mountain Cuvée containing each vintage's best fruit. Gewürztraminer, Chardonnay, and two rosés are also in the mix. You can sample five estate wines in a courtyard with views of vineyards and a pond. For a more comprehensive experience, book a Pinzgauer vehicle vineyard tour or a Heritage Reserve pairing of limited-release old-vine wines. All visits are by appointment only, with same-day tastings often possible. ⊠ *2000 Denmark St., Sonoma* ✛ *At Bundschu Rd., off 8th St. E* ☎ *707/938–5277* ⊕ *www.gunbun. com* 🍷 *Tastings from $55, tours from $80 (includes tasting).*

★ Hamel Family Wines

WINERY | Seeking respite from foggy San Francisco summers, Pam and George Hamel Jr. purchased a vineyard mostly for the scenery but quickly got bitten by the wine bug. The family now owns four biodynamic, mostly dry-farmed (no irrigation) vineyards. Collector-worthy Cabernet Sauvignon, the flagship Isthmus red blend, and carefully crafted Zinfandel and Sauvignon Blanc account for the bulk of production. Pam and George's son John, who makes the wines, also supervises the farming, striving for "purity of fruit" that, he says, requires little of him post-harvest. He's too modest. His choices during fermentation and aging beget magnificent wines. Appointment-only private tastings take place at the family's steel-and-glass Estate House, where guests enjoy indoors or on the broad stone terrace enjoy valley and Sonoma Mountain views. ■ **TIP**➔ **Despite its Sonoma address, the estate is closer to Glen Ellen.** ⊠ *15401 Sonoma Hwy./Hwy. 12, Sonoma* ✛ *At Madrone Rd., 5 miles north of Sonoma Plaza* ☎ *707/996–5800* ⊕ *hamelfamilywines.com* 🍷 *Tastings from $85.*

Hanson of Sonoma Distillery

DISTILLERY | The Hanson family makes grape-based organic vodkas, one traditional, the rest infused with cucumbers, ginger, mandarin oranges, Meyer lemons, or habañero and other chili peppers. A surprise to many visitors, the Hansons make a blended white wine before distilling it into vodka. The family pours its vodkas and a single-malt whiskey in an industrial-looking tasting room heavy on the steel, with wood reclaimed from Deep South smokehouses adding a rustic note. In good weather, some sessions take place on the landscaped shore of a small pond. Per state law, there's a limit to the amount poured, but it's sufficient to get to know the product. ⊠ *22985 Burndale Rd., Sonoma* ✛ *At Carneros Hwy./Hwy. 121* ☎ *707/343–1805* ⊕ *hansonofsonoma.com* 🍷 *Tastings from $35, tours from $75 (includes tasting).*

★ Hanzell Vineyards

WINERY | About a mile and a half from Sonoma Plaza, Lomita Avenue angles off Highway 12, winding north and east to Hanzell, a hillside hideaway whose origin story enchants nearly as much as the winery's collector-worthy Chardonnays and Pinot Noirs. Most tastings take place at metal-roofed outdoor platforms positioned to take maximum advantage of the Sonoma Valley views. James Zellerbach, a businessman and later U.S. ambassador to Italy who became smitten with Chardonnay and Pinot Noir on trips to Burgundy founded Hanzell (his wife's name was Hana) in 1953. At the time, neither grape had much of a foothold in California, but his hunch that each would do well here paid off. A few acres of

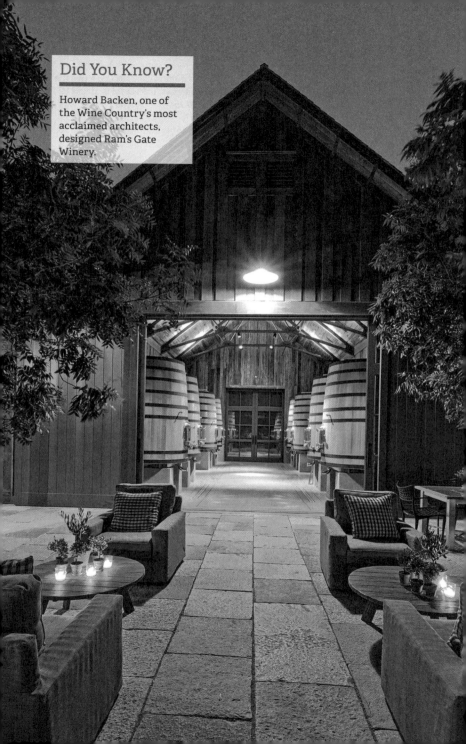

Cabernet Sauvignon planted later provide grapes for the Bordeaux red blend that closes most sessions, led by gracious, well-informed hosts proud of this winery's legacy, organic farming practices, and studiously crafted wines. ⊠ *18596 Lomita Ave., Sonoma ⊹ Off Sonoma Hwy. for 1¾ miles ☎ 707/996–3860 ⊕ hanzell.com ⊡ Tastings from $65.*

Patz & Hall

WINERY | Sophisticated single-vineyard Chardonnays and Pinot Noirs are the trademark of this respected winery that hosts tastings at a fashionable single-story former residence 3 miles southeast of Sonoma Plaza. A Wine Country adage holds that great wines are made in the vineyard—the all-star fields represented here include Hyde, Durell, and Gap's Crown—but the wine-making team routinely surpasses peers with access to the same fruit, proof that discernment and expertise play a role, too. You can sample wines on the vineyard-view back patio in good weather. One tasting focuses on current releases, and the other incorporates older vintages. Appointments are highly recommended; walk-ins are possible, but call first. ⊠ *21200 8th St. E, Sonoma ⊹ Near Peru Rd. ☎ 707/265–7700 ⊕ www.patzhall.com ⊡ Tastings from $40 ☉ Closed Tues. and Wed.*

Ram's Gate Winery

WINERY | Stunning views, ultrachic architecture, and wines made from grapes grown by acclaimed producers make a visit to Ram's Gate an event. The welcoming interior spaces—think Restoration Hardware with a dash of high-style whimsy—open up to outdoor tasting areas and views of the entire western Carneros. In fine weather, cooling breezes waft through the site as guests sip sophisticated wines, primarily Pinot Noirs and Chardonnays but also Pinot Blanc, Sauvignon Blanc, rosé, a sparkling blanc de noirs, Cabernet Sauvignon, Grenache, and Syrah. With grapes from the estate vineyard plus other illustrious sites, the wine-making team focuses on creating balanced wines that express what occurred in nature that year. Appointments are necessary for all tastings, one of which involves a multicourse culinary pairing. ⊠ *28700 Arnold Dr./Hwy. 121, Sonoma ⊹ 2 miles north of Hwy. 37 ☎ 707/721–8700 ⊕ www.ramsgatewinery.com ⊡ Tastings from $50 ☉ Closed Tues. and Wed.*

Robledo Family Winery

WINERY | It's truly a family affair at this winery founded by Reynaldo Robledo Sr., a migrant worker from Michoacán, Mexico, and María de La Luz Robledo. Son and winemaker Everardo Robledo and several of his eight siblings are involved in the winery and vineyard-management company Reynaldo and Maria established. Everardo's lush reds—particularly Tempranillo, Zinfandel, and Cabernet Sauvignon from grapes grown on 350-plus estate acres in several counties—stand out among the wines poured in a modest interior space or on a covered patio that juts into a Pinot Noir vineyard. Los Braceros, a blend, pays tribute to temporary workers from Mexico, including Reynaldo's father and grandfather, who contributed to California agriculture as part of the Bracero Program (1942–64). Over these wines, preceded perhaps by Sauvignon Blanc, Chardonnay, Pinot Grigio, or Pinot Noir, guests hear inspiring multigenerational tales, sometimes firsthand from a family member. ∎**TIP➔ Picnickers and pets are welcome here.** ⊠ *21901 Bonness Rd., Sonoma ⊹ Off Hwy. 116 or E. Bonness Rd. ☎ 707/939–6903 ⊕ www.robledofamilywinery.com ⊡ Tastings from $35.*

★ Sangiacomo Family Wines

WINERY | Several dozen wineries produce vineyard-designate Chardonnays and Pinot Noirs from grapes grown by the Sangiacomo family, whose Italian ancestors first started farming in Sonoma in 1927. The family didn't establish its own label until 2016, but its cool-climate

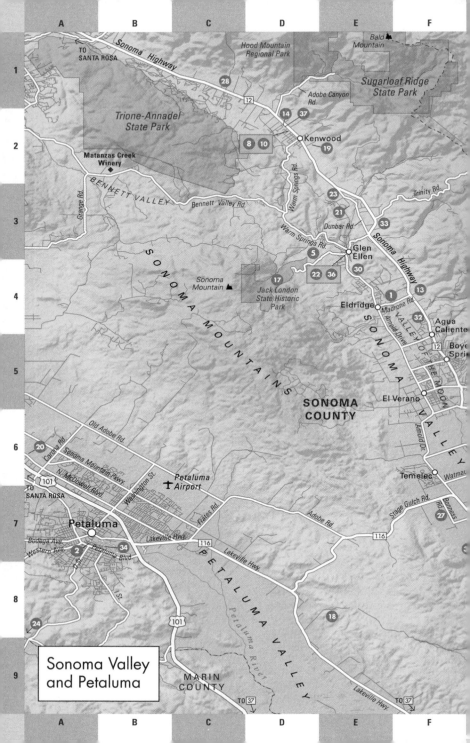

Sonoma Valley and Petaluma

G H I J

Rutherford

NAPA VALLEY

Silverado Trail

29

Oakville

Napa River

Oakville
Grade Rd.

Dry Creek Rd.

NAPA
COUNTY

Yountville

29

Mt.
Veeder ▲

Gehricke Rd.

Hot
gs

16

Downtown
Sonoma
see detail
map

Castle Rd.

4

7

Sonoma

Napa St.

Old Winery Rd.

MacArthur St.

12

Denmark St.

5th St. E

8th St. E.

Napa Rd.

35

Napa
Rd.

Broadway

25

Sonoma
Skypark

TO NAPA →

R Rd.

29

6

12

116

121

3

11

Sonoma
Valley
Airport

Carneros Highway

15

9

12 121

Sonoma Creek

121

Arnold Dr.

N

0   2 mi

0   2 km

26

KEY

1 Sights

G H I J

wines and a Napa Valley Cabernet quickly earned critical plaudits. Chardonnay vines and the Carneros District's western hills form the backdrop for tastings, usually outdoors, at the 110-acre Home Ranch, the first of a dozen-plus vineyards the Sangiacomos acquired or lease. At appointment-only visits, you're apt to encounter one or more third-generation members, all of whom enjoy meeting guests and sharing their family's legacy. ■TIP→ **On Friday from May through September, the winery hosts Sunset on the Terrace, with wines served by the glass, carafe, or bottle (no flights) from 3:30 pm until sundown.** ✉ *21545 Broadway, Sonoma ✛ 2½ miles south of Sonoma Plaza* ☎ *707/934–8445* ⊕ *www.sangiacomowines.com* 🍷 *Tastings from $30.*

Schug Carneros Estate Winery

WINERY | As a young lad in Germany, the late Walter Schug made Pinot Noir, inspiring a lifelong preoccupation with the Burgundian varietal. The founding winemaker at Joseph Phelps, where he developed the flagship Insignia Bordeaux-style blend, in the 1980s he established his namesake winery in the far western reaches of Los Carneros AVA. His children continue his legacy, focusing on Chardonnay, Pinot Noir, Cabernet Sauvignon, and other Bordeaux varietals. There's also a wine from the St. Laurent grape, an offspring of Pinot. To sample current releases with a vineyard view, book a Classic Wine Tasting. The more comprehensive Cave Tour and Tasting includes a brief property walk, seasonal small bites, and current and library wines. ✉ *602 Bonneau Rd., Sonoma ✛ East off Hwy. 116 at Hwy. 121* ☎ *707/939–9363* ⊕ *schugwinery.com* 🍷 *Tastings from $35* ⊘ *Closed Mon.*

★ Serres Ranch

WINERY | You'll always meet a family member at this approximately 200-acre Sonoma Valley ranch established in 1924. The land's history stretches back well further, though, to at least the 1850s, when "Fighting Joe" Hooker, later General Joseph Hooker of Civil War fame, owned it. The Serres family has been growing and selling wine grapes for decades; the fifth generation—a sister and her two brothers—began producing wine in 2017. Merlot and two Bordeaux-style red blends were among the initial bottlings, with Cabernet Sauvignon from 2018 vines growing where Hooker planted his vineyard, expected soon. When the weather's good, tastings, accompanied by cheese and charcuterie, include a UTV ranch tour with a stop at a grove of thick-branched valley oaks. Reservations, best made 48 or more hours ahead, are required. ✉ *16060 Sonoma Hwy./Hwy. 12, Sonoma* ☎ *707/695–9144* ⊕ *www.serresranchwine.com* 🍷 *Tastings $100.*

Sonoma TrainTown Railroad

TRAIN/TRAIN STATION | **FAMILY** | A quarter-scale train at this fun, well-run attraction geared to kids under 10 chugs for 4 miles through tunnels and past a lake, a waterfall, and a miniature town with a petting zoo. Back near the entrance are a turntable and a roundhouse, amusement rides, and a combination snack bar and souvenir stand. ✉ *20264 Broadway, Sonoma ✛ Near Napa Rd.* ☎ *707/938–3912* ⊕ *www.traintown.com* 🍷 *Main park area free, train ride $9; additional fee for amusement rides* ⊘ *Closed rainy days yr-round, weekdays mid-Aug.–mid-June.*

🍴 Restaurants

★ Animo

$$$$ | **ECLECTIC** | Even before charting on *Esquire*'s list of 2022's best new restaurants, the intimate, bungalowlike establishment of New York City transplant Joshua Smookler (formerly chef at his own Mu Ramen and Thomas Keller's Per Se) was already drawing a crowd for its mash-up of Basque, Jewish, and Korean cuisines. Smookler, whose wife, Heidy He, runs the front of the house, consistently delights with idiosyncratic flavor combinations in dishes like feather-cut *ibérico* pork, lobster in XO sauce, grilled whole turbot, and dry-aged rib eye. **Known for:** cheesecake and other desserts; open-hearth kitchen; no web presence so must call for reservations. $ *Average main: $63* ⊠ *18976 Sonoma Hwy., Sonoma* ✛ *Near Verano Ave.* ☎ *707/721–1160* ✆ *Closed Mon. and Tues. No lunch.*

★ Cafe La Haye

$$$ | **AMERICAN** | In a postage-stamp-size open kitchen (the dining room, its white walls adorned with contemporary art, is nearly as compact), chef Jeffrey Lloyd turns out understated, sophisticated fare emphasizing seasonably available local ingredients. Meats, pastas, and seafood get deluxe treatment without fuss or fanfare—and the daily risotto special is always worth trying. **Known for:** Napa-Sonoma wine list with French complements; signature butterscotch pudding; owner Saul Gropman on hand to greet diners. $ *Average main: $27* ⊠ *140 E. Napa St., Sonoma* ✛ *East of Sonoma Plaza* ☎ *707/935–5994* ⊕ *www. cafelahaye.com* ✆ *Closed Sun. and Mon. No lunch.*

Della Santina's

$$$ | **ITALIAN** | After three decades of serving Tuscan-inspired cuisine, this restaurant with a plant-filled heated and tented back patio has developed a homey patina enhanced by brickwork, a fountain, family photos, and other old-school touches. Likewise with the food, you won't find belabored technique or froufrou preparations, only soulful renditions of northern Italy's greatest hits—veal scallopini, mushroom ravioli, pappardelle with rich duck ragout—from two generations of family recipes. **Known for:** adjacent Enoteca Della Santina wine bar; Italian and California wine selections; pillowy gnocchi Nonna. $ *Average main: $27* ⊠ *133 E. Napa St., Sonoma* ✛ *Near 1st St. E* ☎ *707/935–0576* ⊕ *dellasantinas.com.*

★ Edge

$$$$ | **MODERN AMERICAN** | Inside a former residence that received a high-design makeover down to its open-air patio, this restaurant began as an exclusive perk for Stone Edge Farm Estate's wine-club members; though now open to all, it still flies under the radar. Prix-fixe meals built around organically grown ingredients from the winery's nearby farm might include an appetizer like tuna adorned with crispy shallots, kumquats, and cashews followed by a salad of picked-the-same-day greens and a sensitively spiced fish, meat, or vegetarian entrée. **Known for:** regenerative farming techniques employed in the vineyard and culinary garden; prix-fixe rate that includes wine pairings; wine tasting Thursday–Sunday noon–5. $ *Average main: $295* ⊠ *139 E. Napa St., Sonoma* ✛ *Near 1st St. E* ☎ *707/935–6520* ⊕ *edgesonoma.com* ✆ *Closed Sun.–Tues. No lunch.*

El Dorado Kitchen

$$$ | **MODERN AMERICAN** | This restaurant owes its visual appeal to its clean lines and svelte decor, but the eye inevitably drifts westward to the open kitchen, where longtime executive chef Armando Navarro's team crafts dishes full of subtle surprises. The menu might include ceviche or roasted maitake mushrooms as starters and pan-roasted salmon, fettuccine carbonara, or paella awash with seafood among the entrées. **Known for:** subtle tastes and textures; truffle-oil fries with Parmesan; takeout window for Mexican (plus the spicy burger). $ *Average main: $29* ⊠ *El Dorado Hotel, 405 1st St. W, Sonoma* ✛ *At W. Spain St.* ☎ *707/996–3030* ⊕ *eldoradokitchen.com.*

El Molino Central

$ | **MEXICAN** | The goodness at Karen Waikiki's roadside restaurant, which has more tables outside than in, starts with high-quality ingredients and authentic techniques. The stars include tamales (chicken mole and Niman Ranch pork), tacos filled with beer-battered fish or

El Dorado Kitchen's chefs craft flavorful dishes full of subtle surprises.

crispy beef, ahi tostadas poke style, and enchiladas and burritos. **Known for:** crispy three-cheese potato tacos; handmade tortillas and tamales from organic stone-ground heritage corn; breakfast chilaquiles Merida (Friday–Sunday morning). [$] *Average main: $16* ✉ *11 Central Ave., Boyes Hot Springs* ✣ *At Hwy. 12* ☎ *707/939–1010* 🌐 *www.elmolinocentral.com.*

★ The Girl & the Fig

$$$ | **FRENCH** | At this hot spot for inventive French cooking inside the historic Sonoma Hotel bar, you can always find a dish with the signature figs on the menu, whether it's a fig-and-arugula salad or an aperitif blending sparkling wine with fig liqueur. Also look for duck confit, a burger with matchstick fries, and wild flounder meunière. **Known for:** Rhône-wines emphasis; artisanal cheese and charcuterie platters; weekly changing three-course prix-fixe option. [$] *Average main: $30* ✉ *Sonoma Hotel, 110 W. Spain St., Sonoma* ✣ *At 1st St. W* ☎ *707/938–3634* 🌐 *www.thegirlandthefig.com.*

★ LaSalette Restaurant

$$$ | **PORTUGUESE** | Born in the Azores and raised in Sonoma, chef-owner Manuel Azevedo serves cuisine inspired by his native Portugal in this warmly decorated spot with a heated patio out front. The wood-oven whole-roasted fish is always worth trying, and there are usually boldly flavored pork dishes, along with a casserole, pot roast, stew, salted cod, and other hearty fare. **Known for:** authentic Portuguese cuisine; sophisticated spicing; rice pudding with Madeira-braised fig for dessert. [$] *Average main: $31* ✉ *452 1st St. E, Sonoma* ✣ *Near E. Spain St.* ☎ *707/938–1927* 🌐 *www.lasaletterestaurant.com* 🕓 *Closed Wed.*

Oso Sonoma

$$$ | **MODERN AMERICAN** | Chef David Bush, who achieved national recognition for his food pairings at St. Francis Winery, owns this barlike small-plates restaurant inside an 1890s storefront, erected as a livery stable, that incorporates materials reclaimed from the building's prior incarnations. Starters often include oysters, ceviche, and deviled eggs with Dungeness crab and homemade yellow curry, meant to be enjoyed before moving on to braised-pork-shoulder tacos, shrimp and cheesy grits, or an achiote chicken sandwich. **Known for:** plaza location; smart beer and wine selections; Sonoma Dreamer (Griffo gin, St. Germaine, grapefruit, lemon), blood-orange margarita, and other craft cocktails. $ *Average main: $33* ✉ *9 E. Napa St., Sonoma* ✛ *At Broadway* ☎ *707/931–6926* ⊕ *www.oso-sonoma.com* ⊗ *Closed Tues. and Wed.*

Sausage Emporium

$$ | AMERICAN | The owner of this combination restaurant and marketplace escorts her customers on a round-the-world journey via artisanal sausages—traditional links and savory pork, beef, duck, and chicken variations. In her bright storefront edging Sonoma Plaza's southern edge (there's also a patio out back), sausages also appear in sandwiches, tartines, and impressively moist biscuits with creamy sausage gravy. **Known for:** all-day breakfast; sausage and charcuterie flights; local beers and wines. $ *Average main: $18* ✉ *31 E. Napa St., Sonoma* ✛ *At 1st St. E* ☎ *707/934–8814* ⊕ *sausage-emporium.com* ⊗ *Closed Mon. and Tues. No dinner.*

★ Sonoma Eats

$ | MEXICAN | Chef Efrain Balmes attracted such throngs for his "real Mexican food" truck specializing in his native Oaxacan cuisine that he finally went full brick-and-mortar, sharing space with (and pretty much taking over) an existing coffee roastery. The tacos—fish, shrimp, potato, mushroom, pork, and an outstanding lamb one—and the signature mole Oaxaqueño sauce are the must-tries here, the latter with either an enchilada or the "wet supreme burrito." **Known for:** all-day Taco Tuesday specials; tamales with pickled jalapeños; Mexican beers, sodas, and agua frescas. $ *Average main: $14* ✉ *18133 Sonoma Hwy., Sonoma* ✛ *At*

Vallejo Ave. ☎ *707/939–1905* ⊕ *www.sonomaeatsmex.com* ⊗ *Closed Mon.*

Sonoma Grille and Bar

$$$ | AMERICAN | Decorated in shades of brown and white and softly lit at night, the Grille is the type of spot where old schoolers start a meal by washing down oysters on the half shell with a stiff gin martini or cut to the chase with vodka oyster shooters. The menu at lunch and dinner skews heavily surf but covers all the turf bases with grilled, baked, or roasted beef, lamb, pork, chicken, and fish dishes, plus risotto and pasta plates. **Known for:** daily steak and seafood specials; sandwiches and a Niman Ranch quarter-pound burger for lunch; tented patio out back. $ *Average main: $33* ✉ *165 W. Napa St., Sonoma* ✛ *Near 2nd St. W* ☎ *707/938–7542* ⊕ *www.sonomagrilleandbar.com* ⊗ *Closed Mon. and Tues.*

Sunflower Caffé

$ | AMERICAN | Whimsical art and brightly painted walls set a jolly tone at this casual eatery whose assets include the verdant patio out back. Omelets, biscuits, and waffles are the hits at breakfast, with the grilled cheese sandwich and smoked-duck sandwich, the latter served on a sourdough hero roll with garlic aioli, two favorites for lunch. **Known for:** combination café, gallery, and wine bar; local cheeses and hearty soups; no-tipping policy. $ *Average main: $15* ✉ *421 1st St. W, Sonoma* ✛ *At W. Spain St.* ☎ *707/996–6645* ⊕ *www.sonomasunflower.com* ⊗ *No dinner.*

Tasca Tasca Portuguese Tapas Restaurant & Wine Bar

$$ | PORTUGUESE | Sonoma dining—or nibbling, given the portion sizes—received a boost when Azores-born chef Manuel Azevedo opened this retro-contempo tavern dedicated to small Portuguese bites. Dividing his menu into five parts—Cheese, Garden, Sea, Land, Sweet—Azevedo, who also owns the nearby restaurant LaSalette, serves

everything from hearty caldo verde stew, pork sliders, smoked duck breast, and salted codfish cakes to São Jorge cheese topped with marmalade. **Known for:** Portuguese wines; dessert mousses and sorbets; good for lunch. $ Average main: $22 ⊠ 122 W. Napa St., Sonoma ⊹ Near 1st St. W ☎ 707/996–8272 ⊕ www. tascatasca.com ⊗ Closed Wed.

★ **Valley Bar + Bottle**

$$$ | **MODERN AMERICAN** | The team behind this wine shop, bar, and restaurant across from Sonoma Plaza revamped a 19th-century adobe (though inside you'd never know it's this old) and expanded its outdoor patio, where most dining takes place. Sustainably produced seafood and meats find their way into "California home cooking"—summer dishes that might include halibut with corn and cherry tomatoes and winter ones like pork adobo or a half chicken with broccoli. **Known for:** XO deviled eggs, shrimp rolls, and other small plates; organically and biodynamically farmed wines by iconoclastic producers; weekend brunch with traditional fare plus less common alternatives. $ Average main: $32 ⊠ 487 1st St. W, Sonoma ⊹ At W. Napa St. ☎ 707/934–8403 ⊕ www.valleybarand-bottle.com ⊗ Closed Tues. and Wed.

★ **Wit & Wisdom Tavern**

$$$ | **MODERN AMERICAN** | A San Francisco culinary star with establishments worldwide, Michael Mina debuted his first Wine Country restaurant in 2020, its interior of charcoal grays, browns, and soft whites dandy indeed, if by evening vying with outdoor spaces aglow with fire pits and lighted water features. Seasonal regional ingredients—Pacific Coast fish, pasture-raised meats, freshly plucked produce—go into haute-homey dishes, prepared open-fire, that include pizzas, handmade pastas, and the signature lobster potpie with brandied lobster cream and black truffle. **Known for:** 3–5 happy hour's beverage and app selections; many local wines on award-winning list;

prix-fixe Night at the Tavern tasting menu. $ Average main: $35 ⊠ The Lodge at Sonoma, 1325 Broadway, Sonoma ⊹ At Leveroni Rd. ☎ 707/931–3405 ⊕ www. witandwisdomsonoma.com ⊗ Closed Mon. and Tues. No lunch.

 Coffee and Quick Bites

Sweet Scoops

$ | **ICE CREAM** | The scent of waffle cones baking draws patrons into this family-run parlor serving artisanal ice cream made fresh daily. Butter brickle, peach custard, Oreos and cream, and salted caramel are among the alternating flavors that include sorbets and sometimes sherbets, and always vegan options. **Known for:** peppy decor and staffers; husband and wife owners; sister property Darling six blocks away for more of the same, plus ice-cream cakes. $ Average main: $7 ⊠ 408 1st St. E, Sonoma ⊹ Near E. Spain St. ☎ 707/721–1187 ⊕ www.sweetscoop-sicecream.com.

🛏 Hotels

★ **Bungalows 313**

$$$ | **APARTMENT** | The sturdy metal gate of this vacation-rental complex near Sonoma Plaza opens into a leafy courtyard fronting three buildings containing smartly furnished studio, one-bedroom, and two-bedroom accommodations with kitchens or kitchenettes. **Pros:** near shops, restaurants, and tasting rooms, but also hiking and biking trails; hideaway setting; spacious courtyard with lounges, heaters, water feature, barbecue grill, fire pit, and boccie court. **Cons:** no on-site parking (though street parking is easy); no one on property overnight (but manager lives nearby and responds quickly); more like a deluxe Airbnb than a boutique hotel. $ Rooms from: $353 ⊠ 313 1st St. E, Sonoma ☎ 707/996–8091 ⊕ bunga-lows313.com ⇥ 6 rooms ⏐◎⏐ No Meals.

Cottage Inn & Spa

$$$ | B&B/INN | Delivering romance, relaxation, and Zenlike tranquillity is the raison d'être of this courtyard complex 1½ blocks north of Sonoma Plaza. **Pros:** convenient to restaurants, shops, and tasting rooms; quiet location; four suites with double Jacuzzi tubs. **Cons:** books up far ahead for summer weekends; some bathrooms only have a shower; lacks amenities such as room service, restaurant, pool, or gym. $ *Rooms from: $345* ✉ *310 1st St. E, Sonoma* ☎ *707/996–0719* ⊕ *www.cottageinnandspa.com* ⌨ *9 rooms* ⦿ *Free Breakfast.*

El Dorado Hotel

$$ | HOTEL | Guest rooms in this remodeled 1843 building skew contemporary with their Restoration Hardware furnishings, but the Mexican-tile floors hint at Sonoma's mission-era past. **Pros:** stylish for the price; on-site El Dorado Kitchen restaurant; central location. **Cons:** rooms are small, though patios and balconies keep them from feeling claustrophobic; street noise audible in some rooms; parking can be problematic. $ *Rooms from: $264* ✉ *405 1st St. W, Sonoma* ☎ *707/996–3030* ⊕ *www.eldoradosonoma.com* ⌨ *27 rooms* ⦿ *No Meals.*

El Pueblo Inn

$ | MOTEL | A giant pepper tree and a few palms tower over the garden courtyard of this updated 1959 motel whose landscaping, festive pool area, and thoughtful service make a stay here worth considering. **Pros:** festive pool area; expanded continental breakfast buffet; helpful hosts. **Cons:** rates can spike in high season; street noise an issue in some rooms; several blocks west of Sonoma Plaza. $ *Rooms from: $199* ✉ *896 W. Napa St., Sonoma* ⊹ *Off Hwy. 12 near Riverside Dr.* ☎ *707/996–3651* ⊕ *www.elpuebloinn.com* ⌨ *53 rooms.*

Fairmont Sonoma Mission Inn & Spa

$$$$ | RESORT | The draw at this mission-style resort is the extensive spa with its array of massages and treatments, some designed for couples. **Pros:** full-service hotel; enormous spa and other wellness services; Santé restaurant's modern American cuisine. **Cons:** smallish standard rooms; lacks intimacy of similarly priced options; resort fee, though it does include decent perks. $ *Rooms from: $507* ✉ *100 Boyes Blvd./Hwy. 12, Sonoma* ⊹ *2½ miles north of Sonoma Plaza* ☎ *800/540–4499, 707/938–9000* ⊕ *www.fairmont.com/sonoma* ⌨ *226 rooms* ⦿ *No Meals.*

Inn at Sonoma

$$ | B&B/INN | Little luxuries delight at this well-run inn ¼ mile south of Sonoma Plaza whose guest rooms, softly lit and done in pastels, have comfortable beds topped with feather comforters and plenty of pillows. **Pros:** last-minute specials can be a great deal; freshly baked cookies, afternoon wine and cheese; good soundproofing blocks out Broadway street noise. **Cons:** on a busy street rather than right on the plaza; pet-friendly rooms book up quickly; some rooms on the small side. $ *Rooms from: $275* ✉ *630 Broadway, Sonoma* ☎ *707/939–1340* ⊕ *www.innatsonoma.com* ⌨ *27 rooms* ⦿ *Free Breakfast.*

★ Ledson Hotel

$$$ | B&B/INN | With just six rooms the Ledson feels intimate, and the furnishings and amenities—down beds, mood lighting, gas fireplaces, whirlpool tubs, and balconies for enjoying breakfast or a glass of wine—stack up well against Wine Country rooms costing more, especially in high season. **Pros:** convenient Sonoma Plaza location; spacious, individually decorated rooms; whirlpool tub in all rooms. **Cons:** two people maximum occupancy in all rooms; children must be at least 12 years old; front rooms have plaza views but pick up some street noise. $ *Rooms from: $395* ✉ *480 1st St. E, Sonoma* ☎ *707/996–9779* ⊕ *www.ledsonhotel.com* ⌨ *6 rooms* ⦿ *No Meals.*

The Lodge at Sonoma Resort, Autograph Collection

$$$$ | HOTEL | A handsome base for Sonoma Valley wine tasting, this 10-acre, two-story, Mission Revival–style hotel received a makeover completed in 2022 that elevated the property to higher status among the Marriott family's luxury brands. **Pros:** landscaped grounds with many native trees and plants; Michael Mina's Wit & Wisdom Tavern; spa with large outdoor relaxation area. **Cons:** staff's lack of cordiality an issue for some guests; not all rooms have tubs or fireplaces; sizable resort fee (for afternoon wine tasting, free bicycle use, Wi-Fi, and other amenities). [$] *Rooms from: $558* ✉ *1325 Broadway, Sonoma* ☎ *707/935–6600* 🌐 *www.thelodgeatsonoma.com* 🛏 *182 rooms* 🍴 *No Meals.*

★ **MacArthur Place Hotel & Spa**

$$$$ | HOTEL | Guests at this 7-acre boutique property five blocks south of Sonoma Plaza bask in ritzy seclusion in plush accommodations set amid landscaped gardens. **Pros:** verdant garden setting; great for a romantic getaway; appealing common areas. **Cons:** a bit of a walk from the plaza; some traffic noise audible in street-side rooms; pricey in high season. [$] *Rooms from: $705* ✉ *29 E. MacArthur St., Sonoma* ☎ *707/938–2929, 800/722–1866* 🌐 *www.macarthurplace.com* 🛏 *64 rooms* 🍴 *No Meals.*

Sonoma Creek Inn

$ | MOTEL | The exterior of this property between Sonoma and Glen Ellen says "motel," but the design sensibility and customer service are more quaint country inn, with the rates splitting the difference. **Pros:** clean, well-lighted bathrooms; good for travelers on a budget; popular with bicyclists. **Cons:** office not staffed 24 hours; 10-minute drive from Sonoma Plaza; a few rooms cramped. [$] *Rooms from: $130* ✉ *239 Boyes Blvd., Sonoma* ✣ *Off Hwy. 12* ☎ *707/939–9463, 888/712–1289* 🌐 *www.sonomacreekinn.com* 🛏 *16 rooms* 🍴 *No Meals.*

Nightlife

Sigh!

WINE BARS | From the oval bar and walls the color of a fine blanc de blancs to retro chandeliers that mimic Champagne bubbles, everything about this sparkling-wine bar's frothy space screams "have a good time." That owner Jayme Powers and her posse are trained in the fine art of *sabrage* (opening a bottle of sparkling wine with a saber) only adds to the festivity. ■ **TIP→ Sigh! opens at noon, so it's a good daytime stop, too.** ✉ *120 W. Napa St., Sonoma* ✣ *At 1st St. W* ☎ *707/996–2444* 🌐 *www.sighsonoma.com.*

★ **Starling Bar Sonoma**

BARS | Chat up the locals at this neighborhood hangout with a welcoming vibe and bartenders slinging the classics and craft cocktails, some of whose ingredients are grown out back. Noteworthy drinks include the bacon bourbon sour and the pickled martini made with Hanson's organic vodka. Music and comedy acts perform many nights. ✉ *19380 Hwy. 12, Sonoma* ✣ *At W. Spain St.* ☎ *707/938–7442* 🌐 *www.starlingsonoma.com.*

Shopping

FOOD AND WINE

Pomme Cider Shop & Tap Room

OTHER FOOD & DRINK | Reset your palate at this shop whose owners sell more than a hundred ciders (18 on tap) from as near as Sonoma County and as far afield as Slovenia and Austria. They also stock sparklers, rosés, and other light wines. Test drive a few ciders in the tap room, where small bites are also served. ✉ *531 Broadway, Sonoma* ✣ *Near W. Napa St.* ☎ *707/343–7155* 🌐 *www.pommecidershop.com* 🕒 *Closed Wed.*

HOUSEHOLD ITEMS

★ **The Passdoor**

HOUSEWARES | A cross between a design gallery and a museum gift shop, the Passdoor stocks high-quality artworks;

glassware and ceramics; jewelry; and creative home-decor items. ✉ *452 1st St. E, Sonoma* ✛ *100 feet north of Sebastiani Theatre* ☎ *707/634–0015* ⊕ *www.thepassdoor.net.*

Activities

BIKING
Sonoma Adventures
BIKING | Mount a regular bike or one with "pedal assist" on this company's half- and full-day guided tours to area wineries. You can also rent a bike and head off on your own. ✉ *1254 Broadway, Sonoma* ✛ *1/5 mile north of Napa Rd.* ☎ *707/938–2080* ⊕ *www.sonoma-adventures.com* ✑ *½-day tour from $119, not including tasting fees.*

SPAS
The Spa at the Lodge
SPAS | A restful haven in the rear of the 10-acre Lodge at Sonoma property, the spa contains 11 treatment rooms including two for couples. The signature 80-minute Celestial Body Renewal Ritual begins with an exfoliating shea-butter body scrub, followed by a body wrap and a CDB deep-tissue massage, and there are several other 50- or 80-minute options. Facials, eye and lip treatments, and waxing are also on the menu. Before or after sessions, guests can relax in a landscaped outdoor garden with a pool, a hot tub, and a barrel sauna. ✉ *Lodge at Sonoma, 1325 Broadway, Sonoma* ✛ *At Leveroni Rd.* ☎ *707/931–3434* ⊕ *www.thelodgeatsonoma.com/spa* ✑ *Treatments from $210.*

Glen Ellen

7 miles north of Sonoma.

Craggy Glen Ellen epitomizes the difference between the Napa and Sonoma Valleys. Whereas small Napa towns like St. Helena get their charm from upscale boutiques and restaurants lined up along well-groomed sidewalks, Glen Ellen's crooked streets are shaded with stands of old oak trees and occasionally bisected by the Sonoma and Calabazas Creeks. Tucked among the trees of a narrow canyon, where Sonoma Mountain and the Mayacamas pinch in the valley floor, Glen Ellen looks more like a town of the Sierra foothills gold country than a Wine Country village.

Wine has been part of Glen Ellen since the 1840s, when a French immigrant, Joshua Chauvet, planted grapes and later built a winery and the valley's first distillery. Machinery at the winery was powered by steam, and boilers were fueled with wood from local oaks. Other valley farmers followed Chauvet's example, and grape growing took off, although Prohibition took its toll on most of these operations. Today dozens of wineries in the area beg to be visited, but you may find it hard to avoid succumbing to Glen Ellen's slow pace and lounge poolside at your lodging or linger over a leisurely picnic. The renowned cook and food writer M. F. K. Fisher, who lived and worked in Glen Ellen for 22 years until her death in 1992, would surely have approved. Hunter S. Thompson, who lived here for a spell before he became famous, might not: he found the place too sedate. Glen Ellen's most famous resident, however, was Jack London, who personified the town's rugged spirit.

GETTING HERE AND AROUND
To get to Glen Ellen from Sonoma, drive west on Spain Street. After about a mile, take Highway 12 north for 7 miles to Arnold Drive, which, after you take a left, deposits you in the middle of town. Many of Glen Ellen's restaurants and inns are along a half-mile stretch of Arnold Drive. Sonoma Transit buses serve Glen Ellen from Sonoma and Kenwood.

Benziger tram tours take to the fields to show biodynamic farming techniques in action.

Sights

Abbot's Passage Winery & Mercantile

WINERY | For her passion project, sixth-generation vintner Katie Bundschu, who's also involved in her family's historic Gundlach Bundschu winery, focuses on wines made from organic grapes grown in other family-owned, predominantly Sonoma County vineyards. Most of the wines are old-style field blends in which different types of grapes from the same vineyard are fermented and aged together rather than separately, as is more common these days. The wines impress with their balance, approachability, and rich flavors. A recent blend of more or less half-and-half Zinfandel and Petite Sirah with a pinch of Petit Verdot hints at the experimentation going on here. You can sample the wines 2½ miles south of downtown Glen Ellen at a garden estate whose grape-growing history dates back nearly as far as the Bundschu family's. ⊠ *777 Madrone Rd., Sonoma* ✛ *Off Arnold Dr. or Hwy. 12* ☎ *707/939–3017* ⊕ *www.abbotspassage.com* ✉ *Tastings from $40* ⊙ *Closed Tues. and Wed.*

Benziger Family Winery

WINERY | One of the best-known Sonoma County wineries sits on a sprawling estate in a bowl with 360-degree sun exposure. Hosts conducting popular tram tours explain the benefits of the vineyard's natural setting and how biodynamic farming yields healthier, more flavorful fruit. The eco-friendly agricultural practices include extensive plantings to attract beneficial insects and the deployment of sheep to trim vegetation between the vines while simultaneously tilling the soil with their hooves and fertilizing to boot. Known for Chardonnay, Cabernet Sauvignon, Merlot, Pinot Noir, and Sauvignon Blanc, the winery is a beautiful spot for an alfresco tasting, whether you take the tour or not. All visits are by appointment; reserve a tram tour at least a day or two ahead in summer and early fall. ⊠ *1883 London Ranch Rd., Glen Ellen* ✛ *Off Arnold Dr.* ☎ *888/490–2739* ⊕ *www.benziger.com* ✉ *Tastings from $40* ⊙ *Closed Tues. and Wed.*

★ Jack London State Historic Park

STATE/PROVINCIAL PARK | The pleasures are pastoral and intellectual at author Jack London's beloved Beauty Ranch, where you could easily spend the afternoon hiking some of the 30-plus miles of trails that loop through meadows and stands of oaks, redwoods, and other trees. Manuscripts and personal artifacts depicting London's travels are on view at the House of Happy Walls Museum, which provides an overview of the writer's life, literary passions, humanitarian and conservation efforts, and promotion of organic farming. His wife Charmian's equally compelling story is also documented. A short hike away lie the ruins of Wolf House, which burned down just before London was to move in. Also open to visitors are a few outbuildings and the restored wood-frame cottage where London penned many of his later works. He's buried on the property. ■TIP→ **The park hosts hot-ticket musical revues and comedies produced by Transcendence Theatre Company each summer.** ⊠ *2400 London Ranch Rd., Glen Ellen* ✛ *Off Arnold Dr.* ☎ *707/938–5216* ⊕ *www.jacklondonpark. com* ⊠ *Parking $10 ($5 walk-in or bike).*

★ Lasseter Family Winery

WINERY | Immaculately groomed grapevines dazzle the eye at John and Nancy Lasseter's secluded winery, and it's no accident: Phil Coturri, Sonoma Valley's premier organic vineyard manager, tends them. Even the landscaping, which includes an insectary to attract beneficial bugs, is meticulously maintained. Come harvest time, the wine-making team oversees gentle processes that transform the fruit into wines of purity and grace, among them a Sémillon–Sauvignon Blanc blend, the Enjoué rosé, and Bordeaux and Rhône reds. Evocative labels illustrate the tale behind each wine. In good weather, guests hear these well-told stories at tastings on the winery's outdoor patio, whose views include the vineyard and the Mayacamas Mountains, where the Lasseters purchased a second vineyard. All visits to the Glen Ellen property are by appointment. ⊠ *1 Vintage La., Glen Ellen* ✛ *Off Dunbar Rd.* ☎ *707/933–2800* ⊕ *www. lasseterfamilywinery.com* ⊠ *Tastings from $40.*

★ Laurel Glen Vineyard

WINERY | As a longtime wine-industry marketing director, Bettina Sichel knew the potential pitfalls of winery ownership, but when she discovered a uniquely situated volcanic-soiled Sonoma Mountain vineyard for sale, she plunged in enthusiastically. Because her 14 acres of Cabernet Sauvignon vines face east, the mountain shelters the grapes from the hot late-afternoon sun and excessively cool Pacific influences. Sichel's wine-making team includes organic-farming legend Phil Coturri and winemaker Randall Watkins. By appointment at Sichel's tasting room in downtown Glen Ellen, you can taste the impressive estate Cabernet, along with another Cabernet, a rosé from the vineyard's oldest vines, and a Russian River Valley Sauvignon Blanc. ⊠ *13750 Arnold Dr., Glen Ellen* ✛ *At London Ranch Rd.* ☎ *707/933–9877* ⊕ *www.laurelglen. com* ⊠ *Tastings from $40.*

Loxton Cellars

WINERY | Back when tasting rooms were low-tech and the winemaker often poured the wines, the experience at Loxton Cellars unfolded pretty much the way it does today. The personable Australia-born owner, Chris Loxton, who's on hand many days, crafts a Sonoma Coast Chardonnay, along with Zinfandel, Syrah, Cabernet Sauvignon, and a red blend or two. All are quite good, and some regulars swear by the two Syrah Ports. Tastings require an appointment, but the winery generally accommodates weekday walk-ins if guests call ahead. ■TIP→ **To learn more about Loxton's wine-making philosophy and practices, book a Vineyard Walkabout tour, followed by a seated tasting.** ⊠ *11466 Dunbar Rd., Glen Ellen* ✛ *At Hwy. 12* ☎ *707/935–7221*

Jack London Country

Between 1905 and his death in 1916, author Jack London (*The Call of the Wild, White Fang*) bought seven parcels of land totaling 1,400 acres, which he dubbed Beauty Ranch. When he wasn't off traveling, he dedicated most of his time to cultivating the land and raising livestock. He also maintained a few acres of wine grapes for his personal use.

Dreams and Mysteries

In 1913 London rhapsodized about his beloved ranch near Glen Ellen, writing, "The grapes on a score of rolling hills are red with autumn flame. Across Sonoma Mountain, wisps of sea fog are stealing. The afternoon sun smolders in the drowsy sky. I have everything to make me glad I am alive. I am filled with dreams and mysteries."

Much of Beauty Ranch is now preserved as Jack London State Historic Park, worth visiting for its museum and other glimpses into London's life and for trails that skirt vineyards and meander through Douglas firs, coastal redwoods, oaks, and madrones. London and his wife, Charmian, spent two years constructing their dream home, Wolf House, before it burned down one hot August night in 1913, days before they were scheduled to move in. Looking at the remaining stone walls and fireplaces gives you a sense of the building's grand scale. Within, a fireproof basement vault was to hold London's manuscripts. Elsewhere in the park stands the unusually posh pigsty that London's neighbors called the Pig Palace.

⊕ *www.loxtonwines.com* ✉ *Tastings from $20.*

★ Schermeister Winery

WINERY | During the growing season, Robert Schermeister frequently visits the grapes for his wines to observe their progress, focusing on the pick date "to nail it perfectly." The winemaker personally handles all the lab work and ferments using native yeasts, a trickier process than employing commercial ones. This obsession pays off in aromatic Viognier and Chardonnay, intensely flavored Pinot Noirs and Syrahs, and a rosé aged in neutral French oak barrels. A small niche within a historic Glen Ellen building serves as a tasting room—the patio outside faces Sonoma Creek. On a visit, you'll meet Robert or his wife, Laura. The couple's romance began after he charmed her over a bottle of his Pinot Noir. ■TIP➔ **Walk-ins are welcome as space permits, but it's best to make an**

appointment because this highly regarded winery with a small annual production temporarily halts tastings when the wines run out. ✉ *Jack London Village, 14301 Arnold Dr., Studio 28, Glen Ellen* ✛ *¾ mile south of downtown Glen Ellen* ☎ *707/934–8953* ⊕ *schermeister.com* ✉ *Tastings from $40* ⊙ *Closed Mon.–Wed. (and when wine sells out).*

Sonoma Botanical Garden

GARDEN | Rare East Asian trees and plants thrive in this 25-acre woodland garden a little over a mile north of downtown Glen Ellen. There's also a heritage rose garden near the entrance. The colors throughout are most vibrant in spring, but year-round a visit here makes for a pleasant break from wine touring. ✉ *12841 Hwy. 12, Glen Ellen* ✛ *¼ mile north of Arnold Dr.* ☎ *707/996–3166* ⊕ *www.sonomabg.org* ✉ *$12* ⊙ *Closed Tues.*

★ **Talisman Wine**

WINERY | It's "all Pinot, all the time" at Scott and Marta Rich's storefront tasting room inside Glen Ellen's oldest commercial building. The two have well more than half a century of wine-industry experience between them, he in the vineyard and cellar, she on the business end, and their deep knowledge informs their lovingly crafted, predominantly single-vineyard wines. With grapes hailing from several Sonoma County appellations and a few farther afield, the wines are made in small lots, usually a few hundred cases. Scott intervenes as little as possible during wine making to evoke a sense of place in the glass, but his oak-aging and other sage choices elevate the finished product. Talisman releases its Pinots around the four-year mark so they can achieve a little maturity first. ✉ *13651 Arnold Dr., Glen Ellen* ✣ *At Carquinez Ave.* ☎ *707/721–1628* 🌐 *www.talismanwine.com* 🎟 *Tastings from $45.*

🍴 Restaurants

Fig Cafe

$$ | **FRENCH** | The compact menu at this cheerful bistro focuses on California and French comfort food—pot roast and duck confit, for instance, as well as flounder meunière and a few thin-crust pizzas. Steamed mussels are served with crispy fries, which also accompany the Chef's Burger (top sirloin with cheese), two of the many dependable dishes that have made the Fig a downtown Glen Ellen fixture. **Known for:** daily three-course prix-fixe specials; Rhône-oriented wine list; fig and arugula salad. [$] *Average main: $25* ✉ *13690 Arnold Dr., Glen Ellen* ✣ *At O'Donnell La.* ☎ *707/938–2130* 🌐 *www.thefigcafe.com* 🕒 *No lunch.*

★ **Glen Ellen Star**

$$$ | **ECLECTIC** | Chef Ari Weiswasser honed his craft at The French Laundry, Daniel, and other bastions of culinary finesse, but his Sonoma Valley outpost revolves around haute-rustic cuisine, much of it emerging from a wood-fired oven. In 2022, Weiswasser turned the day-to-day reins over to a new chef de cuisine, but the mainstay crisp-crusted, richly sauced Margherita and other pizzas continue to thrive in the oven's torrid heat, as do tender whole fish entrées and vegetables roasted in small iron skillets. **Known for:** outdoor dining area; prix-fixe Wednesday "neighborhood night" menu with free corkage; Weiswasser's sauces, emulsions, and spices. [$] *Average main: $33* ✉ *13648 Arnold Dr., Glen Ellen* ✣ *At Warm Springs Rd.* ☎ *707/343–1384* 🌐 *glenellenstar.com* 🕒 *No lunch.*

★ **The Mill at Glen Ellen**

$$ | **MODERN AMERICAN** | The redwood-timbered main dining space of this comfort-food haven recalls the 19th-century heyday of the former sawmill (later a grist mill) it occupies, though when the weather's nice most patrons take their meals on a plant-filled outdoor deck with timeless Sonoma Creek views. Culinary influences from Latin America to Southeast Asia underlie dishes that might include fire-roasted achiote half chicken, wild poached salmon, and potato patties with red lentils and chutney. **Known for:** steak and Impossible burgers; exotic desserts; owner-chefs of local renown. [$] *Average main: $26* ✉ *Jack London Village, 14301 Arnold Dr., Glen Ellen* ✣ *¾ mile south of downtown* ☎ *707/721–1818* 🌐 *www.themillatglenellen.com* 🕒 *Closed Mon. and Tues.*

☕ Coffee and Quick Bites

★ **Les Pascals**

$ | **CAFÉ** | A bright-yellow slice of France in downtown Glen Ellen, this combination pâtisserie, boulangerie, and café takes its name from its husband-and-wife owners, Pascal and Pascale Merle. Pascal whips up croissants, breads, turnovers, and sweet treats like Napoleons, galettes, and eclairs, along with quiches, potpies, and other savory fare; Pascale creates a cordial environment for customers to enjoy them. **Known for:** memorable French onion soup; shaded back patio; high-test French and Italian coffee drinks. [$] *Average main: $12 ✉ 13758 Arnold Dr., Glen Ellen ✥ Near London Ranch Rd. ☎ 707/934–8378 🌐 www.lespascalspatisserie.com ⏱ Closed Wed. No dinner.*

Hotels

Beltane Ranch
$$$ | **B&B/INN** | On a slope of the Mayacamas range with gorgeous Sonoma Valley views, this working ranch, vineyard, and winery contains charmingly old-fashioned rooms. **Pros:** bountiful breakfasts; relaxed hospitality; ranch setting. **Cons:** downstairs rooms get some noise from upstairs rooms; ceiling fans instead of air-conditioning; may feel too remote or low-key for some guests. [$] *Rooms from: $311 ✉ 11775 Sonoma Hwy./Hwy. 12, Glen Ellen ☎ 707/833–4233 🌐 www.beltaneranch.com 🛏 5 rooms 🍴 Free Breakfast.*

★ Gaige House
$$$ | **B&B/INN** | There's no other place in Sonoma or Napa quite like the Gaige House, which blends the best elements of a traditional country inn, a boutique hotel, and a secluded hideaway. **Pros:** short walk to Glen Ellen restaurants, shops, and tasting rooms; idyllic swimming pool and hot tub area; full breakfast with two hot items. **Cons:** sound carries in the main house; least expensive rooms are on the small side; oriented more toward couples than families with children. [$] *Rooms from: $351 ✉ 13540 Arnold Dr., Glen Ellen ☎ 707/935–0237, 866/207–7146 🌐 www.thegaigehouse.com 🛏 23 rooms 🍴 Free Breakfast.*

★ Olea Hotel
$$$ | **HOTEL** | Husband-and-wife team Ashish and Sia Patel operate this country-casual yet sophisticated boutique lodging. **Pros:** beautiful style; complimentary wine; filling two-course breakfasts. **Cons:** minor road noise in some rooms; fills up quickly on weekends; weekend minimum-stay requirement. [$] *Rooms from: $387 ✉ 5131 Warm Springs Rd., Glen Ellen ✥ West off Arnold Dr. ☎ 707/996–5131 🌐 www.oleahotel.com 🛏 15 rooms 🍴 Free Breakfast.*

Kenwood

4 miles north of Glen Ellen.

Tiny Kenwood consists of little more than a few restaurants, shops, tasting rooms, and a historic train depot, now used for private events. But hidden in this pretty landscape of meadows and woods at the north end of Sonoma Valley are several good wineries, most just off Sonoma Highway. Varietals grown here at the foot of the Sugarloaf Mountains include Sauvignon Blanc, Chardonnay, Zinfandel, and Cabernet Sauvignon.

GETTING HERE AND AROUND

To get to Kenwood from Glen Ellen, head northeast on Arnold Drive and north on Highway 12. Sonoma Transit buses serve Kenwood from Glen Ellen and Sonoma.

Sights

B. Wise Vineyards Tasting Lounge
WINERY | The stylish roadside tasting room of this producer of small-lot reds sits on the valley floor, but owner Brion Wise's winery and vineyards occupy prime acreage high in the Moon Mountain District AVA. The winery made its name crafting big, bold Cabernets, later introducing Pinot Noirs from Sonoma County and Oregon's Willamette Valley. The lineup also includes Chardonnay, a rosé of Pinot Noir that quickly sells out, and the Cabernet-heavy blend Trios, whose grapes, all from the estate, include Bordeaux red grapes plus Syrah and Tannat. There's also a Napa Valley version of Trios. Reservations are recommended, especially on weekends,

but walk-ins are often accommodated. ■TIP→ **A tasting here may whet your appetite for a visit to the estate, done by appointment only.** ✉ *9077 Sonoma Hwy., Kenwood ✛ At Shaw Ave.* ☎ *707/282–9169* ⊕ *www.bwisevineyards.com* 🍷 *Tastings from $25.*

★ En Garde Winery

WINERY | Sommeliers, critics, and collectors extol the Pinot Noirs and Cabernet Sauvignons of Csaba Szakál, En Garde's Hungarian-born winemaker and owner. To create what he describes as "aromatic, complex, lush, and juicy" wines, Szakál selects top Sonoma County vineyards for the Pinots and the Napa Valley's Diamond Mountain, Mt. Veeder, and other high-elevation sites for the Cabernets. Not afraid to heavy up the oak on the Cabernets, he nevertheless achieves elegance as well. The winemaker is equally precise about hiring staffers for his modest highway's-edge tasting room along Kenwood's brief commercial strip. Well-acquainted with his goals and methods, they provide a wealth of knowledge about wine making and California viticulture. If you're lucky, Szakál will be around to discuss his wines (he loves to), which also include Chardonnay, other whites, and rosé of Pinot Noir. Visits are by reservation, with same-day appointments sometimes possible. ✉ *9077 Sonoma Hwy., Kenwood ✛ At Shaw Ave.* ☎ *707/282–9216* ⊕ *www.engardewinery. com* 🍷 *Tastings from $40.*

★ Hamilton Family Wines

WINERY | Olive trees ring the outdoor wine garden attracting most of the action at Greg and Lindsay Hamilton's joyful roadside tasting room. The couple—he's from Scotland, she's a Californian—started their journey as vintners making garage wine together. These days, Sonoma Valley native Jess Wade crafts a sparkling blanc de noirs, Sauvignon Blanc, Pinot Noir, a GSM (Grenache, Syrah, Mourvèdre) blend, and The Phoenix, a lush mix of Cabernet Franc, Cabernet

Sauvignon, and Merlot. The last wine's name refers to Greg and Lindsay's rise from the ashes of the home they lost in the 2017 Wine Country fires. Though a calamity, the Hamiltons credit the blaze with spurring them to achieve more quickly their goal of establishing a wine brand. ■TIP→ **Hamilton Family Wines is next to Vaughn Duffy Wines; the two operations pair well as examples of newer first-generation labels.** ✉ *8860 Sonoma Hwy., Kenwood ✛ Near Greene St.* ☎ *707/408–3090* ⊕ *hamilton.wine* 🍷 *Tastings from $45* ⊗ *Closed Mon. and Tues.*

Kunde Family Winery

WINERY | Founded by its namesake family more than a century ago, this Sonoma Valley operation prides itself on producing 100% estate wines from its 1,850-acre property, which rises 1,400 feet from the valley floor. Kunde's whites, the winery's best offerings, include several Chardonnays and a Sauvignon Blanc, with Cabernet Sauvignon, Merlot, and a Zinfandel from 1880s vines among the reds. Reservations are required; call ahead for same-day visits. ■TIP→ **The Mountain Top Tasting, a vineyard tour by luxury van to a tree-shaded ridge with broad valley views, ends with a sampling of reserve wines. It's offered mid-spring–mid-fall.** ✉ *9825 Sonoma Hwy./Hwy. 12, Kenwood* ☎ *707/833–5501* ⊕ *www.kunde. com* 🍷 *Tastings from $45* ⊗ *Closed Tues. and Wed.*

St. Francis Winery

WINERY | Nestled at the foot of Mt. Hood, St. Francis has earned national acclaim for its pairings of wines and small bites. With its bell tower, red-tile roof, and views of the Mayacamas Mountains to the east, the winery's California Mission–style visitor center occupies one of Sonoma County's most scenic locations. The charm of the surroundings is matched by the wines, among them Cabernet Sauvignon and rich, earthy Zinfandels from the Dry Creek, Russian River, and Sonoma

Valleys. The five-course pairings might include Chardonnay with lobster bisque or Cabernet Sauvignon with wine-braised beef ribs. ✉ *100 Pythian Rd., Kenwood* ✣ *Off Hwy. 12* ☎ *707/833–0242* 🌐 *www.stfranciswinery.com* 🎫 *Tastings from $35.*

★ Vaughn Duffy Wines
WINERY | In 2009, after participating in various aspects of the wine business—working in tasting rooms, as a harvest intern, at a wine shop, and at a custom-crush wine-making facility—Matt Duffy bought a ton of Pinot Noir grapes and launched Vaughn Duffy with his wife, Sara Vaughn. That first Pinot Noir, from a Sonoma coast source, garnered positive reviews. Since then, the two have added several Pinot Noir blends and single-vineyard bottlings to their lineup, along with Sauvignon Blanc, Chardonnay, rosé of Pinot Noir, and Carignane, Zinfandel, and Petite Sirah reds. All the wines are reasonably priced given the quality. At the label's small tasting space (with patio), you'll likely hear the inspiring Vaughn Duffy story firsthand from one of its amiable namesake owners. ✉ *8910 Sonoma Hwy., Kenwood* ✣ *Near Greene St.* ☎ *707/282–9156* 🌐 *vaughnduffywines.com* 🎫 *Tastings from $25* 🕑 *Closed Mon. and Tues.*

🍴 Restaurants

Palooza Gastropub & Wine Bar
$$ | **AMERICAN** | Best for lunch but also open for dinner, Palooza pleases with many beers on tap, jazzed-up pub grub, casual decor, and an often-packed covered outdoor patio. Pulled-pork and crispy-chicken sandwiches and beer-battered fish and fries are among the popular items, with prawn and braised-beef tacos and shredded-kale salads with sliced apples for those seeking lighter fare. **Known for:** many local brews; mostly Sonoma Valley wines; beer-battered fried pickles and mozzarella-ball appetizers. [$] *Average main: $18* ✉ *8910 Sonoma Hwy./Hwy. 12, Kenwood* ☎ *707/833–4000* 🌐 *www.paloozafresh.com* 🕑 *Closed Mon. and Tues.*

Salt & Stone
$$$ | **MODERN AMERICAN** | The menu at this upscale roadhouse with a sloping wood-beamed ceiling focuses on seafood and meat—beef, lamb, chicken, duck, and other options—with many dishes in both categories grilled. Start with the classics, perhaps a martini and oysters Rockefeller, before moving on to well-plated contemporary entrées that might include crispy-skin salmon or duck breast, a fish stew, or grilled rib eye. **Known for:** mountain-view outdoor seating area; weekend brunch; weekday happy hour 2:30–5 except holidays. [$] *Average main: $31* ✉ *9900 Sonoma Hwy., Kenwood* ✣ *At Kunde Winery Rd.* ☎ *707/833–6326* 🌐 *www.saltstonekenwood.com* 🕑 *No lunch Tues. and Wed.*

Tips Roadside
$$$ | **AMERICAN** | The owners of a local-fave tri-tip food trolley opened this comfort-food restaurant in a 90-year-old building originally a gas station and later an inn. In addition to tri-tip, the New Orleans–inspired menu consists of small bites like white-cheddar grits and larger bites that include smoke-braised short ribs, steelhead trout, fried chicken, and a grass-fed burger with cheese and tomato jam. **Known for:** open-air dining with mountain views; full bar's craft cocktails; brunch beignets with Meyer lemon sauce. [$] *Average main: $28* ✉ *8445 Sonoma Hwy./Hwy. 12, Kenwood* ✣ *At Adobe Rd.* ☎ *707/509–0078* 🌐 *www.tipsroadside.com* 🕑 *Closed Mon. and Tues.*

🛏 Hotels

★ Kenwood Inn and Spa
$$$$ | **B&B/INN** | Fluffy feather beds, custom Italian furnishings, and French doors in most cases opening onto terraces or balconies lend this inn's uncommonly spacious guest rooms a romantic

air—more than a few guests are celebrating honeymoons or anniversaries. **Pros:** large rooms; lavish furnishings; romantic setting. **Cons:** far from nightlife; expensive in high season; geared more to couples than families with children. [$] *Rooms from: $420* ✉ *10400 Sonoma Hwy./Hwy. 12, Kenwood* ☎ *707/833–1293, 800/353–6966* 🌐 *www.kenwood-inn.com* 🛏 *29 rooms* 🍴 *Free Breakfast.*

Activities

Spa at Kenwood Inn

SPAS | Done in soft whites and chocolate-brown accents that play off the greenery outside, the intimate spa holds three individual treatment rooms, a room for couples, and a private outdoor terrace (also good for couples) with a tub and shower. The 50-minute Valley of the Moon massage involves aromatherapy oils, while the 80-minute Rest & Renewal treatment focuses on releasing tension and reducing stress. The name of the 110-minute Ultimate Bliss massage telegraphs its goal: deep relaxation. ✉ *10400 Sonoma Hwy./Hwy. 12, Kenwood* ☎ *707/833–1293* 🌐 *www.kenwoodinn.com/spa* 🎟 *Treatments from $165.*

Petaluma

14 miles west of Sonoma; 39 miles north of San Francisco.

The best-known Wine Country gateway towns from San Francisco are Napa and Sonoma, but the sleeper is Petaluma. Despite its population of 60,000, this is a farm town, and the residents are proud of it. Recent years have seen an uptick in the quality of Petaluma cuisine, fueled in part by the proliferation of local organic and artisanal farms and boutique wine production. Since the approval of the Petaluma Gap AVA, the city even has its name on a wine appellation.

Petaluma's agricultural history reaches back to the mid-1800s, when General Mariano Vallejo established Rancho de Petaluma as his vast agrarian empire's headquarters. From the late 1800s into the 1960s, Petaluma marketed itself as the "Egg Capital of the World," and with production totals that peaked at 612 million eggs in 1946, the point was hard to dispute. Although a poultry processor remains one of Petaluma's largest employers, the town has diversified. The adobe, an informative stop, albeit one whose presentation may recall grade-school field trips, was once the area's *only* employer. These days its visitation figures are dwarfed by Lagunitas Brewing Company, whose tour is a hoot. At McEvoy Ranch, which started out making gourmet olive oil before branching into wine, you can taste both products and tour parts of the farm.

GETTING HERE AND AROUND

Petaluma lies west of Sonoma and southwest of Glen Ellen and Kenwood. From Highway 12 or Arnold Drive, take Watmaugh Road west to Highway 116 west. Sonoma Transit buses serve Petaluma from the Sonoma Valley. From San Francisco take U.S. 101 (or Golden Gate Transit Bus 101) north.

VISITOR INFORMATION

CONTACTS Visit Petaluma. ✉ *210 Lakeville St.* ☎ *707/769–0429* 🌐 *visitpetaluma.com.*

Sights

Adobe Road Winery

WINERY | An upbeat atmosphere prevails in the downtown Petaluma tasting areas of this winery founded by former race-car driver Kevin Buckler and his wife, Debra. To produce its portfolio of mostly small-lot wines, Adobe Road sources grapes from top-tier growers, among them Beckstoffer for Napa Valley Cabernet Sauvignon, Malbec, and Merlot; and Sangiacomo for Chardonnay, Pinot

Noir, and Syrah from the Petaluma Gap AVA. The Cabernet and Malbec shine. ■TIP➙ **In 2022, the Bucklers broke ground on a combination tasting room, winery, and car museum along the waterfront at C and 1st Streets that they hope will open in 2024.** ⊠ *6 Petaluma Blvd. N, Petaluma ✛ At B St.* ☎ *707/774–6699* ⊕ *www.adoberoadwines.com* ✉ *Tastings from $30.*

Keller Estate

WINERY | This boutique winery's guests discover why "wind to wine" is the Petaluma Gap AVA's slogan. The steady Pacific Ocean and San Pablo Bay breezes that mitigate the midday heat give the grapes thick "sailor's skin," heightening their tannins and flavor, says Ana Keller, whose parents began planting vineyards here in 1989 on former dairy fields. Keller Estate concentrates on Chardonnay, Pinot Noir, and Syrah wines, many of which receive high marks from critics. Tastings usually take place alfresco on a stone terrace shaded by umbrellas and flowering pear trees. The winery requires reservations for all visits. ■TIP➙ **On most days, hulking garage doors embedded with stained glass created by Ana's sister, Grace, are opened to reveal a few dozen cars collected by their father, Arturo Keller.** ⊠ *5875 Lakeville Hwy., Petaluma ✛ At Cannon La.* ☎ *707/765–2117* ⊕ *www.kellerestate. com* ✉ *Tastings from $50* ☺ *Closed Sun.–Wed.*

Lagunitas Brewing Company

BREWERY | These days owned by Heineken International, Lagunitas began as a craft brewery in Marin County in 1993 before moving to Petaluma in 1994. In addition to its large facility, the company operates a taproom, the Schwag Shop for gifts, and an outdoor beer garden that in good weather bustles even midday. Guides leading the brewery tour, which includes a beer flight, provide an irreverent version of the company's rise to international acclaim. An engaging tale involves the state alcohol board's sting operation commemorated by

Undercover Investigation Shut-down Ale, one of several small-batch brews made here. ⊠ *1280 N. McDowell Blvd., Petaluma ✛ ½ mile north of Corona Rd.* ☎ *707/778–8776* ⊕ *lagunitas.com/taproom/petaluma* ✉ *Tour $10* ☺ *Taproom closed Mon. and Tues.*

★ McEvoy Ranch

FARM/RANCH | The late Nan McEvoy's retirement project after departing as board chair of the *San Francisco Chronicle,* the ranch produces organic extra-virgin olive oil as well as Pinot Noir and other wines, the estate ones from the Petaluma Gap AVA. In good weather, relaxing tastings of oils or wines unfold on a pond's-edge flagstone patio with views of alternating rows of Syrah grapes and mature olive trees. You can preorder lunch to accompany any tasting; for a more private experience, book a pondside cabana. Walkabout Ranch Tours of four guests or more take in vineyards, gardens, and a Chinese pavilion. All visits require an appointment. ⊠ *5935 Red Hill Rd., Petaluma ✛ 6½ miles south of downtown* ☎ *707/778–2307* ⊕ *www. mcevoyranch.com* ✉ *Tastings from $25 (olive oil), $35 (wine); tours from $55.*

Sonoma Portworks

WINERY | In the mid-1990s, Bill Reading got the bright idea to create the world's first chocolate wine. The concept went nowhere, but a later experiment adding dark-chocolate essences to port proved a winner—and became the first Sonoma Portworks product, Deco Port, these days made from Zinfandel, Grenache, and Alicante Bouschet. Reading followed this up by adding hazelnut essences to what's now called Duet Sherry. Individual ports made from Petite Sirah and Petit Verdot are among the additional offerings. You can taste these crowd-pleasing wines where they're made, in a warehouselike space on downtown's southern edge. ⊠ *613 2nd St., Petaluma ✛ Near H St.* ☎ *707/769–5203* ⊕ *portworks.com* ✉ *Tastings from $15* ☺ *Closed Tues. and Wed.*

Restaurants

Brewsters Beer Garden

$$ | AMERICAN | FAMILY | Succulent fried chicken and St. Louis ribs whose meat glides off the bone are among the hits at this open-air, partially covered restaurant where diners sit at sturdy oak picnic or high-top tables. Many of the ingredients come from top artisanal protein and produce purveyors; most of the two dozen beers on tap are by craft breweries. **Known for:** easygoing pace; full bar; good wine selection. $ Average main: $24 ⊠ 229 Water St. N, Petaluma ✦ Near E. Washington St. ☎ 707/981–8330 ⊕ brewstersbeergarden.com.

★ Central Market

$$$ | MODERN AMERICAN | A participant in the Slow Food movement, Central Market serves creative, upscale Cal-Mediterranean dishes—many of whose ingredients come from the restaurant's organic farm—in a century-old building with an exposed brick wall and an open kitchen. The menu, which changes daily depending on chef Tony Najiola's inspiration and what's ripe and ready, might include spicy duck wings as a starter, a slow-roasted-beets salad, pizzas, stews, two or three pasta dishes, and wood-grilled fish and meat. **Known for:** happy hour (5–6 pm) apps, beer, and wine specials; superior wine list; historic setting. $ Average main: $27 ⊠ 42 Petaluma Blvd. N, Petaluma ✦ Near Western Ave. ☎ 707/778–9900 ⊕ www.centralmarket-petaluma.com ⊗ Closed Mon. and Tues. No lunch.

Cucina Paradiso

$$$ | ITALIAN | Long a locals' favorite for traditional Italian-American cuisine, this restaurant has a warmly lit, often packed dining room and a heated back patio with Petaluma River views. The chef, who trained in Italy, prepares several pasta dishes a night, along with mains that might include veal scaloppini or saltimbocca, roasted chicken stuffed with arugula and pancetta, and pork tenderloin with Gorgonzola sauce. **Known for:** antipasti and salads; Italian and Sonoma County wines; tiramisu, crème brûlée, and profiteroles for dessert. $ Average main: $32 ⊠ 114 Petaluma Blvd. N, Petaluma ✦ Near Western Ave. ☎ 707/782–1130 ⊕ cucinaparadisopetaluma.com ⊗ Closed Sun. and Mon.

★ Pearl Petaluma

$$ | MEDITERRANEAN | Regulars of this southern Petaluma "daytime café" with indoor and outdoor seating rave about its eastern Mediterranean–inflected cuisine—then immediately downplay their enthusiasm lest this unassuming gem become more popular. The menu changes often, but mainstays include *shakshuka* (a tomato-based stew with baked eggs) and a lamb burger dripping with fennel tzatziki. **Known for:** weekend brunch; fun beverage lineup, alcoholic and non; menu prices include gratuity. $ Average main: $23 ⊠ 500 1st St., Petaluma ✦ At G St. ☎ 707/559–5187 ⊕ pearlpetaluma.com ⊗ Closed Tues. and Wed. No dinner.

★ Table Culture Provisions

$$$$ | MODERN AMERICAN | The chef-owners of this neighborly restaurant say their fare "walks the line between comfort and haute cuisine"—mostly California-inspired and "hyperseasonal" items that range from vegetarian butter-bean cassoulet (there's also a pork-belly version) to a 30-ounce tomahawk steak. The same could be said for the casual but knowing hospitality and the decor (bare wooden tables yet linen napkins), but it all works: dining here engenders quiet excitement. **Known for:** raw bar and appetizers; weekend brunch (clever updates of the classics); dinner tasting menu. $ Average main: $125 ⊠ 312 Petaluma Blvd. S, Petaluma ✦ Near F St. ☎ 707/559–5739 ⊕ www.tcprovision.com ⊗ Closed Sun. and Mon. No lunch weekdays.

Coffee and Quick Bites

Stockhome

$$ | SCANDINAVIAN | The Petaluma-based owners of this hip-homey counter-service restaurant pay homage to Swedish street food, whose influences, it turns out, include Middle Eastern cuisine. Seasonal ingredients, for the most part locally produced and raised, find their way into kebabs, Swedish meatballs, Wiener schnitzel, gravlax, herring done "grandma's way" (and a few others), and *korv kiosk* (grilled frankfurters or sausages), all prepared with élan. **Known for:** vegetarian and vegan options; artisanal beer, wine, and hard cider selection; Swedish desserts and candy. [$] *Average main: $23* ✉ *220 Western Ave., Petaluma* ✣ *At Liberty St.* ☎ *707/981–8511* 🌐 *www.stockhomerestaurant.com* ⏲ *Closed Mon. and Tues.*

Hotels

Hampton Inn Petaluma

$ | HOTEL | The former Carlson-Currier Silk Mill, its oldest section dating to 1892, houses this atypical Hampton Inn, some of whose guest rooms have 14-foot ceilings and exposed-brick walls. **Pros:** original architectural details in some rooms; classy breakfast area; fitness and business centers. **Cons:** traffic noise (ask for a historic room away from the road); some standard rooms are small; no pool, nondescript neighborhood. [$] *Rooms from: $199* ✉ *450 Jefferson St., Petaluma* ☎ *707/397–0000* 🌐 *www.hampton.com* 🛏 *75 rooms* 🍴 *Free Breakfast.*

★ **Metro Hotel & Café**

$ | HOTEL | A stay at this downtown boutique hotel may leave you cooing *Je l'adore* ("I adore it") for its colorful palette, French-quirky style, and individually decorated standard-sized rooms, larger suites, four Airstream trailers, and two-bedroom cottage. **Pros:** room rate includes self-serve crepes and French-style coffee; largest Airstream popular with honeymooners on a budget; beyond-cordial owners. **Cons:** some travelers may find aesthetic too offbeat; lacks amenities of full-service properties (though owners aim to meet most expectations); 19th-century main building (though restored in 2021). [$] *Rooms from: $179* ✉ *508 Petaluma Blvd. S, Petaluma* ☎ *707/773–4900* 🌐 *metrolodging.com* 🛏 *19 rooms* 🍴 *Free Breakfast.*

Nightlife

★ **Ernie's Tin Bar**

BARS | Ramshackle Ernie's shares a corrugated tin building with a frozen-in-time roadside garage, with part of the bar actually in the garage. Mounted stag heads and a toothy wild boar watch over this rural-neighborhood hangout with a long, narrow bar, a patio outside, and Pliny the Elder and another 20 or so brews on tap. Signs everywhere ban cell phone use, though patrons and even staffers occasionally flout them. ✉ *5100 Lakeville Hwy., Petaluma* ✣ *At Stage Gulch Rd./Hwy. 116* ☎ *707/762–2075.*

★ **Kapu Bar**

BARS | A GM involved with over-the-top Las Vegas Tiki establishments and a chef with a mission to promote authentic Hawaiian cuisine teamed up on this hypertropical bar. Saturated colors out of the Day-Glo school of lighting illuminate a decor heavy on bamboo, rattan, and intricate wood carvings. The rum-leading lineup includes updated takes on Trader Vic's mai tai and Don the Beachcomber's Zombie, along with newer cocktails with equal verve. All play well with the Asian-influenced bar bites. ✉ *132 Keller St., Petaluma* ✣ *Near Washington St.* ☎ *707/559–3665* 🌐 *kapubar.com* ⏲ *Closed Mon. and Tues.*

Chapter 6

NORTHERN SONOMA, RUSSIAN RIVER, AND WEST COUNTY

6

Updated by
Daniel Mangin

● Sights	❶ Restaurants	▣ Hotels	● Shopping	❡ Nightlife
★★★★★	★★★★★	★★★★☆	★★★★☆	★★★☆☆

WELCOME TO NORTHERN SONOMA, RUSSIAN RIVER, AND WEST COUNTY

TOP REASONS TO GO

★ **Back-roads biking:** The region's ultrascenic back roads include gentle hills and challenging terrain you can traverse with a guide or on your own.

★ **Diverse dining:** Area chefs tickle diners' palates with everything from haute-French and Peruvian cuisine to playful variations on American standards.

★ **Hillside Cabs and old-vine Zins:** Alexander Valley hillside Cabernet Sauvignon and Dry Creek Valley old-vine Zinfandel grapes—as far as the eye can see in spots—thrive in the high heat here.

★ **Hip Healdsburg shopping:** Healdsburg wins the shopping wars fair and square, with more captivating galleries, design-oriented shops, and clothing stores than anywhere in the Wine Country.

★ **Pinot aplenty and Chardonnay, too:** Russian River Valley and Sonoma Coast wineries large and small produce some of California's most celebrated Pinot Noirs and Chardonnays.

1 Healdsburg. Its hotels, wineries, restaurants, and shops make this town a tourist hub.

2 Geyserville. Mostly rural Geyserville has a small, engaging downtown.

3 Windsor. Workaday Windsor hosts Russian River Brewing.

4 Forestville. West of Healdsburg, Forestville nestles among redwoods.

5 Guerneville. This lively town has been a vacation retreat for a century-plus.

6 Jenner. The cliffs here overlook the estuary where the Russian River empties into the Pacific.

7 Bodega Bay. Harbor seals bask on Bodega Bay's windswept beaches.

8 Occidental. Redwoods tower over this small burg east of Bodega Bay.

9 Freestone. Its spa, tasting room, and bakery make this tiny town worth investigating.

10 Sebastopol. East of Occidental, Sebastopol contains restaurants, shops, and wineries.

11 Graton. Sebastopol surrounds this hamlet.

12 Santa Rosa. Sonoma County's largest city straddles U.S. 101.

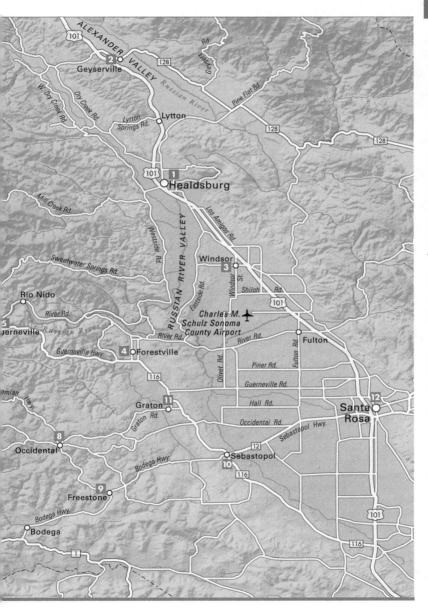

Sonoma County's northern and western reaches are a study in contrasts. Trendy hotels, restaurants, shops, and tasting rooms have transformed Healdsburg into a hot spot. Within a few miles, though, the chic yields to the bucolic, with only an occasional horse ranch, apple or peach orchard, or stand of oaks to interrupt the rolling vineyard hills.

Each of northern and western Sonoma County's regions claims its own micro-climates, soil types, and most-favored varietals, but—except for urban Santa Rosa—all have something in common: peace and quiet. This area is less crowded than the Napa Valley and southern Sonoma. Healdsburg, in particular, is hardly a stranger to overnight visitors, but you'll find less company in many of the region's tasting rooms. The Russian River, Dry Creek, and Alexander Valleys are the grape-growing stars, along with the Sonoma Coast, but smaller appellations like Fort Ross–Seaview also merit investigation.

MAJOR REGIONS

Healdsburg's walkable downtown, swank hotels, and remarkable restaurant scene make it the most convenient base for exploring northern Sonoma County. The wineries here and in Geyserville to the north produce some of the country's best Pinot Noirs, Cabernet Sauvignons, Zinfandels, and Chardonnays.

High-style lodgings and fine dining are in shorter supply in the smaller West County towns of Forestville, Guerneville, Sebastopol, Graton, and Occidental.

Each town has a few charmers, however, along with wineries worth seeking out. The western reaches of Sonoma County, extending all the way to the Pacific Ocean and the towns of Jenner and Bodega Bay, are more sparsely populated, although more and more vineyards are popping up where orchards or ranches once stood.

As the county's—and Wine Country's—largest city, workaday Santa Rosa may lack sex appeal, but it does contain the Charles M. Schulz Museum, Safari West, and other nonwine attractions, and dining and lodging options here and just to the north in Windsor tend to be more affordably priced than in the smaller towns.

Planning

Getting Here and Around

SMART (Sonoma-Marin Area Rail Transit) commuter trains can be helpful if you're visiting the restaurants and tasting rooms of downtown Petaluma and Santa Rosa, but until the tracks are extended to Healdsburg (several years off) it's of minimal use to wine tourists. It's possible to tour by bus, but travel by car remains the best option. One alternative is to book a group or private tour.

BUS

Sonoma County Transit provides transportation to all the main towns in this region. Except for the routes from Santa Rosa to Healdsburg and Sebastopol, service isn't always frequent.

⇨ *For more information about arriving by bus, see the Bus section in the Travel Smart chapter.*

CAR

Driving a car is by far the easiest way to get to and experience this region. From San Francisco, the quickest route to Northern Sonoma is north on U.S. 101 to Santa Rosa and Healdsburg. Highway 116 (aka Gravenstein Highway) heads west from U.S. 101, taking you through Sebastopol and Forestville before depositing you along the Russian River near Guerneville. Traffic can be slow on U.S. 101, especially around Petaluma and Santa Rosa during rush hour and on summer weekends. Parking can be difficult in downtown Healdsburg on busy summer and early fall weekends, when you may have to park in a lot, feed a meter, or walk a few blocks.

Restaurants

Each year at the Sonoma County Harvest Festival and seasonally at local farmers' markets, the remarkable output of Northern Sonoma's farms and ranches is on display. Local chefs often scour the markets for seafood, meats, cheeses, and produce, and many restaurants have their own gardens. With all these fresh ingredients at hand, it should come as no surprise that farm-to-table cuisine predominates here, especially among the high-profile restaurants. Wood-fired pizzas are another local passion, as is modern Italian fare. Gourmet delis and grocery stores in several towns are excellent sources for picnic fare. Except in the region's most expensive restaurants, it's fine to dress casually.

⇨ *Restaurant prices are the average cost of a main course at dinner, or if dinner isn't served, at lunch. Restaurant reviews have been shortened. For full information, visit Fodors.com.*

Hotels

Healdsburg's hotels and inns set this region's standard for bedding down in style, with plush rooms that top $1,000 a night in a few cases. In the more affordable category are traditional bed-and-breakfast inns and small hotels, and there are even some inns and motels with down-to-earth prices. These last lodgings book up well in advance for high season, which is why Santa Rosa—just 15 miles away and home to decent chain and independent inns and hotels—is worth checking out year-round. Several secluded West County inns provide an elegant escape. Smaller properties throughout the region have two-night minimums on weekends (three nights on holiday weekends), though in winter this is negotiable.

⇨ *Hotel prices are the lowest cost of a standard double room in high season. Hotel reviews have been shortened. For full information, visit Fodors.com.*

What It Costs in U.S. Dollars			
$	$$	$$$	$$$$
RESTAURANTS			
under $17	$17–$26	$27–$36	over $36
HOTELS			
under $201	$201–$300	$301–$400	over $400

Planning Your Time

With hundreds of wineries separated by miles of highway, you could wander for weeks here and still not cover everything. To get a taste of what makes this region special, plan on a minimum of two or three days to hit the highlights. Healdsburg and the Russian River Valley are the must-sees, but it's worth venturing beyond them to the Alexander and Dry Creek Valleys. If you still have time, head west toward the coast.

When to Go

High season runs from early June through October, but even then weekday mornings find many wineries blissfully uncrowded. Summers are warm and nearly always pleasant on the coast, and though inland the temperatures often reach 90°F, this is nothing a rosé of Pinot Noir can't cure. Fall brings harvest fairs and other celebrations. Things slow down during winter, but with smaller crowds come more intimate winery visits. Roads along the Russian River are prone to flooding during heavy rains, as are a few in the Alexander Valley. Spring, when the grapevines are budding but the crowds are still thin, is a good time to visit.

Appellations

Covering about 329,000 acres, the **Northern Sonoma AVA,** itself within the larger Sonoma County "appellation of origin," a geopolitical designation, and the even larger multicounty **North Coast AVA,** is divided into smaller subappellations. Three of the most important meet at Healdsburg: the Russian River Valley AVA, which runs southwest along the river; the Dry Creek Valley AVA, which runs northwest of town; and the Alexander Valley AVA, which extends to the east and north. Also in this far northern area

are smaller AVAs whose names you're more likely to see on wine labels than at the few visitable wineries within the appellations themselves: Knights Valley, Chalk Hill, Fountaingrove, Rockpile, and Pine Mountain–Cloverdale Peak.

The cool climate of the low-lying **Russian River Valley AVA,** which extends from Healdsburg west to Guerneville, is perfect for Pinot Noir and Chardonnay. Because of the low elevation, sea fog pushes far inland, dropping temperatures at night (good for maintaining acidity), yet in summer it burns off, giving grapes sufficient sun to ripen fully. The namesake river does its part by depositing layers of gravel that force the vines' roots to push deep down in search of water and nutrients. In the process, the plants absorb trace minerals that add complexity to the grapes' flavors. Three decades ago, this area had as many ranches and apple orchards as vineyards. Now one of Sonoma's most-recognized growing regions, it has a significant subappellation of its own in the Forestville-Sebastopol area, the **Green Valley of the Russian River Valley AVA.**

The **Dry Creek Valley AVA** is a small region—only about 16 miles long and 2 miles wide. The valley's well-drained, gravelly floor is planted with Chardonnay grapes to the south, where an occasional sea fog creeps in from the Russian River and cools the vineyards. Sauvignon Blanc is found in the warmer north. The red decomposed soils of the benchlands bring out the best in Zinfandel—the grape for which Dry Creek is famous—but they also produce excellent Cabernet Sauvignon and Petite Sirah. And these soils are well suited to such white Rhône varietals as Viognier, Roussanne, and Marsanne, along with Grenache, Syrah, and Mourvèdre reds.

As recently as the 1980s, the **Alexander Valley AVA** was mostly planted to walnuts, pears, plums, and bulk grapes, but these days fruit for premium wines, mainly Cabernet Sauvignon but also Sauvignon Blanc, Petite Sirah, and Zinfandel, have largely replaced them. Rhône varietals such as Grenache and Syrah, along with Sangiovese, Barbera, and other Italian grapes, also make great wines here, and certain cooler spots have proven hospitable to Chardonnay and Merlot. In 2022, wineries in the hills and mountains surrounding Alexander Valley proposed the Pocket Peak subappellation to acknowledge the "elevated topography and distinctions in climate, precipitation, and soils." At time of writing, the petition was still pending.

Much of the **Sonoma Coast AVA,** which stretches the length of Sonoma County's coastline, lies within the Northern Sonoma AVA. The classic combination of hot summer days and cooling evening fog and breezes (in some spots even cooler than the Russian River Valley) inspired major Napa Valley wineries to invest in acreage here. The hunch paid off—Sonoma Coast Pinots and Chardonnays have become the darlings of national wine critics. Because the AVA encompasses such varied terrain—the southeastern portion edges into the comparatively warmer Sonoma Valley—some West County growers and vintners have proposed subappellations that express what they promote as the "true" Sonoma Coast geology and microclimates. One subappellation approved was the **Fort Ross–Seaview AVA,** whose hillside vineyards, mostly of Chardonnay and Pinot Noir, occupy land once thought too close to the Pacific Ocean to support grape growing. In 2022, the **West Sonoma Coast AVA,** which encompasses the entire Sonoma coast but not the inland areas of the larger AVA, joined Fort Ross–Seaview as a subappellation.

Mountains surround the idyllic **Bennett Valley AVA** on three sides. Entirely in the Sonoma Valley AVA and overlapping two other AVAs, it bears a Santa Rosa address. Coastal breezes sneak through the wind gap at Crane Canyon, making this area ideal for such cooler-weather grapes as Pinot Noir and Chardonnay. Syrah, Cabernet Sauvignon, and Sauvignon Blanc also do well here.

Healdsburg

17 miles north of Santa Rosa.

Sonoma County's ritziest town and the star of many a magazine spread or online feature, Healdsburg is located at the intersection of the Dry Creek Valley, Russian River Valley, and Alexander Valley AVAs. Several dozen wineries bear a Healdsburg address, and around downtown's plaza you'll find fashionable boutiques, spas, hip tasting rooms, and art galleries, and some of the Wine Country's best restaurants.

Especially on weekends, you're apt to have plenty of company as you tour the downtown area. You could spend a day exploring the tasting rooms and shops surrounding Healdsburg Plaza, but be sure to allow time to venture into the surrounding countryside. With orderly rows of vines alternating with overgrown hills, this is the setting you dream about when planning a Wine Country vacation.

GETTING HERE AND AROUND

To get to Healdsburg from San Francisco, cross the Golden Gate Bridge and continue north for 65 miles on U.S. 101. Take the Central Healdsburg exit and follow Healdsburg Avenue a few blocks north to Healdsburg Plaza. Wineries bearing Healdsburg addresses can be as far apart as 20 miles, so you'll find a car handy. The Dry Creek Valley AVA and most of the Russian River Valley AVA are west of U.S. 101; most of the Alexander Valley AVA is east of the freeway. Sonoma County Transit buses serve Healdsburg from Santa Rosa.

Top Tastings

Tastings

Aperture Cellars, Healdsburg. Its tasting room's ingenious design a nod to the winemaker's father's photography, Aperture clicks with guests even before they sample single-vineyard Cabernets, arguably Sonoma County's best.

Robert Young Estate Winery, Geyserville. The "infinity lawn" of the Young family's hilltop hospitality center gives way to views across the Alexander Valley as captivating as the winery's Chardonnays and Bordeaux-style reds.

Setting

Flowers Vineyard & Winery, Healdsburg. Astonishing architecture blends harmoniously with nature at this showcase for cool-climate Chardonnays and Pinot Noirs.

Iron Horse Vineyards, Sebastopol. The vine-covered hills and valleys surrounding this sparkling wine producer provide such compelling views that the winery hosts all its tastings outside.

Ridge Vineyards, Healdsburg. Patrons of this longtime producer enjoy views of rolling vineyards while tasting intense Zinfandels and other well-rounded wines.

Food Pairing

Cāpo Creek Ranch, Healdsburg. Owner-winemaker and physician Dr. Mary Roy pulls out all the stops for a six-course extravaganza, with dishes like butter-poached lobster tail and a four-cheese tomato tart bringing out the best in her Rhône- and Bordeaux-style wines and Zinfandel.

Bricoleur Vineyards, Windsor. As culinary advisor, chef Charlie Palmer oversees three- and six-course flight pairings, picnic lunches, and seasonal dinners at a verdant estate.

Just Plain Fun

Chenoweth Wines, Sebastopol. Hop aboard a UTV for a rollicking ride through redwoods to taste Pinot Noirs in the hillside vineyards where their grapes are grown. The Chenoweth family has been farming in this area since the mid-1800s.

Westside wineries: To get to wineries along Westside Road, head south on Center Street, then turn right at Mill Street. After Mill Street crosses under U.S. 101, its name changes to Westside Road. After about ½ mile, veer south to continue on Westside Road to reach the Russian River Valley wineries.

Eastside wineries: The route to wineries on Old Redwood Highway and Eastside Road starts out less scenic. Follow Healdsburg Avenue south to U.S. 101. Hop on the freeway, exiting after a mile at Old Redwood Highway. Bear right as you exit, and continue south. Just past the driveway that serves Rodney Strong and J Vineyards, turn southwest to merge onto Eastside Road.

Dry Creek Valley and Alexander Valley wineries: To reach the wineries along Dry Creek Road and West Dry Creek Road, head north from the plaza on Healdsburg Avenue. After about a mile, turn west on Dry Creek Road. Roughly parallel to Dry Creek Road is West Dry Creek Road, accessible by the cross streets Lambert Bridge Road and Yoakim Bridge Road. For Alexander Valley wineries, continue north on Healdsburg Avenue past Dry Creek Road.

VISITOR INFORMATION

CONTACT Healdsburg Chamber of Commerce & Visitors Bureau. ⊠ *217 Healdsburg Ave., Healdsburg* ✥ *North of roundabout* ☎ *707/433–6935* ⊕ *www.healdsburg. com.*

Sights

SIGHTS IN DOWNTOWN HEALDSBURG

BloodRoot Wines

WINERY | How about this for a marketing twist: the folks behind this winery produce outstanding wines using grapes from leading vineyards but reveal neither sources nor winemakers. The novel approach turns the lineup—sparkling wine, Chenin Blanc, rosés, Pinot Noirs, Grenache, and a Syrah-dominant blend, among others—into a who-made-what-from-where guessing game for local oenophiles, who also appreciate prices well below expected for wines so well crafted. (The red blend tops out around $50, and one of the Pinots sells for less than $30.) The tasting space's country-cool decor hints at the panache behind this enterprise, whose servers appear to have been chosen for their ebullience. ⊠ *118 North St., Healdsburg* ✥ *At Center St.* ☎ *707/387–7058* ⊕ *www.bloodrootwines.com* 🍷 *Tastings from $30.*

Breathless Wines

WINERY | The mood's downright bubbly (pardon that pun) at the oasis-like garden patio of this sparkling-wine producer tucked away in an industrial park northwest of Healdsburg Plaza. Established by three sisters in memory of their mother, Breathless sources grapes from appellations in Sonoma, Napa, and Mendocino Counties that find their way into sparklers and a few still wines. The small indoor tasting area was fashioned out of shipping containers, though nearly everyone sips in the umbrella-shaded garden in fine weather. You can sample wine by the glass, flight, or bottle; all visits require an appointment, with same-day reservations sometimes possible. ■ **TIP➔ Splurge on the Sabrage Experience to learn how to open a bottle with a saber, a tradition supposedly initiated by Napoléon's soldiers.** ⊠ *499 Moore La., Healdsburg* ✥ *Off North St.* ☎ *707/395–7300* ⊕ *www. breathlesswines.com* 🍷 *Tastings from $28* ⊗ *Closed Tues. and Wed.*

★ Cartograph Wines

WINERY | The husband-wife team behind Cartograph believes in Pinot Noirs emphasizing "balance, nuance, and complexity, rather than power and intensity." To that end they select vineyard sites based on climate and clone compatibility, harvest their grapes on the early side, and intervene as little as possible during the wine-making process. The resulting wines please on their own and pair well with food. Unlike many Sonoma County Pinot producers, Cartograph eschews Chardonnay for its still whites, opting instead for the Alsatian grape Riesling, done in a refreshingly crisp and dry style. Chardonnay does, however, appear in the winery's sparkling wine. Visits to the storefront space a block northeast of Healdsburg Plaza are by appointment (call for same-day). ⊠ *340 Center St., Healdsburg* ✥ *At North St.* ☎ *707/433–8270* ⊕ *www.cartographwines.com* 🍷 *Tastings from $30* ⊗ *Closed Sun. and Mon.*

★ Jeff Cohn Cellars

WINERY | Rhône-style wines with complex layers and textures have long been the siren song of winemaker Jeff Cohn. The whites might include single-varietal wines and blends, and there's a brut rosé of Grenache, Syrah, and Mourvèdre that's deceptively dry. The Syrahs, from Rockpile, Zio Tony, and other Sonoma County vineyards, are superb. Cohn, who's known to crack wise, also makes Zinfandel and Petite Sirah, endeavoring to avoid making them "over-the-freakin'-top." He's wildly successful with all his wines, which often earn scores in the

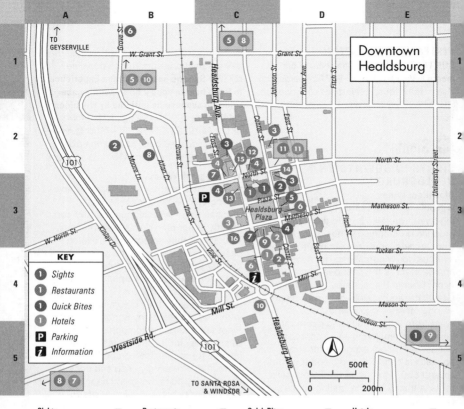

Downtown Healdsburg

KEY

- Sights
- Restaurants
- Quick Bites
- Hotels
- P Parking
- i Information

Sights ▼

1 BloodRoot Wines **C3**
2 Breathless Wines **B2**
3 Cartograph Wines **C3**
4 Jeff Cohn Cellars **C3**
5 Marine Layer Wines.... **D3**
6 Seghesio Family Vineyards **B1**
7 Thumbprint Cellars **C3**
8 Young & Yonder Spirits **B2**

Restaurants ▼

1 Baci Café & Wine Bar... **C3**
2 Barndiva **D4**
3 Bravas Bar de Tapas.... **C2**
4 Guiso Latin Fusion **C2**
5 Hazel Hill................. **C1**
6 KINSmoke **D3**
7 Little Saint **C3**
8 The Madrona Restaurant............... **A5**
9 The Matheson........... **C3**
10 The Parish Café......... **C4**
11 SingleThread Farms Restaurant............... **C2**
12 The Taste of Tea **C2**
13 Troubadour Bread & Bistro **C3**
14 Valette.................... **C3**
15 Willi's Seafood & Raw Bar............... **C2**
16 The Wurst Restaurant............... **C3**

Quick Bites ▼

1 Amy's Wicked Slush..... **E5**
2 Black Oak Coffee Roasters.......... **C3**
3 Costeaux French Bakery **C2**
4 Noble Folk Ice Cream and Pie Bar.............. **C3**

Hotels ▼

1 Harmon Guest House ... **C4**
2 Healdsburg Inn on the Plaza **C3**
3 Hotel Healdsburg **C3**
4 Hôtel Les Mars.......... **C3**
5 Hotel Trio Healdsburg............. **B1**
6 h2hotel **C4**
7 The Madrona........... **A5**
8 Montage Healdsburg.... **C1**
9 River Belle Inn **E5**
10 The Ruse................ **B1**
11 SingleThread Farms Inn **C2**

mid-to-high 90s and effusive praise from guests to his downtown Healdsburg tasting room and patio, where reservations are preferred but walk-ins usually accommodated. ⊠ *34 North St., Healdsburg* ⊹ *Near Healdsburg Ave.* ☎ *707/938–8343* ⊕ *www.jeffcohncellars.com* ✉ *Tastings from $35* ⊘ *Closed Wed.*

★ Marine Layer Wines

WINERY | Sometimes a winery's name or design sensibility hints well at what's in the bottle. In the case of this winery on Healdsburg Plaza's eastern flank, both do. The name references the Sonoma Coast fog rolling off the Pacific, allowing the Chardonnay and Pinot Noir grapes to ripen more slowly than further inland. With spare elegance, the loungelike tasting room's soft lighting, soothing white tones, and alternately gray, dark brown, and light mahogany hues also evoke the shoreline. The winemaker and owner have worked together previously; this project evolved out of a yearning to craft cool-climate, appellation-specific wines from high-pedigree sites. Marine Layer offers as an add-on seasonal mezze plates and similarly adventurous food pairings whose multilayered flavors mirror those of the wines. ■**TIP**➜ **Appointments are recommended for flights, poured until 5, after which hosts serve wines by the glass (no reservations taken) until closing.** ⊠ *308B Center St., Healdsburg* ⊹ *Near Plaza St.* ☎ *707/395–0830* ⊕ *www.marinelayerwines.com* ✉ *Tastings from $35.*

Seghesio Family Vineyards

WINERY | After working nearly a decade at Italian Swiss Colony, then among California's largest wine producers, Edoardo Seghesio purchased land in 1895 and planted some of the Alexander Valley's earliest Zinfandel vines. Fruit from them goes into his namesake winery's highly rated Home Ranch Zinfandel, one of several Zins made here. Wines from Italian varietals are another emphasis, most notably Venom, from what the winery says is North America's oldest Sangiovese vineyard. The whites, Chardonnay and Vermentino, are exceptional, too. At appointment-only tastings, some of which take place on the broad lawn and patio fronting the property, you can learn about the winery's history, farming philosophy, and Sonoma County fruit sources. ⊠ *700 Grove St., Healdsburg* ⊹ *Off W. Grant St.* ☎ *707/433–3579* ⊕ *www.seghesio.com* ✉ *Tastings from $30.*

Thumbprint Cellars

WINERY | With its exposed-brick walls, wine-bottle chandelier, plush booths, and curving bar, this tasting room on Healdsburg Plaza's southern edge has a hip feel. Owner-winemaker Scott Lindstrom-Drake, who believes in selecting good fruit and applying minimal manipulation during fermentation and aging, has received critical acclaim for his single-vineyard Cabernet Franc and Cabernet Sauvignon. He also makes Grenache, Petit Verdot, Pinot Noir, and a few other single-varietal reds, along with Chardonnay, Viognier, Grenache Blanc, and rosé of Cabernet Franc. ⊠ *102 Matheson St., Healdsburg* ⊹ *At Healdsburg Ave.* ☎ *707/433–2393* ⊕ *www.thumbprintcellars.com* ✉ *Tastings from $35.*

Young & Yonder Spirits

DISTILLERY | The husband-and-wife team behind this artisanal distillery forsook gainful employment to produce small-batch vodka, gin, bourbon, and absinthe. A few blocks northwest of Healdsburg Plaza, the two and their crew serve flights and cocktails in a high-ceilinged space whose loungelike decor—dark walls, padded-leather and plush-velvet furniture, and cowskin rugs—hips up the industrial-park setting. ■**TIP**➜ **If it's on the menu, the Modern G&T (gin and tonic), made with the company's superb H.O.B.S. (Heart of Broken Souls), is the must-have cocktail.** ⊠ *449 Allan Ct., Healdsburg* ⊹ *Off North St.* ☎ *707/473–8077* ⊕ *www.*

youngandyonder.com 🖃 Tastings from $12 ⊙ Closed Mon.–Wed.

SIGHTS BEYOND DOWNTOWN HEALDSBURG

Alley 6 Craft Distillery

DISTILLERY | Krystle and Jason Jorgensen make small-batch rye and single-malt whiskey, plus gin, peach liqueur, apple brandy, and candy-cap bitters, at the couple's industrial-park distillery 2 miles north of Healdsburg Plaza. The rye derives its overlapping flavors from its "mash bill" of rye and malted barley aged in heavily charred American oak barrels that add further layers of spice and complexity. The Jorgensens pride themselves on crafting their spirits entirely on-site, from grain milling through bottling, a process they describe with enthusiasm at their apothecarylike tasting room, open on weekends (weekdays by appointment). ⊠ 1401 Grove St., Unit D, Healdsburg ✛ North of Dry Creek Rd. ☎ 707/484–3593 ⊕ www.alley6. com 🖃 Tastings from $20 ⊙ Closed Mon.–Wed.

★ Aperture Cellars

WINERY | As a youth, Jesse Katz tagged along with his photographer father, Andy Katz, to wineries worldwide, stimulating curiosity about wine that led to stints at august operations like the Napa Valley's Screaming Eagle and Bordeaux's Petrús. In 2009, still in his 20s, Katz started Aperture, a success from the get-go for his single-vineyard Cabernets and Bordeaux blends. Among the whites are Sauvignon Blanc and an old-vine Chenin Blanc that's one of California's best. Katz's wines, which benefit from rigorous farming and cellar techniques, are presented by appointment only in an ultracontemporary hospitality center about 2½ miles south of Healdsburg Plaza. One tasting explores Aperture's various wine-growing sites and their soils, the other the single-vineyard wines. The center's shutterlike windows and other architectural elements evoke Andy Katz's photography career; his images of the Russian River Valley and beyond hang on the walls. ⊠ 12291 Old Redwood Hwy., Healdsburg ✛ ¼ mile south of Limerick La. ☎ 707/200–7891 ⊕ www. aperture-cellars.com 🖃 Tastings from $60 ⊙ Closed Tues. and Wed.

★ Arista Winery

WINERY | Brothers Mark and Ben McWilliams own this winery specializing in small-lot Pinot Noirs that was founded in 2002 by their parents. The sons have raised the winery's profile in several ways, most notably by hiring winemaker Matt Courtney, who has earned high praise from Wine Spectator and other publications for his balanced, richly textured Pinot Noirs. Courtney shows the same deft touch with Arista's Chardonnays. Appointment-only introductory tastings focus on Chardonnay, Pinot Noir, and the family's sustainable farming practices; another session examines the single-vineyard wines. The property's Japanese garden predates the winery. ⊠ 7015 Westside Rd., Healdsburg ☎ 707/473–0606 ⊕ www.aristawinery. com 🖃 Tastings from $35.

★ Bacchus Landing

WINERY | The small wineries of this energetic collective pour mostly Sonoma County wines inside and on patios of Spanish Mediterranean–style buildings bordering a large piazza. Music, art, and culinary events lend the dog- and kid-friendly space a village-square feel. Smith Story, Convene by Dan Kosta, Dot Wine, and Montagne-Russe make Pinot Noir; visiting more than one reveals the roles of clones, locations, farming, and cellar strategies in the finished product. The Lopez family of Aldina Vineyards, which developed Bacchus Landing, specializes in Cabernet Sauvignon, as does The Setting, whose partners include Jesse Katz of nearby Aperture Cellars. Aldina and Dot collaborate on California sparkling wines. There's a food market on-site; on Friday and weekend

The Russian River Valley AVA extends from Healdsburg west to Guerneville.

afternoons, you can order a wood-fired pizza to accompany your tasting. ✉ *14210 Bacchus Landing Way, Healdsburg* ✛ *Off Westside Rd., 1 mile west of Healdsburg Plaza* ☎ *707/395–0697* ⊕ *www.bacchuslanding.com* ✉ *Tastings from $25* ⊙ *Closed Tues. and Wed. except by appointment.*

★ Cāpo Creek Ranch

WINERY | Halfway through a wine-and-food pairing at this serenely rustic Dry Creek Valley winery you may find yourself asking not only "How does she do it?"—"she" being Dr. Mary Roy, Cāpo Creek Ranch's proprietor, winemaker, chef, and hostess with the mostest—but also "How does she make it look so easy?" The answer might simply be that running a winery isn't likely to faze someone who raised six kids while operating a bustling radiological imaging center. Whatever the reason, in "retirement" Roy has created a magical showcase for her mostly Rhône-style whites and reds (the stars) along with Cabernet Sauvignon, estate old-vine Zinfandel, and numerous blends. Most tastings occur outdoors facing east toward the heritage-Zin vineyard, with the cave and the tasting room alternative possibilities. ■TIP→ **All tastings involve Roy's food, but a worthwhile splurge is the six-course Ultimate Food & Wine Pairing, which lives up to its name.** ✉ *7171 W. Dry Creek Rd., Healdsburg* ✛ *1¼ miles south of Yoakam Bridge Rd.* ☎ *707/608–8448* ⊕ *www.capocreekranch.com* ✉ *Tastings from $85.*

Chalk Hill Estate

WINERY | At 1,300 acres one of Sonoma County's largest estates, this is the most prominent winery of the Chalk Hill appellation. Most guests taste on the châteaulike production facility's terrace, basking in views of steep, woodsy, vineyard-studded hills. A subappellation of the Russian River Valley AVA, the Chalk Hill AVA is so far east—less than 10 miles from the northern Napa Valley as the crow flies—that it gets much warmer. Although even in summer you might detect the Russian River Valley's cooling Pacific breezes, the estate, which has 15

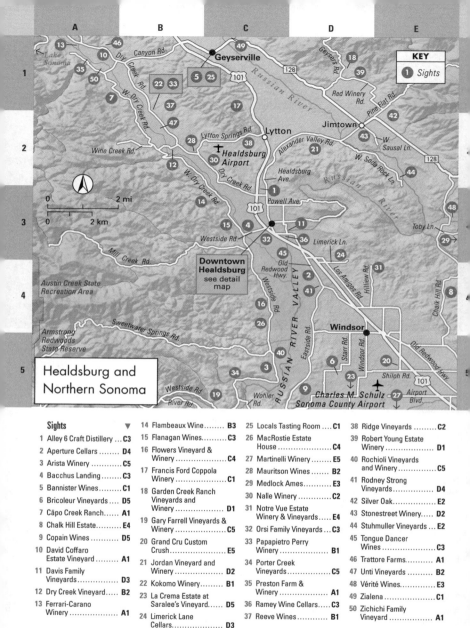

Healdsburg and Northern Sonoma

KEY

1 Sights

Sights

1 Alley 6 Craft Distillery ... **C3**
2 Aperture Cellars **D4**
3 Arista Winery **C5**
4 Bacchus Landing **C3**
5 Bannister Wines **C1**
6 Bricoleur Vineyards **D5**
7 Cäpo Creek Ranch **A1**
8 Chalk Hill Estate **E4**
9 Copain Wines **D5**
10 David Coffaro Estate Vineyard **A1**
11 Davis Family Vineyards **D3**
12 Dry Creek Vineyard **B2**
13 Ferrari-Carano Winery **A1**
14 Flambeaux Wine **B3**
15 Flanagan Wines **C3**
16 Flowers Vineyard & Winery **C4**
17 Francis Ford Coppola Winery **C1**
18 Garden Creek Ranch Vineyards and Winery **D1**
19 Gary Farrell Vineyards & Winery **C5**
20 Grand Cru Custom Crush **E5**
21 Jordan Vineyard and Winery **D2**
22 Kokomo Winery **B1**
23 La Crema Estate at Saralee's Vineyard **D5**
24 Limerick Lane Cellars **D3**
25 Locals Tasting Room **C1**
26 MacRostie Estate House **C4**
27 Martinelli Winery **E5**
28 Mauritson Wines **B2**
29 Medlock Ames **E3**
30 Nalle Winery **C2**
31 Notre Vue Estate Winery & Vineyards **E4**
32 Orsi Family Vineyards ... **C3**
33 Papapietro Perry Winery **B1**
34 Porter Creek Vineyards **C5**
35 Preston Farm & Winery **A1**
36 Ramey Wine Cellars **C3**
37 Reeve Wines **B1**
38 Ridge Vineyards **C2**
39 Robert Young Estate Winery **D1**
40 Rochioli Vineyards and Winery **C5**
41 Rodney Strong Vineyards **D4**
42 Silver Oak **E2**
43 Stonestreet Winery **D2**
44 Stuhmuller Vineyards ... **E2**
45 Tongue Dancer Wines **C3**
46 Trattore Farms **A1**
47 Unti Vineyards **B2**
48 Vérité Wines **E3**
49 Zialena **C1**
50 Zichichi Family Vineyard **A1**

separate microclimates, isn't cool enough for Pinot Noir, so the winery grows it on land nearer the ocean. Many of Chalk Hill Estate's 300 vineyard acres are devoted to Chardonnay—the grape represents more than half of production—with Sauvignon Blanc, Cabernet Sauvignon, a few other Bordeaux varietals (the Malbec's quite good), and Syrah also planted. ✉ 10300 Chalk Hill Rd., Healdsburg ✛ Take Old Redwood Hwy. east off U.S. 101 in Windsor to Pleasant Ave. ☎ 707/657–1809 ⊕ www.chalkhill.com 🍷 Tastings from $50.

Copain Wines

WINERY | The reputation of this winery whose name means "friends" in French rests on its Chardonnays, Pinot Noirs, and Syrahs. Copain occupies an enviable slope in Northern Sonoma County—one that begs guests to sit, sip, and take in the Russian River Valley view—but for years most of its wines derived from grapes grown in hillside vineyards near the coast in Monterey and Mendocino Counties. Since the winery's purchase by Jackson Family Wines, Russian River Valley and Sonoma Coast fruit, including Cabernet Franc, has joined the mix. ✉ 7800 Eastside Rd., Healdsburg ✛ Near Ballard Rd. ☎ 707/837–1101 ⊕ www.copainwines.com 🍷 Tastings from $65.

Davis Family Vineyards

WINERY | Pinot Noir and Rhône-style wines are the specialties at this winery whose prime outdoor tasting areas overlook the Russian River. Owner-winemaker Guy Davis crafts all the Pinots the same way—aiming to let vineyard conditions and the specific clones of Pinot Noir find expression in the bottle—and wine critics routinely praise the results of this humble approach. Other reds of note include the estate Soul Patch Vineyard Syrah and the Sage blend of Cabernet Sauvignon, Syrah, and Merlot. On the lighter side Davis makes Chardonnay, rosé, and the flagship Cuvée Luke blend of Roussanne, Marsanne, and Viognier. All visits are by appointment. ✉ 52 Front St., Healdsburg ✛ At Hudson St. ☎ 707/433–3858 ⊕ www.davisfamilyvineyards.com 🍷 Tastings from $30 ⊘ Closed Tues. and Wed.

Dry Creek Vineyard

WINERY | Loire-style Sauvignon Blanc marketed as Fumé Blanc brought instant success to the Dry Creek Valley's first new winery since Prohibition, but this stalwart established in 1972 also does well with Zinfandel and Cabernet Sauvignon and other Bordeaux-style reds. Founder David Stare's other contributions include leading the drive to develop the Dry Creek Valley appellation and coining the term "old-vine Zinfandel." The winery's history and wine-making evolution are among the topics addressed at tastings—outdoors under the shade of a magnolia and several redwood trees or in the nautical-theme tasting room. ✉ 3770 Lambert Bridge Rd., Healdsburg ✛ Off Dry Creek Rd. ☎ 707/433–1000 ⊕ www.drycreekvineyard.com 🍷 Tastings from $30.

Ferrari-Carano Winery

WINERY | Known for its grand Italian villa and manicured gardens—not a stray blade of grass anywhere here—this winery produces Chardonnay, Sauvignon Blanc, Merlot, Zinfandel, and Cabernet Sauvignon. Although whites have traditionally been the specialty, the reds—particularly the Bordeaux-style blend called Trésor—also garner attention, and some guests come just for the dessert wines. The villa's terrace and sycamore grove host many tastings, which, like the ones that take place indoors, are by appointment. ✉ 8761 Dry Creek Rd., Healdsburg ✛ At Yoakim Bridge Rd. ☎ 707/433–6700 ⊕ www.ferrari-carano.com 🍷 Tastings from $40.

★ Flambeaux Wine

WINERY | A family with deep ties to New Orleans founded this winery named for the dancing torchbearers at Mardi Gras. Zinfandel and Cabernet Sauvignon that go into separate bottlings and jointly into a crisp summery rosé flourish in the iron-rich estate Flambeaux Vineyard, up a winding road on the Dry Creek Valley AVA's western slope. Ryan Prichard, also of Sonoma's Three Sticks Wines, has been making these wines plus a Sonoma Coast Chardonnay, a Cabernet Sauvignon from sourced grapes, and a few others since the first (2014) vintage. Two Flambeaux wines are always on tap at Region wine bar in Sebastopol, but book a terrace tasting at the estate vineyard for a more intimate introduction. The Crescent City hospitality and views across the valley to Geyser Peak uplift the experience all the more. ⊠ *1333 Jack Pine Rd., Healdsburg* ✛ *Off W. Dry Creek Rd.* ☎ *707/637–9019* ⊕ *www.flambeaux-wine.com* ✉ *Contact winery for tasting fee.*

★ Flanagan Wines

WINERY | The back labels outline vintner Eric Flanagan's recipe for creating memorable wines: "Great vineyard sites. Meticulous, sustainable farming. Honest winemaking." Having purchased, upgraded, and sold prestigious vineyards, Flanagan knows how to locate pristine fruit, and once harvested, the grapes receive minimal manipulation from fermentation to bottling. Chardonnay and Pinot Noir are the mainstays, but the winery also produces a fragrant Viognier, along with reds that might include Merlot, Syrah, Cabernet Sauvignon, and a Bordeaux-style blend. As with the winemaking, the hospitality is understated, the hosts eager to educate guests seeking enlightenment or just let them ease back and revel in the views northeast across Dry Creek Valley to Geyserville Peak. Oriented toward serious wine drinkers but welcoming to newbies, the winery prefers visitors to book appointments (required) two days ahead. ⊠ *435 W. Dry Creek Rd., Healdsburg* ✛ *Driveway ½ mile north of Westside Rd.* ☎ *707/723–8800* ⊕ *www.flanaganwines.com* ✉ *Tastings from $65.*

★ Flowers Vineyard & Winery

WINERY | Steel, glass, and wood architecture that discreetly astonishes but ultimately yields to the surrounding gardens, redwoods, vineyards, and distant hills supplies a dramatic backdrop for tastings of this illustrious winery's Chardonnays and Pinot Noirs. Their grapes, grown far to the west in wild Pacific Coast terrain thought years ago too cool and harsh to produce fruit sufficiently ripe, undergo minimal cellar intervention during their transformation into wines recognized for their balance and vibrancy. Tastings take place indoors or out, sometimes accompanied by small bites that illustrate how food-friendly these beautifully crafted wines are. ⊠ *4035 Westside Rd., Healdsburg* ✛ *4 miles south of Healdsburg Plaza* ☎ *707/723–4800* ⊕ *flowerswinery.com* ✉ *Tastings from $75* ⊘ *Closed Tues. and Wed.*

★ Gary Farrell Vineyards & Winery

WINERY | Pass through an impressive metal gate and wind up a steep hill to reach this winery with knockout Russian River Valley views from the two-tiered tasting room and terrace outside. In 2017 *Wine Enthusiast Magazine* named a Gary Farrell Chardonnay wine of the year, one among many accolades for this winery known for sophisticated single-vineyard Chardonnays and Pinot Noirs. Farrell departed in the early 2000s, but current winemaker Theresa Heredia acknowledges that her philosophy has much in common with his. For the Pinots, this means picking on the early side to preserve acidity and focusing on "expressing the site." The Elevation Tasting of single-vineyard wines provides a good introduction; other tastings involve a winery tour or library wines. Visits are by appointment; same-day reservations are possible on weekdays, but call ahead. ⊠ *10701 Westside Rd., Healdsburg* ☎ *707/473–2909* ⊕ *www.garyfarrellwinery.com* ✉ *Tastings from $55.*

The ivy-covered château at Jordan Vineyard looks older than its four-plus decades.

★ Jordan Vineyard and Winery

WINERY | Founders Tom and Sally Jordan erected the French-style château here in part to emphasize their goal of producing Sonoma County Chardonnays and Cabernet Sauvignons—one of each annually—to rival those from the Napa Valley and France itself. Their son John, now at the helm, has instituted numerous improvements, among them the replanting of many vines and a shift to all-French barrels for aging. The signature winery tour and tasting includes a peek at the tank room and its towering oak barrels. The pièce de résistance of the three-hour Estate Tour & Tasting, hosted from spring to early fall, is a stop at a 360-degree vista point overlooking the 1,200-acre property's vines, olive trees, and countryside. As part of these experiences and other seasonal events, the executive chef prepares small bites and dishes whose ingredients come mainly from Jordan's organic garden. Visits are strictly by appointment. ⊠ *1474 Alexander Valley Rd., Healdsburg* ✛ *1½ miles east of Healdsburg Ave.* ☎ *707/431–5250* ⊕ *www.jordanwinery.com* 🖾 *Tastings from $90* ⊘ *Closed Tues. and Wed. Dec.–Mar.*

★ Kokomo Winery

WINERY | Since decamping for California, Hoosier winemaker Erik Miller, who named his winery after his Indiana hometown, has raked in awards for his single-vineyard wines, most notably Chardonnay, Merlot, Pinot Noir, and Zinfandel. A few years back, one of the Pinots scored 100 points at a prestigious local competition, capturing top honors for its varietal and among all the reds entered. Fans of the Pauline's Vineyard Grenache Rosé snag most of the supply within weeks of release. Some guests sit amid the potted plants fronting the industrial-parklike production facility, though the banter in the main tasting area, high rows of oak aging barrels its focal point, lures many inside. (The adjacent room for club members is a veritable party even midweek on some summer days.) Appointments are highly recommended; same-day visits are possible, but call first.

✉ *4791 Dry Creek Rd., Healdsburg* ✛ *At Timber Crest Farms* ☎ *707/433–0205* ⊕ *www.kokomowines.com* 🍷 *Tastings from $25.*

★ Limerick Lane Cellars

WINERY | The rocky, clay soils of this winery's northeastern sliver of the Russian River Valley combine with foggy mornings and evenings and hot, sunny afternoons to create the swoon-worthy Zinfandels (critics love 'em) produced here. The estate 1910 Block Zinfandel comes from old-style head-trained vines planted more than a century ago. Fruit from this block adds richness and depth to the flagship Russian River Zinfandel, whose grapes also come from nearby sources. You can taste Limerick Lane's Zins and a few other wines at a restored stone farm building with views of the vineyards and the Mayacamas Mountains. Tastings are by appointment; call ahead for same-day visits, which are easier on weekdays than weekends. ✉ *1023 Limerick La., Healdsburg* ✛ *1 mile east of Old Redwood Hwy.* ☎ *707/433–9211* ⊕ *www.limericklanewines.com* 🍷 *Tastings from $40.*

MacRostie Estate House

WINERY | A driveway off Westside Road curls through undulating vineyard hills to this longtime Chardonnay and Pinot Noir producer's steel, wood, and heavy-on-the-glass tasting space. Moments after you've arrived and a host has offered a glass of wine, you'll already feel transported into a genteel realm. Hospitality is clearly a priority, but so, too, is seeking out top-tier grape sources—30 for the Chardonnays, 15 for the Pinots—among them Dutton Ranch, Sangiacomo, and owner Steve MacRostie's Wildcat. With fruit this renowned, current winemaker Heidi Bridenhagen downplays the oak and other tricks of her trade, letting the vineyard settings, grape clones, and vintage do the talking. Tastings, inside or on balcony terraces with views across the Russian River Valley, are all seated and

by appointment. ✉ *4605 Westside Rd., Healdsburg* ✛ *Near Frost Rd.* ☎ *707/473–9303* ⊕ *macrostiewinery.com* 🍷 *Tastings from $35.*

★ Mauritson Wines

WINERY | Winemaker Clay Mauritson's Swedish ancestors planted grapes in what is now the Rockpile appellation in the 1880s, but it wasn't until his generation, the sixth, that wines bearing the family name first appeared. Much of the original homestead lies submerged under human-made Lake Sonoma, but the remaining acres produce the distinctive Zinfandels for which Mauritson is best known. Cabernet Sauvignon, other red Bordeaux grapes, Syrah, and Petite Sirah grow here as well, but the Zinfandels in particular illustrate how Rockpile's varied climate and hillside soils produce vastly different wines—from the soft, almost Pinot-like Westphall Ridge to the more structured and tannic Pritchett Peaks. The Mauritsons also grow grapes in Dry Creek Valley, where the winery and tasting room are located, and Alexander Valley. ✉ *2859 Dry Creek Rd., Healdsburg* ✛ *At Lytton Springs Rd.* ☎ *707/431–0804* ⊕ *www.mauritsonwines.com* 🍷 *Tastings from $30.*

★ Medlock Ames

WINERY | A participant in a worldwide movement promoting earth-friendly regenerative farming techniques, this winery established in 1998 produces small-lot wines from organic grapes grown at 338-acre Bell Mountain Ranch. Most of the hilly property is in the southeastern Alexander Valley, but a portion spills into the Russian River Valley AVA. The estate Cabernet Sauvignons garner the most acclaim, but the other wines—Cabernet Franc, Malbec, and Merlot reds, Sauvignon Blanc and Chardonnay, and brut-style sparklers—are also well made. In addition to a standard tasting, you can book an evocative self-guided audio tour or experience the ranch on an excursion led by a wine educator.

Ames Morison, the winery's eloquent cofounder and winemaker for the first two decades, leads enlightening vineyard walks on Fridays. All visits require an appointment. ■ TIP→ **Closer to Healdsburg, Medlock Ames operates a tasting room in a converted century-old country store.** ⊠ *13414 Chalk Hill Rd., Healdsburg* ✛ *2½ miles south of Hwy. 128, take Toby La. east* ☎ *707/431–8845* ⊕ *www.medlockames.com* ⊡ *Tastings from $50 at tasting room, $65 at ranch (less for self-guided tour).*

★ Nalle Winery

WINERY | Established in 1984 on a ranch farmed by the same family for five generations, this resolutely old-school winery produces restrained low-alcohol Zinfandels. Aged in French oak and elegant in ways Zinfandel often is not, they score well in competitions and with critics. How well? In 2022, the flagship Dry Creek Valley Zinfandel was the *only* Zin on *Wine Spectator* magazine's list of the world's top 100 wines. Two other notable bottlings are a Russian River Pinot Noir from Swan clone grapes and the estate Dry Creek Valley Cabernet. These crackerjack wines would be worth a trip on their own, but getting to know the family behind them—Doug and Lee Nalle, who founded this small operation, and their son Andrew, the current winemaker, and daughter-in-law April, a viticulturist—makes a visit all the more fulfilling, as does seeing the aboveground rosemary-covered "living roof" wine-aging "cellar." ⊠ *2383 Dry Creek Rd., Healdsburg* ✛ *About ½ mile south of Lytton Springs Rd.* ☎ *707/433–1040* ⊕ *nallewinery.com* ⊡ *Tastings from $35* ⊙ *Closed Sun.–Tues.*

Orsi Family Vineyards

WINERY | Sunny weekends at this farmhouse-style tasting venue less than a mile from Healdsburg Plaza have a lawn-party vibe. Guests seated in cabanas or at teak tables shaded by candy-apple-red umbrellas sip wines from Italian varietals, occasionally pausing to play cornhole or ogle the 70 acres of vineyards surrounding the property. Orsi, whose motto is "Italian roots in Sonoma County soil," makes whites like Biancolella and Fiano, but the reds—Aglianico, Barbera, Montepulciano, Nebbiolo, Negroamaro, Primitivo, Sangiovese, and Schioppettino among them—are the highlight. Many of their grapes are grown at the family's hillside Dry Creek Valley ranch to the north. ⊠ *2306 Magnolia Dr., Healdsburg* ✛ *¼ mile south of Mill St./Westside Rd. off Kinley Rd.* ☎ *707/732–4660* ⊕ *orsifamilyvineyards.com* ⊡ *Tastings from $35* ⊙ *Closed Tues. and Wed.*

Papapietro Perry Winery

WINERY | The mood is almost always upbeat on the vineyard-view patio at Papapietro Perry as regulars and first-timers sip Pinot Noirs, most from Russian River Valley grapes. A Chardonnay, a Zinfandel, and a rosé of Pinot Noir also grace the lineup. The house style is to pick early and shoot for elegance rather than the "overexpression" that can result from using riper fruit. The consistency of approach allows guests to discern the differences between wines from multiple fruit sources, a single vineyard, or a particular clone, or variant, of Pinot Noir. ■ TIP→ **Papapietro Perry is one of several tasting rooms in the Family Wineries complex; Kokomo is another fun stop with exemplary wines.** ⊠ *4791 Dry Creek Rd., Healdsburg* ✛ *At Timber Crest Farms* ☎ *707/433–0422* ⊕ *www.papapietro-perry.com* ⊡ *Tastings from $30.*

Porter Creek Vineyards

WINERY | About as down-home as you can get—the easygoing tastings at this modest family farm take place in or just outside a small redwood-beamed structure—Porter Creek makes notably good wines, some from estate biodynamically grown Chardonnay and Pinot Noir. Its vineyards climb up steep hillsides of volcanic soil that is said to impart a slight mineral note to the Chardonnay; cover crops planted between the vines provide erosion control in addition to nutrients. Winemaker Alex Davis—son of George Davis, who founded the winery—also makes two wines from old-vine grapes, Carignane from Mendocino County and Zinfandel from Sonoma County, and his lineup includes Viognier and Syrah. ⌧ *8735 Westside Rd., Healdsburg* ⌖ *Look for sign at sharp bend in road* ☎ *707/433–6321* ⊕ *www.portercreekvineyards.com* ⌨ *Tastings $30.*

Preston Farm & Winery

WINERY | The long driveway at homespun Preston, flanked by vineyards and punctuated by the occasional olive tree, winds down to farmhouses encircling a large shady yard. Year-round, a small shop near the tasting room sells organic produce grown in the winery's gardens; house-made bread and olive oil are also available. Owners Lou and Susan Preston are committed to organic growing techniques. They use only estate-grown grapes in their wines, which include Sauvignon Blanc, Barbera, Petite Sirah, Grenache, Viognier, and Zinfandel. All visits are by appointment, with walk-ins often possible on weekdays (call ahead, though). ⌧ *9282 W. Dry Creek Rd., Healdsburg* ⌖ *At Hartsock Rd. No. 1* ☎ *707/433–3372* ⊕ *www.prestonfarmandwinery.com* ⌨ *Tastings from $35* ⊘ *Closed Mon.*

★ Ramey Wine Cellars

WINERY | Anointed by *Wine Spectator* a "legend of California Chardonnay," David Ramey has been making acclaimed, ageworthy wines for four-plus decades. Collectors and wine lovers appear daily at his spick-and-span industrial space, where hosts convey the passion, artistry, and deep knowledge of wine-making chemistry underlying his output. The seated sessions (book well ahead in summer) begin with a few Chardonnays, followed by equally accomplished reds. Cabernet Sauvignon receives the most accolades of the latter, but Ramey also does well by Pinot Noir and has a soft spot for Syrah. Scrupulously farmed Napa and Sonoma sources supply the grapes for most of the wines, the exception being a Chardonnay from Westside Farms, the estate Russian River Valley vineyard. Ramey's children own and run his operation now—he chuckles that he's become their employee—and a longtime associate handles the day-to-day wine making, but the vision remains emphatically his. ⌧ *25 Healdsburg Ave., Healdsburg* ⌖ *¾ mile south of Healdsburg Plaza, near Front St.* ☎ *707/433–0870* ⊕ *www.rameywine.com* ⌨ *Tastings $50.*

Reeve Wines

WINERY | A narrow driveway leads up a forested hill to the secluded hilltop tasting enclave where Kelly and Noah Dorrance present their expressive cool-climate wines. With views of vineyards fanning magic carpet–like to the south, the outdoor tables here often spark daydreams accelerated by the dry Riesling commencing many sessions. (If the day's brisk, the indoor space's country-chic sensibility—high wood-beamed ceilings, black walls, dried and fresh flowers, and handcrafted furniture, all courtesy of Kelly—inspires reveries as well.) You're here for winemaker Noah Dorrance's Pinot Noirs, though, all terrific and in ways that illuminate the differences among clone types and variations in vineyards' soils, elevations, and weather. Tastings are by appointment only; same-day guests should call ahead rather than arrive unannounced. ■**TIP**→ **If a visit leaves you yearning to contemplate the views (or wines) further, ask about overnight stays at Reeve's villa.** ⌧ *4551 Dry Creek Rd., Healdsburg* ⌖ *1¼ miles north of Lambert Bridge Rd.* ☎ *707/235–6345* ⊕ *www.reevewines.com* ⌨ *Tastings from $50.*

★ Ridge Vineyards

WINERY | Ridge stands tall among local wineries, and not merely because its 1971 Monte Bello Cabernet Sauvignon rated second-highest among California

The focus at Ridge Vineyards is on single-vineyard estate wines.

reds competing with French ones at the famous Judgment of Paris blind tasting of 1976. The winery built its reputation on Cabernets, Zinfandels, and Chardonnays of unusual depth and complexity, but you'll also find blends of Rhône varietals. Ridge makes wines using grapes from several California locales—Sonoma County, Dry Creek Valley, the Napa Valley, and Paso Robles among them—but the focus is on single-vineyard estate wines such as the Lytton Springs Zinfandel from fruit grown near the tasting room. In good weather, you can sit outside, taking in views of rolling vineyard hills while you sip. ■TIP→ **The educational Century Tour & Library Tasting, a solid value, begins with a spin around the property in an electric cart, followed by a comparative tasting of current and older wines.** ⊠ *650 Lytton Springs Rd., Healdsburg* ✛ *Off U.S. 101* ☎ *408/867–3233* ⊕ *www.ridgewine.com/ visit/lytton-springs* 🍷 *Tastings from $30.*

Rochioli Vineyards and Winery
WINERY | Claiming one of the prettiest sites in the area, with patio tables overlooking the vineyards, this winery has an airy tasting room with an equally romantic view. Production is small, and fans on the winery's mailing list snap up most of the bottles, but Rochioli is still worth a stop to sample wines that might include the estate Sauvignon Blanc, Chardonnay, Pinot Noir, and Valdigiué (a red grape from southern France). Because of the cool growing conditions in the Russian River Valley, the whites' flavors are intense and complex, and the Pinot Noir, which helped cement the Russian River's status as a varietal powerhouse, is consistently excellent. Tastings are by appointment only. ⊠ *6192 Westside Rd., Healdsburg* ☎ *707/433–2305* ⊕ *www. rochioliwinery.com* 🍷 *Tastings from $25* ⊙ *Closed Tues.*

Rodney Strong Vineyards
WINERY | The late Rodney Strong was among the first winemakers to plant Pinot Noir in the Russian River Valley. His namesake winery still makes Pinot Noirs, but it's known more for Cabernet Sauvignon. The large brand has a stylish

tasting room, though from April through October many guests sit on an umbrella-shaded vineyard-view terrace sipping Cabs, Pinots, and other wines from several Sonoma County appellations. Some tastings include Davis Bynum Pinot Noirs (like Strong, Bynum was a pioneer of this varietal here) or the Cabernet-heavy Bordeaux-style Rowen Wine blends from a hilly ranch in far northern Sonoma County. Appointments are recommended, with same-day visits often possible. ■ TIP➔ **The winery hosts summer outdoor concerts; Alanis Morissette, Colbie Caillat, Blues Traveler, and Smokey Robinson have performed in recent years.** ✉ *11455 Old Redwood Hwy., Healdsburg* ✛ *North of Eastside Rd.* ☎ *707/431–1533, 800/678–4763* ⊕ *www.rodneystrong.com* ⛶ *Tastings from $40* ⊗ *Closed Tues. and Wed.*

★ Silver Oak

WINERY | The views and architecture are as impressive as the wines at the 113-acre Sonoma County outpost of the same-named Napa Valley winery. As in Napa, the Healdsburg facility—an ultramodern, environmentally sensitive winery with a glass-walled tasting pavilion—produces just one wine each year: a well-balanced Alexander Valley Cabernet Sauvignon aged in American rather than French oak barrels. One tasting includes the current Alexander Valley and Napa Valley Cabernets, plus an older vintage. Two or more wines of sister operation Twomey Cellars, which produces Sauvignon Blanc, Pinot Noir, and Merlot, begin a second offering that concludes with the current Cabernets. Hosts at a third pour current and older Cabernets from Napa and Sonoma. Make a reservation for all visits. ✉ *7300 Hwy. 128, Healdsburg* ✛ *Near Chaffee Rd.* ☎ *707/942–7082* ⊕ *www.silveroak.com* ⛶ *Tastings from $50.*

Stonestreet Winery

WINERY | From the broad patio that fronts the Stonestreet Alexander Mountain Estate's stablelike building you can see some of the steep, rugged terrain where grapes for the winery's full-bodied Chardonnays and tannic, wild-as-a-stallion Cabernet Sauvignons are grown. At 5,100 acres (900-plus planted), this is among the world's largest mountain vineyards. Farming these steep hills is difficult and labor-intensive, but the hard-won output finds its way into top boutique wines in addition to Stonestreet's. One seated tasting focuses on current-release single-vineyard wines. A session showcasing older vintages demonstrates the Cabernets' ageability. All visits require a reservation. ■ TIP➔ **Book a mountain excursion for stunning views and to experience the vineyards close up.** ✉ *7111 Hwy. 128, Healdsburg* ✛ *Off W. Sausal La.* ☎ *800/355–8008* ⊕ *www.stonestreetwines.com* ⛶ *Tastings from $75* ⊗ *No mountain tour on weekends.*

Stuhlmuller Vineyards

WINERY | Chardonnay and Cabernet Sauvignons from estate-grown grapes are the specialties of this slightly off-the-beaten-path winery whose tasting room and production facility occupy a stained-redwood former barn. Standout wines include the Summit Chardonnay and the Estate Cabernet Sauvignon, the latter from Stuhlmuller's oldest vines. Other wines to look for are the Estate Zinfandel and the Starr Ridge Vineyard Pinot Noir. Some tastings (by appointment; same-day visits possible) take place in a room adjoining the aging cellar, but in good weather you can sip outdoors on a patio near the vines. The dog-friendly winery invites guests to picnic while on the property. ■ TIP➔ **Picnickers are welcome at this dog-friendly winery.** ✉ *4951 W. Soda Rock La., Healdsburg* ✛ *Off Alexander Valley Rd.* ☎ *707/431–7745* ⊕ *www.stuhlmullervineyards.com* ⛶ *Tastings from $30.*

★ Tongue Dancer Wines

WINERY | Down a country lane less than 2 miles south of Healdsburg Plaza, James MacPhail's modest production facility seems well away from the upscale fray.

The Russian River Valley's hot summer days and cool nights create ideal conditions for growing Chardonnay and Pinot Noir.

MacPhail makes wines for The Calling, Sangiacomo, and other labels, but Tongue Dancer's Chardonnays and Pinot Noirs are his handcrafted labors of love. Made from small lots of grapes from choice vineyard sites, the wines impress, sometimes stun, with their grace, complexity, and balance. The flagship Sonoma Coast Pinot Noir, a blend from two or more vineyards, is poured at most tastings, in a mezzanine space above oak-aging barrels or on an outdoor patio. Either the winemaker or his co-owner and wife, Kerry Forbes-MacPhail—she's credited on bottles as the "Knowledge-able One" (and she is)—will host you. As James describes it, they aim to "create an approachable experience for guests we hope will leave as friends." Appointment-only visits are best made a day or more ahead. ⊠ *851 Magnolia Dr., Healdsburg* ⊹ *Off Westside Rd.* ☎ *707/433–4780* ⊕ *tonguedancerwines. com* ⊡ *Tastings $30* ⊗ *Closed Sun. and Mon.*

Unti Vineyards

WINERY | There's a reason why Unti, known for Zinfandel and wines made from sometimes obscure Rhône and Italian varietals, often bustles even when business is slow elsewhere in Dry Creek: this is a fun, casual place. You'll often find sociable cofounder Mick Unti chatting up guests and pouring wine in or outside the rustic-not-trying-to-be-chic tasting room. The Rhône reds, particularly two Syrahs and Cuvée Foudre (Grenache, Syrah, Mourvèdre), tend to garner more critical notice than the Italians—Aglianico, Sangiovese, and Montepulciano—but all are well made. Appointments are necessary, with same-day ones usually possible on weekdays. ⊠ *4202 Dry Creek Rd., Healdsburg* ⊹ *¾ mile north of Lambert Bridge Rd.* ☎ *707/433–5590* ⊕ *www. untivineyards.com* ⊡ *Tastings from $25.*

★ Vérité Wines

WINERY | Sixth-generation French winemaker Pierre Seillan and the late Jess Jackson of Jackson Family Wines cofounded this winery set amid Chalk

Hill's rolling countryside. Grapes for three soulful Bordeaux-style blends—La Muse (Merlot-forward), La Joie (Cabernet Sauvignon), and Le Désir (Cabernet Franc)—come from estate properties in four Sonoma County appellations: Chalk Hill and the Alexander, Knights, and Bennett Valleys. Since 2013, Seillan has crafted Vérité's collector-quality gems with his daughter, Hélène, and with no drop-off in quality: a well-respected wine critic bestowed 100-point scores on her debut blends. Hosts at the tile-roofed château greet guests with Champagne, directing them to large comfortable sofas for a bit of conversation before the tasting. The French-style hospitality, overseen by Pierre's wife, Monique, makes a visit here enchanting. Appointments, required, are best made a week ahead. ✉ *4611 Thomas Rd., Healdsburg* ✥ *Off Chalk Hill Rd.* ☎ *707/433–9000* 🌐 *www.veritewines.com* 🎫 *Tastings from $200.*

★ Zichichi Family Vineyard
WINERY | Most winery owners would love to be in Steve Zichichi's shoes: wines from his flagship vineyard, some of whose vines were planted in the 1920s during Prohibition, are largely sold out before they're bottled. As a result, customers of this northern Dry Creek Valley operation taste some wines while they're still aging in barrels and purchase "futures" available for shipping or pickup months or more later. The highlight, only sometimes available for tasting, is the Old Vine Zinfandel. Zichichi makes another Zinfandel and a Petite Sirah from his main vineyard, and one of each from another Dry Creek property. There's also a 100% Cabernet from the Chalk Hill appellation. The amiably paced tastings, all by appointment, often take place on a porch overlooking the historic vines. ✉ *8626 W. Dry Creek Rd., Healdsburg* ✥ *At Yoakim Bridge Rd.* ☎ *707/433–4410* 🌐 *www.zichichifamilyvineyard.com* 🎫 *Tastings from $30.*

🍴 Restaurants

Baci Café & Wine Bar
$$$ | **ITALIAN** | A neighborhood trattoria with cream-yellow walls, zinc-top tables, and colorful artwork and banners, Baci bustles with tourists during high season, but after things die down, locals continue dropping by for pasta dishes, gnocchi, risotto, and osso buco, saltimbocca, and other stick-to-your-ribs Italian standards. The Iranian-born chef, Shari Sarabi, applies a pan-Mediterranean sensibility to area-sourced, mostly organic ingredients, and his dishes satisfy without being overly showy. **Known for:** wine selection by Lisbeth Holmefjord, the chef's sommelier wife; enthusiastic owners; many gluten-free dishes. [$] *Average main: $33* ✉ *336 Healdsburg Ave., Healdsburg* ✥ *At North St.* ☎ *707/433–8111* 🌐 *www.bacicafeandwinebar.com* 🕒 *Closed Tues. and Wed. No lunch.*

★ Barndiva
$$$$ | **AMERICAN** | Not one to rest on her laurels, the creative director of this urban-rustic restaurant responded to winning a prestigious fine-dining award by welcoming a new chef, mixologist, and wine lead, all with impressive credentials themselves. The worth-the-splurge cuisine, hinging on hyperfresh local ingredients from superstar purveyors, comes off even more intricate than before in dishes that might include kanpachi crudo or goat-cheese croquette apps or a smoked pork chop with Japanese sweet potato entrée. **Known for:** open-air front and back patios; ornate, well-built cocktails; Friday and weekend brunch. [$] *Average main: $45* ✉ *231 Center St., Healdsburg* ✥ *Near Matheson St.* ☎ *707/431–0100* 🌐 *www.barndiva.com* 🕒 *Closed Mon. and Tues. No lunch weekdays.*

Bravas Bar de Tapas
$$$ | **SPANISH** | Spanish-style tapas and an outdoor patio in perpetual party mode make this restaurant, headquartered in a restored 1920s bungalow, a popular

downtown perch. Contemporary Spanish mosaics set a perky tone inside, but unless something's amiss with the weather, nearly everyone heads out back for flavorful croquettes, paella, *jamón ibérico, pan tomate* (tomato toast), grilled octopus, skirt steak, and crispy fried chicken. **Known for:** casual small plates; specialty cocktails, sangrias, and beer; Spanish and Sonoma County wines. [$] *Average main: $33* ✉ *420 Center St., Healdsburg* ✥ *Near North St.* ☎ *707/433–7700* 🌐 *www.barbravas.com.*

★ Guiso Latin Fusion

$$$ | LATIN AMERICAN | Shortly after graduating from a local college's culinary program, chef Carlos Mojica opened this warmly lit Latin American–Caribbean restaurant with a handful of tables inside and out. Loyalists pine for enchiladas with salsa *verde* and *pupusas* (corn tortillas stuffed with cheese and pork or vegetables), a prelude to signature entrées like *pescado en salsa con coco* (fish in sweet coconut) and Caribbean-style paella suffused with smoky-garlicky tomato broth. **Known for:** attentive service; distinctive flavors; neighborhood feel. [$] *Average main: $33* ✉ *117 North St., Healdsburg* ✥ *Near Center St.* ☎ *707/431–1302* 🌐 *guisolatinfusion.com* 🕓 *Closed Sun. and Mon.*

Hazel Hill

$$$$ | MODERN AMERICAN | Even before diners settle in their seats, the Montage resort's glass-walled destination restaurant captures the imagination with exterior views of vineyards, oaks, and far-off Mt. St. Helena and interior haute-luxury touches like chandeliers of locally hand-blown Czech glass. The Cali-Continental connection comes full circle in dishes—Pacific oysters with a spicy mignonette, perhaps, or halibut with shrimp, corn, and chanterelles—whose French flourishes elevate the seasonal ingredients. **Known for:** chef's tasting menu; Wagyu with foraged mushrooms and sauce au poivre (or go full-tilt with a Wagyu tomahawk); embrace of area wines on food-friendly international list. [$] *Average main: $47* ✉ *Montage Healdsburg, 100 Montage Way, Healdsburg* ✥ *Off Healdsburg Ave.* ☎ *707/354–6900* 🌐 *www.montagehotels.com/healdsburg/dining.*

KINSmoke

$$ | BARBECUE | Beef brisket and St. Louis ribs are the hits at this saloon-like, order-at-the-counter joint whose house-made sauces include espresso barbecue, South Carolina mustard, and the sweet-and-sourish KIN blend. Along with the expected sides of potato salad, corn bread muffins, and baked beans (the latter bourbon-infused), the spiced sweet-potato tater tots and Granny Smith–and-horseradish slaw stand out. **Known for:** pulled smoked chicken with Alabama white sauce; beer selection; sensibly priced local wines. [$] *Average main: $17* ✉ *304 Center St., Healdsburg* ✥ *At Matheson St.* ☎ *707/473–8440* 🌐 *www.kinsmoke.com.*

Little Saint

$$$ | VEGETARIAN | Inside a metal-and-glass structure design writers have described as industrial grange-hall chic, the chefs at this "farm-forward gathering place" prepare satisfying plant-based cuisine supporting the founders' goal of creating Healdsburg's first entirely vegan restaurant. With most ingredients rushed over from Little Saint's nearby 8-acre Russian River farm, the menu items change often. **Known for:** live music and events upstairs some nights; coffee bar, wine shop, and mercantile with made-to-go salads, sandwiches, and dips; sensitive wine pairings, plus beers, ciders, and cocktails alcoholic and non. [$] *Average main: $29* ✉ *25 North St., Healdsburg* ✥ *At Foss St.* ☎ *707/433–8207* 🌐 *www.littlesainthealdsburg.com* 🕓 *Closed Tues. and Wed.*

The Madrona Restaurant

$$$ | MODERN AMERICAN | Owner-designer Jay Jeffers initiated a top-to-bottom makeover of this restaurant and its same-named hotel but retained the farm-to-table, French-inspired cuisine, the chef freshening it up a little to reflect The Madrona's flashy-elegant look. Inside a 19th-century mansion, with ornate molding and high ceilings but ultracontemporary to the max, diners feast in chic splendor on multifaceted preparations that make ample use of locally raised proteins and the on-site organic garden's fruits and vegetables. **Known for:** global wine offerings; Hannah's Bar for predinner (here or elsewhere) craft cocktails; Palm Terrace for alfresco dining, especially sunny-day weekend brunch. [$] *Average main: $36* ✉ *The Madrona Hotel, 1001 Westside Rd., Healdsburg* ✣ *At W. Dry Creek Rd.* ☎ *707/395–6700* 🌐 *themadronahotel.com/dine-drink.*

★ The Matheson

$$$$ | **MODERN AMERICAN** | The location of Dustin Valette's farm-to-table restaurant holds a special place in his heart: the bar and its Wine Wall taps dispensing mostly Sonoma County wines occupy the space where the Geyserville native's great-grandfather ran a bakery a century ago. Valette describes the menu—aged meats creatively adorned, local fish with recently plucked vegetables—as a "love letter" to local agriculture, a point driven home by the large, bright paintings of farm and culinary activity hanging above the dining-room floor. **Known for:** ingredients harvested for peak ripeness; rooftop bar for craft cocktails and bar bites; see-and-be-seen dining. [$] *Average main: $43* ✉ *106 Matheson St., Healdsburg* ✣ *Near Healdsburg Ave.* ☎ *707/723–1106* 🌐 *www.thematheson.com* 🕒 *No lunch.*

The Parish Café

$$ | **AMERICAN** | A few blocks south of Healdsburg Plaza at the busy roundabout, Parish's chefs whip up beignets, gumbo, muffulettas, and heapin' po'boys—from fried oyster, shrimp, or catfish to roast beef, turkey, or ham and cheese—along with other New Orleans delights. Borderline decadent breakfasts served inside a white-trimmed yellow house or on its patio include bananas Foster French toast, egg po'boys, and the crawfish and andouille omelet slathered in Creole sauce. **Known for:** beignets all day; regular and "king" po'boy portions; fried sides—pickles, okra, green tomatoes. [$] *Average main: $18* ✉ *60 Mill St., Healdsburg* ✣ *At Healdsburg Ave. roundabout* ☎ *707/431–8474* 🌐 *theparishcafe.com* 🕒 *Closed Tues. No dinner.*

★ SingleThread Farm Restaurant

$$$$ | **ECLECTIC** | The seasonally oriented Japanese dinners known as kaiseki inspire the 10-course prix-fixe vegetarian, meat, and seafood menu at the spare, elegant restaurant—redwood walls, walnut tables, mesquite-tile floors, muted-gray yarn-thread panels—of internationally renowned culinary artists Katina and Kyle Connaughton (she farms, he cooks). As Katina describes the endeavor, the micro-seasons of their nearby farm plus SingleThread's rooftop garden of fruit trees and greens dictate Kyle's rarefied fare, prepared in a theatrically lit open kitchen. **Known for:** impeccable wine pairings; dishes customized based on guests' preferences; instinctive service. [$] *Average main: $425* ✉ *131 North St., Healdsburg* ✣ *At Center St.* ☎ *707/723–4646* 🌐 *www.singlethread-farms.com* 🕒 *Closed Tues. and Wed. No lunch.*

The Taste of Tea

$$ | **JAPANESE** | At this storefront a block north of Healdsburg Plaza, Japanese-style prints and furniture offset the mildly industrial feel of an enterprise whose offerings include tea flights, light cuisine, and a spalike tea treatment involving a foot soak and a facial mask. Ramen cold or hot and rice bowls are the highlights, the former accompanied by shoyu-marinated egg, fish cake, tofu, and other ingredients as desired. **Known for:** vegan variations on most dishes; milk tea and matcha drinks; last dinner seating at 7 pm. [$] *Average main: $21* ✉ *109 North*

St., Healdsburg ✥ Near Healdsburg Ave. ☎ 707/431–1995 🌐 www.thetasteoftea.com ⏲ Closed Tues. and Wed.

★ Troubadour Bread & Bistro

$$$$ | MODERN AMERICAN | The founders of Quail & Condor, both formerly of SingleThread Farms, followed up the success of their small bakery in town with this shop and restaurant that by day showcases their naturally fermented sourdough breads in sandwiches ($–$$) distinguished by their expressive flavors. Come evening, the kitchen shifts into fine-dining mode, producing multicourse prix-fixe French-inspired "Le Dîner" meals, served at counters and a communal table, that quickly evolved into a local hot ticket. **Known for:** reservations essential for dinner; sensational breads; Dungeness crab and other seasonal sandwiches. [$] *Average main: $125 ✉ 381 Healdsburg Ave., Healdsburg ✥ Near North St. ☎ 707/756–3972 🌐 www.troubadourhbg.com ⏲ Closed Sun. and Mon.*

★ Valette

$$$$ | MODERN AMERICAN | Northern Sonoma native Dustin Valette opened this homage to the area's artisanal agricultural bounty with his brother, who runs the high-ceilinged dining room, where the playful contemporary lighting tempers the austerity of the exposed concrete walls and butcher-block-thick wooden tables. Charcuterie is an emphasis, but also consider the signature day-boat scallops *en croûte* (in a pastry crust) or dishes that might include coriander-crusted duck breast, Duroc pork tenderloin, or pan-roasted trout. **Known for:** "Trust me" (the chef) tasting menu; mostly Northern California and French wines; pot de crème and other desserts worth saving room for. [$] *Average main: $38 ✉ 344 Center St., Healdsburg ✥ At North St. ☎ 707/473–0946 🌐 www.valettehealdsburg.com ⏲ No lunch.*

Willi's Seafood & Raw Bar

$$$ | SEAFOOD | Willi's occupies a corner storefront with street-side outdoor seating and a compact dining room that curls around the full bar. The warm Maine lobster roll with garlic butter and fennel remains a hit among the small, primarily seafood-oriented plates, with the ceviches, local barbecued oysters (also Buffalo-style crispy), and bacon-wrapped scallops among its worthy rivals. **Known for:** eight types of oysters daily; "Kale Caesar!" salad with toasted capers; butterscotch pudding with miso caramel and ginger snaps. [$] *Average main: $34 ✉ 403 Healdsburg Ave., Healdsburg ✥ At North St. ☎ 707/433–9191 🌐 www.willisseafood.net.*

The Wurst Restaurant

$ | AMERICAN | "The Wurst is the best" is the motto at this glass-fronted fast-food joint with a menu of sausages and dogs with specific toppings like the Detroit Polish (with sauerkraut, beer mustard, and onion rings) or augmented with (choose two) caramelized onions, sweet peppers, hot peppers, or kraut. Burgers are another specialty, with the blue-cheese and smoked bacon and barbecue ones from a local beef purveyor among the top sellers patrons enjoy at communal and single tables inside and on the front patio. **Known for:** Not Dog vegan sausage; 15 beers on tap and midwestern pop (soda) selection; turkey, falafel, and smash burgers with fries or onion rings. [$] *Average main: $12 ✉ 22 Matheson St., Healdsburg ✥ Near Healdsburg Ave. ☎ 707/395–0214 🌐 thewurst.com.*

Coffee and Quick Bites

Amy's Wicked Slush

$ | ICE CREAM | Boston-style slush in flavors from root beer to raspberry that change with the season are the specialty of this shack in southern Healdsburg across from the beach. The owner's nostalgia for New England summers past extends to soft-serve ice cream in ever-changing flavors. **Known for:** half slush, half soft-serve "Split"; waffle cones and bowls; festive sprinkles. $ *Average main: $6* ✉ *13840 Healdsburg Ave., Healdsburg* ✥ *Across from Memorial Beach Park* ☎ *707/431–9253* 🌐 *www.amyswickedslush.com.*

★ Black Oak Coffee Roasters
$ | **CAFÉ** | Skilled baristas churn out a dizzying array of coffee drinks—drip, cold brew, nitro cold brew, all the fave espresso options—in a clean downtown space with white walls and teal wainscoting. Pastries, tartines, avocado toast, quiche, and egg-inflected sandwiches (some vegan or gluten-free) are the breakfast hits, with banh mi and the like added for lunch. **Known for:** superior bean sources and roasting methods; matcha, chai, and other teas and tea drinks and kombucha; seasonal drinks and pastries. $ *Average main: $11* ✉ *324 Center St., Healdsburg* ✥ *Near Plaza St.* ☎ *866/390–1427* 🌐 *blackoakcoffee.com/pages/healdsburg* ⏲ *No dinner.*

Costeaux French Bakery
$ | **FRENCH** | Breakfast, served all day at this bright-yellow French-style bakery and café, includes the signature omelet (sun-dried tomatoes, bacon, spinach, and Brie) and French toast made from thick slabs of cinnamon-walnut bread. French onion soup and cranberry-turkey, chicken with Jarlsberg, and (on the cinnamon-walnut bread) Monte Cristo sandwiches are among the lunch favorites. **Known for:** breads, croissants, and fancy pastries; quiche and omelets; front patio. $ *Average main: $16* ✉ *417 Healdsburg Ave., Healdsburg* ✥ *At North St.* ☎ *707/433–1913* 🌐 *www.costeaux.com* ⏲ *Closed Mon. and Tues. No dinner.*

★ Noble Folk Ice Cream and Pie Bar
$ | **BAKERY** | Seasonal pies including blood-orange custard with graham-cracker crust are the specialty of this white-walled, brightly lit pie palace with a few tables and barstool window seating. The bakers use heritage grains like buckwheat and farro in the crusts, filling them with local fruits and other ingredients, and, if desired, topping the ensemble with ice cream in flavors from Swiss chocolate and vanilla bean to Thai tea, salted caramel, and almond cardamom. **Known for:** trad and rad cupcakes; cookies and whoopie pies; macarons and cookie sandwiches. $ *Average main: $12* ✉ *116 Matheson St., Healdsburg* ✥ *Near Center St.* ☎ *707/395–4426* 🌐 *www.thenoblefolk.com* ⏲ *No dinner.*

Hotels

★ Harmon Guest House
$$$$ | **HOTEL** | A boutique sibling of the h2hotel two doors away, this downtown delight that debuted in 2018 earned instant LEED Gold status for its eco-friendly construction and operating practices. **Pros:** rooftop bar's cocktails, food menu, and views; connecting rooms and suites; similarly designed sister property h2hotel two doors south. **Cons:** minor room-to-room noise bleed-through; room gadgetry may flummox some guests; minimum-stay requirements some weekends. $ *Rooms from: $519* ✉ *227 Healdsburg Ave., Healdsburg* ☎ *707/922–5262* 🌐 *harmonguesthouse.com* 🛏 *39 rooms* 🍴 *Free Breakfast.*

Healdsburg Inn on the Plaza
$$$ | **B&B/INN** | A sensible choice if you'll be dining in town during your stay, this inn across from Healdsburg Plaza occupies a 19th-century office building whose former tenants include a Wells, Fargo & Co. Express office and stagecoach stop. **Pros:** central location; freshly baked cookies; late-afternoon wine and hors d'oeuvres. **Cons:** garish room lighting; slightly impersonal feel for this type of inn; street noise audible in plaza-facing rooms. $ *Rooms from: $349* ✉ *112 Matheson St., Healdsburg* ☎ *707/433–6991* 🌐 *www.healdsburginn.com* 🛏 *12 rooms* 🍴 *Free Breakfast.*

Hotel Healdsburg

$$$$ | **RESORT** | Across the street from the tidy town plaza, this full-service hotel has an upscale restaurant, a gourmet pizzeria, a spa, a pool, and a fitness center. **Pros:** minimalistic aesthetic, soothing tones; several rooms overlook town plaza; most rooms have private balconies. **Cons:** exterior rooms get some street noise; some sound bleed-through between rooms; smallest rooms pricey. $ *Rooms from: $699* ✉ *25 Matheson St., Healdsburg* ☎ *707/431–2800, 707/922–5256 reservations* ⊕ *www.hotelhealdsburg.com* ⇄ *55 rooms* ⏍ *Free Breakfast.*

Hôtel Les Mars

$$$$ | **HOTEL** | This Relais & Châteaux property takes the prize for opulence with guest rooms, spacious and elegant enough for French nobility, furnished with 18th- and 19th-century antiques and reproductions, canopy beds dressed in luxe linens, and gas-burning fireplaces. **Pros:** large rooms; luxurious feel; just off Healdsburg's plaza. **Cons:** expensive most of the year; minimum-stay requirement on weekends; no pool or spa. $ *Rooms from: $749* ✉ *27 North St., Healdsburg* ☎ *707/433–4211* ⊕ *www.hotellesmars.com* ⇄ *16 rooms* ⏍ *Free Breakfast.*

★ Hotel Trio Healdsburg

$$ | **HOTEL** | Named for the three major wine appellations—the Russian River, Dry Creek, and Alexander Valleys—whose confluence it's near, this Residence Inn by Marriott 1¼ miles north of Healdsburg Plaza caters to families and extended-stay business travelers with spacious rooms equipped with full kitchens. **Pros:** cute robot room service; full kitchens; rooms sleep up to four or six. **Cons:** 30-minute walk to downtown; corporate feel; pricey in high season. $ *Rooms from: $282* ✉ *110 Dry Creek Rd., Healdsburg* ☎ *707/433–4000* ⊕ *www.hoteltrio.com* ⇄ *122 rooms* ⏍ *Free Breakfast.*

h2hotel

$$$$ | **HOTEL** | Eco-friendly touches abound at this hotel, from the plant-covered "green roof" to wooden decks made from salvaged lumber. **Pros:** stylish modern design; free bikes for use around town; relaxing pool and public areas. **Cons:** least expensive rooms lack bathtubs; lacks on-site fitness center; can get pricey in high season. $ *Rooms from: $469* ✉ *219 Healdsburg Ave., Healdsburg* ☎ *707/922–5251* ⊕ *h2hotel.com* ⇄ *36 rooms* ⏍ *Free Breakfast.*

The Madrona

$$$$ | **HOTEL** | An 1881 mansion lauded in its early decades as Healdsburg's finest residence remains the centerpiece of this 8-acre estate of wooded and landscaped grounds co-owner and celebrity designer Jay Jeffers has transformed into a colorful boutique property dripping with ultraluxe style. **Pros:** secluded and romantic; 1¼ miles from Healdsburg Plaza; destination restaurant. **Cons:** can be a bit of a scene; geared more toward couples than families; two-night minimum on weekends. $ *Rooms from: $600* ✉ *1001 Westside Rd., Healdsburg* ☎ *707/395–6700* ⊕ *themadronahotel.com* ⇄ *22 rooms* ⏍ *No Meals.*

★ Montage Healdsburg

$$$$ | **RESORT** | Its bungalowlike guest rooms deftly layered into oak- and Cabernet-studded hills a few miles north of Healdsburg Plaza, this architectural sensation that opened fully in 2021 significantly upped Sonoma County's ultraluxury game. **Pros:** vineyard views from spa, restaurant, and swimming pool; outdoor living spaces with daybeds and fire pits; recreational options on-property or nearby. **Cons:** expensive year-round; hefty resort fee; car trip required for off-property visits. $ *Rooms from: $1000* ✉ *100 Montage Way, Healdsburg* ☎ *707/979–9000* ⊕ *www.montagehotels.com/healdsburg* ⇄ *130 bungalows* ⏍ *No Meals.*

Some rooms at Montage Healdsburg face oak-laden hills, others a young Cabernet vineyard.

★ **River Belle Inn**
$$$$ | **B&B/INN** | An 1875 Victorian with a storied past and a glorious colonnaded wraparound porch anchors this boutique Russian River property affiliated since 2022 with SingleThread Farms. **Pros:** riverfront location near tasting rooms; cooked-to-order full breakfasts; attention to detail. **Cons:** about a mile from Healdsburg Plaza; minimum-stay requirement on weekends; lacks pool, fitness center, and other amenities. [$] *Rooms from: $425* ✉ *68 Front St., Healdsburg* ☎ *707/955–5724* 🌐 *www.riverbelleinn.com* 🛏 *11 rooms* 🍴 *Free Breakfast.*

The Ruse
$$$$ | **B&B/INN** | An 1883 Italianate Victorian anchors this luxury inn on 3 lush acres in a residential area a mile from Healdsburg Plaza, which received a top-to-bottom makeover completed in early 2023. **Pros:** full breakfast with hot entrée; near town but away from Healdsburg's bustle; pool, hot tub, 18-hole putting green,and boccie and pickle ball courts. **Cons:** steep stairs to mansion rooms; unappealingly lighting in guest-room sleeping area; light hum of traffic in street-side rooms. [$] *Rooms from: $595* ✉ *891 Grove St., Healdsburg* ☎ *707/569–2800, 866/857–7873* 🌐 *theruse.com* 🛏 *11 rooms* 🍴 *Free Breakfast.*

★ **SingleThread Farm Inn**
$$$$ | **B&B/INN** | A remarkable Relais & Châteaux property a block north of Healdsburg Plaza, SingleThread is the creation of husband-and-wife team Kyle and Katina Connaughton, who operate the ground-floor destination restaurant and the four guest rooms and a suite above it. **Pros:** multicourse breakfast; spacious bathrooms with luxurious touches; rooftop garden. **Cons:** expensive year-round; no pool or fitness center; no spa. [$] *Rooms from: $1222* ✉ *131 North St., Healdsburg* ☎ *707/723–4646* 🌐 *www.singlethreadfarms.com* 🛏 *5 rooms* 🍴 *Free Breakfast.*

Nightlife

Duke's Spirited Cocktails

BARS | Fruity and savory "farm-to-bar" cocktails, many powered by local artisanal spirits and organically farmed ingredients, are among the specialties of this bar on Healdsburg Plaza's northern periphery. The old-school-in-a-fresh-setting vibe suits the inventive libations, but the bartenders at this happening hangout fashion the classics with equal aplomb. ⊠ *111 Plaza St., Healdsburg* ⊹ *Near Healdsburg Ave.* ☎ *707/431–1060* ⊕ *www.drinkatdukes.com.*

★ Lo & Behold Bar and Kitchen

BARS | Two cocktail all-stars and a chef with a fascination for international comfort food opened this bar where patrons wash down fish tacos, kimchi noodles, crispy pork spare ribs, and chicken tenders with craft cocktails that include the Phatty Margarita ("phattened" up with avocado and coconut oil). Good beer and wine list, too. Everything's best enjoyed out back on the patio. ⊠ *214 Healdsburg Ave., Healdsburg* ⊹ *Near Mill St.* ☎ *707/756–5021* ⊕ *loandbeholdca.com* ⊘ *Closed Tues. and Wed.*

★ Roof 106

BARS | The elevator at the back of The Matheson restaurant whisks patrons up to Roof 106, Healdsburg's hot spot for craft cocktails enjoyed with or without pizzas, small plates, and desserts. The vibe here is jolly and hip, with luxury patio furniture for lounging and fire pits and overhead heaters to keep the open-air space toasty when there's a chill. The rooftop's a fun stop for lunch, except on Monday and Tuesday when the bar opens at 5. ■ **TIP→ Ask about the Best of Chef menu (two-person minimum) of the upstairs chef's favorite dishes.** ⊠ *The Matheson, 106 Matheson St., Healdsburg* ⊹ *Near Healdsburg Ave.* ☎ *707/723–1106* ⊕ *www.thematheson.com/roof-106.*

The Rooftop

BARS | Though not the scene as its rooftop rival Roof 106, the fourth-story bar at the Harmon Guest House offers a more laid-back setting, arguably better views, and a seafood-oriented menu. The mostly small bites pair well with specialty cocktails like the signature The Rooftop (vodka, mixed berries, lemon, mint, and soda). ⊠ *Harmon Guest House, 227 Healdsburg Ave., Healdsburg* ⊹ *Near Matheson St.* ☎ *707/922–5442* ⊕ *harmonguesthouse.com/the-rooftop.*

Shopping

ART GALLERIES

★ Gallery Lulo

ART GALLERIES | A collaboration between a local artist and jewelry maker and a Danish-born curator, this gallery presents changing exhibits of jewelry, sculpture, and objets d'art. ⊠ *303 Center St., Healdsburg* ⊹ *At Plaza St.* ☎ *707/433–7533* ⊕ *www.gallerylulo.com.*

BOOKS

Copperfield's Books

BOOKS | In addition to magazines and best-selling books, this store, part of a local indie chain, stocks a wide selection of discounted and remaindered titles, including many cookbooks. ⊠ *104 Matheson St., Healdsburg* ⊹ *Near Healdsburg Ave.* ☎ *707/433–9270* ⊕ *www.copperfieldsbooks.com/healdsburg.*

CRAFTS

★ JAM JAR Goods

CRAFTS | Local artisans that include the two owners—one a painter, the other a jewelry maker—create many of the crafts, clothing, and other items, some vintage, sold at this smartly curated shop a block north of the plaza. ⊠ *126 North St., Healdsburg* ⊹ *At Center St.* ☎ *707/508–6664* ⊕ *jamjargoods.com* ⊘ *Closed Mon. and Tues.*

Dry Creek General Store sells gourmet sandwiches and picnic supplies.

FOOD AND WINE

Dry Creek General Store

FOOD | For breakfasts, sandwiches, bread, cheeses, and picnic supplies, stop by the general store, established in 1881 and still a popular spot for locals to hang out on the porch or in the bar. Beer and wine are also for sale, along with artisanal sodas, ciders, and juices. ⊠ *3495 Dry Creek Rd., Healdsburg* ✛ *At Lambert Bridge Rd.* ☎ *707/433–4171* ⊕ *www. drycreekgeneralstore1881.com.*

SingleThread Farm Store

FOOD | The owners of the award-winning SingleThread Farms Restaurant opened a fancy stand at the 24-acre farm that supplies much of the produce for their same-named dining spot. In addition to mindfully tended fruits, vegetables, and herbs grown, the store sells sauces, flowers, kitchen supplies, and wine. Weekend workshops cover farming and other topics. This place is so ag au courant it's worth checking out even if you're not interested in buying anything. ⊠ *2836 Dry Creek Rd., Healdsburg* ✛ *At*

Lytton Springs Rd. across from Maurit-son Winery ☎ *707/723–4646* ⊕ *www.sin-glethreadfarms.com/farm/store* ☉ *Closed Mon.–Wed.*

Activities

BICYCLING

Getaway Adventures / Wine Country Bikes
BIKING | This shop several blocks southeast of Healdsburg Plaza is perfectly located for setting up single or multiday treks into the Dry Creek and Russian River valleys by bike, kayak, or both. Private and group tours might include winery stops. If you prefer to explore on your own, you can rent equipment. ⊠ *61 Front St., Healdsburg* ✛ *At Hudson St.* ☎ *800/499–2453* ⊕ *getawayadventures. com* ⊠ *Daily rentals from $39 per day, full-day tours from $144.*

BOATING

Russian River Adventures
BOATING | This outfit open from mid-April through mid-November rents inflatable canoes for self-guided, full- and half-day

trips down the Russian River. Pack a swimsuit, pick up a picnic lunch, and shove off. You'll likely see wildlife on the shore and can stop at fun swimming holes and even swing on a rope above the water. The fee includes a shuttle ride back to your car. Ask about dog-friendly trips. ⊠ *20 Healdsburg Ave., Healdsburg* ⊹ *At S. University St.* ☎ *707/433–5599, 800/280–7627* ⊕ *www.russianriveradventures.com* ⊠ *From $75.*

HIKING

Healdsburg Ridge Open Space Preserve

HIKING & WALKING | The preserve's easy to navigate trails wind past oaks, manzanitas, Douglas firs, and redwoods on the way to an overlook with postcard views of the Russian River. ⊠ *Bridle Path and Arabian Way, Healdsburg* ⊹ *2 miles north from plaza on Healdsburg Ave., then east ¾ mile on Parkhill Farms Blvd.* ☎ *707/431–3317* ⊕ *www.ci.healdsburg. ca.us/741/open-space* ⊠ *Free.*

SPAS

★ A Simple Touch Spa

SPAS | Skilled in Swedish, deep-tissue, sports, and other massage modalities, this soothing but unpretentious day spa's therapists routinely receive post-session raves. The most popular treatment involves heated basalt stones applied to the client's body, followed by a massage of choice. Foot reflexology, reiki, and facials are among the other specialties. ■**TIP**→ **Couples can enjoy any of the massages performed side-by-side by two therapists.** ⊠ *239 Center St., Suite C, Healdsburg* ⊹ *Near Matheson St.* ☎ *707/433–6856* ⊕ *asimpletouchspa.com* ⊠ *Treatments from $60.*

The Spa Hotel Healdsburg

SPAS | Taking a page from its restaurant's farm-to-table approach, the Hotel Healdsburg's spa also sources many of its treatments' ingredients from area farms. Swedish-style massage techniques are central to the Healdsburg Signature Massage, which also involves aromatic oils. Deep-tissue and hot-stone

massages are among the other modalities. The signature facial uses biodynamic botanicals and concludes with a cool-stone facial massage. ⊠ *327 Healdsburg Ave., Healdsburg* ⊹ *At Matheson St.* ☎ *707/433–4747* ⊕ *www.hotelhealdsburg.com/spa* ⊠ *Treatments from $150.*

Geyserville

8 miles north of Healdsburg.

Several high-profile Alexander Valley AVA wineries, including the splashy Francis Ford Coppola Winery, can be found in Geyserville, a small portion of which stretches west of U.S. 101 into northern Dry Creek. Tasting rooms, shops, and restaurants do business along or, in the case of chef Douglas Keane's sophisticated Cyrus, near the two-block commercial drag. But for the most part, this town with fewer than 1,000 full-time residents, retains its dusty rural character.

GETTING HERE AND AROUND

From Healdsburg, the quickest route to downtown Geyserville is north on U.S. 101 to the Highway 128/Geyserville exit. Turn right at the stop sign onto Geyserville Avenue and follow the road north to the small downtown. Sonoma County Transit buses serve Geyserville from Healdsburg.

VISITOR INFORMATION

CONTACT Geyserville Chamber of Commerce. ⊠ *Geyserville* ☎ *707/276–6067* ⊕ *visitgeyserville.com.*

 Sights

Bannister Wines

WINERY | Brook Bannister's appreciation for his mother's wine-industry achievements inspired him to, as he puts it, forsake his career as a furniture maker "to keep her dream alive." That dream, which Martha "Marty" Bannister initiated in 1989, was to make layered, graceful ageworthy wines. Brook continues this tradition with the core lineup of Chardonnay, Riesling, several Pinot Noirs, and Zinfandel, supplemented in recent years by wines from lesser-known grapes. In 2022, Bannister Wines opened a gallery-style tasting room in the 1901 Geyserville Bank structure. Full of stories all its own, it's a fanciful space to sample Brook's well-crafted wines and learn more about this multigenerational labor of love. ✉ *21035 Geyserville Ave., Geyserville ✛ At Hwy. 128* ☎ *707/387–0124* ⊕ *bannisterwines.com* ☙ *Tastings from $35* ⊘ *Closed Tues. and Wed.*

David Coffaro Estate Vineyard

WINERY | One of the Dry Creek Valley's least pretentious wineries, David Coffaro specializes in red blends and single-varietal wines from grapes grown on a 20-acre estate. Zinfandel and Petite Sirah are strong suits, but Coffaro and his team also make wines using Lagrein, Aglianico, and other less familiar grapes. These also find their way into his unique blends, including the Rhône-style Terre Melange, with Peloursin and Carignane added to the usual Grenache, Syrah, and Mourvèdre mix. ✉ *7485 Dry Creek Rd., Geyserville ✛ Near Yoakim Bridge Rd.* ☎ *707/433–9715* ⊕ *www.coffaro.com* ☙ *Tasting from $10* ⊘ *Closed Tues. and Wed.*

Francis Ford Coppola Winery

WINERY | The fun at what the film director has called his "wine wonderland," since 2021 owned by Delicato Family Wines, is all in the excess. You may find it hard to resist having your photo snapped standing next to Don Corleone's desk from *The Godfather* or beside other movie memorabilia. A bandstand reminiscent of one in *The Godfather Part II* is the centerpiece of a large pool area where you can rent a changing room, complete with shower, and lounge poolside, perhaps ordering food from the adjacent café. A more elaborate restaurant, Rustic, overlooks the vineyards. As for the wines, the excess continues in the cellar, where the team produces several dozen single-varietal bottlings and blends. You don't need an appointment to taste at the bar but do for seated experiences. All memorabilia may not be on display when you visit—items are sometimes on loan. ✉ *300 Via Archimedes, Geyserville ✛ Off U.S. 101* ☎ *707/857–1400* ⊕ *www.franciscoppolawinery.com* ☙ *Tastings from $30.*

★ Garden Creek Ranch Vineyards and Winery

WINERY | During private tastings at this 100-acre property, you may find yourself swept away by husband-and-wife Justin Miller and Karin Warnelius-Miller's passion for their land and determination to craft collector-worthy wines. Justin grew up on the ranch, which his father purchased in 1963; Karin's Swedish-born parents owned vineyards and a winery nearby. Just as his father became an early Alexander Valley adopter of Cabernet Sauvignon, well before many of his peers, Justin embraced sustainable practices early on. Chardonnay, Grenache Blanc, Marsanne, Roussanne, and the rare-in-California Scheurebe are among the white grapes grown here; Cabernet Sauvignon and other Bordeaux varietals go into the flagship Tesserae red blend. Justin and Karin jointly make their small label's wines, only releasing the red after eight years in bottle. Supple upon release, it's built to last. ■ **TIP→ Appointment-only two-hour tastings (book well ahead) include a vineyard tour; there's also a 2½-hour Cabernet library session.** ✉ *2335 Geysers Rd., Geyserville ✛ Off Hwy. 128* ☎ *707/433–8345* ⊕ *gardencreekvineyards.com* ☙ *Tastings from $125* ⊘ *Closed Sun.–Tues.*

Locals Tasting Room

WINERY | If you're serious about wine, this tasting room is worth the trek 8 miles north of Healdsburg Plaza to downtown Geyserville. Connoisseurs who appreciate the owners' ability to spot up-and-comers head here regularly to sample the output of 10 or so small wineries, most without their own tasting rooms. There's no fee to sip—extraordinary for wines of this quality—and the well-versed staffers are happy to pour you a flight of several wines so you can compare, say, different Cabernet Sauvignons. ⊠ *21060 Geyserville Ave.* ✛ *At Hwy. 128* ☎ *707/814–0713* ⊕ *www. localstastingroom.com* ☒ *Tastings free* ⊗ *Closed Sun.–Tues.*

★ Robert Young Estate Winery

WINERY | Panoramic Alexander Valley views unfold at Scion House, the stylish yet informal knoll-top tasting space of this longtime Geyserville grower. The first Youngs began farming this land in the mid-1800s, raising cattle and growing wheat, prunes, and other crops. In the 1960s the late Robert Young, of the third generation, began cultivating grapes, eventually planting two Chardonnay clones now named for him. Grapes from them go into the Area 27 Chardonnay, among the best whites. The reds—small-lot Cabernet Sauvignons plus individual bottlings of Cabernet Franc, Malbec, Merlot, and Petit Verdot—shine even brighter. Tastings at Scion House, named for the fourth generation, whose members built on Robert Young's legacy and established the winery, are by appointment. Call ahead for same-day reservations. ■ **TIP**→ **Cab fanatics should consider the Ultimate Cabernet Lovers Experience of top-tier estate wines.** ⊠ *5120 Red Winery Rd., Geyserville* ✛ *Off Hwy. 128* ☎ *707/431–4811* ⊕ *www.ryew.com* ☒ *Tastings from $40* ⊗ *Closed Tues.*

Trattore Farms

WINERY | The tectonic shifts that created the Dry Creek Valley reveal themselves at this winery atop one of several abruptly rolling hills tamed only partially by grapevines and olive trees. Food offerings vary by day and time of year but might include cheeses, charcuterie, panini, and wood-fired pizzas. The main events, though, are the views and the Rhône-style wines, among them a Marsanne-Roussanne white blend and reds that range from Grenache to the Proprietor's Reserve GSM (Grenache, Syrah, Mourvèdre). Trattore Farms also makes Cabernet Sauvignon and a Cab-Zinfandel blend. You'll get a feel for the rollicking terrain on the fun (by appointment only) Get Your Boots Dirty vineyard, olive orchard, and mill tour in a Kawasaki 4x4. Reservations for tastings are recommended, especially on weekends. ■ **TIP**→ **To fully enjoy those valley views, book a seated outdoor tasting.** ⊠ *7878 Dry Creek Rd., Geyserville* ✛ *¾ mile north of Yoakim Bridge Rd.* ☎ *707/431–7200* ⊕ *www.trattorefarms. com* ☒ *Tastings from $30.*

★ Zialena

WINERY | Sister-and-brother team Lisa and Mark Mazzoni (she runs the business, he makes the wines) debuted their small winery's first vintage in 2014, but their Italian American family's wine-making heritage stretches back more than a century. Named for the siblings' great aunt Lena, known for her hospitality, Zialena specializes in estate-grown Zinfandel and Cabernet Sauvignon, some of whose lush mouthfeel derives from techniques Mark absorbed while working for the international consultant Philippe Melka. The Zin and Cab grapes, along with Chardonnay and Sangiovese for the seductive rosé, come from the 120-acre Mazzoni Vineyard, from which larger labels like Jordan also source fruit. Tastings are by appointment only, with same-day visits often possible. ⊠ *21112 River Rd., Geyserville* ✛ *Off Hwy. 128* ☎ *707/955–5992* ⊕ *www.zialena.com* ☒ *Tastings from $30.*

🍽 Restaurants

★ Catelli's

$$$ | ITALIAN | Cookbook author and *Iron Chef* judge Domenica Catelli returned home to revive her family's American-Italian restaurant, a Geyserville fixture. Contemporary abstract paintings, reclaimed-wood furnishings, and muted

Zialena's tasting patio edges the Geyserville winery's vineyard.

gray and chocolate-brown walls signal the changing times, but you'll find good-lovin' echoes of traditional cuisine in the sturdy meat sauce that accompanies the signature lasagna paper-thin noodles and ricotta-and-herb-cheese filling. **Known for:** three-meat ravioli and other pasta dishes; festive back patio; organic gardens. [$] *Average main: $28* ✉ *21047 Geyserville Ave., Geyserville* ✣ *At Hwy. 128* ☎ *707/857–3471* 🌐 *www.mycatellis.com* 🕘 *Closed Mon. and Tues.*

Corner Project Ales & Eats

$$ | **AMERICAN** | Two microbrewing brothers' longtime dream, this storefront gastropub along Geyserville's slim commercial row serves their ales and other area craft brews, plus a rotating lineup of kombuchas, ciders, stouts, seltzers, and sours. The beverages beguile, as do the flavors in animal- and plant-based dishes that might include farro salad, cheddar cauliflower muffulettas, lamb burgers, roasted-mushroom melts, pickled vegetables, and pork belly sliders (good with the potent house IPA). **Known for:** weekend brunch with egg dishes and waffles; family-run business; live music some evenings. [$] *Average main: $17* ✉ *21079 Geyserville Ave., Geyserville* ☎ *707/814–0110* 🌐 *cornerprojectales.com* 🕘 *Closed Mon. and Tues.*

★ **Cyrus**

$$$$ | **MODERN AMERICAN** | A decade after his beloved, same-named Healdsburg restaurant closed, celebrity chef Douglas Keane of *Top Chef Masters* and other fame reopened a "2.0" version inside an 8,000-square-foot steel, glass, and concrete structure set in an Alexander Valley vineyard. Keane bills his prix-fixe culinary experience as a "dining journey," with guests (couples'-rate only; single diners charged double) changing rooms a few times for multiple internationally inspired courses based on hyper-seasonal mostly Northern California ingredients. **Known for:** reservations (essential) released in monthly blocks two months in advance; architectural stunner in a rural setting; Bubbles Lounge for cocktails and small bites à la carte (no reservations).

ⓢ *Average main: $295* ✉ *275 Hwy. 128, Geyserville* ⊹ *Near Railroad Ave.* ☎ *707/318–0379* ⊕ *www.cyrusrestaurant.com* ◷ *Closed Mon.–Wed. No lunch.*

Diavola Pizzeria & Salumeria

$$ | **ITALIAN** | A dining area with hardwood floors, a pressed-tin ceiling, and exposed-brick walls provides a fitting setting for the rustic cuisine at this Geyserville mainstay. Chef Dino Bugica studied with artisanal cooks in Italy before opening this restaurant specializing in wood-fired pizzas and house-cured meats, with a few salads and meaty main courses rounding out the menu. **Known for:** talented chef; prime rib sandwich for lunch; chicken under a brick for dinner; outdoor patio. ⓢ *Average main: $26* ✉ *21021 Geyserville Ave., Geyserville* ⊹ *At Hwy. 128* ☎ *707/814–0111* ⊕ *www.diavolapizzeria.com.*

 Hotels

Geyserville Inn

$$ | **HOTEL** | Give the Healdsburg hubbub and prices the heave-ho but still have easy access to outstanding Dry Creek and Alexander Valley wineries from this modest, motel-like inn with a boutique-hotel sensibility. **Pros:** outdoor pool; vineyard-view decks from second-floor rooms in back; picnic area. **Cons:** rooms facing pool or highway can be noisy; minimum-stay requirement on weekends; not worth price on weekends in high season. ⓢ *Rooms from: $239* ✉ *21714 Geyserville Ave., Geyserville* ☎ *707/857–4343, 877/857–4343* ⊕ *www.geyservilleinn.com* ⤴ *41 rooms* ◎ *No Meals.*

 Nightlife

Geyserville Gun Club Bar & Lounge

BARS | Two doors down from Diavola Pizzeria (same ownership), this long, skinny bar in Geyserville's Odd Fellows Building wows locals and tourists with classic cocktails and a bar menu of international comfort food. Hardwood floors, exposed brick, taxidermied animals, and contemporary lighting set the mood at this cool spot. ✉ *21025 Geyserville Ave., Geyserville* ⊹ *At Hwy. 128* ☎ *707/814–0036* ⊕ *www.geyservillegunclub.com.*

Windsor

6 miles south of Healdsburg.

Founded in 1855 but unincorporated until 1992, Windsor lies between Healdsburg to the north and Santa Rosa to the south. Heavily rural into the mid-20th century and known for oak trees and wine-grape, prune, and beer-hops farms, the town, with a population of 26,300, consists these days of suburban-style developments straddling U.S. 101 and a small downtown, with vineyards still in abundance.

Many wineries in Santa Rosa's orbit, among them La Crema and Martinelli, actually bear a Windsor address. Russian River Brewing Company, home of Pliny the Elder and other exalted brews, operates a combination brewery, pub, and tasting space here.

GETTING HERE AND AROUND

To get to Windsor from Santa Rosa, head north on U.S. 101; from Healdsburg take the highway south. Sonoma County Transit serves Windsor from both towns. Once here, a car will be most convenient.

VISITOR INFORMATION

CONTACT Windsor Chamber of Commerce and Visitors Center. ✉ *9001 Windsor Rd., Windsor* ⊹ *At Emily Rose Circle* ☎ *707/838–7285* ⊕ *www.windsorchamber.com/visitors.*

6

Northern Sonoma, Russian River, and West County WINDSOR

◉ Sights

★ Bricoleur Vineyards

WINERY | According to cofounders Mark and Beth Hanson, the French word *bricoleur* loosely translates to "flying by the seat of the pants," the feeling the two experienced when they purchased a 40-acre estate southwest of Windsor's town green and set about establishing a winery and lavish hospitality center. The Hansons enlisted several Wine Country veterans to develop wine-making and culinary programs, and—voilà! (well, almost)—a star was born. The Windsor property produces Chardonnay and Pinot Noir, with vineyards in Alexander Valley (Zinfandel, Carignane) and Fountaingrove (Sauvignon Blanc, Viognier, and Grenache for rosé) supplying additional varietals. By appointment, hosts pour these self-assured wines in a 10,000-square-foot barn, a courtyard shaded by London plane trees, an open-air pavilion, and other settings with vineyard, garden, or Russian River Valley views (sometimes all three). All tastings involve food pairings overseen by the winery's culinary advisor, chef Charlie Palmer. ☒ *7394 Starr Rd., Windsor* ✛ *1¾ miles south of Windsor River Rd.* ☎ *707/857–5700* ⊕ *www.bricoleurvineyards.com* ☜ *Tastings from $75* ⊙ *Closed Tues. and Wed.*

★ Grand Cru Custom Crush

WINERY | Wineries without production equipment of their own often make wine at communal "custom-crush" facilities. Most such places don't have tasting rooms open to the public, but by appointment at Grand Cru (walk-ins often possible on weekdays), you can reserve a Vintners' Selection of several wineries' offerings or book a private tasting with one label. If you go the latter route, **Black Kite, Maritana, Bucher,** and **Bruliam** for Pinot Noir and Chardonnay (also Zinfandel for the last two) are worth seeking out, as is **Edaphos** for wines from rare white and red grapes. Vintners or winemakers often host their winery's tastings. ■TIP➡ **Some visitors pair a stop here with beer tasting and lunch at Russian River Brewing Company, a block away.** ☒ *1200 American Way, Windsor* ✛ *From U.S. 101 Exit 496, head west on Shiloh Rd. and north on Conde La.* ☎ *707/687–0904* ⊕ *www.grandcrucustomcrush.com* ☜ *Tastings from $35.*

La Crema Estate at Saralee's Vineyard

WINERY | The high-profile brand's multistory tasting space occupies a restored early-1900s redwood barn used over the years for hops, hay storage, and as a stable. With its cool Russian River Valley maritime climate, the celebrated Saralee's Vineyard, named for a former owner, fits the preferred La Crema profile for growing Chardonnay and Pinot Noir. By reservation (required, but walk-ins are accommodated when possible), you can sample wines on the patio or hop aboard a golf cart for a vineyard tour followed by a tasting. ☒ *3575 Slusser Rd., Windsor* ✛ *¾ mile north of River Rd.* ☎ *800/314–1762* ⊕ *www.lacrema.com* ☜ *Tastings from $40.*

Martinelli Winery

WINERY | In a century-old hop barn with the telltale triple towers, Martinelli has the feel of a traditional country store, but sophisticated wines are made here. The winery's reputation rests on its complex Pinot Noirs, Syrahs, and Zinfandels, including the Jackass Hill Vineyard Zin, made with grapes from vines planted mainly in the 1880s by the current owners' ancestors. Noted winemaker Helen Turley set the Martinelli style—fruit-forward, easy on the oak, reined-in tannins—in the 1990s, and the 21st-century team continues this approach. Tastings held (weather permitting) on a vineyard's-edge terrace survey the current releases. All visits are by appointment, best made online. ■TIP➡ **Terrace and Hop Barn tastings survey the portfolio, but serious wine drinkers should consider the Collector's Flight of top-drawer Chardonnays, Pinot Noirs, and Zinfandels.** ☒ *3360*

River Rd., Windsor ✣ East of Olivet Rd. ☎ 707/525–0570, 800/346–1627 🌐 www.martinelliwinery.com 🎟 Tastings from $35.

★ Notre Vue Estate Winery & Vineyards
WINERY | The estate's name means "our view," and you'll likely deem the perspective magnificent wherever you taste. The Russian River Valley sprawls below the Block 23 Terrace tasting area; egrets and otters cavort in the Lakeshore Pavilion, where bottle service is offered private experiences unfold; and Mt. St. Helena looms eastward at The Summit, the 710-acre property's highest point. Chardonnay and Rhône-style reds are two strengths, and there's a vibrant Pinot Noir. The best of the Rhônes, the G-S-M (Grenache, Syrah, Mourvèdre), comes from the slice of Notre Vue in the Chalk Hill AVA (the rest is Russian River Valley). Visits are by appointment. **■ TIP→ The owners encourage hiking on the estate's trails; with the rise in elevation from 200 to 1,200 feet, a stroll here can range from easy to strenuous.** ✉ *11010 Estate La., Windsor ✣ Off Arata La. east of U.S. 101 ☎ 707/433–4050 🌐 www.notrevueestate.com 🎟 Tastings from $35.*

🍴 Restaurants

Grata Italian Eatery
$$ | **ITALIAN** | **FAMILY** | A chef formerly with the Stark organization (Willi's Seafood and others) opened this casual restaurant—a good bet for families—whose decor of rich pastels sets a placid tone. Hits here include Parmesan arancini, fried calamari, and *burrata* with lemon honey starters, as well as shrimp *diavolo* pasta and halibut piccata entrées. **Known for:** spacious patio; weekday happy hour menu (focaccia, sliders, oysters); reasonable prices. [$] *Average main: $24* ✉ *186 Windsor River Rd., Windsor ✣ Near Bell Rd. ☎ 707/620–0508 🌐 gratawindsor.com ⏲ No lunch.*

★ Himalayan Restaurant of Windsor
$$ | **NEPALESE** | Asian tapestries, Nepalese tunes, images of precipitous peaks, and the fragrant scent of curries transport patrons of this storefront restaurant to the Himalayas, at least for an hour. Locals enamored of the flavorful cuisine and solicitous service often pack the place for dinner, served indoors and on the adjoining patio. **Known for:** varied menu; neighborhood atmosphere; many dishes vegan and gluten-free. [$] *Average main: $21* ✉ *810 McClelland Dr., Windsor ✣ At Marshall Way ☎ 707/838–6746 🌐 www.himalayanrestaurantwindsor.com ⏲ Closed Mon.*

★ Pizzaleah
$$ | **PIZZA** | A longtime member of the United States Pizza Team, chef-owner Leah Scurto has won national and international awards for creations like the Mush-a-Roni (pepperoni, cremini), the Nico (olive oil, mozzarella, roasted garlic, Parmesan), and the spicy Old Grey Beard (two kinds of cheese, sausage, Calabrian peppers, honey, orange zest). She serves her pies—plus salads, calzones, meatballs, and a few other items—in a minimally decorated strip-mall storefront with a spacious entryway patio. **Known for:** square pan pies serving four; local wines and craft beers; choose-your-own ingredients option. [$] *Average main: $21* ✉ *9240 Old Redwood Hwy., Windsor ✣ Across from Windsor Town Green ☎ 707/620–0551 🌐 www.pizzaleah.com ⏲ Closed Mon.*

Russian River Brewing Company Windsor
$$ | **AMERICAN** | The makers of Pliny the Elder and the Younger operate this cavernous brewpub with a vast lawn and outdoor patio on the site of their state-of-the-art brewing facility. Choose among 20 beers on tap to wash down beer-compatible pub grub—chicken wings with Pliny sauce, a malted-bacon burger with cheddar fondue, fish-and-chips, pulled-pork sliders and sandwiches, and a few salads. **Known for:**

year-round and seasonal beers; beers to go; casual atmosphere. $ *Average main: $17* ✉ *700 Mitchell La., Windsor* ✢ *At Conde La. (Shilo Rd. exit west off U.S. 101)* ☎ *707/545–2337* 🌐 *russianriverbrewing.com* ⏲ *Pub closed Mon. and Tues. in winter (beer garden open for drinks only). No lunch Mon. and Tues.*

Activities

BIKING

Ace It Bike Tours

BIKING | Join an easygoing beer, wine, or Sonoma coast tour or reserve a rental and head out on your own on one of this downtown shop's hybrid, electronic-assist, or road bikes. The equipment's in tip-top shape, the guides charming and well-informed. ✉ *367 Windsor River Rd., Windsor* ✢ *East of rotary* ☎ *707/688–4063* 🌐 *aceitbiketours.com* 🎫 *Rentals from $79 a day, tours from $169.*

Forestville

9 miles southwest of Windsor.

To experience the Russian River AVA's climate and rusticity, follow the river's westward course to the town of Forestville, home to a highly regarded restaurant and inn and a few wineries producing Pinot Noir from the Russian River Valley and well beyond.

GETTING HERE AND AROUND

To reach Forestville from U.S. 101 near Windsor, take Exit 494/River Road and head west. From Healdsburg, follow Westside Road to River Road and then continue west. Sonoma County Transit buses serve Forestville.

Sights

★ Hartford Family Winery

WINERY | Pinot Noir lovers appreciate the subtle differences in the wines Hartford's team crafts from grapes grown in several Sonoma County AVAs, along with fruit from nearby Marin and Mendocino Counties and Oregon. The winery also produces highly rated Chardonnays and old-vine Zinfandels. If the weather's good, enjoy a flight on the patio outside the main winery building. At private library tastings, guests sip current and older vintages. All visits are by appointment; call ahead on the same day. ✉ *8075 Martinelli Rd., Forestville* ✢ *Off Hwy. 116 or River Rd.* ☎ *707/904–6950* 🌐 *www.hartfordwines.com* 🎫 *Tastings from $40.*

★ Joseph Jewell Wines

WINERY | Pinot Noirs from the Russian River Valley and Humboldt County to the north are the strong suit of this winery sourcing from prestigious vineyards like Bucher and Hallberg Ranch. Owner-winemaker Adrian Manspeaker, a Humboldt native, spearheaded the foray into Pinot Noir grown in the coastal redwood country. His storefront tasting room in downtown Forestville (visits by appointment; walk-ins welcomed when possible) provides the opportunity to experience what's unique about the varietal's next Northern California frontier. Manspeaker also makes two Zinfandels; lighter wines include two Chardonnays, Pinot Gris, Vermentino, a sparkling Vermentino, and rosé of Pinot Noir. ■ **TIP→ From spring to mid-fall, a private wine educator accompanies small parties on engaging vineyard tastings involving a tour or picnic lunch.** ✉ *6542 Front St., Forestville* ✢ *Near 1st St.* ☎ *707/820–1621* 🌐 *www.josephjewell.com* 🎫 *Tastings from $35* ⏲ *Closed Mon.–Wed.*

Russian River Vineyards

WINERY | Live music on Fridays and weekends attracts an eclectic clientele to this winery specializing in single-vineyard Russian River Valley Pinot Noirs, but it's worth a stop anytime. In good weather, most guests enjoy tastings under pergolas, shade trees, and umbrellas as woodpeckers pilfer acorns from nearby oaks, caching their booty in the redwood roof

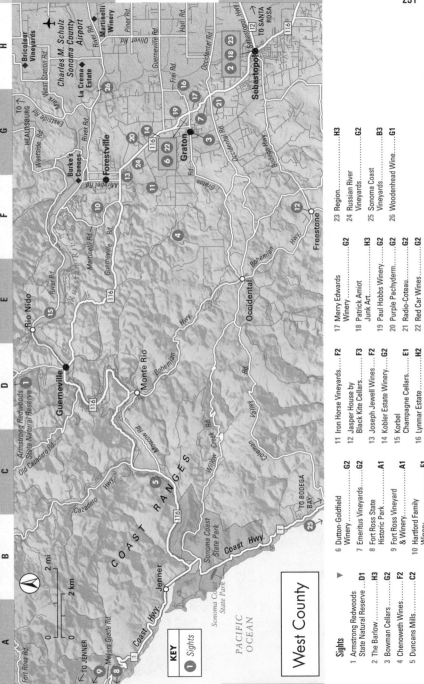

6

Northern Sonoma, Russian River, and West County

FORESTVILLE

Sights

1 Armstrong Redwoods
State Natural Reserve ...D1
2 The Barlow...............H3
3 Bowman Cellars G2
4 Chenoweth Wines.......F2
5 Duncans Mills...........C2

6 Dutton-Goldfield
Winery.................G2
7 Emeritus Vineyards.......G2
8 Fort Ross State
Historic Park...........A1
9 Fort Ross Vineyard
& Winery..............A1
10 Hartford Family
Winery.................F1

11 Iron Horse Vineyards....F2
12 Jasper House by
Black Kite Cellars.......F3
13 Joseph Jewell Wines....F2
14 Kobler Estate Winery....G2
15 Korbel
Champagne Cellars.....E1
16 Lynmar Estate..........H2

17 Merry Edwards
Winery.................G2
18 Patrick Amiot
Junk Art...............H3
19 Paul Hobbs Winery......G2
20 Purple Pachyderm......G2
21 Radio-Coteau..........G2
22 Red Car Wines.........H2

23 Region.................H3
24 Russian River
Vineyards..............G2
25 Sonoma Coast
Vineyards..............B3
26 Woodenhead Wine......G1

West County

KEY
1 Sights

of the property's hop-barn-style structure. The countrified setting has been known to induce "couch lock," causing patrons to while away hours sipping wine and nibbling on gourmet food boards, sandwiches, and salads (lunch is served daily). Some folks even settle in with a book, an option that wine service by the glass or bottle makes all the more tempting. Appointments are preferred, but walk-ins are usually welcome. ✉ *5700 Hwy. 116 N* ✣ *¾ mile south of town* ☎ *707/887–2300* 🌐 *www.russianrivervineyards.com* 🎟 *Tastings from $25.*

Woodenhead Wine

WINERY | A former girlfriend bestowed the nickname "Wooden Head" on Nikolai Stez for his stubborn nature, but he's also got a sense of humor, resurrecting the name years later for his winery. The meticulous if idiosyncratic winemaker has an impeccable pedigree, having begun his education working harvests for Burt Williams of the acclaimed Williams Selyem Winery, eventually becoming assistant winemaker there. In 1999, he established Woodenhead. Pinot Noir and Zinfandel are the focus, but don't miss the French Colombard, Chardonnay, and other whites. Tastings are reasonably priced and relatively old school, with most patrons perched on a deck overlooking Pinot Noir vines, a Russian River Valley panorama unfolding beyond them. Reservations are recommended, but the cheerful hosts usually accommodate walk-ins. ✉ *5700 River Rd., Forestville* ✣ *At Trenton Rd.* ☎ *707/887–2703* 🌐 *woodenheadwine.com* 🎟 *Tastings from $25* 🕒 *Closed Tues. and Wed.*

🍴 Restaurants

Farmstand

$$$ | **MODERN AMERICAN** | Anchored by a large heated patio adjoining the pool, the Farmhouse Inn's casual all-day restaurant serves farm-to-table cuisine with ingredients as local as the herbs and vegetables from the on-site culinary garden and livestock from an owners' nearby ranch. Look for avocado toast, brioche French toast, and the hearty farmer's plate (eggs, meat, potatoes) for breakfast, smoked salmon salad and the sandwich du jour for lunch, and quail, bass, or a pork chop for dinner. **Known for:** splendid for a sunny-day lunch; clean-on-the-palate cuisine; Farmhouse Inn Restaurant for prix-fixe fine dining (evening only). [$] *Average main: $36* ✉ *Farmhouse Inn, 7871 River Rd., Forestville* ✣ *At Wohler Rd.* ☎ *707/887–3300* 🌐 *www.farmhouseinn.com/farmstand* 🕒 *No dinner Sun. and Mon.*

Sonoma Pizza Co.

$$ | **PIZZA** | "Gorgeous, mouth-watering, over-the-top incredible" pizzas are the mission of this casual-contemporary, wide-windowed restaurant in downtown Forestville. The two types of pies—thicker ones cooked in a wood-fired oven and thinner ones with cold-fermented dough baked in an electric oven—live up to their billing, with tapas, meatballs, salads like the seasonal burrata-and-beets, and other small plates among the nonpizza alternatives. **Known for:** seasonal pizzas like one starring peaches and pork-cheek bacon; vegan, vegetarian, and gluten-free options; Gooey Butter Cake Bar for dessert. [$] *Average main: $22* ✉ *6615 Front St., Forestville* ✣ *At 1st St.* ☎ *707/820–1031* 🌐 *www.sonomapizzaco.com* 🕒 *Closed Mon. and Tues.*

☕ Coffee and Quick Bites

A La Heart Kitchen

$ | **AMERICAN** | A longtime Bay Area caterer opened this retail shop serving soups, salads, sandwiches, and a few entrées to go or eat indoors or on the front patio. Supplementing staples like turkey, tri-tip, and roasted portobello sandwiches—the Caesar salad is a town favorite—are surprise items, says the owner, "we just feel like cooking, like pot roast when it rains or Thai wraps on sunny days." **Known for:** house-made blueberry-bacon maple scones; good stop for picnic fixings or dining back at lodging; espresso drinks, chai tea, kombucha, Italian sodas. $ *Average main: $14* ✉ *6490 Mirabel Rd., Forestville* ✦ *Off Hwy. 116* ☎ *707/527–7555* ⊕ *www.alaheart.com* ⊗ *Closed Mon. and Tues. No dinner.*

Hotels

★ The Farmhouse Inn

$$$$ | B&B/INN | With a farmhouse-meets-modern-loft aesthetic, this low-key but upscale getaway with a pale-yellow exterior contains spacious rooms filled with king-size four-poster beds, whirlpool tubs, and hillside-view terraces. **Pros:** on-site Farmhouse Inn Restaurant (fine dining) and Farmstand (upscale casual); luxury bath products; full-service spa. **Cons:** mild road noise audible in rooms closest to the street; two-night minimum on weekends; pricey, especially during high season. $ *Rooms from: $1182* ✉ *7871 River Rd., Forestville* ☎ *707/887–3300, 800/464–6642* ⊕ *www.farmhouseinn. com* ⇄ *25 rooms* ⦿ *Free Breakfast.*

Activities

Burke's Canoe Trips

CANOEING & ROWING | You'll get a real feel for the Russian River's flora and fauna on a leisurely 10-mile paddle downstream from Burke's to Guerneville. A shuttle bus returns you to your car at the end of the journey, which is best taken on a weekday—summer weekends can be crowded and raucous. ✉ *8600 River Rd., Forestville* ✦ *At Mirabel Rd.* ☎ *707/887–1222* ⊕ *www.burkescanoetrips.com* ▣ *From $55 (kayak), $90 (canoe)* ⊗ *Closed mid-Oct.–late May.*

Guerneville

7 miles northwest of Forestville; 15 miles southwest of Healdsburg.

Guerneville's tourist demographic has evolved over the years—Bay Area families in the 1950s, lesbians and gays starting in the 1970s, and these days a mix of both groups, plus techies and outdoorsy types—with coast redwoods and the Russian River always central to the town's appeal. The area's most famous winery is Korbel Champagne Cellars, established nearly a century and a half ago. Even older are the shady stands of trees that make Armstrong Redwoods State Natural Reserve such a perfect respite from wine tasting on hot summer days.

GETTING HERE AND AROUND

To get to Guerneville from Healdsburg, follow Westside Road south to River Road and turn west. From Forestville, head west on Highway 116; alternatively, you can head north on Mirabel Road to River Road and then head west. Sonoma County Transit serves Guerneville.

VISITOR INFORMATION

CONTACT Guerneville Visitor Center.
✉ *16209 1st St., Guerneville* ✦ *At Armstrong Woods Rd.* ☎ *707/869–9000* ⊕ *www.russianriver.com.*

Sights

★ Armstrong Redwoods State Natural Reserve

STATE/PROVINCIAL PARK | FAMILY | Here's your best opportunity in the western Wine Country to wander amid *Sequoia sempervirens,* also known as coast redwood trees. The oldest example in this 805-acre state park, the Colonel Armstrong Tree, is thought to be more than 1,400 years old. A half mile from the parking lot, the tree is easily

On a hot summer day the shady paths of Armstrong Redwoods State Natural Reserve provide cool comfort.

accessible, and you can hike a long way into the forest before things get too hilly. ■TIP→ **During hot summer days, Armstrong Redwoods's tall trees help the park keep its cool.** ✉ *17000 Armstrong Woods Rd., Guerneville ✢ Off River Rd.* ☎ *707/869-2015* ⊕ *www.parks.ca.gov* ✉ *$10 per vehicle, free to pedestrians and bicyclists.*

Duncans Mills

TOWN | Halfway between Guerneville and the Pacific Ocean, this small town named for a sawmill that thrived here in the late 1800s is a popular pit stop for cyclists jonesing for coffee and aficionados of quirky retail. Antiques and gift shops can be found on the highway's north side, along with a general store, a petite bookstore, and a longtime local's casual wine-tasting venue. Guerneville and Jenner have better food options, though Cape Fear Café (north side) and the Gold Coast Bakery and Blue Heron Restaurant (south) have their adherents. ✉ *Duncans Mills ✢ On River Rd./Hwy. 116 8 miles west of Guerneville, 8 miles east of Jenner* ⊕ *duncansmillsvillage.com.*

Korbel Champagne Cellars

WINERY | The brothers Korbel (Joseph, Francis, and Anton) planted Pinot Noir grapes in the Russian River Valley in the 1870s, pioneering efforts duly noted during tastings at the well-known brand's Guerneville facility. Korbel makes still wines, but the core business is producing dry to sweet bubblies using the French *méthode champenoise,* for which the second fermentation takes place in the bottle. ■TIP→ **If it's open when you visit, stroll through the rose garden, home to more than 250 varieties.** ✉ *13250 River Rd., Guerneville ✢ West of Rio Nido* ☎ *707/824-7000* ⊕ *www.korbel.com/winery* ✉ *Tastings free–$20.*

🍽 Restaurants

★ boon eat+drink

$$ | **AMERICAN** | A casual storefront restaurant on Guerneville's main drag, boon eat+drink has a menu built around salads, smallish shareable plates, and entrées that might include a vegan bowl, chili-braised pork shoulder, and local cod with shiitakes. Like many of chef-owner Crista Luedtke's dishes, the signature polenta lasagna—creamy ricotta salata cheese and polenta served on greens sautéed in garlic, all of it floating upon a spicy marinara sauce—deviates significantly from the lasagna norm but succeeds on its own merits. **Known for:** adventurous culinary sensibility; Sonoma County wine selection; sister restaurant Brot for German cuisine in same block. $ *Average main: $25* ⊠ *16248 Main St., Guerneville* ✛ *At Church St.* ☎ *707/869–0780* ⊕ *eatatboon.com* ⊗ *Closed Mon. and Tues.*

Pat's International

$$ | ECLECTIC | On Main Street for several generations, Pat's got a new lease on life when a pop-up chef known for gooey-delicious, highly addictive Korean fried chicken (aka "Korean Fried Crack") bought the place and broadened its menu to include chicken pozole, huevos rancheros, and other international comfort food items. The setting—diner with counter and booths on one side, "dining room" with fake grass and picnic tables on the other, and plenty of cabinlike wood paneling all around—is peppy ersatz retro. **Known for:** playful ambience; artful spin on American classics; KFT (with tofu), noodle bowls, and other nonmeat options. $ *Average main: $22* ⊠ *16236 Main St., Guerneville* ✛ *Near Church St.* ☎ *707/604–4007* ⊕ *patsinternational.com* ⊗ *Closed Wed. No dinner Thurs.*

Stumptown Brewery

$ | AMERICAN | Microbrews and river views make a stop at this rough-hewn, overgrown shack enjoyable, especially on sunny days while sipping punchy-named beers like Rat Bastard Pale Ale, Dirty Rat IPA, and Donkey Punch Pils on the patio out back. The pub grub's predictable—chili con carne, garlic fries, corn dogs, hot dogs, and chicken wings starters, plus pork sliders, tacos, and several burgers and sandwiches—but reasonably well executed. **Known for:** bar open late on Friday and Saturday night; dog-friendly lawn near river; Stumptown Beer Revival and Barbecue Cookoff in August. $ *Average main: $13* ⊠ *15045 River Rd., Guerneville* ✛ *1 mile east of town* ☎ *707/869–0705* ⊕ *stumptown.com.*

☺ Coffee and Quick Bites

Big Bottom Market

$ | MODERN AMERICAN | Foodies love this grocery for its breakfast biscuits, clever sandwiches, and savory salads to go or eat here. Everything from butter and jam and mascarpone and honey to barbecue pulled pork with pickles and slaw accompanies the biscuits, whose mix made Oprah's Favorite Things list, and the sandwiches include the Colonel Armstrong (curried chicken salad with currants and cashews on brioche). **Known for:** biscuits and heartier breakfast fare; Wine Country lunches; excellent for a quick bite. $ *Average main: $13* ⊠ *16228 Main St., Guerneville* ✛ *Near Church St.* ☎ *707/604–7295* ⊕ *www.bigbottommarket.com* ⊗ *Closed Tues. No dinner.*

Nimble & Finn's

$ | ICE CREAM | An architecturally significant century-old bank now houses an artisanal ice cream parlor, a wine bodega, and a room with exhibits by the Russian River Historical Society. Along with the expected cups and cones of ice cream handmade from local organic dairy products, the former bank's main event, Nimble & Finn's, also sells pies, cakes, candy, shakes, floats, and coffee drinks. **Known for:** Wine Vault for wines from Sonoma County and beyond, plus microbrews; velvety triple-chocolate ice-cream sandwiches; bonus scoop of Guerneville history. $ *Average main: $7* ⊠ *Guerneville Bank Club, 16290 Main St., at Church St., Guerneville* ☎ *707/666–9411* ⊕ *www.nimbleandfinns.com* ⊗ *Closed Wed. (sometimes other days in winter; check first).*

Hotels

AutoCamp Russian River

$$$ | **B&B/INN** | **FAMILY** | Guests at this spot along the Russian River camp (well, sort of) in luxury under the redwoods in cute-as-a-button Airstream trailers decked out with top-notch oh-so-contemporary beds, linens, and bath products, with smaller "Happier Camper" and tent options (not year-round) only for two. **Pros:** retro feel; comfortable down beds; campfire and barbecue pit for each Airstream. **Cons:** lacks room service and other hotel amenities; fee for housekeeping; tents late spring–mid-fall only, with two-guest maximum including children. [$] *Rooms from: $324* ✉ *14120 Old Cazadero Rd., Guerneville* ☎ *888/405–7553* 🌐 *autocamp.com/russian-river* 🛏 *26 rooms* 🍴 *No Meals.*

boon hotel+spa

$$ | **HOTEL** | Redwoods, Douglas firs, and palms supply shade and seclusion at this lushly landscaped resort ¾ mile north of downtown Guerneville. **Pros:** filling breakfasts; pool area and on-site spa; complimentary bikes. **Cons:** lacks amenities of larger properties; pool rooms too close to the action for some guests; can be pricey in high season. [$] *Rooms from: $244* ✉ *14711 Armstrong Woods Rd., Guerneville* ☎ *707/869–2721* 🌐 *boonhotels.com* 🛏 *15 rooms* 🍴 *Free Breakfast.*

★ **Dawn Ranch**

$$$ | **RESORT** | A historic, woodsy 15-acre property that reopened in 2022 as a deluxe, reconnect-with-nature variation on mid-century roadside resorts, Dawn Ranch provides accommodations ranging from one-room, cedar-shingled cabins and larger "chalets" with sitting areas to a cottage and a bungalow. **Pros:** emphasis on unplugging and unwinding; high-quality beds, linens, and bath products; on-site restaurant and full bar with live music some nights. **Cons:** no TVs or phones in rooms (but solid Wi-Fi); some cabins are small; two-night minimum for some stays. [$] *Rooms from: $399* ✉ *16467 Hwy. 116, Guerneville* ☎ *707/869–0656* 🌐 *www.dawnranch.com* 🛏 *53 rooms* 🍴 *No Meals.*

The Highlands

$ | **B&B/INN** | Two hoteliers with an eye for woodsy low-budget panache teamed up to rejuvenate the decades-old cabins at this redwood-studded hillside property not far from downtown and the main Russian River beach. **Pros:** free continental breakfast; LGBTQ friendly; 11 glamping tents available mid-spring to mid-fall. **Cons:** weekend minimum-stay requirement; some rooms small (check website before booking) and only three pet friendly; parent or guardian must accompany guests under age 18 at all times. [$] *Rooms from: $159* ✉ *14000 Woodland Dr., Guerneville* ☎ *707/869–0333* 🌐 *www.highlandsresort.com* 🛏 *15 cabins* 🍴 *Free Breakfast.*

★ **The Stavrand**

$$$ | **HOTEL** | Redwoods tower over this secluded, romantic boutique resort convenient to Guerneville restaurants, Sonoma Coast and Russian River wineries, and Armstrong Woods and other outdoorsy attractions. **Pros:** pool and hot tub under the redwoods; exemplary service; full hot breakfast, evening apéritif, other upscale amenities. **Cons:** car necessary for most outings; smallest rooms can feel cramped; minimum-stay requirement on weekends. [$] *Rooms from: $356* ✉ *13555 Hwy. 116, Guerneville* ☎ *707/869–9093* 🌐 *thestavrand.com* 🛏 *21 rooms* 🍴 *Free Breakfast.*

Nightlife

El Barrio

BARS | Mescal-powered craft cocktails, classic tequila margaritas, and artisanal bourbons are the mainstays of this serape-chic watering hole. A festive downtown spot to begin or end the evening or to park yourself while waiting for a table at nearby restaurants, El Barrio serves ceviche, guacamole, cheese dips, tacos, and other small bites. ✉ *16230 Main St., Guerneville ✛ Near Church St.* ☎ *707/604–7601* ⊕ *www.elbarriobar.com* ⊘ *Closed Tues. yr-round, Mon. mid-fall–early spring.*

 Activities

TUBING

R2T2 Taxi and River Rentals

LOCAL SPORTS | Floating west down the Russian River in an inner tube is an area tradition dating back nearly to the advent of the automobile. This downtown vendor rents single and double tubes (the latter equipped with ice chests) seasonally and picks up clients at beaches downriver. Stand-up paddleboards and kayaks are also available, and R2T2 runs a taxi service, more dependable than Uber or Lyft this far west. ✉ *16297 Main St., Suite A, Guerneville ✛ Entrance on Church St.* ☎ *707/849–6802* ⊕ *www.r2t2taxi.org* ✑ *From $30 (single inner tube).*

Jenner

10 miles north of Bodega Bay.

The Russian River empties into the Pacific Ocean at Jenner, a wide spot in the road where houses dot a mountainside high above the sea. Facing south, the village looks across the river's mouth to Sonoma Coast State Park's Goat Rock Beach. North of town, Fort Ross State Historic Park provides a glimpse into Russia's early-19th-century foray into California. South of the fort, a winery named for it grows Chardonnay and Pinot Noir above the coastal fog line. North of the fort lie more beaches and redwoods to hike and explore.

GETTING HERE AND AROUND

Jenner is north of Bodega Bay on Highway 1. From Guerneville head west on Highway 116 (River Road). Mendocino Transit Authority buses serve Jenner.

 Sights

Fort Ross State Historic Park

STATE/PROVINCIAL PARK | FAMILY | With its reconstructed Russian Orthodox chapel, stockade, and officials' quarters, Fort Ross looks much the way it did after the Russians made it their major California coastal outpost in 1812. Russian settlers established the fort on land they leased from the native Kashia people. The Russians hoped to gain a foothold in the Pacific coast's warmer regions and to produce crops and other supplies for their Alaskan fur-trading operations. In 1841, with the local marine mammal population depleted and farming having proven unproductive, the Russians sold their holdings to John Sutter, later of goldrush fame. The land, privately ranched for decades, became a state park in 1909. One original Russian-era structure remains, as does a cemetery. The rest of the compound has been reconstructed to look much as it did during Russian times. An excellent small museum documents the history of the fort, the Kashia people, and the ranch and state-park eras. No dogs are allowed past the parking lot and picnic area. ✉ *19005 Hwy. 1, Jenner ✛ 11 miles north of Jenner village* ☎ *707/847–3437* ⊕ *www.fortross.org* ✑ *$10 per vehicle.*

Fort Ross Vineyard & Winery

WINERY | The Russian River and Highway 116 snake west from Guerneville through redwood groves to the coast, where Highway 1 twists north past rocky cliffs to this windswept ridgetop winery. Many experts deemed the weather this far west too chilly even for cool-climate varietals, but Fort Ross Vineyard and other Fort Ross–Seaview AVA wineries proved that Chardonnay and Pinot Noir could thrive above the fog line. The sea air and rocky soils here produce wines generally less fruit-forward than their Russian River Valley counterparts but equally sophisticated and no less vibrant. With its barnlike tasting room and outdoor patio overlooking the Pacific, Fort Ross provides an appealing introduction to its region's wines. Tastings include small bites (vegetarian options possible). Appointments are required; for same-day visits, call before 11 am. ✉ *15725 Meyers Grade Rd., Jenner* ✣ *Off Hwy. 1, 6 miles north of Jenner* ☎ *707/847–3460* 🌐 *www.fortrossvineyard.com* 🎫 *Tastings from $60* 🕘 *Closed Wed. and Thurs.*

🍴 Restaurants

★ Café Aquatica

$ | **AMERICAN** | In a weather-beaten shack that doesn't look like much but whose outdoor tables perch over the Russian River Estuary near the Pacific, this order-at-the-counter health-oriented café attracts meandering tourists, serious cyclists tackling curvy Highway 1, and West County residents soaking up the views and countercultural vibe. Sandwiches and salads, many incorporating locally caught fish and seafood, are the lunch mainstays, with avocado toast, eggs cooked various ways, and yogurt-granola parfait among the breakfast selections. **Known for:** organic ingredients; true-trade coffee, prebiotic sodas; live music on weekends. [$] *Average main: $13* ✉ *10439 Hwy. 1, Jenner* ✣ *1 mile north of Hwy. 116* ☎ *707/865–2251* 🌐 *www.cafeaquaticajenner.com* 🕘 *No dinner.*

★ River's End

$$$$ | **AMERICAN** | The hot tip at this low-slung cliff's-edge restaurant is to come early or reserve a window table, where the Russian River and Pacific Ocean views alone, particularly at sunset, might make your day (even more so if you're a birder). Seafood is the specialty—during the summer the chef showcases local king salmon—but filet mignon, duck, elk, a vegetarian napoleon, and pasta with prawns are often on the dinner menu. **Known for:** majestic setting; raw oysters and wine pairing; burgers, fish-and-chips for lunch. [$] *Average main: $37* ✉ *11048 Hwy. 1, Jenner* ✣ *1½ miles north of Hwy. 116* ☎ *707/865–2484* 🌐 *www.ilovesunsets.com* 🕘 *Closed Wed. and Thurs.*

🛏 Hotels

★ Timber Cove Resort

$$$$ | **RESORT** | Restored well beyond its original splendor, this resort anchored to a craggy oceanfront cliff is by far the Sonoma coast's coolest getaway. **Pros:** dramatic sunsets; grand public spaces; patio dining at Coast Kitchen restaurant. **Cons:** some service lapses; pricey ocean-view rooms; far from nightlife. [$] *Rooms from: $467* ✉ *21780 Hwy. 1, Jenner* ☎ *707/847–3231* 🌐 *www.timbercoveresort.com* 🛏 *46 rooms* 🍴 *No Meals.*

Bodega Bay

23 miles west of Santa Rosa.

Pockets of modernity notwithstanding, this commercial fishing town retains the workaday vibe of its cinematic turn in Alfred Hitchcock's *The Birds* (1963). Little from the film's era remains save the windswept bay and ocean views. To the east in the town of Bodega, the film's schoolhouse still stands, at Bodega Lane off Bodega Highway.

GETTING HERE AND AROUND

To reach Bodega Bay, exit U.S. 101 at Santa Rosa and take Highway 12 west (called Bodega Highway west of Sebastopol) 23 miles to the coast. A scenic alternative is to take U.S. 101's East Washington Street/Central Petaluma exit and follow signs west to Bodega Bay; just after you merge onto Highway 1, you'll pass through down-home Valley Ford, where Valley Ford Cheese & Creamery is worth a stop if it's open. Mendocino Transit Authority buses serve Bodega Bay.

Sights

Sonoma Coast Vineyards

WINERY | This winery with an ocean-view tasting room makes small-lot wines from grapes grown close to the Pacific. The Petersen Vineyard Chardonnay and Antonio Mountain Pinot Noir stand out among cool-climate bottlings that also include Sauvignon Blanc, rosé of Pinot Noir, and a blanc de noirs sparkler. ✉ *555 Hwy. 1, Bodega Bay* ☎ *707/921–2860* 🌐 *www.sonomacoastvineyards.com* 🎫 *Tastings from $10 glass.*

Beaches

★ Sonoma Coast State Park

BEACH | The park's gorgeous sandy coves stretch for 17 miles from Bodega Head to 4 miles north of Jenner. Bodega Head is a popular whale-watching perch in winter and spring, and Rock Point, Duncan's Landing, and Wright's Beach, at about the halfway mark, have good picnic areas. Rogue waves have swept people off the rocks at Duncan's Landing Overlook, so don't stray past signs warning you away. Calmer Shell Beach, about 2 miles north, is known for beachcombing, tidepooling, and fishing. Walk part of the bluff-top Kortum Trail or drive about 2½ miles north of Shell Beach to Blind Beach. Near the mouth of the Russian River just north of here at Goat Rock Beach, you'll find harbor seals; pupping season is from March through August. Bring binoculars and walk north from the parking lot to view the seals. During summer, lifeguards are on duty at some beaches, but strong rip currents and heavy surf keep most visitors onshore. **Amenities:** parking (fee); toilets. **Best for:** solitude; sunset; walking. ✉ *Park Headquarters/Salmon Creek Ranger Station, 3095 Hwy. 1, Bodega Bay* ✣ *2 miles north of Bodega Bay* ☎ *707/875–3483* 🌐 *www.parks.ca.gov* 🎫 *$8 per vehicle.*

Restaurants

Drakes Sonoma Coast

$$$$ | MODERN AMERICAN | Conversation softens around sunset at this ocean-view restaurant whose chefs pride themselves on preparing meals from mostly local ingredients, as diners' eyes drift westward to often spectacular light shows. With such fresh source materials—seafood from the day's Bodega Bay catch, cheeses crafted as near as 5 miles east, and some vegetables grown even closer—the house culinary philosophy mirrors that of many a Sonoma coast winery: minimal but wise intervention to bring out the best in them. **Known for:** reservations difficult when resort is full; among the best area restaurants open daily; usually one vegan or vegetarian dish, other plates adapted on request. [$] *Average main: $42* ✉ *103 Coast Hwy. 1, Bodega Bay* ✣ *At Doran Park Rd.* ☎ *707/377–5010* 🌐 *drakesbodegabay.com* ⏲ *No lunch.*

★ Fishetarian

$$ | SEAFOOD | Ask Bodega Bay residents where they go for superfresh, reasonably priced seafood in a casual setting, and many will suggest this unassuming order-at-the-counter shack. Boston clam chowder, seafood tacos and sandwiches, and fish (or calamari, crab cakes, or prawns)—and— chips are the hands-down favorites, along with raw or cooked oysters. **Known for:** closes early evening; tented open-air dining area; taffy, toffee, root beer floats, and other desserts. [$] *Average main: $21* ✉ *599 Hwy. 1, Bodega Bay* ✣ *¼ mile south of Inn at Tides Rd.* ☎ *707/875–9092* 🌐 *fishetarian-fishmarket.com.*

★ Ginochio's Kitchen

$$ | ECLECTIC | The eye-level bay perspective steals the show at this low-slung self-described barbecue and Italian restaurant whose outdoor seating areas fill up quickly in good weather. For breakfast the kitchen turns out oh-so-moist caramel-bacon monkey bread and burritos with scrambled eggs and brisket; lunchtime brings Italian-style scallop-and-clam chowder, fish tacos, pulled-pork sandwiches, and, in season, Dungeness crab sandwiches awash in molten Havarti cheese. **Known for:** Alicia's Crackling Nachos with or without meat; 14-hour cherrywood-smoked beef and brisket; wine list favoring small Sonoma County producers. [$] *Average main: $18* ✉ *1410 Bay Flat Rd., Bodega Bay* ✥ *Off Eastshore Rd. west off Hwy. 1* ☎ *707/377–4359* 🌐 *ginochioskitchen.com* 🕘 *No dinner.*

★ Terrapin Creek Cafe & Restaurant

$$$ | **MODERN AMERICAN** | Intricate but not fussy cuisine based on locally farmed ingredients and *fruits de mer* has made this casual yet sophisticated restaurant with an open kitchen a West County darling. Start with raw oysters, rich potato-leek soup, or (in season) Dungeness crab before moving on to halibut or other fish pan-roasted to perfection. **Known for:** intricate cuisine of chefs Liya and Andrew Truong; many locally sourced ingredients; signature hamachi crudo and Mediterranean fish stew. [$] *Average main: $36* ✉ *1580 Eastshore Rd., Bodega Bay* ✥ *Off Hwy. 1* ☎ *707/875–2700* 🌐 *www.terrapincreekcafe.com* 🕘 *Closed Tues. and Wed. No lunch.*

Coffee and Quick Bites

Fisherman's Cove

$ | **SEAFOOD** | Brave the lines at this seafood shack that doubles as a bait-and-tackle store to feast on crab sandwiches on sourdough, catch-of-the-day fish tacos, and fresh Tomales Bay oysters raw or barbecued (the latter with sauces that include piquant chorizo butter). The family owners place a premium on quality and sustainably produced ingredients, so you'll pay top dollar, but most patrons find the offerings well worth the price. **Known for:** indoor and outdoor seating; hearty clam chowder and Portuguese fish stew; vegetarian options including salads and beer-batter avocado and fries. [$] *Average main: $16* ✉ *1850 Bay Flat Rd., Bodega Bay* ✥ *Follow Eastshore Rd. west from Hwy. 1* ☎ *707/377–4238* 🌐 *www.fishermanscovebodegabay.com* 🕘 *No dinner.*

Spud Point Crab Company

$ | **SEAFOOD** | Crab sandwiches, New England or Manhattan clam chowder, and homemade crab cakes with roasted red-pepper sauce star on this food stand's brief menu. Place your order and enjoy your meal to go or, when possible, at one of the marina-view picnic tables outside. **Known for:** family operation; opens at 9 am; seafood cocktails, superb chowder. [$] *Average main: $14* ✉ *1910 Westshore Rd., Bodega Bay* ✥ *West off Hwy. 1, Eastshore Rd. to Bay Flat Rd.* ☎ *707/875–9472* 🌐 *www.spudpointcrab-co.com* 🕘 *No dinner.*

Hotels

Bodega Harbor Inn

$ | **HOTEL** | As humble as can be, this is among the few places on this stretch of the coast with rooms for around $100 a night. **Pros:** budget choice; rooms for larger groups; ocean views from public areas and some rooms. **Cons:** older facility; nondescript rooms; behind a shopping center. [$] *Rooms from: $145* ✉ *1345 Bodega Ave., Bodega Bay* ☎ *707/875–3594* 🌐 *www.bodegaharborinn.com* 🛏 *16 rooms* 🍴 *No Meals.*

★ The Lodge at Bodega Bay

$$$ | **HOTEL** | Looking out to the ocean across a wetland, the lodge's shingle-and-river-rock buildings contain Bodega Bay's finest accommodations. **Pros:** spacious rooms with ocean views; on-site Drakes Sonoma Coast restaurant for sunsets and seafood; fireplaces and patios or balconies in most rooms. **Cons:** pricey in season; parking lot in foreground of some rooms' views; must drive to other fine dining. [$] *Rooms from: $349* ✉ *103*

Coast Hwy. 1, Bodega Bay ☎ 707/875–3525 🌐 www.bodegabaylodge.com 🛏 83 rooms 🍴 No Meals.

Occidental

11 miles south of Guerneville; 14 miles east of Bodega Bay.

A village surrounded by redwood forests, orchards, and vineyards, Occidental is a former logging hub with a bohemian vibe. The small downtown, which contains several handsome Victorian-era structures, has a whimsically decorated B&B inn, a few restaurants, and a handful of art galleries and shops worth poking around.

GETTING HERE AND AROUND

From Guerneville, head west on Highway 116 for 4 miles to the town of Monte Rio, then turn south on Church Street and travel past the old Rio Theater and over the bridge spanning the Russian River. By this point, the road is signed as the Bohemian Highway, which takes you into town, where the road's name changes to Main Street. From Bodega Bay, head south and then east on Highway 1, continuing east on Bodega Highway at the town of Bodega; at Freestone, head north on the Bohemian Highway. Public transit is not a convenient way to travel here.

🍴 Restaurants

★ Altamont General Store

$$ | AMERICAN | Spouses Andzia and Jenay Hofftin opened this organic restaurant, retail and wine shop, and community gathering spot inside Occidental's oldest building (1872). The "farm-fresh comfort food" menu encompasses everything from egg sandwiches and a yogurt and grain, free granola parfait for breakfast to vegan bowls and pork melts for lunch and (three days a week) early dinner until 7. **Known for:** children's menu; ingenious ingredients and spicing; groceries, handmade jewelry, bath products, books, and ceramics. [$] *Average main: $20* ✉ *3703 Main St., Occidental* ✥ *At 3rd St.* ☎ *707/874–6053* 🌐 *www.altamontgeneralstore.com* 🕘 *Closed Tues. and Wed. No dinner Sun. and Mon.*

★ Hazel

$$$ | MODERN AMERICAN | Pizza and pastries are the specialties of this tiny restaurant whose owner-chefs, Jim and Michele Wimborough, forsook their fancy big-city gigs for the pleasures of small-town living. Jim's mushroom pizza, adorned with feta, mozzarella, and truffle oil, and the pie with sausage and egg are among the headliners, with Michele's chocolate *pot de crème* among the enticements for dessert. **Known for:** flavorful seasonal cuisine; roasted chicken with lemon vinaigrette entrée; outdoor seating area. [$] *Average main: $29* ✉ *3782 Bohemian Hwy., Occidental* ✥ *At Occidental Rd.* ☎ *707/874–6003* 🌐 *www.restauranthazel.com* 🕘 *Closed Mon. and Tues. No lunch.*

Howard Station Cafe

$ | AMERICAN | The mile-long list of morning fare at Occidental's neo-hippie go-to breakfast and weekend brunch spot includes order-at-the-counter huevos rancheros, omelets, eggs Benedict, waffles, pancakes, French toast, and "healthy alternatives" such as oatmeal, housemade granola, and quinoa and brown rice bowls with kale and eggs. Soups, salads, burgers, and monstrous sandwiches are on the menu for lunch at this laid-back space with seating inside a 19th-century gingerbread Victorian and outside on its wooden front porch and covered back patio. **Known for:** mostly organic ingredients; juice bar; vegetarian and gluten-free items. [$] *Average main: $15* ✉ *3611 Main St./Bohemian Hwy., Occidental* ✥ *At 2nd St.* ☎ *707/874–2838* 🌐 *www.howardstationcafe.com* 🕘 *No dinner.*

The decor at the Inn at Occidental is whimsically tasteful.

Hotels

The Inn at Occidental

$$ | B&B/INN | Quilts, folk art, and original paintings and photographs fill this colorful inn up the hill from tiny Occidental's shops and restaurants. **Pros:** whimsical decor; most rooms have private decks and jetted tubs; quiet setting. **Cons:** not for those with minimalist tastes; not for kids; no pool. [$] *Rooms from: $269* ✉ *3657 Church St., Occidental* ☎ *707/874–1047* 🌐 *www.innatoccidental.com* 🛏 *17 rooms* 🍴 *Free Breakfast.*

Activities

ZIPLINE

Sonoma Zipline Adventures

ZIP LINING | Zip through the trees with the greatest of ease—at speeds up to 25 mph—at this ziplining center 2½ miles north of Occidental. Friendly guides prepare guests well for their 2½-hour natural high. Overnight stays in one of six treehouses include two ziplining adventures. ■ **TIP→ Participants must be at least 10 years old and weigh between 70 and 250 pounds.** ✉ *6250 Bohemian Hwy., Occidental* ✣ *2½ miles north of Occidental* ☎ *888/494–7868* 🌐 *www.sonomacanopytours.com* 🎟 *From $119* ⏲ *Closed some midweek days in winter.*

Freestone

4 miles south of Occidental; 6 miles west of Sebastopol.

Freestone (population less than 100) retains a laid-back feel. Wild Flour Bread (come early or the sticky buns will be all gone) and, for Japanese-inspired treatments, the Osmosis spa, are two reasons to drop by. A third reason is the Black Kite Cellars tasting room, opened in 2023 to showcase the winery's Chardonnays and Pinot Noirs.

GETTING HERE AND AROUND

To get to Freestone from Occidental, drive south on the Bohemian Highway. From central Sebastopol, drive west on Highway 12 and turn north on the

Bohemian Highway. Public transit is not a convenient way to travel here.

Sights

★ Jasper House by Black Kite Cellars

WINERY | A boutique operation with a loyal following, Black Kite makes cool-climate Chardonnays and Pinot Noirs critics often score in the mid-90s. The reds come from prestigious Sonoma Coast and Anderson Valley sites and the 8-acre estate Jasper Freestone Vineyard. Planted in 2014 across the Bohemian Highway from the wood-clad hospitality house the winery is scheduled to open by summer 2023, the vineyard also contains Chardonnay. The Freestone vineyard and tasting space are named for surveyor Jasper O'Farrell, who owned much of the town in the 19th century. Longtime winemaker Jeff Gaffner crafts the Black Kite wines to last, but they're drinkable upon release. You can find out for yourself at the Freestone facility, where tastings include an older vintage for comparison. All visits are by appointment. ✉ *12747 El Camino Bodega, Freestone ✛ At Bohemian Hwy.* ☎ *707/312–1678* ⊕ *blackkitecellars.com* 🍷 *Tastings from $65* ⌚ *Closed Tues. and Wed.*

☕ Coffee and Quick Bites

Wild Flour Bread

$ | BAKERY | The sticky buns at Wild Flour are legendary in western Sonoma—they're often all gone by the early afternoon on weekends—as are the rye bread and sock-it-to-me scones in flavors like double chocolate, espresso, and hazelnut. The coffee at this roadside stop is good, too. **Known for:** pastry lineup; fougasse (Provençal flatbread), rye, and other breads; roadside setting. 🗓 *Average main: $8* ✉ *140 Bohemian Hwy., Freestone ✛ At El Camino Bodega, 4 miles south of Occidental* ☎ *707/874–2938* ⊕ *www.wildflourbread.com* ⌚ *Closed Tues.–Thurs. No dinner.*

Activities

SPAS
Osmosis Day Spa Sanctuary

SPAS | The signature treatment at this locally beloved spa is a traditional Japanese detoxifying bath. After sipping the preparatory diuretic herbal tea, you'll slip into a deep redwood tub filled with damp cedar shavings and rice bran naturally heated by the action of enzymes. Attendants bury you up to the neck, and throughout the 20-minute session bring sips of water and place cool cloths on your forehead. After a shower, you can lie down and listen to brain-balancing music through headphones or have a massage, perhaps in one of the creekside pagodas, or a facial. Reservations are recommended. ✉ *209 Bohemian Hwy., Freestone ✛ Near Bodega Hwy.* ☎ *707/823–8231* ⊕ *www.osmosis.com* 🍷 *Treatments from $145.*

Sebastopol

6 miles east of Occidental; 7 miles southwest of Santa Rosa.

A stroll through downtown Sebastopol—a town formerly known more for Gravenstein apples than for grapes but these days a burgeoning wine hub—reveals glimpses of the distant and recent past and perhaps the future, too. Many hippies settled here in the 1960s and '70s and, as the old Crosby, Stills, Nash & Young song goes, they taught their children well: the town remains steadfastly—if not entirely—countercultural.

Sebastopol has long had good, if somewhat low-profile, wineries, among them Iron Horse, Lynmar Estate, and Merry Edwards. With the replacement in 2016 of the town's beloved Fosters Freeze location with an industrial-chic venue for California coastal cuisine and the evolving cluster of artisanal producers at

The Barlow, the site of a former apple cannery, the town always seems poised for a Healdsburg-style transformation. Then again, maybe not—stay tuned (in, not out).

GETTING HERE AND AROUND

Sebastopol can be reached from Occidental by taking Graton Road east to Highway 116 and turning south. From Santa Rosa, drive west on Highway 12. Sonoma County Transit buses serve Sebastopol.

VISITOR INFORMATION

CONTACT Sebastopol Visitor Center. ✉ 265 S. Main St., Sebastopol ✧ At Willow St. ☎ 707/823–3032 ⊕ www.sebastopol.org.

Sights

★ The Barlow

MARKET | A multibuilding complex on a 12½-acre former apple-cannery site, The Barlow celebrates Sonoma County's "maker" culture with tenants who produce or sell wine, beer, spirits, crafts, clothing, art, and artisanal foods. The anchor wine tenant, Kosta Browne, receives only club members and allocation-list guests, but other tasting rooms are open to the public, among them Region wine bar, which promotes small Sonoma County producers. Crooked Goat Brewing makes and sells ales, Golden State Cider pours apple-driven beverages, and you can have a nip of vodka, gin, sloe gin, or wheat and rye whiskey at Spirit Works Distillery. Over at Fern Bar, the zero-proof (as in nonalcoholic) cocktails entice as much as the traditional ones. The bar serves food, as do Blue Ridge Kitchen (Southern-influenced comfort fare), Acme Pizza, Red Bird Bakery (excellent breakfast and lunch fare), Sushi Koshō, and the affiliated Oyster Bar, and a few other spots. ✉ 6770 McKinley St., Sebastopol ✧ At Morris St., off Hwy. 12 ☎ 707/824–5600 ⊕ www.thebarlow.net ⊠ Complex free; fees for tasting.

★ Chenoweth Wines

WINERY | Distinguished producers like Patz & Hall and Kosta Browne make wines from grapes farmed by the Chenoweth family, whose ancestors settled in the redwood-studded hills northwest of Sebastopol in the mid-1800s. In 2000, Charlie Chenoweth converted apple orchards to vineyards, in recent years reserving some of the fruit for his wife, Amy, to craft the namesake Pinot Noirs and rosé of Pinot Noir. Her excellent wines alone warrant a visit to the several hundred–acre property, but the lofty Russian River Valley perspectives, down-home hospitality, and hardworking but fun-loving family vibe elevate the experience exponentially. Appointment-only tastings, often conducted by the gregarious Amy herself, include a rollicking UTV tour to sip Pinots where their grapes were grown. ■ TIP➔ **If you can't make it to the ranch, Region wine bar in The Barlow pours two Chenoweth wines.** ✉ 5550 Harrison Grade Rd., Sebastopol ✧ Off Green Valley Rd. ☎ 707/829–3367 ⊕ www.chenowethwines.com ⊠ UTV tour and tasting $150 ⊗ Closed Fri. and Sun.

★ Dutton-Goldfield Winery

WINERY | An avid cyclist whose previous credits include developing the wine-making program at what's now Hartford Family Winery, Dan Goldfield teamed up with fifth-generation farmer Steve Dutton to establish this small operation devoted to cool-climate wines. Goldfield modestly strives to take Dutton's meticulously farmed fruit and "make the winemaker unnoticeable," but what impresses the most about these wines, which include Chardonnay, Pinot Blanc, Pinot Noir, and Zinfandel, is their sheer artistry. Among the ones to seek out are the Angel Camp Pinot Noir, from Anderson Valley (Mendocino County) grapes, and the Morelli Lane Zinfandel, from fruit grown on the remaining 1.8 acres of an 1880s vineyard Goldfield helped revive. Lauded as a top Sonoma County winery by *Wine &*

Iron Horse produces sparklers that make history.

Spirits and Food & Wine magazines, Dutton-Goldfield is open by appointment but accepts walk-ins when possible. ✉ 3100 Gravenstein Hwy. N/Hwy. 116, Sebastopol ✛ At Graton Rd. ☎ 707/827–3600 ⊕ www.duttongoldfield.com ✉ Tastings from $40.

Emeritus Vineyards
WINERY | Old-timers recall the superb apples grown at Hallberg Ranch, since 2000 an elite Pinot Noir vineyard. Founder Brice Jones coveted this land for its temperate climate and layer of Goldridge sandy loam soil atop a bed of Sebastopol clay loam. Along with dry-farming (no irrigation), this soil combination forces vine roots to work hard to obtain water, yielding berries concentrated with flavor. Emeritus sells grapes to boutique and larger wineries, reserving much of the remainder for the flagship Emeritus Hallberg Ranch Pinot Noir. Less than 10 miles away, the winery farms the estate 30-acre Pinot Hill Vineyard, whose wines are often denser and more complex. You can sample the Pinots at a structure whose floor-to-ceiling windows are retracted in good weather to create an extended open-air space steps from the vines. Tastings are by appointment, with same-day visits sometimes possible. ✉ 2500 Gravenstein Hwy. N, Sebastopol ✛ At Peachland Ave. ☎ 707/823–9463 ⊕ www.emeritusvineyards.com ✉ Tastings and tours from $40.

★ Iron Horse Vineyards
WINERY | A meandering one-lane road leads to this winery known for its sparkling wines and estate Chardonnays and Pinot Noirs. The sparklers have made history: Ronald Reagan served them at his summit meetings with Mikhail Gorbachev; George H. W. Bush took some along to Moscow for treaty talks; and Barack Obama included them at official state dinners. Despite Iron Horse's brushes with fame, a casual rusticity prevails at its outdoor tasting area (large heaters keep things comfortable on chilly days), which gazes out on acres of rolling, vine-covered hills. Tastings are by appointment only. ✉ 9786 Ross

Station Rd., Sebastopol ✛ Off Hwy. 116 ☎ *707/887-1507* ⊕ *www.ironhorsevineyards.com* ✉ *Tastings from $35.*

Kobler Estate Winery

WINERY | Find out what makes small family-owned wineries tick at this operation producing fewer than 2,000 cases annually. In northern Sebastopol almost to Forestville, Michael Kobler farms 4½ acres of Viognier and Syrah. His son Mike makes wines from these grapes, along with Chardonnay and Pinot Noir purchased from the esteemed Bacigalupi Vineyard. Michael's wife (and Mike's mom), Debbie, keeps everything running smoothly at the family's 1870 Victorian farmhouse, where guests enjoy tastings on a vineyard's-edge patio. With an old water tower looming overhead, chickens clucking in a nearby coop, and views west to Green Valley's wooded hills, the setting is laid back and idyllic. Visits are by appointment. If you can't get one, try Region wine bar in downtown Sebastopol, which always pours a white and a red. ✉ *4630 Gravenstein Hwy. N/ Hwy. 116, Sebastopol ✛ ¼ mile north of Guerneville Rd.* ☎ *707/329-5474* ⊕ *koblerestatewinery.com* ✉ *Tastings from $50* ☉ *Closed Tues. and Wed.* .

★ Lynmar Estate

WINERY | *Elegant* and *balanced* describe Lynmar's landscaping and contemporary architecture, but the terms also apply to the wine-making philosophy. Expect handcrafted Chardonnays and Pinot Noirs with long, luxurious finishes, especially on the Pinots. The attention to refinement and detail extends to the tasting spaces, where well-informed pourers serve patrons enjoying garden and vineyard views. The Quail Hill Vineyard Pinot Noir, a blend of some or all of the 15 Pinot Noir clones grown in the vineyard just outside, consistently performs well. Also exceptional are La Sereinité Chardonnay and the Five Sisters, Anisya's Blend, and Lynn's Blend Pinot Noirs. Most wines can be bought only by belonging to the allocation list or at the winery. Tastings are by appointment only. ✉ *3909 Frei Rd., Sebastopol ✛ Off Hwy. 116* ☎ *707/829-3374* ⊕ *www. lynmarestate.com* ✉ *Tastings from $65* ☉ *Closed Tues. and Wed.*

Merry Edwards Winery

WINERY | Winemaker Merry Edwards has long extolled the Russian River Valley as "the epicenter of great Pinot Noir." The winery that bears her name, since 2019 owned by the Roederer Estate sparkling-wine house, produces single-vineyard and blended wines that express the unique characteristics of the soils, climates, and grape clones from which they derive. (Edwards's research into Pinot Noir clones has been so extensive that one is named after her.) Edwards preferred the Russian River as a growing site, believing that the warmer-than-average daytime temperatures encouraged more intense fruit, with the evening fogs mitigating the extra heat's potentially adverse effects. The winery also makes Chardonnay and Sauvignon Blanc. ■ **TIP→ The Appellation Tasting provides a three-wine, 30-minute introduction to the brand and the Russian River Valley, but consider stepping up to the Terroir Tasting of several Pinot Noirs.** ✉ *2959 Gravenstein Hwy. N/Hwy. 116, Sebastopol ✛ Near Oak Grove Ave.* ☎ *707/823-7466* ⊕ *www. merryedwards.com* ✉ *Tastings from $45.*

Patrick Amiot Junk Art

PUBLIC ART | The whimsical sculptures of local junk artist Patrick Amiot and his wife, Brigitte Laurent (he creates them, she paints them), can be seen all over Sonoma County, but you can see many works on Florence Avenue three blocks west of Main Street. Amiot reclaims old car parts, abandoned appliances, and the like, refashioning them into everything from pigs, dogs, and people to mermaids and Godzilla. ✉ *Florence Ave., Sebastopol ✛ Between Bodega Ave./Hwy. 12 and Healdsburg Ave.* ⊕ *www.patrickamiot.com.*

Patrick Amiot's "junk art" sculptures liven up three blocks in Sebastopol.

Paul Hobbs Winery

WINERY | Wine critics routinely bestow high-90s scores on the Chardonnays, Pinot Noirs, and Cabernet Sauvignons produced at this appointment-only winery set amid gently rolling vineyards in northwestern Sebastopol. Owner-winemaker Paul Hobbs's university thesis investigated the flavors that result from various oak-barrel toasting levels. He continued his education at Robert Mondavi Winery, Opus One, and other storied establishments before striking out on his own in 1991. Tastings take place in a space designed by winery specialist Howard Backen's architectural firm. Guests on a Signature Tasting visit the winery and sip several wines; the Vineyard Designate Experience includes the tour plus small bites paired with limited-edition single-vineyard wines. ✉ *3355 Gravenstein Hwy. N, Sebastopol* ✣ *Near Holt Rd.* ☎ *707/824–9879* ⊕ *www. paulhobbswinery.com* ✉ *Tastings from $95* ⏱ *Closed Sun.*

Purple Pachyderm (*Claypool Cellars*)

WINERY | "Come for the Primus, stay for the wines" is the unspoken motto of this winery the funk-metal band Primus's bassist and lead vocalist, Les Claypool, founded (as Claypool Cellars) with his wife, Chaney. The trailer hot dog stand out back and the 21st-century hippie-casual tasting room—a former boat-repair shack with an unpainted-wood interior and catchy Craigslist-castoff furnishings—are two signs this isn't an aren't-we-fabulous vanity project. So, too, are the cool-climate Pinot Noirs from Sonoma Coast grapes. Made by Ross Cobb, a local master of the genre, these wines would earn serious consideration no matter who was fronting them. The only upscale touch is the welcome wine, Champagne from a French producer Claypool admires. ■ **TIP→ Frivolity reigns at Wines and Weiners, the latter gourmet Niman Ranch hot dogs, on Friday and weekends.** ✉ *5425 Gravenstein Hwy. N/Hwy. 116, Sebastopol* ✣ *Near Ross Station Rd.* ☎ *707/820–1263* ⊕ *www.purplepachyderm.com* ✉ *Tastings from $35* ⏱ *Closed Mon. and Tues.*

★ Radio-Coteau

WINERY | Connoisseurs of coastal cool-climate wines gravitate to this small operation that's made *Wine & Spirits Magazine*'s list of the world's top 100 wineries annually for nearly a decade. The estate lineup—Chardonnay, Pinot Noir, Riesling, Syrah, and Zinfandel—comes from a 42-acre, biodynamically farmed hilltop vineyard in Occidental. Owner-winemaker Eric Sussman sources fruit from similar marine-influenced sites for the rest of his wines. A visit to his warehouselike Sebastopol production facility isn't about glam or fabulous vineyard views or the mythical Wine Country lifestyle. But if you want to experience "true Sonoma Coast" wines grown with precision and sculpted with minimal intervention by a master craftsman, try to score one of the few weekday appointments (very much required). Chardonnay, Pinot Noir, and Syrah are Radio-Coteau's stars, though the estate Lemorel Zinfandel, from 1946 vines, shines nearly as bright. ✉ *2040 Barlow La., Sebastopol* ✣ *½ mile west of Hwy. 116* ☎ *707/823–2578* 🌐 *radiocoteau.com* 🎫 *Tasting fee varies; ask when booking* 🕒 *Closed weekends.*

Red Car Wines

WINERY | Some ex–movie folks started Red Car as the new millennium dawned, naming it for Los Angeles's old streetcars and producing wines out of Southern California before moving operations to Sonoma County. Coastal, cool-climate wines are the specialty. The Estate Vineyard Chardonnay, Pinot Noir, and Syrah, among the best, come from grapes grown in the far-coastal Fort Ross–Seaview AVA. Other wines that consistently shine include the Sonoma Coast Chardonnay, the rosé of Pinot Noir ("hits the mark year after year," enthused one critic), and Heaven & Earth Pinot Noir. The tasting room's hip country-casual decor pairs well with the rock playlist and the hosts' low-key approach. On a sunny afternoon the shaded outdoor patio is the place to be. ■ **TIP→ Red Car shares a parking lot with Dutton-Goldfield, making this an excellent two-for-one stop.** ✉ *8400 Graton Rd., Sebastopol* ✣ *At Gravenstein Hwy./Hwy. 116* ☎ *707/829–8500* 🌐 *redcarwine.com* 🎫 *Tastings from $35.*

Region

WINERY | "Drink your region" is the motto of this combination wine bar and shop whose self-serve stations dispense two wines by 25 small Sonoma County producers in 1-, 2½-, and 5-ounce pours. Each week a different operation takes center stage, with vintners, winemakers, or staffers from the featured winery discussing wines during meet-the-makers happy hours. Convene by Dan Kosta and Michael Browne's Chev, the new (separate) projects by the founders of Kosta Browne are among the labels represented, along with Chenoweth, Eric Kent, Trombetta, Young Hagen, and other local brands worth learning about. (If you've never heard of them, there's your reason to check this place out.) ■ **TIP→ Region, which encourages appointments but strives to accommodate same-day guests, opens at 1 pm and closes at 8.** ✉ *The Barlow, 180 Morris St., Suite 170, Sebastopol* ✣ *At McKinley St.* ☎ *707/329–6724* 🌐 *drinkyourregion.com* 🎫 *Tastings from $7 for a 5-oz pour.*

🍴 Restaurants

Blue Ridge Kitchen

$$$ | MODERN AMERICAN | Artfully plated Southern-inspired cuisine piques the palate at this farm-to-table restaurant inside a vast industrial-looking space whose garagelike doors open up to unite the dining/bar area and spacious patio. Dishes that might include ahi tuna tartare, truffle fries, and cioppino owe as much to California as Carolina (fried chicken with collard greens, once-a-week shrimp and grits special), while options like Cajun shrimp pasta and the portobello muffuletta straddle both coasts. **Known for:** smash burgers; vegan roasted cauliflower steak; Mississippi mud pie ("kinda"). [$] *Average* *main: $31 ✉ The Barlow, 6770 McKinley St., Suite 150, Sebastopol ✣ Off Morris St. ☎ 707/222–5040 🌐 brkitchen.com.*

★ Fern Bar

$$$ | MODERN AMERICAN | The mixologists at this verdant "bar-focused restaurant" whip up creative "garden-to-glass" cocktails meant for pairing with neo-comfort food whose ingredients, especially the produce, are primarily cultivated in west Sonoma County. "Umami bomb" mushrooms with sticky rice and the tofu with turmeric and peanut velouté entice vegans and vegetarians at dinner, but with lamb sausage, roasted chicken, a smash burger, and pan-seared fish, there's plenty for meat eaters, too. **Known for:** inviting 21st-century tavern feel; low-alcohol and spirit-free drink options; sandwiches at lunch and weekday brunch. [$] *Average main: $28 ✉ The Barlow, 6780 Depot St., Suite 120, Sebastopol ✣ Near McKinley St. ☎ 707/861–9603 🌐 fernbar.com 🕒 No lunch Mon. and Tues.*

Gravenstein Grill

$$$ | MODERN AMERICAN | Tablecloths, cut flowers, and the soft glow of liquid paraffin candles and strings of lights overhead draw most diners to this casual-elegant restaurant's expansive outdoor patio. Chef Bob Simontacchi relies on local sources for the organic, sustainable ingredients in vegan, vegetarian, and omnivore bistro-style dishes like beet salad, braised red cabbage with bacon and Sebastopol apples, vegetable stew, foraged-mushroom risotto, and duck confit. **Known for:** patio atmosphere; artisanal wines, beers, and ciders; barbecued chicken from massive smoker. [$] *Average main: $27 ✉ 8050 Bodega Ave., Sebastopol ✣ At Pleasant Hill Ave. N ☎ 707/634–6142 🌐 www.gravensteingrill.com 🕒 Closed Mon. and Tues.*

Handline

$$ | MODERN AMERICAN | FAMILY | Sebastopol's former Foster's Freeze location, now a 21st-century fast-food palace, won design awards for its rusted-steel frame and translucent panel-like windows. The menu, a paean to coastal California cuisine, includes oysters raw and grilled, fish tacos, ceviche, tostadas, three burgers (beef, vegetarian, and fish), and, honoring the location's previous incarnation, chocolate and vanilla soft-serve ice cream. **Known for:** upscale comfort food; outdoor patio; sustainable seafood and other ingredients. [$] *Average main: $17 ✉ 935 Gravenstein Hwy. S, Sebastopol ✣ Near Hutchins Ave. ☎ 707/827–3744 🌐 www.handline.com.*

★ Khom Loi

$$ | THAI | The chefs behind this open-kitchen storefront eatery have mastered the art of fusing northern Thai and Northern California techniques without sacrificing authenticity. Hits such as whole fried chili-pepper fish, green papaya salad, and spicy and sour seafood curry captivate even before the first bite with their fragrant aromas, colorful presentation, and obviously fresh locally cultivated ingredients. **Known for:** casual vibe; patio seating area; vegan, vegetarian, and gluten-free dishes. [$] *Average main: $23 ✉ 7385 Healdsburg Ave., Sebastopol ✣ At Florence Ave. ☎ 707/329–6917 🌐 www.khomloisonoma.com 🕒 Closed Mon. and Tues.*

Oyster

$$$$ | SEAFOOD | Building on the success of Sushi Koshō across the street, chef Jake Rand opened this "Champagne and bivalves" sidewalk café specializing in raw and cooked seafood accompanied by sides like marvelously crispy duck-fat fries and an iceberg salad Louie with rock shrimp, avocado, smoked bacon, and confit tomato. Straddling two garagelike industrial spaces with indoor and outdoor seating, Oyster opens at 2 pm, making it a good stop for a late lunch or early dinner. **Known for:** chef with finesse; canny Champagne and still-wine choices; small plates for sharing. [$] *Average main: $37 ✉ The Barlow, 6751 McKinley St.,*

Suite 130, Sebastopol ✥ Near Morris St. ☎ 707/503–6003 🌐 www.oystersebastopol.com.

Ramen Gaijin

$$ | JAPANESE | Inside a tall-ceilinged, brick-walled, industrial-looking space with reclaimed wood from a coastal building backing the bar, the chefs at Ramen Gaijin turn out richly flavored ramen bowls brimming with pork belly, wood ear mushrooms, seaweed, and other well-proportioned ingredients. *Izakaya* (Japanese pub grub) dishes like *donburi* (meat and vegetables over rice) are another specialty, like the ramen made from mostly local proteins and produce. **Known for:** artisanal cocktails, beer, wine, and cider; gluten-free, vegetarian options on request; karaage (fried chicken) and other small plates. [$] *Average main: $21* ✉ *6948 Sebastopol Ave., Sebastopol ✥ Near Main St.* ☎ *707/827–3609* 🌐 *www.ramengaijin.com* ⏲ *Closed Sun. and Mon.*

Sushi Koshō

$$$ | JAPANESE | The owner-chef at this industrial-looking high-ceilinged spot pushes the envelope with crowd-pleasers like the 15-spice spare ribs with hoisin barbecue sauce and salmon tartare tacos with crispy wonton shells. He and his team also present sushi classics with style, the intricacy enticing as much as the freshness of the mostly local ingredients. **Known for:** sake selection; beer, wine, and mocktails; outdoor seating area with fire pit. [$] *Average main: $34* ✉ *The Barlow, 6750 McKinley St., Sebastopol ✥ Off Morris St.* ☎ *707/827–6373* 🌐 *www.koshosushi.com.*

Coffee and Quick Bites

★ Pascaline Patisserie & Café

$ | CAFÉ | Delicate pastries and quiches, croques monsieur, and other bistro bites have made locals as passionate about this Highway 116 café as its executive and pastry chefs, who previously worked at establishments in Paris, San Francisco, and elsewhere, are about their cuisine and hospitality. Pastel-green walls, a wood-burning stove, and tables from reclaimed wood lend the small interior space a French-country feel; on sunny days the best seating is on the wooden deck outside. **Known for:** kouign-amann French pastry; French-style coffee; joyous atmosphere. [$] *Average main: $14* ✉ *4552 Gravenstein Hwy. N ✥ Almost to Forestville* ☎ *707/823–3122* 🌐 *pascalinepatisserieandcafe.com* ⏲ *No dinner.*

Nightlife

Third Pig Bar

BARS | West County natives who also own Bowman Cellars in Graton attract a craft-cocktail-loving crowd to this downtown Sebastopol watering hole also serving beers, ciders, and wines by the glass. The place, whose name and red-brick interior pay homage to "The Three Little Pigs," stays open a little later than most neighboring bars. ✉ *116 S. Main St., Sebastopol ✥ Near Bodega Ave.* ☎ *No phone* 🌐 *thirdpigbar.com* ⏲ *Closed Mon. and Tues.*

Graton

½ mile west of Sebastopol.

Steps from Sebastopol and near Occidental, tiny Graton has a one-block main drag one can stroll in two minutes—although it's possible to while away a few hours at the artist-run gallery, nostalgia-inducing antiques shop, tasting rooms, and two notably fine restaurants.

GETTING HERE AND AROUND

To reach Graton from Sebastopol, head west from Highway 116 ½ mile on Graton Road. Sonoma County Transit buses pass through Graton.

Sights

Bowman Cellars

WINERY | Winemaker Alex Bowman learned his craft as a lad, making hobby wines with his father, an electrical contractor with deep West County roots. By his late 20s the wine-making bug had bitten Alex hard, inspiring him to make wines "for real." His debut wine won a double-gold ribbon at the local county fair, prompting him to draw on the experience of several wine-industry relatives to establish Bowman Cellars with his wife, Katie, whose family has long owned a roadside produce market in Sebastopol. The two pour their wines (reservations required, same-day possible) in a casual tasting room fronted by a patio twice as large. Alex shows a light but knowing touch with Russian River Valley Chardonnay and Pinot Noir, the winery's two stars. ✉ *9010 Graton Rd., Graton* ✥ *At Edison St.* ☎ *707/827–3391* 🌐 *bowmancellars.com* 🎫 *Tastings from $20* 🕒 *Closed Mon.–Wed.*

Restaurants

★ Underwood Bar & Bistro

$$$ | **AMERICAN** | The same people who operate the Willow Wood Market Cafe across the street run this restaurant with a Continental atmosphere and a seasonal menu based on smaller and larger dishes. Entrées might include anything from hoisin-glazed ribs and seared scallops to "Thai Life" staples like chicken curry and crispy five-spice duck leg. **Known for:** oyster of the day, French onion soup, and flatbread starters; old-style cocktails, ports, and cognacs; outdoor patio with heaters. [$] *Average main: $29* ✉ *9113 Graton Rd., Graton* ✥ *About ½ mile west of Hwy. 116* ☎ *707/823–7023* 🌐 *www.underwoodgraton.com* 🕒 *Closed Mon. No lunch Sun.–Thurs.*

Willow Wood Market Cafe

$$ | **AMERICAN** | Salads, several hot sandwiches, and filling signature entrées like chicken potpie, the French dip, and spaghetti and meatballs appear on this pale-yellow and lime-green eatery's lunch and dinner menus. Sunday brunch is elaborate, and breakfast the rest of the week—specialties include hot, creamy polenta and house-made granola—is American down-home solid. **Known for:** casual setting; outdoor back patio; ragouts on polenta. [$] *Average main: $21* ✉ *9020 Graton Rd., Graton* ✥ *About ½ mile west of Hwy. 116* ☎ *707/823–0233* 🌐 *willowwoodgraton.com* 🕒 *No dinner Sun.*

Santa Rosa

6 miles east of Sebastopol; 55 miles north of San Francisco.

Urban Santa Rosa isn't as popular with tourists as many Wine Country destinations—which isn't surprising, seeing as there are more office parks than wineries within its limits. Nevertheless, this hardworking town is home to a couple of interesting cultural offerings and a few noteworthy restaurants and vineyards. The city's chain motels and hotels can come in handy if everything else is booked up, especially since Santa Rosa is roughly equidistant from Sonoma, Healdsburg, and the western Russian River Valley, three heavily visited wine-tasting destinations.

GETTING HERE AND AROUND

To get to Santa Rosa from Sebastopol, drive east on Highway 12. From San Francisco, cross the Golden Gate Bridge and continue north on U.S. 101. Santa Rosa's hotels, restaurants, and wineries are spread over a wide area; factor in extra time when driving around the city, especially during morning and evening rush hour. To get here from downtown San Francisco, take Golden Gate Transit Bus

A familiar-looking hat provides shade at the Charles M. Schulz Museum.

101. Several Sonoma County Transit buses serve the city and surrounding area.

VISITOR INFORMATION

CONTACT Visit Santa Rosa. ⊠ *9 4th St., Santa Rosa ✛ At Wilson St.* ☎ *800/404–7673* ⊕ *visitsantarosa.com.*

 Sights

Balletto Vineyards

WINERY | A few decades ago Balletto was known more for quality produce than grapes, but the new millennium saw vineyards emerge as the core business. About 90% of the fruit from the family's 800-plus acres goes to other wineries, with the remainder destined for Balletto's estate wines. The house style is light on the oak, high in acidity, and low in alcohol content, a combination yielding exceptionally food-friendly wines. Sipping Pinot Gris, rosé of Pinot Noir, or a brut rosé sparkler on the outdoor patio can feel transcendent on a warm day, though the Chardonnays and Pinot Noirs steal the show. The winery also makes

Gewürztraminer, Sauvignon Blanc, Syrah, and Zinfandel. ⊠ *5700 Occidental Rd., Santa Rosa ✛ 2½ miles west of Hwy. 12* ☎ *707/568–2455* ⊕ *www.ballettovine-yards.com* 🍷 *Tastings from $25.*

★ Belden Barns

WINERY | Experiencing the enthusiasm this winery's owners radiate supplies half the pleasure of a visit to Lauren and Nate Belden's Sonoma Mountain vineyard, where at elevation 1,000 feet they grow fruit for their all-estate lineup. Grüner Veltliner, a European white grape, isn't widely planted in California, but the crisp yet softly rounded wine they produce from it makes a case for an increase. Critics also hail the Grenache, Pinot Noir, Syrah, and a nectarlike late-harvest Viognier, but you're apt to like anything poured. Tastings take place in a high-ceilinged former milking barn whose broad doorway frames a view of grapevines undulating toward a hilltop. The Beldens tailor visits to guests' interests but will nearly always whisk you into the vineyard, past a 2-acre organic garden, and over to a wishing tree whose results Lauren swears by. ✉ *5561 Sonoma Mountain Rd., Santa Rosa ✛ 10 miles south of downtown off Bennett Valley Rd.; 5½ miles west of Glen Ellen off Warm Springs Rd.* ☎ *415/577–8552* ⊕ *www.beldenbarns.com* ⌨ *Tastings from $20.*

★ **Benovia Winery**

WINERY | Winemaker-partner Mike Sullivan's Chardonnays and Pinot Noirs would taste marvelous even in a toolshed, but guests to Benovia's unassumingly chic Russian River Valley ranch house will never know. Appointment-only tastings of his acclaimed wines—Benovia also produces Grenache, Zinfandel, and Cabernet Sauvignon—take place in the brown-hued living room or on the open-air patio. From either vantage point, views of the estate Martaella Vineyard all the way to Mt. St. Helena draw the eye. Wine educators leading vineyard tours focus on Benovia's earth-friendly farming practices; a production tour tracks the wine-making process from vineyard to barrel to glass. Sullivan's handling of two Chardonnays from Martinelli-family grapes typifies his minimalistic approach. He subtly emphasizes minerality in a wine from the Three Sisters Vineyard in the coastal Fort Ross–Seaview AVA. By contrast, a hint of California ripeness emerges in La Pommeraie, from Zio Tony Ranch in the warmer Russian River Valley. ✉ *3339 Hartman La., Santa Rosa ✛ Off Piner Rd.* ☎ *707/921–1040* ⊕ *benoviawinery.com* ⌨ *Tastings from $45.*

Carol Shelton Wines

WINERY | It's winemaker Carol Shelton's motto that great wines start in the vineyard, but you won't see any grapevines outside her winery—it's in an industrial park 4 miles north of downtown Santa Rosa. What you will find, and experience, are well-priced Zinfandels from grapes grown in vineyards Shelton, ever the viticultural sleuth, locates from Mendocino to Southern California's Cucamonga

Valley. With coastal, hillside, valley, inland, and desert's-edge fruit, the Zins collectively reveal the range and complexity of this varietal that so arouses Shelton's passion. Although Zinfandel gets most of the attention, Shelton also crafts Cabernet Sauvignon, Petite Sirah, other reds, and Chardonnay and Viognier. Two wines to look for are Coquille Blanc, a Rhône-style white, and Coquille Rouge, a blend of Rhône and other red grapes. It's best to make an appointment, but walk-ins are welcome. ✉ *3354B Coffey La., Santa Rosa ✛ Off Piner Rd.* ☎ *707/575–3441* ⊕ *www.carolshelton.com* ⌨ *Tastings $20.*

★ **Charles M. Schulz Museum**

ART MUSEUM | **FAMILY** | Fans of Snoopy and Charlie Brown will love this museum dedicated to the late Charles M. Schulz, who lived his last three decades in Santa Rosa. Permanent installations include a re-creation of the cartoonist's studio, and temporary exhibits often focus on a particular theme in his work. ■ **TIP→ Children and adults can take a stab at creating cartoons in the Education Room.** ✉ *2301 Hardies La., Santa Rosa ✛ At W. Steele La.* ☎ *707/579–4452* ⊕ *www.schulzmuseum.org* ⌨ *$14* ⊙ *Closed Tues. early Sept.–late May.*

Inman Family Wines

WINERY | "The winemaker is in," reads a driveway sign when owner Kathleen Inman, who crafts her winery's Chardonnay, Pinot Noir, and other Russian River Valley wines, is present. She's often around, and it's an extra treat to learn directly from the source about her farming, fermenting, and aging methods. Her restrained, balanced wines complement sophisticated cuisine so well that top-tier restaurants include them on their lists. Inman shows equal finesse with rosé of Pinot Noir, sparkling wines, and Pinot Gris. Her zeal to recycle is evident everywhere, most conspicuously in the tasting room, where redwood reclaimed from an on-site barn was incorporated into the design, and crushed wine-bottle

6

Sights ▼

1 Balletto Vineyards **A9**
2 Belden Barns....................... **J8**
3 Benovia Winery.................... **B4**
4 Carol Shelton Wines **F5**
5 Charles M. Schulz Museum **F6**
6 Inman Family Wines............... **A5**
7 J. Cage Cellars **J6**
8 Luther Burbank Home
   & Gardens **H8**
9 Matanzas Creek Winery........... **J8**
10 Safari West......................... **H1**

Restaurants ▼

1 Grossman's Noshery and Bar.... **H7**
2 John Ash & Co **E3**
3 Rosso Pizzeria & Wine Bar **I7**
4 Sazón Peruvian Cuisine........... **G8**
5 The Spinster Sisters............... **H8**
6 Stark's Steak & Seafood.......... **G7**
7 Walter Hansel Wine & Bistro **B6**
8 Warike Restobar................... **H7**
9 Willi's Wine Bar.................... **I6**

Hotels ▼

1 Astro Motel........................ **H8**
2 Flamingo Resort.................... **J6**
3 The Gables Wine Country Inn..... **I9**
4 Hotel E **H7**
5 Vintners Resort **E3**

glass was fashioned into the bar. Tastings, some held on an outdoor patio, are by appointment only. ✉ *3900 Piner Rd., Santa Rosa* ✛ *At Olivet Rd.* ☎ *707/293–9576* ⊕ *www.inmanfamilywines.com* 🍷 *Tastings from $35* 🕙 *Closed Tues. and Wed.*

★ J. Cage Cellars

WINERY | Wine writers turned vintners Roger Beery and his late wife Donna parlayed their passion for Pinot Noir into a boutique winery that benefits from connections they made while reporting on the industry. They met their consulting winemaker, Adam Lee, even before he cofounded Siduri Wines, and their vineyard lineup includes stellar sites like El Coro, La Cruz, van der Kamp, and the Martinelli family's The Wedding Block. J. Cage also produces Sauvignon Blanc, rosé of Pinot Noir, and the Craftsman's blend of Sangiovese, Zinfandel, and Petite Sirah. Considering the caliber of the vineyards involved, the wines, poured at the production facility where they are made, are very reasonably priced. ✉ *Sugarloaf Crush, 6705 Cristo La., Santa Rosa* ✛ *At Hwy. 12* ☎ *707/318–6323* ⊕ *www.jcage.com* 🍷 *Tastings from $25.*

Luther Burbank Home & Gardens

GARDEN | Renowned horticulturist Luther Burbank lived and worked on these grounds and made significant advances using modern selection and hybridization techniques. The 1.6-acre garden and greenhouse showcase the results of some of Burbank's experiments to develop spineless cacti and such flowers as the Shasta daisy. ■**TIP**➔ **Use your cell phone on a free self-guided garden tour, or from April through October take a docent-led tour (required to see the house).** ✉ *204 Santa Rosa Ave., Santa Rosa* ✛ *At Sonoma Ave.* ☎ *707/524–5445* ⊕ *www.lutherburbank.org* 🍷 *Gardens free, tour $10* 🕙 *No house tours Nov.–Mar. (unless staff available).*

Matanzas Creek Winery

WINERY | The visitor center at Matanzas Creek sets itself apart with an understated Japanese aesthetic, extending to a tranquil fountain and a vast field of lavender. The winery makes Sauvignon Blanc, Chardonnay, Merlot, Pinot Noir, and Cabernet Sauvignon under the Matanzas Creek name, and three equally well-regarded wines—a Bordeaux red blend, a Chardonnay, and a Sauvignon Blanc—bearing the Journey label. The winery, owned by Jackson Family Wines, encourages guests to enjoy a picnic on the property with a bottle of Matanzas wine. Visits and picnicking are by appointment. Same-day reservations are usually possible except on summer weekends, but call ahead. ■**TIP**➔ **An ideal time to visit is from late June to mid-August, when lavender perfumes the air.** ✉ *6097 Bennett Valley Rd., Santa Rosa* ☎ *707/528–6464, 800/590–6464* ⊕ *www.matanzascreek.com* 🍷 *Tastings from $35.*

★ Safari West

WILDLIFE REFUGE | **FAMILY** | An unexpected bit of wilderness in the Wine Country, this preserve with African wildlife covers 400 acres. Begin your visit with a stroll around enclosures housing lemurs, cheetahs, giraffes, and rare birds like the brightly colored scarlet ibis. Next, climb with your guide onto open-air vehicles that spend about two hours combing the expansive property, where more than 80 species—including gazelles, cape buffalo, antelope, wildebeests, and zebras—inhabit the hillsides. ■**TIP**➔ **If you'd like to extend your stay, lodging in semi-glam Botswana-made tent cabins is available.** ✉ *3115 Porter Creek Rd., Santa Rosa* ✛ *Off Mark West Springs Rd.* ☎ *707/579–2551, 800/616–2695* ⊕ *www.safariwest.com* 🍷 *From $105 Sept.–May, from $126 June–Aug.*

Rare zebras are among the animals on view at Santa Rosa's Safari West.

🍴 Restaurants

Grossman's Noshery and Bar

$$ | SANDWICHES | The menu at this homage to Jewish delicatessens plays the greatest hits—blintzes, latkes, lox, chopped liver, and knishes, plus pastrami, corned beef, and Reuben sandwiches all on house-made breads—but mashes things up with chicken shawarma kebabs, fish-and-chips, and other atypical deli dishes. It's all executed with panache, and the retro-eclectic decor (black-and-white ceramic tile floors, colorful tropical-bird-print wallpaper, chunky stone fireplace) feels nostalgic yet of the moment. **Known for:** full bar; meats and fish cured and smoked in-house; picnic-table seating beside the building. $ *Average main: $18* ⊠ *Hotel La Rose, 308½ Wilson St., Santa Rosa* ✛ *Near 4th St.* ☎ *707/595–7707* ⊕ *grossmanssr.com.*

John Ash & Co.

$$$$ | MODERN AMERICAN | A dress-up multiroom special-occasion establishment that debuted in 1980, John Ash bills itself as Sonoma County's first farm-to-table restaurant, but its legacy extends even further: the namesake founder, no longer involved, was among several pioneering Wine Country chefs who tailored their cuisine to the region's wines. Though eclipsed as a destination restaurant by rivals in Healdsburg and elsewhere, this remains a worthy stop for well-crafted dishes like rack of lamb, pan-seared dayboat scallops, and brick chicken. **Known for:** raw and cooked oysters and other apps; happy hour (3–5 pm) beverages and small bites; Sonoma-centric wine list with international selections. $ *Average main: $43* ⊠ *Vintners Resort, 4350 Barnes Rd., Santa Rosa* ✛ *At River Rd.* ☎ *707/527–7687* ⊕ *vintnersresort.com/dining/john-ash-co* ⊗ *Closed Mon. and Tues. No lunch.*

Rosso Pizzeria & Wine Bar

$$ | PIZZA | Ask local wine pourers where to get the best pizza, and they'll often recommend Rosso, a sprawling strip-mall restaurant whose chefs hold center stage in the large open kitchen.

Two perennial Neapolitan-style pizza favorites are the Moto Guzzi, with house-smoked mozzarella and spicy Caggiano sausage, and the Funghi di Limone, with oven-roasted mixed mushrooms and Taleggio and fontina cheese. **Known for:** wine selection; fried chicken with caramelized pancetta glaze; salumi and salads. $ *Average main: $21* ✉ *Creekside Center, 53 Montgomery Dr., Santa Rosa* ✥ *At Brookwood Ave.* ☎ *707/544–3221* ⊕ *www.rossopizzeria.com* ⊘ *Closed Sun.*

Sazón Peruvian Cuisine

$$ | PERUVIAN | Join Peruvian locals enjoying a taste of back home at this strip-mall restaurant whose name means "flavor" or "seasoning." Several ceviche appetizers—including one with ponzu sauce for a Japanese twist—show the range of tastes the chefs conjure up, as do the empanadas, *lomo saltado* (steak and fries), and *arroz con mariscos,* a velvety, turmeric-laced seafood paella. **Known for:** skillfully spiced Peruvian food; small and large plates for sharing family-style; deli annex with salads and sandwiches. $ *Average main: $24* ✉ *1129 Sebastopol Rd., Santa Rosa* ✥ *At Roseland Ave.* ☎ *707/523–4346* ⊕ *www.sazonsr.com.*

The Spinster Sisters

$$$ | MODERN AMERICAN | The versatile chef of this concrete-and-glass grazing spot anchoring the SOFA Santa Rosa Arts District satisfies her diverse devotees with American standards and playful variations on international cuisines. Separated on the menu into three main categories—ocean, garden, and pasture, each with a selection of appetizers, salads, and entrées—the dishes change often but might include trout with French lentils, hanger steak with kale gratin, Tuscan-style St. Louis ribs, and mushroom hand pie with leeks and ricotta. **Known for:** thought-provoking flavors; dessert pastries; local and international wines. $ *Average main: $31* ✉ *401 S. A St., Santa Rosa* ✥ *At Sebastopol Ave.*

☎ *707/528–7100* ⊕ *thespinstersisters. com* ⊘ *Closed Sun. and Mon. No lunch.*

Stark's Steak & Seafood

$$$$ | STEAKHOUSE | The low lighting, well-spaced tables, and gas fireplaces at this Railroad Square Historic District restaurant create a congenial setting for dining on steak, raw-bar seafood, and sustainable fish. With entrées including 20-ounce prime rib and dry-aged rib eye—plus a shareable 56-ounce rib eye—there's no chance meat eaters will depart unsated, and nonsteak options like ahi tuna tartare and tamarind barbecue prawns surpass those at your average temple to beef. **Known for:** old-school steak-house atmosphere; high-quality seafood; weekday happy hour (3–6) often tops best-of-county polls. $ *Average main: $43* ✉ *521 Adams St., Santa Rosa* ✥ *At 7th St.* ☎ *707/546–5100* ⊕ *www.starkssteak-house.com* ⊘ *No lunch weekends.*

★ Walter Hansel Wine & Bistro

$$$$ | FRENCH | Tabletop linens and lights softly twinkling from this ruby-red road-house restaurant's low wooden ceiling raise expectations the Parisian-style bistro cuisine consistently exceeds. A starter of cheeses or French onion soup awakens the palate for entrées like chicken cordon bleu, steak au poivre, or seafood dishes that might include scallops in a rich yet somehow delicate gastrique or subtly sauced wild Alaskan halibut. **Known for:** romantic setting for classic cuisine; prix-fixe option; vegan and vegetarian dishes. $ *Average main: $38* ✉ *3535 Guerneville Rd., Santa Rosa* ✥ *At Willowside Rd., 6 miles northwest of downtown* ☎ *707/546–6462* ⊕ *walterhanselbistro.com* ⊘ *Closed Mon. and Tues. No lunch.*

Warike Restobar

$$$ | PERUVIAN | A Cali take on a Peruvian *cevicheria,* this downtown Santa Rosa restaurant with exposed-brick walls and a dizzying tile floor beguiles patrons with nimbly spiced ceviches, empanadas, and other starters that demand one of the

Many rooms at Vintners Resort have vineyard views.

two-dozen citrusy craft cocktails on offer. The mains include classics like steak and fries, bean stew, paella, a few pasta dishes, and shredded chicken in a yellow pepper sauce. **Known for:** signature scallop, salmon, and shrimp ceviche with corn, cucumbers, and avocado; grilled octopus and fried wonton stuffed with crab or pork apps; house salad with grilled chicken breast, oyster mushrooms, fried garlic, and mint. $ *Average main: $27* ✉ *527 4th St., Santa Rosa* ✛ *Near Mendocino Ave.* ☎ *707/536–9201* ⊕ *warikesf.com.*

★ Willi's Wine Bar

$$$$ | ECLECTIC | First in a historic roadside haunt that perished in the 2017 wildfires and now in a strip mall location more urbane than its exterior suggests, Willi's serves inventive globe-trotting small plates paired with international wines. Pork-belly pot stickers represent Asia, the Mediterranean inspires Tunisian roasted local carrots and Moroccan-style lamb chops, and curried crab tacos straddle two, maybe three, continents. **Known for:**

patio seating; inspired wine selection; 2-ounce pours so you can pair a new wine with each dish. $ *Average main: $39* ✉ *1415 Town and Country Dr., Santa Rosa* ✛ *At Terrace Way* ☎ *707/526–3096* ⊕ *williswinebar.net.*

Hotels

Astro Motel

$ | MOTEL | The '60s are back splashier than ever at this tastefully and whimsically restored motel diagonally next to a park and across from the Luther Burbank Home & Gardens. **Pros:** vintage mid-century modern furnishings; well-designed rooms; nearby Spinster Sisters restaurant (same owners) anchors neighborhood arts district. **Cons:** no pool, gym, spa, or other amenities; about a mile from Railroad Square Historic District; surrounding area mildly scruffy. $ *Rooms from: $183* ✉ *323 Santa Rosa Ave., Santa Rosa* ☎ *707/200–4655* ⊕ *theastro.com* ➦ *34 rooms* ⦿ *No Meals.*

Flamingo Resort

$$ | **HOTEL** | If Don Draper from *Mad Men* popped into this 1950s motel-hotel hybrid 2¼ miles northeast of downtown Santa Rosa, he'd feel right at home. **Pros:** movie star Jayne Mansfield partied here in the 1960s; retro vibe; zippy poolside Lazeaway Club restaurant and bar. **Cons:** 30-minute walk to downtown; service lapses; feels more motor lodge than resort. $ *Rooms from: $216* ✉ *2777 4th St., Santa Rosa* ☎ *707/545–8530, 800/848–8300* ⊕ *www.flamingoresort. com* ⇌ *170 rooms* ¶◎¶ *No Meals.*

★ The Gables Wine Country Inn

$$ | **B&B/INN** | Guests at this circa-1887 Gothic Victorian inn set on 3½ bucolic acres slip back in time inside high-ceilinged, period-decorated pastel-painted rooms, some with four-poster beds and all with comfortable mattresses and high-quality sheets. **Pros:** Victorian style and hospitality; three-course gourmet breakfasts; country vibe yet 4 miles from downtown. **Cons:** period look may not work for all guests; slightly off the beaten path; weekend minimum-stay requirement April–mid-November. $ *Rooms from: $249* ✉ *4257 Petaluma Hill Rd., Santa Rosa* ☎ *707/585–7777* ⊕ *www. thegablesinn.com* ⇌ *8 rooms* ¶◎¶ *Free Breakfast.*

Hotel E

$ | **HOTEL** | This downtown hotel's developer renovated a four-story 1908 Beaux Arts former bank into a boutique property within walking distance of restaurants, bars, and shops and less than a 10-minute drive to vineyards and tasting rooms. **Pros:** appealing room decor; convenient to downtown restaurants; lobby doubles as wine bar. **Cons:** lacks small-town Wine Country feel; no on-site parking (valet service provided); some rooms are smallish (but thoughtfully organized). $ *Rooms from: $152* ✉ *37 Old Courthouse Sq., Santa Rosa* ☎ *707/481–3750* ⊕ *hotelesantarosa.com* ⇌ *39 rooms* ¶◎¶ *No Meals.*

★ Vintners Resort

$$$ | **HOTEL** | With a countryside location, a reserved sense of style, and spacious rooms with comfortable beds, the Vintners Resort further seduces with a slew of amenities and a scenic vineyard landscape. **Pros:** café and John Ash & Co. restaurant; vineyard jogging and walking path; facials, massages at Vi La Vita spa. **Cons:** occasional noise from adjacent events center; trips to Healdsburg or downtown Santa Rosa require a car; pricey on summer and fall weekends. $ *Rooms from: $364* ✉ *4350 Barnes Rd., Santa Rosa* ☎ *800/421–2584* ⊕ *www. vintnersresort.com* ⇌ *78 rooms* ¶◎¶ *No Meals.*

Nightlife

BREWPUBS

Russian River Brewing Company

BARS | It's all about Belgian-style ales, "aggressively hopped California ales," and barrel-aged beers at this famous brewery's Santa Rosa pub. The lineup includes Pliny the Elder (and Younger, but only for a short period), Blind Pig IPA, Supplication sour (aged 12 months in used Pinot Noir barrels), and many more. ■**TIP→ A second, larger pub (more seats, more beers) operates out of RRBC's production facility in Windsor.** ✉ *725 4th St., Santa Rosa* ✛ *Near D St.* ☎ *707/545–2337* ⊕ *www.russianriverbrewing.com.*

Index

Photo Credits

Front Cover: Alexandra Latypova / Alamy Stock Photo [Description: Sunrise in the vineyards of Napa Valley]. **Back cover, from left to right:** FloridaStock/Shutterstock, Kent Sorensen/Shutterstock, Cheng Cheng/Shutterstock. **Spine:** Juancat/Shutterstock. **Interior, from left to right:** Ljupco Smokovski/Shutterstock (1). Rebecca Gosselin Photography (2-3). **Chapter 1: Experience Napa and Sonoma:** Courtesy of Inglenook (6-7). Michael Warwick/Shutterstock (8-9). Israel Valencia/Infinity Visuals (9). Courtesy of the Napa Valley Wine Train (9). Mariana Marakhovskaia/Shutterstock (10). Courtesy of Sonoma County Tourism (10). Shea Evans/Longmeadow Ranch (10). Courtesy of Wine Country Botanicals (10). Joseph Phelps Vineyards (11). Nat and Cody Gantz 2018/Hanson of Sonoma Distillery (11). Courtesy of Sonoma County/Smugmug (12). Donum Estate (12). CIA at Copia (12). Valentina_G/ Shutterstock (12). Courtesy of Sonoma County Tourism (13). Zack Frank/Shutterstock (13). Lisovskaya Natalia/Shutterstock (16). Steven Freeman 2016 (16). Courtesy of Sonoma County/Smugmug (16). Jeff Bramwell (16). New Africa/Shutterstock (17). Tubay Yabut Photography/KollarChocolates (17). Bob McClenahan/Courtesy of Charlie Palmar (17). Richard Ault/ZazieSF (17). Natalie and Cody Gantz (18). Garrett Rowland (18). Harmon Guesthouse (18). SF Weekly (18). Christophe Genty Photography/Goose & Gander (19). Bob McClenahan/Courtesy of Sky & Vine Rooftop Bar (19). Courtesy of Sonoma County Tourism (19). El Barrio Bar (19). Kirkman Amyx/McEvoy Ranch (20). Jay Jeffers (20). Courtesy of Makers Market (20). Carlos Yudica/Shutterstock (20). Zeljko Radojko/Shutterstock (20). Nikovfrmoto/Dreamstime (21). Napa Soap Company (21). Natalia Svistunova/Shutterstock (21). Napa Wine Candles (21). McEvoy Ranch (21). Sara Sanger/Robert Rauschenberg and Francis Bacon (22). Israel Valencia/Infinity Visuals (23). **Chapter 3: Visiting Wineries and Tasting Rooms:** Getty Images/iStockphoto (45). Megan Reeves Photography/Napa Valley scenic (48). Courtesy of Napa Valley Balloons, Inc. (51). Andy Dean Photography/Shutterstock (56). **Chapter 4: Napa Valley:** Courtesy of the Napa Valley Wine Trai (65). Randy andy/Shutterstock (73). Life Atlas Photography/Shutterstock (74). Di Rosa Center for Contemporary Art (83). Robert Holmes (84). Victor M.Samuel (97). Chung Chung/Shutterstock (99). Open Kitchecn Photography/Domaine Chandon (101). Far Niente+Dolce+Nickel & Nickel (112). Jason Tinacci/Sonoma (114). Olaf Beckman/Round Pond (118). Scott Chebagia (131). Courtesy of Long Meadow Ranch (136). Smcfeeters/Dreamstime (142). TimCarlPhotography/Embrace Calligosta (150). **Chapter 5: Sonoma Valley and Petaluma:** Wildly Simple Productions (153). Julie Vader/Shutterstock (164). Rocco Ceselin/Ram's Gate Winery (168). Leo Gong (174). Benziger Family Winery (180). **Chapter 6: Northern Sonoma, Russian River, and West County:** Danita Delimont/Shutterstock (191). Joe Becerra/Shutterstock (203). Matt Armendariz/Jordan Vineyard and Winery (207). Robert Holmes/Ridge Vineyards (211). Warren H White/Russian River Valley Wine Growers (213). Christian Horan Photography/Montage Healdsburg (220). Sonoma County Tourism (222). Zialena Winery (226). Sonoma County Tourism/Armstrong Wood State Park (234). Inn at Occidental (242). Laurence G. Sterling/Iron Horse Vineyards (245). Ed Aiona Photography/Patrick Amiot/Sonoma County/Smugmug (247). Joe Shlabotnik/Flickr (252). R. Mabry Photography 2017/Safari West (257). Vintners Resort/Sonoma County/Smugmug (259). **About Our Writer:** Photo is courtesy of the writer.

Every effort has been made to trace the copyright holders, and we apologize in advance for any accidental errors. We would be happy to apply the corrections in the following edition of this publication.

Notes

Fodor's NAPA AND SONOMA

Publisher: Stephen Horowitz, *General Manager*

Editorial: Douglas Stallings, *Editorial Director;* Jill Fergus, Amanda Sadlowski, *Senior Editors;* Brian Eschrich, Alexis Kelly, *Editors;* Angelique Kennedy-Chavannes, *Assistant Editor;* Yoojin Shin, *Associate Editor*

Design: Tina Malaney, *Director of Design and Production;* Jessica Gonzalez, *Senior Designer*

Production: Jennifer DePrima, *Editorial Production Manager;* Elyse Rozelle, *Senior Production Editor;* Monica White, *Production Editor*

Maps: Rebecca Baer, *Senior Map Editor;* David Lindroth, Mark Stroud (Moon Street Cartography), *Cartographers*

Photography: Viviane Teles, *Senior Photo Editor;* Namrata Aggarwal, Neha Gupta, Payal Gupta, Ashok Kumar, *Photo Editors;* Eddie Aldrete, *Photo Production Intern;* Kadeem McPherson, *Photo Production Associate Intern*

Business and Operations: Chuck Hoover, *Chief Marketing Officer;* Robert Ames, *Group General Manager*

Public Relations and Marketing: Joe Ewaskiw, *Senior Director of Communications and Public Relations*

Fodors.com: Jeremy Tarr, *Editorial Director;* Rachael Levitt, *Managing Editor*

Technology: Jon Atkinson, *Director of Technology;* Rudresh Teotia, *Associate Director of Technology;* Alison Lieu, *Project Manager*

Writer: Daniel Mangin

Editor: Douglas Stallings

Production Editor: Elyse Rozelle

5th Edition

ISBN 978-1-64097-614-6

ISSN 2375-9453

All details in this book are based on information supplied to us at press time. Always confirm information when it matters, especially if you're making a detour to visit a specific place. Fodor's expressly disclaims any liability, loss, or risk, personal or otherwise, that is incurred as a consequence of the use of any of the contents of this book.

SPECIAL SALES

This book is available at special discounts for bulk purchases for sales promotions or premiums. For more information, e-mail SpecialMarkets@fodors.com.

PRINTED IN CANADA

10 9 8 7 6 5 4 3 2 1

About Our Writer

 Daniel Mangin returned to California, where he's maintained a home for three decades, after two stints at the Fodor's editorial offices in New York City, the second one as the Editorial Director of Fodors.com and the Compass American Guides. While at Compass he was the series editor for the *California Wine Country* guide and commissioned the *Oregon Wine Country* and *Washington Wine Country* guides. A wine lover whose earliest visits to Napa and Sonoma predate the Wine Country lifestyle, Daniel is delighted by the evolution in wines, wine making, and hospitality. With several dozen wineries less than a half-hour's drive from home, he often finds himself transported as if by magic to a tasting room bar, communing with a sophisticated Cabernet or savoring the finish of a smooth Pinot Noir.